Hi Faey,

Thanks for coming to my launch.

Lots of love
always

Simon

Security, Conflict and Cooperation in the Contemporary World

Edited by **Effie G. H. Pedaliu**, LSE-Ideas and **John W. Young**, University of Nottingham

The Palgrave Macmillan series Security, Conflict and Cooperation in the Contemporary World aims to make a significant contribution to academic and policy debates on cooperation, conflict and security since 1900. It evolved from the series Global Conflict and Security edited by Professor Saki Ruth Dockrill. The current series welcomes proposals that offer innovative historical perspectives, based on archival evidence and promoting an empirical understanding of economic and political cooperation, conflict and security, peace-making, diplomacy, humanitarian intervention, nation-building, intelligence, terrorism, the influence of ideology and religion on international relations, as well as the work of international organisations and non-governmental organisations.

Series editors

Effie G. H. Pedaliu is Fellow at LSE IDEAS, UK. She is the author of *Britain, Italy and the Origins of the Cold War*, (Palgrave Macmillan, 2003) and many articles on the Cold War. She is a member of the peer review college of the Arts and Humanities Research Council.

John W. Young is Professor of International History at the University of Nottingham, UK, and Chair of the British International History Group. His recent publications include *Twentieth Century Diplomacy: A Case Study in British Practice, 1963–76* (2008) and, co-edited with Michael Hopkins and Saul Kelly, *The Washington Embassy: British Ambassadors to the United States, 1939–77* (Palgrave Macmillan, 2009).

Titles include:

Martín Abel González and Nigel J. Ashton
THE GENESIS OF THE FALKLANDS (MALVINAS) CONFLICT
Argentina, Britain and the Failed Negotiations of the 1960s

Christopher Baxter, Michael L. Dockrill and Keith Hamilton
BRITAIN IN GLOBAL POLITICS VOLUME 1
From Gladstone to Churchill

Pablo Del Hierro Lecea
SPANISH-ITALIAN RELATIONS AND THE INFLUENCE OF THE MAJOR POWERS, 1943–1957

Aaron Donaghy
THE BRITISH GOVERNMENT AND THE FALKLAND ISLANDS, 1974–79

Rui Lopes
WEST GERMANY AND THE PORTUGUESE DICTATORSHIP
Between Cold War and Colonialism

Malcolm Murfett
SHAPING BRITISH FOREIGN AND DEFENCE POLICY IN THE TWENTIETH

CENTURY
A Tough Ask in Turbulent Times

Simon A. Waldman
ANGLO-AMERICAN DIPLOMACY AND THE PALESTINIAN REFUGEE
PROBLEM, 1948–51

John W. Young, Effie G. H. Pedaliu and Michael D. Kandiah
BRITAIN IN GLOBAL POLITICS VOLUME 2
From Churchill to Blair

Security, Conflict and Cooperation in the Contemporary World
Series Standing Order ISBN 978-1-137-27284-3 (Hardback)
(*outside North America only*)

You can receive future titles in this series as they are published by placing a standing order. Please contact your bookseller or, in case of difficulty, write to us at the address below with your name and address, the title of the series and the ISBN quoted above.

Customer Services Department, Macmillan Distribution Ltd, Houndmills, Basingstoke, Hampshire RG21 6XS, England

Anglo-American Diplomacy and the Palestinian Refugee Problem, 1948–51

Simon A. Waldman
King's College London, UK

First published 2015 by
PALGRAVE MACMILLAN

Palgrave Macmillan in the UK is an imprint of Macmillan Publishers Limited, registered in England, company number 785998, of Houndmills, Basingstoke, Hampshire RG21 6XS.

Palgrave Macmillan in the US is a division of St Martin's Press LLC, 175 Fifth Avenue, New York, NY 10010.

Palgrave Macmillan is the global academic imprint of the above companies and has companies and representatives throughout the world.

Palgrave® and Macmillan® are registered trademarks in the United States, the United Kingdom, Europe and other countries.

ISBN 978–1–137–43150–9

This book is printed on paper suitable for recycling and made from fully managed and sustained forest sources. Logging, pulping and manufacturing processes are expected to conform to the environmental regulations of the country of origin.

A catalogue record for this book is available from the British Library.

A catalog record for this book is available from the Library of Congress.

Contents

Acknowledgements

I owe many debts of gratitude. Thanks are due to the University of London Central Research Fund for the grant that enabled me to visit the United States National Archives in Washington.

King's College London has been my academic home since 2006. I have been overwhelmed by the support of the faculty at the Centre for Middle East and Mediterranean Studies. Thanks are due to professors Paul Janz and Michael Kerr for their support, advice and encouragement, while Professor Rory Miller has been a superb supervisor and colleague, a good friend and my academic role model and mentor. Thank you.

I have benefited from the helpful advice given to me by professors Clive Jones of Durham University and Colin Shindler of the School of Oriental and African Studies as well as the comments by the first and second readers of this manuscript. I thank Dr Neil Caplan of Vanier College for his advice and for helping me locate an elusive document. Thanks are also due to Clare Mence and Angharad Bishop at Palgrave Macmillan.

I thank Teri Sisa for her positive encouragement, Maya for her support and sacrifice and Aseel for insights into US presidential politics and many excuses for breaks!

My biggest debt of gratitude is to Bonnie and Anthony Waldman, my dear parents. Their love and support is always unconditional and it is to them that this book is affectionately dedicated.

Acronyms and Abbreviations

AHC	Arab Higher Committee
AHE	Arab Higher Executive
ALA	Arab Liberation Army
BMEO	British Middle East Office
CIA	Central Intelligence Agency
CIGS	Chief of the Imperial General Staff
COS	Chiefs of Staff
DP	Displaced Persons
DRO	Disaster Relief Organization
ECOSOC	Economic and Social Council (UN)
EFENDI	Economic and Financial Development Institute of Near East
ESM	Economic Survey Mission (UN)
FAO	Food and Agriculture Organization (UN)
IDF	Israel Defense Forces
IRO	International Refugee Organization
JCS	Joint Chiefs of Staff
MAC	Mixed Armistice Commissions
NEDI	Near East Development Institute
NESDA	Near East Settlement and Development Authority
NSU	Palestine Negotiations Support Unit
PA	Palestinian Authority
PCC	Palestine Conciliation Commission
PLO	Palestine Liberation Organization
UN	United Nations
UNICEF	United Nations International Children's Emergency Fund
UNRPR	United Nations Relief for Palestine Refugees
UNRRA	United Nations Relief and Rehabilitation Administration
UNRWA	United Nations Relief and Works Agency for Palestine Refugees in the Near East
UNSCOP	United Nations Special Committee on Palestine
WHO	World Health Organization

Introduction: The Palestinian Refugee Problem as an Impediment to Peace

In his report published posthumously in September 1948, Count Folke Bernadotte, the assassinated United Nations Mediator in Palestine, wrote the following:

> A new and difficult element has entered into the Palestine problem as a result of the exodus of more than 300,000 Arabs from their former homes in Palestine...The right of innocent people, uprooted from their homes by the present terror and ravages of war, to return to their homes, should be affirmed and made effective, with assurance of adequate compensation for the property of those who may choose not to return.[1]

The recommendation became the basis of UN General Assembly Resolution 194 which stated that, 'The refugees wishing to return to their homes and live at peace with their neighbours should be permitted to do so at the earliest practicable date, and that compensation should be paid for the property of those choosing not to return.'[2]

Bernadotte's proposal was made despite his earlier call to Israel on 26 July 1948 that the refugees be permitted to return to their homes. Israel's position was that there would be no such return while there was war,[3] and the Israeli Ministry of Foreign Affairs responded to the proposal by stating that the problem could only be considered when the Arab states were ready to conclude a peace treaty with Israel, citing security and military concerns.[4] This Israeli position, together with the insistence by Arab states and the Palestinians that Resolution 194 be upheld, has been the basis of the Arab–Israeli impasse over the settlement of the refugee problem until this very day and an obstacle that generations of mediators have failed to overcome. Several examples in the decades since the 1948 War illustrate the point.

Speaking in 1958 in his capacity as a member of the Saudi Arabian Mission to the UN, Ahmed Shuqayri, who would later become the first chairman of the Palestine Liberation Organisation (PLO), stated that the right of Palestinian refugees to return to their homes was 'natural, inherent and self-existing' and that the solution to the problem was 'repatriation and nothing but repatriation'.[5] In stark contrast, during the same year, Abba Eban, the senior Israeli representative to the UN, stated that the only solution to the problem was the resettlement of the refugees among host countries.[6] Countless peace talks and negotiations since 1948 have faltered over the question of the fate of the refugees. For example, with the signing of the Declaration of Principles in 1993 which ushered in the Oslo peace process between Israel and the PLO, 'final status' issues, including the question of refugees, were deferred to later permanent status negotiations.[7] When final status talks eventually took place at Camp David in 2000, they stumbled over the issue of refugees as well as Jerusalem and territory.[8] Later in September 2000, the US convened the Millennium Summit in New York to revive discussions. Dennis Ross, the chief US Middle East negotiator, put forward ideas for the settlement of the Palestinian refugee issue. The refugees would have the right to apply to return to Israel and there would be an agreed number of refugees who could return to Israel for humanitarian purposes with priority given to those living in Lebanon.[9] Fearing that this proposal would only continue the myth that refugees could return to Israel, the response by Israeli negotiators was lukewarm, while Palestinian negotiators sought to increase the numbers of these refugees who could return.[10] Then, for their part, in response to President Bill Clinton's proposal which envisioned his conception of a final Israeli–Palestinian settlement which called for the Palestinians to waive their right to return to their pre-1948 homes, the December 2000 'Clinton Parameters', the Palestine Negotiations Support Unit (NSU) wrote that the proposals supported the Israeli position and negated Resolution 194 which called for the refuges to be returned to their homes.[11] No settlement was reached.

Another opportunity, the Arab Peace Plan, which was first introduced by the Arab League in Beirut in 2002, offered Israel 'normal relations' if Jerusalem would withdraw from lands it had occupied since the 1967 Arab–Israeli War.[12] However, Israel was unable to accept this proposal because it also made reference to there being 'a just solution to the problem of Palestinian refugees…in accordance with the UN General

Assembly Resolution No 194'.[13] There were similar Israeli reservations to the 2007 Arab League Initiative which reiterated many of the points of the earlier 2002 proposal.[14] The question of Resolution 194 is based on the interpretation of the resolution with the Arab states deeming it a recognition of the wholesale right to repatriation. However, Ruth Lapidoth of the Jerusalem Institute of Israel Studies has argued that the resolution does not guarantee a 'right', but recommends that the refugees 'should' be 'permitted' to return if there is a wish to live at peace with their neighbours.[15] Meanwhile, in response to a call by the then Israeli Prime Minister Ehud Olmert that the Palestinians recognize Israel as a Jewish state, in November 2007, just days ahead of the Annapolis Conference,[16] the Palestine NSU advised against doing so, primarily on the grounds that it would negate the right of return for Palestinian refugees and recognize Israel's demographic objections to the right of Palestinians to return to their pre-1948 homes.[17] However, this did not stop Prime Minister Benjamin Netanyahu, after his 2009 election victory, from proposing 'a demilitarised Palestinian state' that would 'recognize the one and only Jewish state' – an allusion to the demographic imbalance if Palestinian refugees were to be repatriated.[18]

Today, as peace talks stall between Israel and the PLO, the refugee issue still remains a crucial obstacle. Writing in *The Guardian* in 2010, the Palestinian Authority's (PA) chief negotiator, Saeb Erekat, was unequivocal in his insistence that a future agreement with Israel must provide the basis for the settlement of the Palestinian refugee problem, highlighting the Arab demand that they be allowed to return to their homes. 'Return and restitution' Erekat argued, is 'the remedy of choice [that] has a strong international precedent'.[19] The problem, however, with this position, is that Jerusalem is adamant that only a small number of refugees can return. Meanwhile, PA President and PLO Chairman Mahmoud Abbas has said that the Palestinians are seeking an independent state on the terms of Resolution 194.[20]

However, between 1948 and 1951, the period covered by this volume, there was a significant opportunity to find a solution to the Palestinian refugee problem, at a time in which the US and Britain considered the refugee crisis as a significant strategic concern and a foreign policy priority. Together they led a concerted diplomatic campaign to solve the crisis under the auspices of the United Nations Palestine Conciliation Commission (PCC), a body designed to build an Arab–Israeli agreement. They discussed at length the questions of resettlement, relief, repatriation, compensation and rehabilitation, and even designed and attempted to employ mechanisms to facilitate and enforce them. As this study of international diplomacy towards the refugee problem will high-light, Washington and London's strategies and tactics were flawed and ill-conceived, and they ultimately failed.

The Palestinian refugee problem and its origins

The Palestinian refugee problem was a product of the 1948 Arab–Israeli War. The conflict was first waged between Zionist forces and Palestinian militias supported by Arab irregulars and the Arab Liberation Army (ALA) after the passing of the 1947 Partition Resolution on 29 November 1947. After Israel's Declaration of Independence, which followed the termination of the British Mandate in May 1948, the war was fought between the newly established Israel Defense Forces (IDF) and the invading armies of Egypt, Transjordan, Iraq, Lebanon and Syria. The origins, reasons and responsibility for the mass exodus of Palestinian refugees are highly disputed by historians. Some scholars contend that the Palestinian refugees were victims of premeditated ethnic cleansing and deliberate transfer.[21] Nur Masalha, for example, has argued that the notion of transfer is 'as old as the early Zionist colonies in Palestine and the rise of political Zionism' and was embraced by almost all shades of opinion within the Zionist movement. In his study *Expulsion of the Palestinians: The Concept of 'Transfer' in Zionist Political Thought, 1882–1948*, Masalha documents instances where the Zionist leadership discussed or debated the transfer of the Arab Palestinians as a potential policy from 1882 until 1948, and he highlights Jewish Agency debates following the Peel Commission Report of 1937, early transfer proposals prior to 1930 and the British Labour Party Resolution of 1944 which put forward transfer as its official policy.[22] Similarly, David Hirst contends that 'population transfer' was 'never far from their [Zionist] hearts'.[23]

Central to the claim that the Zionists deliberately expelled and eth-nically cleansed Palestine of its Arab inhabitants, thus leading to the refugee problem, is the question of Plan D, a Zionist military strategy adopted in April 1948 by the Haganah (the defence arm of the Yishuv or Jewish community in mandatory Palestine) to secure territorial con-tingency in anticipation of a future Arab attack. The contentious section of Plan D that precipitated the ethnic cleansing charge reads:

> In the conquest of villages in your area, you will determine – whether to cleanse or destroy them – in consultation with your Arab affairs advisers and HIS officers...You are permitted to restrict – insofar as you are able – cleansing, conquest and destruction operations of enemy villages in your area.[24]

Masalha argues that although Plan D was not a blueprint for expulsion, it was the realization of the political-ideological concept of the transfer scheme.[25] Revisionist Israeli historian Benny Morris, in his 2004 study into the Palestinian refugee problem, contended that the plan was not a political blueprint for the expulsion of Palestine's Arabs. Rather, Morris asserted, it was based on military considerations for the purpose of achieving military ends. Furthermore, it was neither used nor regarded by Haganah commanders as a blanket instruction for the country's expulsion of Arab residents. Nevertheless, Morris continued, it 'constituted a strategic-doctrinal basis and *carte blanche* for expulsion by front, brigade, district and battalion commanders ... and it gave commanders, *post facto*, formal persuasive cover for their actions'.[26] Avi Shlaim, another revisionist, echoes Morris' latter contention.[27] The basis of these claims was the plan's objective of removing potentially hostile elements from captured Arab villages in anticipation of the invasion by the Arab armies.[28] It has been countered by Israeli historian Yoav Gelber that Plan D was only systematically employed in Upper Galilee, and the plan's instructions stipulated that if no resistance was met by the Arab residents, then they should remain under military rule.[29] Meanwhile, in an earlier study, Nadav Safran has argued that during the period until the end of May 1948 and June, the refugees under Jewish control left by themselves. It was only after that time in areas newly acquired by Israel after May 1948 that they were expelled from new territories that had been conquered.[30]

In another older study into the refugee problem, Joseph B. Schechtman argued that during the civil war stage of the conflict, wealthy Arabs left the country expecting to return in the wake of an Arab victory. He added that there was also pressure by the Arab leadership for Palestinians to leave their homes.[31] Schechtman asserts that Arab over-confidence turned into panic, and the Arab population started to flee in large numbers, as what started as a 'precautionary evacuation' turned into a 'stampede'.[32] Using the example of Haifa, Jon and David Kimche have argued that there was evidence that the Arab leadership had ordered the Arabs to abandon their homes either by direct or indirect instruction.[33] Morris adds that the Arab Higher Executive (AHE), the main organization of the Palestinian Arab leadership, made no effort to halt the exodus, adding that the evacuation from Haifa in April 1948, Palestine's major port city with a large Arab population, was not a new development; it had happened earlier in Tiberias in the same month of April.[34] Morris further argues that during April–May 1948, more than 20 Arab villages were largely or completely evacuated because of orders from Arab leaders.[35]

However, in a 1961 article that appeared in *The Spectator*, Erskine Childers argues that no primary evidence of evacuation orders was ever produced, even though Israel claimed that Arab radio broadcasts ordered the evacuation of Palestinian residents. Childers therefore concludes that Arab panic was deliberately induced. Together with reports of forced expulsions, he continues to argue, 'It is clear beyond all doubt that official Zionist forces were responsible for expulsion of thousands upon thousands of Arabs.'[36] Similarly, Walid Khalidi has argued that the general theme running through the 'Zionist' account of the Palestinian refugee problem is that there were orders broadcasted to Arab residents to leave the country to pave the way for invading Arab armies. However, Khalidi contends that this account is false, having found no record of such broadcasts in Zionist sources. Like Childers before him, Khalidi also did not find such orders in the Arab press. If anything, it was the reverse; there were orders to stay.[37] This assertion is backed by Morris, who wrote that he also found no blanket orders by radio or otherwise instructing the Palestinian Arabs to flee.[38]

American historian Dan Kurzman levels the claim that, in his view, the exaggerated Arab response to the massacre in the village of Deir Yassin[39] on 9 April 1948 helped propel the flight of hundreds of thousands of Palestinian refugees.[40] Arthur Koestler, in his early study of the Zionist movement until the creation of Israel, also highlighted the Deir Yassin incident as a psychological factor for the refugee problem.[41] Aharon Cohen argues that a cluster of Zionist military successes in the early part of 1948 convinced the Arabs that the Jews were winning, thus leading to their exodus, especially after Deir Yassin.[42] However, Cohen alleges that the panic and flight was largely caused by the Arab Higher Committee (AHC) which made them believe that a 'bloodbath' was approaching. Furthermore, there was low morale and the mass hysteria was contagious.[43] In William R. Polk *et al*'s 1957 study *Backdrop to Tragedy: The Struggle for Palestine*, the authors contend that until April 1948, the number of refugees was about 30,000, but a refugee 'atmosphere' developed after the Deir Yassin massacre.[44] The authors note both instances where Arab propaganda portraying Zionist terrorists as merciless and fanatical had the reverse effect. Instead of rallying the Arab population, it caused mass panic.[45] Morris agrees with this contention that the retelling of the horrors of Deir Yassin added to the flight.[46]

In his study of the Palestinian exodus between 1 April and 31 October 1948 from the Galilee region of what was Palestine, Nafez Nazzal argues that to some extent the Palestinian refugee problem could have been a result of normal wartime panic; however, he adds that there were additional factors such as incidences between December 1947 and April 1948 of 'Zionist terrorism'. He also argues that rumours and psychological pressures were utilized in Zionist siege tactics in cities such as Safed, Tiberias, Beisan and Acre in April 1948, as well as direct attacks on civilians in several villages from July to October 1948. There were also incidences of direct expulsion in some villages, forcing inhabitants to flee towards the Syrian border.[47] Morris writes of a 'whispering campaign' by the Haganah in the case of some Arab villages.[48] Rony E. Gabbay argues that the Haganah employed psychological measures such as announcements on loud speakers that Arab villagers would be killed and their homes burnt down.[49] Furthermore, the panic induced by psychological factors was exacerbated after the massacre at Deir Yassin where reports of civilian deaths spread across Palestine. Reminiscent of Gabbay's earlier analysis, David Hirst contends that it was the combination of a physical and psychological 'blitz' that brought on the Palestinian exodus.[50] Morris refers to a 'psychosis of flight' which was heightened following the fall of Arab towns such as Tiberias, Safed, Haifa and Beisan. But there was also a small but significant proportion due to Jewish expulsion orders and Jewish psychological warfare ploys.[51]

The extent of the psychological factor employed by the Zionists and the documentary evidence to support such claims as recorded by Benny Morris have been vehemently contested by Shabtai Teveth, who additionally emphasizes the lack of use of Arabic sources in Morris' narrative.[52] Efraim Karsh argues that Arab leaders inflated death tolls, going so far as to report non-existent massacres, the aim being to obtain sympathy for the Arab Palestinians, a tactic that spectacularly backfired.[53] In contrast, Jewish leaders withheld describing gruesome attacks on their own people to avoid such panic.[54]

Some scholars have argued that the flight of the Arab residents of Palestine occurred in several distinct phases. Benny Morris identifies four such phases,[55] while other much earlier writers such as Gabbay and Schechtman identified three.[56] Others, notably Teveth, have rejected this, arguing instead that only 'two phases are necessary': the civil war stage and the Arab military invasion after 15 May 1948. Furthermore, Teveth argues that the dates of the phases used by Morris avoided patterns which would suggest that there was a domino effect in the exodus, thus overemphasizing the Zionist-induced factors for the refugee problem.[57]

The dispute between Morris and Teveth highlights the debate within Israeli historiography that has emerged in recent decades over Israel's role in the 1948 Palestine War. Since the 1980s, following the opening of

British and Israeli archives, a group of Israeli revisionist historians have questioned what they deem to be the 'standard Zionist version' which had been 'largely unchallenged' outside of the Arab world.[58] Indeed, the aforementioned works by Childers, Kurzman, Schechtman, Safran and the Kimches were published at a time when archival sources remained closed. The revisionist academics have often been referred to as the 'New Historians', a blanket term that accounts for studies that have focused on the events surrounding Israel's establishment, although they often cover different aspects of this period. For example, Avi Shlaim's *Collusion across the Jordan: King Abdullah, the Zionist Movement, and the Partition of Palestine*, focuses on secret diplomacy between the Zionists and King Abdullah of Jordan over the partitioning of Palestine at the expense of the Palestinian Arabs.[59] Meanwhile, Ilan Pappé's *Britain and the Arab-Israeli Conflict, 1947–51*, which challenges conventional views of British hostility towards Zionism and its alleged attempt to prevent the establishment of Israel, argues that Britain's policy was based on support for Jordan and pragmatism.[60] On the question of the origins of the Palestinian refugee problem, foremost among these 'New Historians' is Benny Morris. In his study *The Birth of the Palestinian Refugee Problem* and his aforementioned revised version *The Birth of the Palestinian Refugee Problem Revisited*, Morris investigated how and why approximately 700,000 Palestinians fled their homes during the 1948 War and challenged traditional Israeli and Arab narratives that they had left voluntarily or that they were victims of a planned expulsion.

Within the 'New Historians' there are indeed significant differences between them, as highlighted by Morris' scathing critique of the scholarship of his one-time fellow traveller Ilan Pappé on the basis of Pappé's factual errors and partisanship in his historical methodological approach fuelled by his far left ideological beliefs. Furthermore, Morris asserts that contrary to 'the conspiratorial image projected by our critics', the 'New Historians' were never a close-knit or monolithic school of intellectuals; some barely knew each other, but rather all had written histories focusing on Israel and Palestine in the 1940s that demonstrated that the conflict could not be properly understood in black-and-white and good vs evil terms.[61]

The work of Morris himself was not without critics. In addition to Teveth, one of Morris' most stern critics, is Efraim Karsh, who has countered that Morris' claim that transfer was mainstream in Zionist thinking is based on only a few meetings of the Jewish Agency Executive taken out of context and from documents which have been either twisted or misinterpreted.[62] Partly as a result, but also because of the release of additional Israeli archival sources and the use of Arab diaries and books based on interviews, Morris repeated his earlier study in the updated *The Birth of the Palestinian Refugee Problem Revisited*.[63] In this work, he dedicated a chapter to Zionist transfer thinking before 1948 as a result of criticism from scholars such as Nur Masalha, who claim that it was a pillar of Zionist ideology,[64] and Anita Shapira and Shabtai Teveth, who claim that the Zionists did not support it nor take it seriously.[65] Morris adds that evidence of support for transfer thinking before 1948 was unambiguous.[66]

Issa Khalaf has argued that as Britain was coming towards the end of the Mandate, and was engaged in the evacuation of its personnel and transferring power to Arab and Jew, the Arabs of Palestine were unprepared to take over governmental tasks, functions and responsibilities in key sectors such as health, education, water, sanitation, social welfare, agriculture, etc. And the meagre Arab efforts to take over such functions were insufficient and badly organized.[67] In contrast, the Yishuv was not only prepared to take over the functions of the state, but it was serving many of these functions already. Moreover, Palestinian society was not yet established enough to produce stable, interconnected socio-economic relationships.[68] British archival documents also show that there was a lack of social and national cohesion and solidarity in Palestinian society and that morale was low. As early as March 1947, over seven months before the initial 'civil war' stage of the conflict, there were signs of the exodus that was soon to come. British reports noted large-scale movements of Arabs from the south of the country as a result of drought. Estimating that 30 per cent of cattle and flocks had died or had been slaughtered, it was reported that:

> 20,000 Arabs are moving North in search of grazing and work... As the fellaheen move they graze their flocks on any pasture they can find, with the result that clashes with Jewish settlements and even with Arab villages are occurring. This sort of thing will increase, and as the shortage of food is felt the temper of the fellaheen will rise, and a degree of civil unrest must be expected.[69]

Indeed, this drought in the south of Palestine saw migrations of not just Bedouin Arabs but also permanently domiciled Arabs who were leaving for the north of the country.[70] Before the start of the civil war stage of the conflict, there were reports that among Christian and more 'moderate' elements of Arab Palestine, there was fear that if there was a British withdrawal, unemployment would result as well as strife, not just between Jew and Arab, but also between Arab factions.[71] While it was reported by the British in March 1947 that personal feuds and petty rivalries prevented the ability of Arab organizations to run,[72] it was also asserted in November 1947 that Hajj Amin al-Husseini, the Grand Mufti of Jerusalem, was still unable to obtain cohesion among the various Arab parties.[73] In a note about Arab politics in Palestine, it was reported that although the majority of Palestinians acknowledged that al-Husseini was their leader, numerous Arabs had little enthusiasm for his leadership or programme, or for that matter, faith in the AHC.[74] By December–January 1947–48, the British reported that the AHC appeared to have little influence over its followers and that some parts of the country were falling into the hands of 'unscrupulous adventurers and brigands', leading to a disruption of the administrative and economic life of Arab Palestine.[75] Meanwhile, in January 1948, it was being reported from Amman that the Jordanian city was being 'crowded with Arab refugees from Palestine' and that Arab partisans were only now appearing to get into their stride.[76]

Morale was low among the Palestinian Arabs. Reporting on his talks with a local Arab Sheikh, a British officer, noting that the Arabs did not have an equivalent of the Jewish Haganah, wrote that:

> he even went so far as to say that in two months, unless the Arab League sent in really substantial numbers of men and arms and money, the Palestine Arabs would slop [sic] ... in the Sheikh's view, there is not an all-out, do or die, feeling in the Arabs of Palestine as their leaders would have us believe.[77]

Indeed, there were also examples of tribal affiliation overriding national sentiment. During the 'civil war' stage, when the Zionist forces were on the defensive, particularly from November 1947 to March 1948, there were incidents where residents in areas close to the Syrian frontier fled north to join their tribesmen. For example, in the Arab village of El Khisas (home to a Sheikh who also owned land in Syria), 90 Arab families sought refuge with their 'fellow-tribesmen' in Syria.[78]

The lack of social and national cohesion was exacerbated by the departure of middle-class Palestinians who could afford to leave the country during the early stages of the Palestine War. For example, in January 1948, British intelligence reported that the AHE was becoming concerned about the large number of Arab families leaving Arab areas. The report also stated, 'this evacuation is by no means confined only to the lower classes but even such leading personalities as members of

the Nashashibi family have left Jerusalem'.[79] Meanwhile, British reports
noted in February 1948 that in Arab rural areas there was a steady
diminution of government authority.[80] On 16 April it was reported
from Amman that Arab Legion sources noted a general collapse of Arab
morale in Palestine.[81] Similarly, by 1 May 1948, it was noted by Britain's
high commissioner in Jerusalem, General Sir Alan Cunningham, that
wherever the Arabs are in contact with the Jews, 'their morale has practically collapsed and we are finding increasingly difficultly in bolstering
them up'.[82] Reporting in April 1948, one month before the scheduled
termination of the Mandate, a British official opined that:

> The collapsing Arab morale in Palestine is in some measure due
> to the increasing tendency of those who should be leading them
> [Palestinian Arabs] to leave the country. For instance in Jaffa the
> Mayor went on four days leave twelve days ago and has not returned
> and half the national committee has left.[83]

Nowhere was the evacuation of Arab leaders from towns and cities more
destructive to Palestinian society than in the city of Haifa, which by the
end of April 1948 had fallen to Zionist forces. Tens of thousands of Arab
residents left the city after British military officers led by General Hugh
Stockwell were unable to successfully broker a truce. Reporting on the
battle for Haifa, British intelligence wrote that the Haganah expected the
battle to last four days after the talks between the two sides broke down,
but were surprised by their sudden victory. The reason given was that:

> The Arab leaders, including Amin Ezzadin [sic], who was supposed
> to command the Haifa ALA, had been warned of the attack the day
> before, and without further ado had fled to Acre. The desertion of
> their leaders and the sight of so much cowardice in high places
> completely unnerved the inhabitants.[84]

Indeed, Consul-General Cyril Marriott reported on the events which
occurred in Haifa and on Britain's role. During the critical stage on
21 April when both sides were 'spoiling for a fight', Ahmed Bey Khalil,
Chief Magistrate and the only AHC representative in Haifa and in whom
General Stockwell had great confidence in the handling of Arab affairs,
left the town by sea. So did another Arab official, Amin Izz al-Din, as did
Yunis Nafa'a the following day. 'The actual leaders had left at the crucial
stage', reported Marriott.[85] Many of the Arab refugees from Haifa fled to

Acre, but it was reported on 11 May, almost three weeks later, that many of these refugees were trying to get to Lebanon.[86]

In Jaffa, it was reported that the 'Arab inhabitants were leaving fast'.[87] It was stated that the Arab collapse of Haifa and Jaffa was accelerated by the early flight of Arab leaders, but then exploited by Jewish publicity which exaggerated the refugee figures.[88] Many of these refugees fled to Gaza where it was becoming increasingly difficult to shelter and feed them.[89] It was also reported that a number of refugees obtained passage to Belgium on a ship belonging to a Lebanese firm.[90] And following a Jewish offensive in Safed and Samakh in May 1948, it was noted that Arab morale was low and 'cracking up in [the] whole northern sector'.[91] Some British officials appeared to have contempt for the Palestinian Arabs. Commenting in May 1948, two weeks before Israel's Declaration of Independence and the Arab invasion of Palestine, High Commissioner Cunningham commented that many Arab leaders were fleeing the country and that the effendi class 'did not seem to be ashamed of watching the contest from the sidelines'.[92]

What emerges from the scholarly literature and British documents on the Palestinian refugee problem is a multi-faceted explanation of the reasons for the flight and expulsion of Palestine's Arab population. There were incidents of massacres and expulsions committed by Zionists. There were psychological factors such as 'whispering campaigns' on the part of the Zionist forces which increased panic in the Arab population of Palestine. There was a failure on the part of the Arab leadership, many of whom left the country at a time when their presence in Palestine was most needed. In contrast to the Zionist leaders, they publicized massacres in the hope of inciting their population to action, a tactic which dramatically backfired, and instead, news of the horrors of war added to the 'psychosis of flight'.[93] Meanwhile, Palestinian Arab society was suffering from low morale and a lack of unity and cohesiveness. It was a society lacking strong leaders and its fabric unravelled under the burden of war, exacerbating population migrations that are typical in times of conflict and war.

According to a report published by the UN's PCC, 720,000 Palestinian Arabs were made refugees during the course of the fighting.[94] The exact number of Palestinian refugees varies from diplomatic sources. Using UN records, a 1949 study by the Royal Institute of International Affairs put the figure at 713,000.[95] The Technical Committee of the UN's PCC estimated the total as 711,000.[96] In an interview with the *New York Times*, Israeli Foreign Minister Moshe Sharett estimated the total number as 520,000.[97]

British and US officials, when discussing the problem in the following years, often used varying estimates. For example, Sir D.
Norton of the British Treasury estimated the total number as 800,000.[98] However,
the British delegation to the UN noted that the latest estimate they had
received put the refugee number at 815,000, but other estimates put
the number between 800,000 and 900,000. In order to avoid a 'battle
of figures', the British delegation suggested that they be given justifica-
tions for the generally accepted estimate.[99] The Foreign Office enclosed
a Research Department paper which estimated 600,000 refugees. In the
Foreign Office's explanation, it was noted that three agencies in the
field estimated there were 1,040,000 refugees. Meanwhile, the number of rations that were being issued by the United Nations Relief for
Palestine Refugees (UNRPR) was 940,000, and the maximum estimate
for the number of refugees according to the Technical Committee of
the PCC was 766,000. The reasons for the higher figures from the aid
agencies were put down to refugee families trying to get the maximum
number of rations and people who were destitute going to the refugee
camps. It was also admitted that on the actual number of refugees, there
was not enough reliable information in possession to reach a final judgment. Further, it was mentioned that while the Research Department's
estimate was 600,000 (with a 5 per cent margin of error either way),
'All that can be said', the Foreign Office admitted that the number was
therefore 'between 600,000 and 760,000'.[100]

On 15 March 1949, the US State Department estimated the number of
refugees to be 725,000, but noted that 'No accurate statistical breakdown
of the refugees exists.'[101] Although the State Department had estimated
the number of refugees to be 725,000, when Secretary of State Dean
Acheson discussed the problem with Sharett in New York in April 1949,
Acheson talked of 'some 800,000' refugees. And US Assistant Secretary
of State for Near Eastern and African Affairs George McGhee conceived
that although the number of Palestinian refugees and destitute persons receiving relief stood at 950,000, the number of bona fide refugees
who would need to be repatriated or resettled stood at no more than
700,000.[102]

Structure and content of the volume

This volume is a study of international diplomacy towards the Middle East. It examines US and British attempts to solve the Palestinian
refugee problem. In addition to charting the developments in the negotiating process, it analyses London and Washington's attitudes towards

the negotiations between 1948 and 1951 during which time major diplomatic initiatives were spearheaded by the two powers. The volume investigates why, despite there being a concerted diplomatic effort on the part of the US and Britain to find a solution to the Palestinian refugee problem during the period in question, a solution was not forthcoming. Ultimately, it will identify the reasons why these efforts were unsuccessful, with each chapter examining developments and initiatives to bring about a settlement to the Arab–Israeli conflict and the refugee problem specifically. The US and Britain faced a highly difficult challenge; the differences between the local parties were vast, making a third-party attempt to solve the problem an almost unattainable task. However, the US and Britain made significant mistakes that made this near-unattainable task impossible. It created even more distance between Israel and the Arab states and led to a diplomatic stalemate that would last for decades to come.

Chapter 1 argues that although Britain and the US were both motivated by shared Cold War strategic interests in developing their respective Middle East policies, they diverged significantly over the question of Palestine. Both were concerned about Soviet encroachment into the region, and both recognized the importance of maintaining Arab goodwill. However, the US staunchly supported the entry of 100,000 Jewish displaced persons into Palestine; something Britain, with troops stationed on the ground, would not accept. Britain feared that the entry of such a large number of Jews would enrage the Arabs of Palestine – this at a time when it was facing an uprising by Jewish militants. While the US had decided to favour the UN partition plan after the Soviet Union had declared its support for this solution, Britain abstained. These policy differences put a strain on ties, which would later need to be healed in order to diplomatically engage in the aftermath of the Palestine conflict and maintain Western strategic interests in the Middle East.

Nevertheless, despite their differences over the Palestine question, Chapter 2 highlights how mutual self-interest drove Britain and the US to cooperate in facilitating a programme of emergency aid and relief under the auspices of the UN as established under General Assembly Resolution 212. Meanwhile, Resolution 194 was drafted to set up the PCC to mediate between the parties to work out a diplomatic settlement. However, although there was much debate on the wording of the resolution in the paragraphs referring to territory, scant attention was devoted to the paragraph on the refugees which was originally part of the late Mediator's proposals that featured in his posthumous report. The phraseology of the refugee paragraph would later prove to be a significant obstacle to diplomatic efforts, and represented either

a major oversight by British and US officials or a short-sighted strategic calculation, because the resolution which called for the right of
Palestinian refugees to return to their homes would later polarize the
sides in diplomatic forums and eventually grind diplomatic efforts to
a halt.

Chapters 3 and 4 analyse the work of the PCC. It was through this
body that Britain and the US pursued their diplomatic initiatives during
subsequent years. Both chapters argue that London and Washington,
particularly the latter, made major strategic and tactical errors in pursuing peace between Israel and the Arab states. Chapter 3 addresses
why US and British diplomatic efforts, under the auspices of the PCC,
ground to a halt in the first half of 1949. It argues that multilateral diplomacy in the pursuit of an all-encompassing Arab–Israeli peace mediated
by the PCC was the objective; however, in doing so, the Arab states
were grouped together into a bloc. This hardened the Arab position
towards the fate of the Palestinian refugees, which emerged as the primary obstacle for PCC diplomacy. The Arab states insisted on full refugee
repatriation to Israel in accordance with their interpretation of General
Assembly Resolution 194. This was something Israel resisted with equal
vigour. Chapter 4 argues that in order to break this impasse, London
and Washington pursued another failed policy, which was to create an
economic incentive for the Arab states to agree to the resettlement of
the Palestinian refugees. This was manifested through the work of the
Economic Survey Mission (ESM). The main reason for the failure of the
ESM was that it was launched, with the strong backing of the US and
Britain, without there being a political agreement on the resettlement
of Palestinian refugees. The work of the ESM was therefore compro-
mised, watered down and unable to follow through on its intended
purpose. This led to much debate between US and British officials on
the tactics and role of the ESM. The ESM was greeted with suspicion and
mistrust by the Arab states and Israel. This was the complete opposite
of what the US and Britain hoped to achieve. Instead of incentivizing
the local parties to reach an agreement, the effect of their policy was
that the ESM was viewed as a back-door operation to the resettlement
of Palestinian refugees in Arab countries before an agreement had been
reached between the parties.

Chapter 5 argues that although Britain and the US were fully aware
that Middle Eastern states despised and mistrusted the PCC, they still
continued to work under its auspices, despite contrary advice from
the field. This represented a tactical error that hampered the effectiveness of diplomatic efforts and was a significant reason for the
continued impasse. Meanwhile, Britain, the US and the PCC believed

that compensation for Palestinian refugees could offer a potential means to overcome the Arab–Israeli negotiating deadlock. Although there was considerable thought and possibilities in British and US discussions over compensation, the PCC was unable to put this forward in concrete terms because it was unable to overcome the political stalemate that had developed during the Lausanne Conference. By the end of 1951, Washington, without London's knowledge, instructed the PCC to facilitate a conference in Paris. This was another tactical blunder as it was mistimed and rushed. There had been little indication that the parties were ready for such a meeting, as their attitudes had stayed rigid. The mistake Britain and the US made was to commence with the conference without a significant indication of flexibility among the parties, and allowing the PCC to continue to be the mechanism to mediate Arab–Israeli talks despite it being a mistrusted and increasingly despised body. The failed Paris Conference brought to a close US and British involvement in substantive peace talks to solve the refugee problem for a generation and made Anglo-American discussions over compensation immaterial.

Chapter 6 examines the extent to which there was an opportunity to solve the Palestinian refugee problem through direct Arab–Israeli dialogue. It argues that in the cases of Syria, Egypt and Jordan, the refugee problem was less of a factor than in PCC-mediated forums. This highlights that when grouped as a bloc, the Arab states were less forthcoming in their position towards the refugees than they were in direct bilateral diplomacy. Britain and the US, although generally supportive of these discussions, were unwilling to get directly involved in mediation. Instead, such direct talks were referred to the PCC. The reasoning behind this was fear that if the talks proved unsuccessful or had an unsatisfactory conclusion, it was the Western powers who could face the blame or even ownership of the problem.

Chapter 7 examines the work of the United Nations Relief and Works Agency (UNRWA), an organization which was the culmination of three years of US, British and international diplomacy. The US and Britain initially conceived this organization as being a mechanism to help find a solution to the problem of the resettlement of Palestinian refugees. Instead, it became an agency that perpetuated aid dependency in the absence of a political agreement. The ESM, which was itself conceived to study possibilities in the region to rehabilitate and resettle Palestinian refugees through public works projects, recommended establishing UNRWA in its interim report. The idea was to have a body that would take over the function of providing aid and relief to refugees, but then slowly wean them off aid and into work through public development projects that would enhance the growth of their host nations. However, UNRWA failed in its task. This chapter explains why and goes on to argue that this represented the major failing of US and British diplomacy. By the end of 1951 with political talks at a standstill, refugee dependency through UNRWA had become entrenched. This lasts to the present day.

What emerges from this study is that the US and Britain had a unique opportunity between 1948 and 1951 to solve the Palestinian refugee problem. Both powers recognized the importance and significance of the refugee issue and made it a high priority. They were committed to finding a solution and spearheaded concerted and focused diplomatic efforts. However, these efforts were ultimately in vain. The reason why Britain and the US were unable to bring about a solution to the refugee crisis was that the differences between the local parties were momentous, which made the task of third-party involvement complex and intricate. In addition, the strategy adopted by the US and Britain did not help to break the stalemate that had emerged between Israel and the Arab states. The mistake that the powers made was in grouping the Arab states into one bloc during PCC-orchestrated negotiations. This hardened the Arab position because, when grouped together, the Arabs states became less likely to show flexibility in negotiations. Meanwhile, pressure was being exerted on Israel to return 200,000 refugees as a gesture to the Arab states. Britain and the US knew this crossed Israeli red lines and was unlikely to bear fruit, yet this tactic of trying to create an Israeli gesture of goodwill was adhered to.

Eventually, PCC talks ground to a halt by July 1949. Still the US and Britain insisted on using this vehicle for discussions. At the same time, Britain and the US attempted to use economic incentives and initiatives through public works programmes to resettle the refugees on the grounds that it was through resettlement and compensation that the refugee crisis would be solved. This tactic spectacularly backfired, as the Arab states, and to some extent Israel, saw this as an underhanded Western attempt to solve the refugee crisis without a political agreement. Subsequently, UNRWA was unable to fulfil the original task for which it was conceived, to resettle and rehabilitate Palestinian refugees through public works programmes in their host nations. Instead, UNRWA became a body which perpetuated the refugee problem, a problem that remains a primary obstacle towards peace in the Middle East to this very day.

1
The Palestine Factor in Anglo-American Post-War Middle Eastern Policy, 1945–48

Introduction

On one of the coldest days ever recorded in British history, 25 February 1947, in a month which saw minus degree temperatures, just 17 hours of sunlight and the freezing over of the River Thames, the British Foreign Secretary Ernest Bevin told parliament, 'The course of events has led His Majesty's Government to decide that the problem of Palestine must be referred to the United Nations...The Mandatory Power cannot go on for ever.'[1]

Bevin added that the UN would have to decide whether Palestine should be a Jewish state, an Arab state or a Palestinian state, with safeguards for all communities.[2] Although his decision on Palestine had already been reached on 14 February 1947,[3] it was not until April 1947 that London sent an official letter to UN Secretary-General Trygve Lie informing him of the verdict.[4] This conclusion was reached after attempts had been made by London to bring about a diplomatic solution through the 'Bevin Plan'. The plan had followed 'round table' discussions with Arab leaders in July 1946 and January 1947, as well as separate meetings with the Jewish Agency, although the Zionists boycotted talks in December 1946.[5] The plan sought to bridge competing Zionist and Arab visions for the future of Palestine. Bevin was a trade unionist leader who had progressed to the Minister of Labour in 1940. Upon his appointment as Foreign Secretary in 1945, Bevin soon became a despised figure among Zionists and their sympathizers, who felt betrayed by the maintenance of the 1939 White Paper that severely restricted Jewish immigration into Palestine. The White Paper contradicted the Labour Party's pledges to support the establishment

18

of a Jewish home in Palestine that had been renewed at ten party conferences including the last one in May 1945.[6]

Labour's December 1944 conference adopted as policy a resolution that there should be a Jewish majority in Palestine, the voluntary transfer of populations and the extension of Palestine's boundaries. The resolution emphasized as 'irresistible' the need for Jewish immigration in the wake of the 'unspeakable' Nazi atrocities.[7] Bevin's refusal to lift the White Paper led to charges that his policy was motivated by anti-Semitism and that he held conspiratorial views of Jews.[8] Prior to being foreign secretary, Bevin was neither strongly committed nor opposed to Zionist goals. Upon taking up office, Bevin had to deal with greater difficulties in Palestine in the post-war period than when Labour was in opposition. Jewish passion for the creation of a Jewish state was high, mixed with both desperation and preparation for armed struggle against the British. Bevin also had to contend with the potential regional consequences of the Zionist demand for a state.[9] Bevin furthermore believed that Jews, unlike the Arabs, were not a nation and therefore did not need a state of their own, even commenting that Jews should not 'get too much ahead of the queue' in the post-war period, despite having survived the Holocaust.[10]

Bevin, together with Colonial Secretary Arthur Creech-Jones, envisaged a unitary state with Jewish immigration permitted at a rate of 4,000 Jews per month for two years. Eventual independence would be granted, but only after a (suggested) five-year period of British trusteeship during which time both Arab and Jewish populations would be integrated under a central government.[11] Partition leading to a Jewish state in part of Palestine was not recommended, as it would be opposed by the Arab world and would not necessarily placate the Jews.[12] Bevin's proposal was rejected by both Zionists and Arab leaders, who refused to discuss any proposals other than their own.

It had been decided by Britain that if the plan was rejected, the problem would be referred to the UN.[13] The question of the future of Palestine put a great strain on Anglo-American relations in the period after World War II.[14] Although both Britain and the US formulated their Palestine policies on the basis of Cold War strategic interests, there were considerable policy differences which brought the two allies into conflict. Britain, concerned about Soviet encroachment into the Middle East and the need to maintain Arab goodwill, was wary of US calls to allow Jewish immigration into Palestine. However, facing economic difficulties as well as intense US pressure, Britain resigned itself to retreating from Palestine. The US, under President Harry Truman, saw Jewish immigration into Palestine as a means to alleviate the problem of Jewish displaced persons in post-war Europe.[15] This chapter evaluates US and British policy towards the question of Palestine during the final years of the Mandate in the context of the post-war strategic environment.

Britain and the Middle East: An easterly extension of the American continent?

In a paper written in March 1946, the new Labour Prime Minister Clement Atlee argued that Britain should now be viewed as an eastern extension of a strategic area which was the American continent rather than a separate power looking eastwards. Attlee maintained that air forces and bases were now required rather than a naval strategy for the maintenance of the Mediterranean route to India.[16] Foreign Secretary Ernest Bevin did not agree with this world view. He was concerned that it would damage British prestige and hurt the security of the Mediterranean route of the Empire.[17] The Chiefs of Staff (COS), apprehensive about the consequences of a British evacuation from the region, supported Bevin. Specifically, they argued that Atlee's position risked the Soviets replacing Britain in the area and the subsequent loss of British influence in the region. This would then lead Egypt to question whether to allow Britain to have bases around the Canal Zone.[18]

The debate led to a reformulation of how the COS positioned the Middle East in terms of their global strategy. Field Marshal Bernard Law Montgomery, for example, wrote a paper shortly after being appointed Chief of the Imperial General Staff (CIGS) in June 1946, which argued that while the Middle East and Mediterranean were important for the launch of an offensive, the region was also vital, because if Britain's defence was limited to the British Isles alone, an attacker would be unimpeded by danger to its own front. The Middle East's oil and the potential for the Soviets to have bases in the area were also highlighted.[19] Not only was the Arab Middle East the source of energy and commodities that were fundamental for Britain's post-war economic recovery where a withdrawal could interrupt the oil supply from Iraq, but the region was also the gateway to and centre of Britain's communications with its global imperial interests. As such, the COS viewed Britain's presence in Egypt and Palestine as fundamental to the defence of the whole Middle East.[20]

Meanwhile, at the close of World War II, Bevin wanted Britain to maintain its Great Power position by leading a Euro-African 'third world force' which would be a significant actor on the world stage, independent of the US and Soviet Union.[21] Treaties with Egypt, Iraq and Transjordan would provide sovereign status but with mutually advantageous ties that bound them to Britain so as to maintain British power from the Mediterranean Sea to the Indian Ocean.[22] Bevin envisaged plans for the economic development of the Middle East to raise the living standards of 'peasants not pashas'. Not only would this undermine the arguments of radicals and communists in this strategically vital region, but it would also create a productive area which would help Britain's economic growth.[23]

However, this ambitious foreign policy objective was tempered by Britain's financial circumstances. Britain's post-war economic and currency crises had started from Truman's decisive Lend Lease cancellation, and Britain's subsequent need for a US$3.75 billion US loan that eventually led to the British acknowledgement of US dependency.[24] During World War II, the British Foreign Office was adamant that Britain's role as a Great Power as well as its 'World Wide Mission' should be maintained, but because of Britain's weakened condition, US support was needed. So while Bevin commented that 'I'm not going to have Britain barged about', the Foreign Secretary soon awoke from his delusions of grandeur. Realizing that Britain did not have the resources to act on its own, he turned to the US. 'Financial weakness', Bevin finally conceded, 'has necessarily increased the need to coordinate our foreign policy with that of the only country which is able effectively to wield extensive economic influence – namely the United States'.[25] However, in the eyes of the British foreign policy makers, all was not lost. Although Britain would be a junior partner in its alliance with the US, it would possess infinitely more experience. Britain could therefore harness and guide US power for its own foreign policy orientations.[26]

The decision to refer Palestine to the UN was taken despite protests by the British COS as well as Secretary of Defence Albert Alexander.[27] Palestine was of significance because Britain feared that, if forced from the Mandate, its position in Suez, Egypt and the region would be challenged. Palestine was also crucial to the defence of Egypt.[28] Palestine's importance was heightened by the breakdown in negotiations with Egypt in December 1946, leading to the COS insistence that, with the evacuation of British forces (excluding the Canal Zone), Britain had to station troops in Palestine whose airbases were also needed for imperial communications.[29] Britain's withdrawal from Palestine threatened to unearth a power vacuum which, it was feared, would be filled by the Soviet Union. This could materialize through the establishment of a Jewish state which would become a bulwark for Bolshevism as a result of far left elements already in Palestine and through 'communist indoctrinated immigrants'.[30] Britain was also anxious about the possible establishment of an Arab Palestinian state, as it could be dominated by Haj Amin al-Husseini, the former Grand Mufti of Jerusalem who had collaborated with the Nazis during World War II.[31] Worse still, a Jewish state in Palestine threatened the goodwill of the Arab states whose military bases the British army required. The loss of Arab goodwill not only threatened to result in Soviet dominance in the Middle East, but also to communism spreading to other traditional areas of British dominance such as India, Burma, Malaya and Africa.[32]

Meanwhile, Britain was seeking to redraft and negotiate the terms of treaties with several Arab states. Although the revised Anglo-Jordanian Treaty was signed in March 1948, there were difficulties redrafting treaties elsewhere. In January, rioting crowds prevented amendments to the Anglo-Iraqi Treaty from being made. With the impending withdrawal from Palestine, the importance of relations with Egypt intensified and increased the necessity of bases in the Suez Canal, the status of which was also being negotiated.[33]

Some scholars have argued that the decision to leave Palestine was really due to Britain's expectation that the UN would redetermine the terms of the Mandate rather than recommend its abolition, especially as observers would not support partition because a Jewish state could precipitate a civil war. Instead, the UN would give Britain either a clear mandate to enforce its trusteeship over Palestine, a binational state, or establish a unitary Arab state absorbed or dominated by Transjordan.[34] However, by January 1946, Britain was already considering the possibility of turning over its mandates to the UN, although it had not yet decided on the question of Palestine.[35] On 12 October 1946, the ambassador to the US, Archibald Clark Kerr, 1st Baron Invernchapel, noted that such suggestions were being reported in the US press. Foreign Office official Harold Beeley responded that such a move would not be wise unless it was on the basis of a clearly defined policy.[36]

On a visit to New York in November 1946, Bevin told the US Secretary of State James Byrnes that Britain was considering either giving the Mandate to the US or to the UN. Byrnes implied that of the two options, Britain should refer it to the UN.[37] Britain was certainly in a difficult position. If it sought a solution on Arab terms, the US would be alienated and the Yishuv would launch a full-scale insurrection. On the other hand, agreeing to partition or to the establishment of a Jewish state would enflame the Arab world.[38] Illegal immigration and the British policy of intercepting ships sending immigrants to camps in Cyprus, according to the British High Commissioner in Palestine, Sir Alan Cunningham in February 1947, was plunging the Yishuv into a state of 'hysterical emotional tension', thus uniting Zionist moderates and extremists.[39]

Meanwhile, the interception strategy was breaking down and becoming an increasing burden on financial resources.[40] In addition, the number of illegal immigrants was potentially higher than the capacity to detain them in Cyprus.[41] The Zionist revolt against British rule had also taken its toll and sapped morale. A British quarterly report of October 1946 cited that the number of incidents such as road mines had forced men to stay in their quarters.[42] Other events damaging to morale included British sergeants being flogged by dissident Zionist groups and the bombing of the British Mandate Headquarters at the King David Hotel.[43] These incidents also affected public opinion back home, where the British press reported the story of the two hanged British sergeants with an anti-American angle over funding of the underground organizations coming from private groups in the US.[44]

However, the primary factors in Britain's decision to relinquish the Mandate were Britain's dire economic circumstances as well as US pressure. The financial burden of maintaining the Mandate was heavy. Dealing with the deteriorating security situation in Palestine cost £100 million between January 1945 and November 1947.[45] Britain's retreat was not limited to Palestine. It represented a general trend of British withdrawal from its international presence. Despite opposition from the COS and the importance of the Middle East and Mediterranean to British strategic interests, the decline of Britain in the region was irrevocable. By February 1947, Britain informed the US that it would be withdrawing military support from Greece and Turkey,[46] for financial reasons. The British economy was indeed in dire straits. Britain's overseas debt had multiplied six fold, and by 1947, half of its overseas investment had been lost, while exports had fallen by two thirds. Commodity prices were further reducing Britain's purchasing power from the US loan they had received. Even worse, the British Isles was facing its worst winter in 66 years. On a weekly basis, Hugh Dalton, the Chancellor of the Exchequer, was calling for a reduction of Britain's financial commitments, and Bevin was unable to rally enough support to counter Dalton's demands.[47] Not only had Britain informed the US of its inability to maintain support for Greece, but there was also the drafting of the Indian Independence Bill. This made Palestine's relevance to communication lines along the route to India less of a priority. With India about to gain independence, new strategic lines were being drawn, and while treaty negotiations with Egypt were being contemplated, Palestine also became more expendable.[48] Further, the idea that Palestine could be an alternative base in case troop numbers in Egypt were exceeded was offset by the possibility that other parts of the region could be used instead. Britain had determined that it would remain in Egypt and secure facilities in Cyrenaica.[49]

Rebuilding the dam: US containment strategy in the Middle East and Eastern Mediterranean

On 9 February 1946, following the UN Security Council's demand that the Soviet Union withdraw from Iran, Stalin declared that capitalism and communism were incompatible. Dean Acheson, the then US Undersecretary of State, would later label the speech an announcement of the Soviet Union's offensive against the US.[50] The speech was influential in changing US calculations towards Soviet intentions and determining that Soviet foreign policy was ideologically motivated. Previously, there had been a certain degree of uncertainty. For example, in a report released just one month before the speech, which assessed ideological factors in Soviet foreign policy, it was argued that most evidence suggested that the Soviet Union was no longer motivated by communist ideals.[51] Following Stalin's speech, the ideological aspect was again emphasized in strategic assessments. For example, in one memorandum, it was commented that Stalin's address bore 'comparison with certain speeches of Adolph Hitler of the 1930s' and that the contours of Soviet thinking would continue to be Marxist, although with sufficient leeway to accommodate relations with other Great Powers.[52]

On 12 February, George F. Kennan, the Deputy Chief of Mission of the United States to the Soviet Union, wrote that the speech was a 'straight Marxist interpretation' of the two world wars.[53] Ten days later, Kennan penned the 'Long Telegram'. The following year, under the name 'X', the telegram was refined and published in *Foreign Affairs*. Entitled 'The Sources of Soviet Conduct', Kennan, in summary, argued that the Soviet Union was 'a political force committed fanatically to the belief that with US there can be no permanent modus vivendi'. In Kennan's interpretation of Soviet strategic thinking, only by disrupting the internal stability and traditional way of life of the West would Soviet power be secure.[54] In order to combat this threat, Kennan argued that the US had to initiate a policy of containment which would confront the Russians with an unalterable counter-force at every point where the Soviets attempted to encroach it.[55]

Kennan's views were later echoed in another memorandum that argued that the Soviets also sought to acquire the 'warm water' of the Middle East where it could control oil-rich areas. Not only would the Soviets deny this precious resource to Britain and the US, but it would also gain power from possessing the oil fields. Ultimately, the memorandum concluded, the Soviet Union's ambition was to supplant Britain as the dominant political, economic and military power in the region.[56] This was a significant threat. As Acheson recalled, it centred on territory considered most favourable to the Soviet Union's exterior lines where its military power was superior and where US power was at its weakest: the Middle East and Eastern Europe.[57]

Truman commissioned another report in the summer of 1946 under the direction of Special Counsel Clark Clifford. In compiling his report, Clifford consulted the Departments of State, War, Navy, the Joint Chiefs of Staff and the Director of the Central Intelligence. The report concluded that there was a persistent pattern in Soviet behaviour which would either unilaterally implement agreements in a way to serve its own interests or encourage its satellites to do so. Therefore, the Clifford Report continued, the Soviet Union had no intention of cooperating with the West and instead sought to expand its influence as much as possible without regard for the security concerns of its wartime allies.[58] Upon receiving the Clifford Report, Truman ordered all copies to be locked in the White House safe. In all probability, Truman's reaction was not because he disagreed with Clifford's assessment, but because he was concerned that its public release could further damage relations with the Soviet Union.[59]

In March 1946, the American Joint War Plans Committee warned that Soviet pressure on Iran and Turkey could be the spark to ignite World War III, as Soviet success in Turkey would threaten British interests in Suez as well as oil reserves.[60] In December 1945, Loy Henderson, Director of Near East and African Affairs at the State Department, argued that British interests in the Middle East were acting as a dam against Russian expansion while protecting its own communication lines. The Soviets, Henderson believed, wanted to break down the existing structure in order to extend their influence into the Mediterranean, Iran and towards the Indian Ocean.[61] By 26 July 1946, the Joint Chiefs of Staff (JCS) assessed that the Soviet Union desired to have Greece, Turkey and Iran in her orbit.[62]

Following the end of the Iran crisis in which the US offered an ultimatum to the Soviet Union for prolonging its military presence in Azerbaijan, and the subsequent Soviet withdrawal, it appeared to confirm that US resoluteness would pay off against Soviet actions.[63] Coupled with the Iranian crisis were concerns over Soviet designs on Turkey. Recently appointed Undersecretary of State Dean Acheson interpreted a note Stalin had written to Turkey over redefining the status of the strategic Dardanelles as a Soviet threat to Turkey, Greece and the Middle East. Left unchallenged, Acheson feared it would lead to the collapse of the Middle East and then possibly India and China.[64] Truman informed the Soviets that Turkey would maintain primary responsibility for the Dardanelles. The aircraft carrier Franklin D. Roosevelt was sent into the area for good measure.[65]

If Britain was acting as a dam against Soviet encroachment in the region, London's inability to maintain its obligations meant that the US was obliged to fill the void. In a similar vein to relinquishing Palestine to the UN, also in February 1947, Britain declared that it would be withdrawing military support for Greece and Turkey. Recently appointed Secretary of State George Marshall later called the British declaration tantamount to a British abdication of its role in the Eastern Mediterranean.[66] State Department officials were apparently surprised at the announcement, even doubting the sincerity of the British reason for the withdrawal of aid to Greece. Francis Williams, Downing Street's press secretary, later commented that he thought Bevin deliberately withdrew aid as a means to force the US to engage in the international arena.[67] However, there were some State Department officials who had already alluded to Britain's move. As early as August 1945, a State Department memorandum noted that Britain had admitted that it was no longer able to keep the Middle East in order without US help.[68] According to Cold War historian Walter Lafeber, in early 1947, the US knew that British attempts to regain control of Greece had become bogged down in the civil war, and as the Tito-supported communist-led National Liberation Front grew, the US was becoming involved, siding with the British and sending US$260 million in aid in 1946. Therefore, Truman's later US$400 million request was not a sudden departure in US policy.[69] Clark Clifford recalled that by late 1946, the administration had received word that Britain would have to pull out of Greece and Turkey.[70] On 3 February 1947, the US ambassador in Athens reported the rumour that Britain would soon be pulling out.[71] And indeed, later that month, Britain did exactly that, signifying the beginning of the end of British dominance in the Middle East and ushering in an era of US influence in the region.

The basis of what became known as the Truman Doctrine emanated from the president's speech of 12 March 1947, which requested congressional support for urgent requests from Greece for financial and economic assistance, and also for aid to Turkey. Truman reasoned that 'one of the primary objectives of the foreign policy of the United States is the creation of conditions in which we and other nations will be able to work out a way of life free from coercion'.[72]

While not mentioning the Soviet Union by name, Truman argued that there were two alternative ways of life, one embodying the will of the majority, with guarantees of liberty, freedom of speech and religion and freedom from political oppression; and the other of minority rule, terror and oppression. 'The policy of the United States is to support free peoples who are resisting attempted subjugation by armed minorities or by outside pressures',[73] and that help should be extended through financial aid. Truman also highlighted the danger of Greece falling to an armed minority and the effect it would have on its neighbour Turkey.[74]

It was in this context that the US State Department considered the Palestine problem an immediate concern to the US government, stressing that the necessity of finding a settlement was a 'real concern for security' in the Middle East.[75] Although Washington recognized in early 1945 that a solution to the Palestine question was 'most important' and 'urgent', some quarters in Washington considered the country to be primarily a British responsibility.[76] However, others such as James Landis, the American Director of Economic Relations in the Middle East, believed that the Palestine problem should be an international responsibility as the British could not carry the burden alone.[77] In 1945, the State Department feared that pro-Zionist sentiments expressed by the president could lead to bloodshed in the Middle East and endanger the security of US oil interests in Saudi Arabia.[78] This was especially the case after President Roosevelt had met Ibn Saud on board the *USS Quincy* following the Yalta Conference, and his subsequent April letter to the Saudi king which stated that no action would be taken on Palestine that might prove hostile to the Arab peoples.[79] Meanwhile, from the field it was noted that the Soviet Union was being looked at by Arab nationalists for help against Zionism.[80] Loy Henderson, Director of the Office of Near Eastern and African Affairs, highlighted what was at stake for US interests. If the US were to support a Jewish state in Palestine, it could lead to the boycott of trade, with US oil interests, especially in Saudi Arabia, being affected. Furthermore, long-established US educational and cultural institutions would be placed at risk and the US might also lose its 'moral prestige' in the region.[81] Similar sentiments were expressed by Gordon Merriam, Chief of the Division of Near Eastern Affairs, later in May 1946, highlighting the anger in Arab states over the possible entry of 100,000 Jewish displaced persons to Palestine and the repercussions of a 'very serious nature' that might follow.[82]

Jewish immigration to Palestine

Despite the strategic importance of Palestine to both British and US interests, the country's future became a source of tension between the two allies, particularly over Britain's policy towards Jewish immigration. An estimated 200,000 Jewish displaced persons were in Europe by the end of World War II. With nothing left for them in Europe and with a lack of options for immigration, the vast majority of them wanted to leave for Palestine. Britain had 100,000 troops stationed in Palestine and was facing a significant insurgency by the Jewish population as well as general Arab unrest and dissatisfaction with British rule. Deteriorating security in a Palestine facing insurgency and on the brink of civil war was coupled with opposition to British policy, particularly over immigration, from the White House. President Truman saw a solution to the Jewish displaced persons problem, and as early as July 1945, asked Winston Churchill at the Potsdam Conference to lift restrictions on Jewish entry into Palestine. The following month Truman sent a letter to the new British Prime Minister Clement Attlee enclosing the Harrison Report. Commissioned by Truman to assess the conditions and needs of displaced persons in liberated Western Europe, it recommended 100,000 entry certificates for Jews to Palestine[83] on compassionate grounds.[84] In an attempt to bridge the differences between Britain and the US and to find a joint solution, the Anglo-American Committee of Inquiry into the Problem of European Jewry and Palestine was set up.

Its report, published in April 1946, called for the immediate transfer of 100,000 displaced persons to Palestine and was supported by President Truman,[85] much to the dissatisfaction of Britain. Increasing the pressure, a White House press release of 2 July 1946 detailed a meeting with US members of the Jewish Agency for Palestine such as Rabbi Stephen Wise and Rabbi Abba H. Silver, and mentioned that the president wanted to press for the entry of 100,000 refugees without further delay.[86] Then, on the Jewish holiday of Yom Kippur, October 1946, Truman stated that the entry of 100,000 refugees to Palestine and partition was something the American public could accept.[87] Britain was highly reluctant to ease Jewish immigration into Palestine, believing that the entry of 100,000 Jewish refugees would 'set aflame the whole Middle East'. Bevin went as far as to quip that Truman's refugee policy was because he did not want the Jews to enter the US,[88] and that 'certain Jewish groups were exercising great influence upon public opinion in the United States at a time when public issues are about to be brought to the test of a Congressional election'.[89]

The dilemma Britain faced was that in order to remain a dominant power in the region, it was essential to maintain good and cooperative relations with both the Arab states and the US.[90] Meanwhile, the displaced persons impasse threatened the passing in Congress of a US\$3.75 billion loan to Britain which was already unpopular with the majority of Americans.[91] In one discussion over the US loan to Britain, Adolph J. Sabath, the Chairman of the House of Representatives Rules Committee and a staunch Zionist, alleged that Britain was now under a 'fascist government'.[92] While facing pressure from the White House, a Cabinet report stated that all of Britain's defence requirements, including maintaining oil supplies and lines of communications, were dependent on the goodwill of the Arabs.[93] Still, demands from Washington persisted; Truman continued to press Britain over its Palestine policy following the publication of the Anglo-American Committee of Inquiry Report.[94] On 14 June, Truman told Attlee that although he understood Britain's reservations in allowing 100,000 refugees into Palestine, a detailed plan for their transfer should nevertheless be urgently made.[95] Washington even offered to finance and provide the ships for the entry of the Jewish immigrants.[96] However, London insisted that such a policy could not be implemented without first examining the repercussions.[97] Washington continued to insist, and even as Britain announced its referral of Palestine to the UN, Truman made another call for Jewish immigration.[98]

In the summer of 1947, tensions continued to sour. Acting Secretary of State Robert Lovett noted that large sections of US public opinion had been angered over the Exodus affair, during which the ill-fated ship containing hundreds of Jewish immigrants, including many Holocaust survivors, had been forced to return by the British to Hamburg, Germany. Lovett warned that the incident had done significant harm to Britain's public position in the US.[99] An additional factor for the US public outcry was that many of the crew were US citizens.[100] Anti-British sentiment was so high in the US that some pro-Zionist propagandists such as Ben Hecht were equating Britain with the Nazis.[101] It was this increasing public sentiment that prompted British Undersecretary of State Sir Orne Sargent to protest to the US Ambassador Lewis Douglas that the New York press was inciting violence.[102] The public outcry against Britain soon impacted on diplomatic relations. In August, when Bevin requested that the US do more to help prevent illegal Jewish immigration, he was rebuffed and told by Secretary of State General George Marshall that the US would 'study the matter'.[103]

The divergent positions of Britain and the US over the future of Jewish displaced persons severely strained the transatlantic relationship. Indeed, British advisor Harold Beeley blamed the US for much of Britain's troubles in Palestine, arguing that 'the impotence of our policy in Palestine has been due to the contrary pressure upon us from the Arab states and from the United States'.[104] Relations with the US were therefore an important element in British Cabinet deliberations on Palestine in the period leading up to the decision to refer Palestine to the UN. For example, in a 15 January 1947 Cabinet meeting, Bevin commented that even if Britain did not think it necessary to refer Palestine to the UN, he had 'no doubt' that it would be referred to by 'some government which disliked the solution which we adopted'.[105] The country to which Bevin was in all probability referring was the US, because the statement was made in the context of referring to the Anglo-American Committee of Inquiry and Truman's opposition to British policy.[106]

Active neutrality: Britain's response to the United Nations Special Committee on Palestine's recommendations

Following Britain's referral of Palestine to the UN in May 1947, the United Nations Special Committee on Palestine (UNSCOP) was established. The committee was comprised of delegates from 11 UN states and was headed by Swedish Supreme Court Judge Emile Sandstrom.[107] In the following months, the committee, which was accompanied by Harold Beeley, visited Palestine to investigate potential solutions for the future of Palestine. The committee heard from representatives of the Jewish Agency and other proponents of the Zionist cause. Although the Arabs officially boycotted UNSCOP, the committee members heard from King Abdullah of Jordan and Musa Alami, a relative of the former Grand Mufti of Jerusalem Haj Amin al-Husseini and head of the Arab Office, the Arab League's information bureau based in London, Washington and Jerusalem.[108]

Anticipating UNSCOP's report, a draft paper was prepared by the Foreign Office detailing four possible recommendations for the future of Palestine arranged in the order of preference from a strategic point of view. They were British trusteeship, a unitary independent state, partition and an international trusteeship scheme.[109] The paper cited the need to maintain the use of Haifa or possibly Gaza as a supply port and the use of airfields, freedom of movement and the free flow of oil to Palestine's Mediterranean terminals.[110] Although Britain was aware that a unanimous recommendation by UNSCOP was highly unlikely, it predicted that the committee would most likely propose some form of partition, although not concede to the Jewish Agency's 'unreasonable demands'. This would be opposed by the Arabs and therefore Anglo-Arab relations would be damaged if Britain voted in favour of partition.[111]

UNSCOP failed to put forward a unanimous proposal for the future of Palestine. However, it did unanimously agree that the Mandate should be terminated and that there should be a short transitional period before independence. The report by the majority of UNSCOP members proposed that Palestine be partitioned into two states, one Jewish and one Arab, with the city of Jerusalem internationalized. The two states would be bound in an economic union and gain independence after a transitional period of two years. Britain would continue to administer Palestine but under the auspices of the UN. During this transitional period, 150,000 Jewish immigrants would be permitted entry into Palestine.[112] The Negev, eastern Galilee, the Huleh Basin, the coastal plain from Acre down to Jaffa and Tel Aviv would be part of the Jewish state. The majority proposal was accepted by the Jewish Agency but rejected by the Arabs. Nevertheless, the proposal was put forward to the UN General Assembly, which voted in favour of it on 29 November 1947. When the partition vote was held at the UN and passed by a two-thirds majority,[113] Britain abstained and was the only Great Power not to vote in favour of partition.

Britain was concerned about the possibility that Soviet policy aimed to establish a Zionist state. The Jewish state could potentially become a Soviet vassal through the influence of far left elements already in Palestine and through 'communist-indoctrinated immigrants' entering the Jewish state.[114] A source from the field added that the Soviets were in fact producing a large number of communist-indoctrinated citizens to enter Palestine.[115]

Later, Bevin told his US counterpart that many indoctrinated communists were moving into Palestine from the Balkans, presenting a real threat to Middle East stability.[116] He also told Labour MP Richard Crossman, who had been a member of the 1946 Anglo-American Committee of Inquiry, that he had information that 'the Russians have massed an army of Jews at Odessa, ready for the attack!'[117] Crossman was unable to convince Bevin that it was precisely because the Jews were from Russia that they were unlikely to spread communism to the Middle East.[118] Moreover, the internal Jewish question in the Soviet Union and its support for a Jewish state needed to be separated, as not only was Stalin preventing Soviet Jews from identifying with the Zionist cause, but he was also barring Jewish emigration to Palestine, leading to wholesale arrests, even executions of leading Jewish writers and intellectuals from 1949. Plans were already in place in 1946 to close the Jewish Anti-Fascist Committee, established in 1942 to garner world Jewish support for the Soviets against Nazi Germany.[119]

Meanwhile at the UN, the Soviet Ambassador Andrei Gromyko had made a favourable speech towards Zionism in May 1947 critiquing British behaviour and rule.[120] Later in November 1947, he put forward a policy in favour of partitioning Palestine. On 13 October 1947, Semen Tsarapkin, the Soviet delegate to the Ad Hoc Committee on Palestine, announced Moscow's endorsement of partition, leaving the US 'mystified', to use the words of Lovett.[121] Soviet motives for this apparent support of Zionist aspirations can be summed up by Gromyko, who once commented that there was only one logic in foreign affairs, that being what was 'best for the Soviet Union'.[122] Indeed, Moscow was motivated by its determination to oust Britain in the region and to prevent the US from filling the void while doubling as an opportunity to create a rift in the Anglo-American post-war alliance, not to mention the advantages of winning its long-coveted warm sea port, with Haifa serving such a purpose.[123] It was also speculated by some British officials that Moscow would advocate similar national claims for Kurds and Armenians in order to capitalize on the geographical position of Turkish Armenia and Kurdistan to British and US oil areas.[124] As will be seen, this apparent Soviet reversal of its earlier Palestine policy[125] would later be a determining factor for US support for partition.

Britain calculated that a solution unfavourable to the Arab nations, and partition as proposed by the UNSCOP majority report especially, could also push the Arab world towards the Soviet Union. This particularly concerned Britain, not least because of the need to maintain military positions, sustain strategic depth in the region and ensure the steady flow of oil. Britain also feared that the Soviets could gain influence as partition would lead to a decline in Britain's military presence.[126] A warning of growing Arab discontent with Western powers and a possible shift to the Soviet Union was given by the Iraqi prime minister to Britain. He stated that the US and Britain should be under no illusions about what would be the repercussions of a UN solution unacceptable to the Arabs, 'serious trouble, political and economic'.[127] Indeed, Arab prime ministers convening in Lebanon to discuss UNSCOP's proposals put forward the idea of initiating economic sanctions against Britain and the US.[128] The continuous supply of oil was at stake which was vital to rebuild Europe after the devastation wrought by World War II and fundamental to the success of the Marshall Plan. On October 1947, the British ambassador to the US relayed Britain's fears to Undersecretary of State Robert Lovett that the security situation in Palestine would deteriorate and that Arab hostility towards Britain and the US could last indefinitely affecting both nations' interests in the area.[129]

Britain also had genuine sympathy for the Arab position. For example, Ernest Bevin told the British Cabinet that 'the majority proposal is so manifestly unjust to the Arabs it is difficult to see how in Sir Alex Cadogan's words "we could reconcile it with our conscience" '.[130] Beeley echoed these sentiments, contending that the partition proposal would have involved a serious injustice to the Arabs.[131] However, the crux of British concern over the future of Palestine was the need to maintain Arab 'goodwill'. For self-interested reasons, Beeley argued that Britain could neither accept responsibility nor agree to implement it principally because it would be harmful to Anglo-Arab relations unless changes were made to the majority solution, which would probably be unacceptable to the Jews anyway.[132] The challenge facing British diplomacy was providing an impression of neutrality while at the same time finding a position that would maintain Arab goodwill.

In the wider Arab world, partition could also upset the geopolitical balance in the region, with Abdullah seeking to capitalize on his ambitions for a Greater Syria.[133] Britain also predicted that relations with oil-rich Saudi Arabia would be damaged, as King Abdul Aziz Ibn Saud, who advised the Arabs to trust Britain during the early stages of World War II, would feel betrayed.[134] King Abdullah's 'ambitions', a reference supposedly to plans to expand his territory to include Arab Palestine, associated with partition might curb any anti-British actions in Jordan, and British influence in the Gulf Sheikdoms was believed to be strong enough to maintain.[135] However, in was what termed 'advanced' Arab nations such as Syria, Iraq and Egypt, Britain's position would be unstable. Throughout 1947, Britain was negotiating treaty rights with Iraq and Egypt and Britain feared that the growth of Arab nationalism and calls for treaty amendments were already putting a strain on relations.[136] Importantly, this growing revolutionary sentiment made these 'developed' Arab nations susceptible to Soviet propaganda which was already being disseminated across the Arab world with the aim of dislodging Britain's position. And if a solution to the Palestine question was unacceptable to the Arabs, Britain's position would be undermined and open to further Soviet penetration.[137]

Britain therefore tried to maintain the impression of neutrality at the UN, but behind the scenes, it looked to make amendments to the UNSCOP recommendations. For example, two weeks after the release of UNSCOP's report, the Colonial Office was considering modifications that could be made to the majority report to make the scheme more palatable to the Arabs, especially regarding the Negev and Jaffa, even with the possibility of getting an agreement with the former Mufti.[138] Indeed, Bevin had instructed the Eastern Department to look into ways that UNSCOP's majority proposals could be modified in case Britain was approached by the Arab states following the passing of a resolution at the UN.[139]

On 26 September 1947, the British Colonial Secretary Arthur Creech-Jones walked the diplomatic tightrope as he addressed the second meeting of the Ad Hoc Committee on Palestine discussing UNSCOP's recommendations for Palestine. The colonial secretary crucially stated that if the General Assembly were to recommend a policy that was unacceptable to both Jews and Arabs, the British government would feel unable to endorse it and would not contemplate upholding a proposal by force of arms.[140] This was a fundamental point designed to hide British intransigence and create the appearance that Britain was amicable to a UN decision, but at the same time not to a solution unacceptable to the Arabs who had expressed their fierce opposition to UNSCOP's proposals. It also served as a warning to any party considering voting in favour of partition because a positive vote would now risk creating a crisis in implementation. The speech had the desired effect with its target audience as it 'made a very good impression on all Arab states'.[141] Britain's position was reiterated by Creech-Jones again at the Ad Hoc Committee on 16 October stating that 'if the Assembly should recommend a policy which is not acceptable to the Jews and Arabs, some authority alternative to the United Kingdom must be provided in order to implement the United Nations policy'.[142] And later at the 25th Ad Hoc Committee meeting, the UK representative Sir Alexander Cadogan restated his government's policy that the UK could not play a role in the implementation of a plan that was not accepted by both parties, and that Britain would soon decide when it would withdraw troops from the Mandate without approval by the Security Council. He also implied that authority would only be handed over to a UN commission after withdrawal.[143] In other words Britain was refusing to participate in the proposed solution as it had been rejected by the Arab side. Furthermore, it was leaving Palestine, regardless, indicating the possibility that a solution determined by force of arms would be the likely result.

Humanitarianism and Cold War interests: President Truman's partition policy

The US administration of Harry Truman drifted significantly from the British position on partition. Unlike Britain, the US not only voted in favour of partition at the UN General Assembly, but it even lobbied other governments to do the same.[144] However, US policy was not monolithic and there was a significant gap between White House policy and that of the State Department and key figures in the administration. They included the Secretary of State George Marshall, Undersecretaries Dean Acheson and Robert Lovett, Defence Secretary James Forrestal and the Director of the Policy Planning Staff George Kennan and Loy Henderson in the Near East Department. Indeed, it was one thing for Washington to support the entry of 100,000 Jewish displaced persons and be critical of the British approach to the Palestine problem, but quite another to support the partitioning of Palestine and face intense Arab opposition and an opportunity for Soviet infiltration into the region.

This apparent split in Washington over the correct Palestine policy has led scholars to suggest multiple reasons why Truman seemingly ignored the advice of his staff. Some have argued that domestic factors influenced Truman; by pursuing a favourable policy towards partition (and later recognizing Israel), Truman would clinch the crucial Jewish vote during the 1948 presidential elections while he was also under pressure from Jewish lobbying groups.[145] This in itself was not a new argument. Suggestions that electoral politics were influencing Truman's Palestine policy were alleged as early as 1946.[146] Some have even argued that Truman's religious background and belief in the authority of Holy Scripture influenced his pro-partition policy and subsequent recognition of the State of Israel.[147] Steven L. Spiegel contends that Truman was caught between an articulated public opinion that was supported by most of Congress and key White House staff, but opposed by the majority in the national security bureaucracy.[148] However, their differences reflected a tactical, rather than strategic divergence. Truman's commitment to the goals of the Zionist movement was limited. For example, despite calls by personal friends such as Eddie Jacobson to announce US support for the partition plan ('Harry, my people need help and I am appealing to you to help them'), Truman replied that because it was before the UN General Assembly, it would not be right to interfere.[149] In another letter to Jacobson, Truman stressed that the Zionists had wanted the US to support them with a 'big stick approach' only to be disappointed.[150] Evan M. Wilson, a former US foreign officer, has argued that a Jewish state was of secondary importance to Truman, who only placed the US government in favour of a Jewish state in October 1947.[151]

Two weeks after the release of the UNSCOP report, the US delegation to the UN debated what US policy should be ahead of Secretary of State Marshall's address to the UN on the matter. In a view similar to that of the British Foreign Office, Marshall argued that adopting the majority report would lead to a very violent Arab reaction and that the US should avoid arousing the Arabs and precipitate their rapprochement with the Soviet Union. Marshall also highlighted the concerns of Loy Henderson who feared that if the US committed itself to partition and obtaining the necessary two-thirds majority, it might have to take part in its practical implementation.[152] In reply to a question by Eleanor Roosevelt, US delegate to the UN, about whether it was evident that the Soviets would oppose the majority report, it was argued that it did appear so;[153] a prediction which would not only prove incorrect but would also shift US policy. Delegates General Hilldring and Mrs Roosevelt expressed support for partition and advocated that the US should accept the report, but should also remain willing to amend it following debate in the General Assembly. Meanwhile Roosevelt outlined a point in favour of supporting partition by stressing the importance of promoting the success of the UN.[154] Marshall feared that the US might have to follow through with its commitment by putting its own troops on the ground.[155]

In general, US opponents of the UN partition plan argued it would damage relations with the Arabs whose oil was vital for the success of the Marshall Plan and the profits of US oil companies.[156] The US might also have to contribute militarily and financially for partition to work. Meanwhile, the Soviets would benefit because either the new Jewish state would become a Soviet ally or the Arabs would be pushed towards Russia, and the plan would lead to an increase of Arab extremism.[157] One particularly vocal opponent of partition was Loy Henderson. He was of the view that nearly every member of the Foreign Service or the State Department with Near East experience believed that the Palestine question at the UN would have far-reaching consequences for US efforts to promote regional stability and cause further Soviet penetration.[158] For Henderson, the 'overwhelming majority of non Jewish Americans who are intimately acquainted with the situation' thought it not in US national interests to advocate a partition plan leading to a Jewish state.[159] Henderson further stated that as well as undermining relations with the Arab world, it would also affect Britain's ability to maintain bases and remain a stabilizing power in the area. Further, Arab friendship was vital for the US in order to draw upon regional resources to benefit US economic interests and its stake in the reconstruction of Europe.[160] Henderson was not alone in his views. Undersecretary of State Acheson believed that a Jewish state capable of receiving over a million Jewish inhabitants would imperil US interests in the Middle East.[161] Some of Henderson's assertions were repeated by King Abdul Aziz Ibn Saud in a message to President Truman. 'Without doubt the results of this decision will lead to a deathblow to American interests in the Arab countries and will dissolve the Arab's confidence in the friendship, justice and fairness of the United States.'[162]

Henderson was called to a meeting with President Truman to discuss his views. Also present were Clark Clifford and David Niles, advisors to the president who were sympathetic to the majority report. Henderson, who later recalled that he felt that his hosts were trying to humiliate him, was asked by Clifford for the sources of his views and whether his views were simply his opinions. For example, did he think the opinions of him and his staffs were superior to the experts of UNSCOP? As the questioning became more heated, Truman had had enough and left the room.[163] However, Clifford's opposition to Henderson was a significant factor as Clifford had been one of the most important advocates of the containment policy. He played a fundamental role in drafting the Truman Doctrine.[164] Therefore, he undoubtedly had the confidence of Truman in matters of strategic importance. All the more so as Truman was deeply suspicious of the State Department who he referred to as the 'striped pants boys'.[165] According to Clifford, Truman even suspected that the British had influenced some State Department officials in matters pertaining to Palestine.[166]

But foremost, it was Cold War factors and the need to contain the Soviet Union that was the primary factor behind Truman's Palestine policy. Previously, the general assumption was that the Soviets would not be in favour of partition. Indeed, following the aforementioned discussion by the US delegation to the UN on 24 September, Secretary of State Marshall decided that the US representative to the Ad Hoc Committee on Palestine would support an open discussion and ascertain the views of Britain, the Jewish Agency and the Arab Higher Committee. After these discussions, the US representative would present US views. Taking into account the views expressed, the US representative would embrace the UNSCOP majority report but with amendments to make it workable.[167]

In Truman's memoirs, he conceded that the main difference in his position to that of the State Department was more about pace and speed rather than the direction of movement, but that Marshall, Lovett and US Ambassador to the UN Austin saw eye to eye with him.[168] Michael Ottolenghi has argued that actually there was some consensus between the White House and the State Department over the Palestine issue. Decisions on Palestine were based on no US troops being deployed to Palestine and that the country should be denied Soviet penetration.[169] Just as importantly, Truman calculated that Saudi oil was tied to the US and would not be affected by US policy towards Palestine. He therefore pursued the middle line between his advisors and the State Department where opposition to partition rested on the assumption that the Soviet Union would not support it. Truman instructed his UN delegation to support partition (but ruled out sending US troops) on 11 October 1947, and two days later the Soviet Union announced its support for partition, altering the US concern that the Arab states would turn to the Soviets in response to the US position.[170]

Furthermore, Truman recalled that the Palestine question had been placed in the hands of the UN, and the UN, he believed, had to be a success.[171] Even when the US temporarily reversed its policy in favour of partition to support trusteeship, it was due to fears of the necessity of a US troop presence in Palestine as a result of increasing Arab statements of belligerency and reports from the Central Intelligence Agency (CIA) and the State Department's Policy Planning Staff.[172] But the majority of the American press[173] as well as Congress had become highly supportive of the UN, believing that the organization could maintain world peace; therefore, a reversal of the UN-sponsored partition plan for Palestine could undermine and damage the organization at a critical time in the Cold War, and it was with 'outrage' that the press reacted to Truman's policy reversal.[174] This apparent about face in policy occurred as Czechoslovakia fell to communist forces and there was a 'war scare' mentality in the US. Questions of Truman's steadfastness and ability to lead the country during the Cold War were now being asked by the press.[175]

Conclusion

Despite Britain and the US being, for the most part, in agreement on the necessity of checking perceived Soviet expansion, the two wartime allies drifted apart in their respective policies towards Palestine. Britain considered the maintenance of Arab goodwill as essential for the West to prevent Soviet encroachment into the Middle East. However, Britain found itself in a quandary. In the post-war period, Britain became increasingly reliant on the US to advance its strategic interests, especially because of the financial burden of maintaining its presence in the Middle East and Mediterranean. Moreover, Britain's Palestine policy was at odds with that of the White House. This was a time when good relations with the US were an essential pillar of British foreign policy. The relationship between Britain and the US was severely strained and tested over the question of Palestine. The US under President Truman saw Jewish immigration into Palestine as a means to alleviate the problem of Jewish displaced persons in post-war Europe. Humanitarian aspects concerning Europe's Jewish displaced persons as well as Cold War concerns, specifically Soviet infiltration in to the region explained Truman's Palestine policy. The Soviet Union's support for partition and later a Jewish state, further pushed Washington into supporting partition and a policy which further distanced her from Britain.

As the following chapter will reveal, after partition and the outbreak of violence between Jew and Arab in Palestine, what would emerge was compromise in the positions of Britain and the US in an effort to maintain Arab goodwill. This became a particular concern following the emergence of the Palestinian refugee crisis. However, although both the US and Britain were quick to recognize the potential fallout of the refugee problem, and together took decisive action, the scars following the policy divergence during the final years of the Mandate were not fully healed and would resurface.

2
Friends Reunited? Britain and the US Respond to the Palestinian Refugee Problem

Introduction

The previous chapter demonstrated how Cold War strategic interests influenced the policies of both Britain and the US towards the question of Palestine between 1945 and 1948. It showed that despite there being a general agreement on the importance of maintaining Arab goodwill and preventing the Soviet Union from exploiting the void left by Britain's withdrawal from the region, there was neither a unified nor a coordinated policy approach towards the future of Palestine. In fact, there were major disagreements which put great strain on the transatlantic alliance. When UN General Assembly Resolution 181 calling for the partition of Palestine into a Jewish and Arab state was tabled on 29 November 1947, Britain and the US voted differently. The latter voted favourably alongside the Soviets; the former abstained.

Despite their differences on the Palestinian refugee crisis, a major consequence of the 1948 War meant that Britain and the US had to deal with both a humanitarian problem as well as a political impasse almost immediately. Ultimately, it was through UN General Assembly Resolution 212, which called for a major relief effort, that both cooperated to spearhead a short-term initiative to alleviate the suffering of the refugees. This provided aid for the hundreds of thousands of refugees made homeless following the 1948 Palestine War. Resolution 212 called for US$29.5 million financial assistance to the Palestinian refugees plus an additional US$2.5 million for administrative and local operational expenses.[1] The resolution also called for all member states to make voluntary contributions and invited the assistance of specialized agencies of the UN, the United Nations International Children's Emergency Fund (UNICEF), the International Committee of the Red

Cross, the International Refugee Organization (IRO), the League of Red Cross Societies and other voluntary organizations.[2] Meanwhile, UN General Assembly Resolution 194 established the mechanism through which the outstanding political differences between Israel and the Arab states would be discussed. Among them were the potential return, resettlement and rehabilitation of the refugees. The resolution established the PCC; a body which took over the role of mediator and was given the authority to assist the parties in reaching a final settlement of all outstanding questions between them.[3] However, in order to implement these initiatives, Britain and the US had to overcome their own internal differences about how such a mechanism would and should work, and how aid could be administered and organized. They also had to identify the basis for negotiations between Israel and the Arab states.

This chapter will show that despite continued differences over Palestine, both Britain and the US managed jointly to launch a diplomatic initiative which would influence Middle East diplomacy for the next three years. However, in the course of doing so, they had to overcome considerable differences in terms of focus and emphasis and even the feasibility of such projects. This chapter will assess the different positions in the formation of the two aforementioned resolutions which were the basis for aid and diplomatic initiatives in subsequent years. What becomes apparent was that although Britain and the US successfully led the way in terms of aid and diplomacy, both countries still made serious errors of judgment regarding the refugee question. Although they acknowledged that the Palestinian refugee issue was a political problem with ramifications for the future, they both discussed it, primarily, in its humanitarian context. Instead of tackling it as a significant outstanding issue between Arabs and Israelis, this aspect of the problem was simply referred to the proposed conciliation commission without detailed consideration. Britain and the US were preoccupied with launching a humanitarian effort to help the refugees because they feared continued Palestinian hardship would be detrimental to their own strategic interests. When the UN resolution to launch a diplomatic effort was discussed, Britain and the US were concerned with the question of territorial adjustments, as recommended by the late Mediator Count Folke Bernadotte, and paid much less attention to the refugee issue. Ultimately, the failure to address the extent to which the refugee issue threatened to be a diplomatic obstacle would have lasting repercussions for future efforts to bring about peace between Israel and the Arab states and would perpetuate the Palestinian refugee crisis in the subsequent decades.

The blame game

One of the reasons why Britain and the US urgently addressed the humanitarian aspect of the refugee problem was because of the proliferation of Arab anti-Western sentiment during the 1948 Palestine War, which saw the emergence of the refugee problem.[4] As the refugee crisis developed, so too did hostility towards the West. This was noted by Foreign Office and State Department officials as reports emerged from the field that Britain was being accused of complicity in the Palestinian exodus. For example, after the fall of Haifa in April 1948, it was reported that Arab leaders, in an attempt to save face, were blaming Britain for the departure of Arabs from the city. Such claims had caused anti-British sentiment to run so high that it was considered inadvisable for British personnel to use the Jerusalem–Nablus–Jenin road.[5] By this time, May 1948, the number of Arab refugees stood at between 250,000 and 300,000.[6] An Arab broadcast from Ramallah reported an account of one man who 'bitterly' stated that Britain had 'left us Palestinians very useless against the Jews'.[7]

Accusations were circulated that there had been an agreement between Britain and the Haganah to expel Arabs from their homeland. 'We shall never forget your disapproved of attitude', read one typical Arab communication after the fall of Haifa to Zionist forces several days earlier.[8] Even though the US did not have soldiers on the ground or administrative responsibility, like Britain, it saw the potential of increased Arab anger because of the refugee problem. For example, when the US ambassador to Egypt reported on the conditions of the refugees, he stated that with US prestige in the country at a low ebb, the State Department would be best advised to extend aid to Arab refugees in the region.[9] There had already been outbreaks of anti-American incidents in Jordan, Syria, Lebanon and Egypt following the passing of the 1947 partition plan.[10] As such, while it may be cynical to suggest that British and US aid had no benevolent intentions, their main motive was to impress upon the Arabs concern for their cause and to regain goodwill. As one British official noted, there was no such financial appeal made for Indian and Pakistani refugees.[11] Another British official, while agreeing with Sir Hugh Dow, consul-general in Jerusalem, that there was little chance of the refugees being allowed to return, commented that although the refugee issue was a problem, it might well point to a solution to 'one of the greatest difficulties in the way of a satisfactory implementation of partition'. The official was referring to the demographic imbalance in the Jewish state under the partition plan of 1947.[12] While Dow was correct that it solved the problem of demographic instability, it did not lead to a solution between Israel and the Arabs.

As war continued, the international community became increasingly aware of the humanitarian crisis facing the Palestinian refugees. The UN Mediator Count Bernadotte, in his interim proposals published on 18 June 1948, just as the warring parties had re-established a truce, called for the 250,000–300,000 refugees to 'return to their homes without restriction'.[13] Discussing the matter, the Israeli Cabinet on 16 June came to accept the views of the prime minister. In a speech in response to the Marxist oriented Mapam Party's resolution to support the return of 'peace minded' refugees, Ben-Gurion argued that it would be foolish to allow the return of the Palestinian refugees while the war was taking place, stating that he would be against them returning even after hostilities had ended.[14] Foreign Minister Sharett spoke against their return with equal vigour, although adding that Israel should be ready to pay compensation for their resettlement.[15]

Although no formal vote was taken on Cabinet level, Morris argues that the line that no refugees should be allowed back had now become Israeli policy, placating representatives of Mapam as it did not entirely rule out the return of refugees after the war.[16] Nevertheless, the policy to bar the return of refugees went down to the IDF chain of command.[17] In subsequent talks with Bernadotte the following day, Sharett said that the refugees could not return while the war was on, leaving the possibility open that they may return after hostilities had ended.[18] This position would mutate by the end of July; Sharett informed Bernadotte that not only would there be no return during hostilities, but also after the war it could only be discussed in the context of an overall peace settlement.[19] This would become a consistent Israeli position later in negotiations. When the second truce went into effect on 18 July, after ten days of fighting an additional 100,000 refugees were created. During this period, Ben-Gurion and IDF commanders were left on their own, without Cabinet deliberations, to determine the fate of conquered Palestinian communities. Decisions were made in an inconsistent and haphazard fashion depending on strategic objectives and the demographic nature of conquered communities.[20]

However, by this time, one of the Arab League's three conditions was the return of refugees plus a halt to Jewish immigration.[21] The US transmitted its concerns to Britain about how the refugee problem could have repercussions on the truce and noted that reports had suggested that Britain had helped refugees to flee to Jordan and Lebanon.[22] The US delegation to the UN, concerned that the refugee issue could disrupt the truce, sought Britain's attitude towards the possible repercussions of the refugee problem.[23] In an informal capacity, Foreign Office official Harold Beeley estimated that at minimum there were 250,000 refugees whose presence in Arab countries was beginning to have serious economic and social repercussions.[24] Foreign Secretary Bevin laid the blame squarely at Washington's feet on the grounds that it was US policy towards Palestine that had aroused anti-American resentment from the Arabs.[25]

That aside, what was clear was that both Britain and the US were facing serious repercussions from the Palestine War and the refugee crisis. Reports were coming into the British Foreign Office of warm feelings towards the Soviet Union across local populations being influenced by local communists. Individuals were being quoted as saying that they were hoping that one day Russia would 'smash' Great Britain.[26] The US was also the target of Arab anger.[27] The US was made aware of the British view that Arab bitterness over the 'imposition' of a Jewish state in the Middle East could be minimized by providing aid for the Arab refugees.[28] The US also saw the refugee crisis as an opportunity to display goodwill and to 'mend our own fences with the Arabs'.[29] Robert M. McLintock, Special Assistant to the UN Affairs Director Dean Rusk, summed up US attitudes very frankly when he wrote:

> I do not care a dried camel's hump [about the refugees]. It is, however, important to the interests of this country that these fanatical and over-wrought people do not injure our strategic interests through reprisals against our oil investments and through the recision [sic] of our air base rights in that area.[30]

Old scars resurface

While there was an emerging Anglo-American consensus that self-interest demanded action towards alleviating the refugee problem, there was initial disagreement on how this should be announced and if it should be linked to the issue of Jewish refugees from Europe. As the previous chapter showed, the entry into Palestine of these Jewish displaced persons had already caused tension between Britain and the US. In accepting the 18 July truce, the Arab League went on record in stating that 'Zionist terrorists' had forced Arabs to leave their homes while bringing in Jewish immigrants to take their place.[31] This, no doubt, struck a chord with Ernest Bevin, who wrote that partition was meant to solve the problem of Jewish displaced persons, but instead had only created a bigger one.[32] The British foreign secretary believed that the

Arab refugee crisis warranted attention as a major factor in the Palestine problem.[33] Alexander Cadogan, Britain's representative to the UN, went a step further. He directly linked the Arab refugee problem with Jewish displaced persons, telling the US ambassador to London that, because there was a similar number of Jewish displaced persons in Europe to that of the Arab refugees (200,000 and 250,000 were the figures cited, respectively), the problem of the Arab refugees should be a major element in UN deliberations just as the Jewish refugee problem had been in previous years.[34] In fact, this linkage did not stop there. Cadogan further argued that if there were an opportunity for Jewish displaced persons in Europe to be settled somewhere other than Palestine, they would be less inclined to go to Israel. Therefore, there should be a 'serious effort on an international scale to dispose of all European displaced persons, Jews and non-Jews... this would "remove feelings that the world is trying to solve problem, that Arabs had no part in creating, at expense of Arabs alone" '.[35] In other words, if Jewish displaced persons were either rehabilitated or resettled in Europe or North America and international action was to be taken on behalf of Palestinian refugees, anti-Western hostility in the Arab world would decline. What this position amounted to was a reopening of the old wounds between Britain and the US detailed in the previous chapter, with Britain reiterating Bevin's past accusation that the entry to Palestine of these Jewish refugees would 'set aflame the whole Middle East' and that Truman's demand that 100,000 Jewish displaced persons enter Palestine was intended to prevent Jews from entering the US.[36]

Not only did Bevin instruct the British delegation at the UN to initiate a discussion at the Security Council about the Arab refugees,[37] he also wanted this discussion to make reference to Jewish displaced persons in order to induce the Security Council to take up the matter with the relevant authorities.[38] It was, therefore, not surprising that the US was firmly opposed to this for several reasons, not least because the US did not consider the Security Council the proper forum to discuss the issue.[39] Moreover, Washington considered the refugee problem to be primarily a humanitarian issue and therefore not suited to the politically focused Security Council. The US also feared it would give the Soviet Union, as well as the temporary member Ukraine, a platform to speak.[40] In the view of Philip Jessup, US delegate to the UN, the British intention of linking Jewish displaced persons and Arab refugees could prove to be self-defeating, as it would be detrimental to President Truman's attempt to liberalize US policy towards Jewish immigration. According to Jessup, hostile members of Congress could interpret Security Council involvement as a British attempt to bring the displaced persons to the US. Further still, Israel would oppose such a move and protest that Britain was attempting to impair Jewish sovereignty.[41]

In an attempt to meet Britain halfway, Jessup suggested that, in coordination with President Truman's legislative programme on Jewish displaced persons, the transatlantic allies could jointly encourage philanthropic groups to organize large-scale relief operations and ask the mediator to request the advice and assistance of the UN Economic and Social Council (ECOSOC) or the IRO.[42] Britain's response to this idea was lukewarm. While agreeing to delay temporarily bringing the refugee question before the Security Council, the British delegation was instructed that it should abbreviate the statement relating to the Jewish displaced persons. The delegation was simply to state that the implications of the displaced persons problem on the Palestine situation were well known and emphasize the need to consider further measures. The foreign secretary added that it should be explained to the US that, while Britain wished to meet them in their views, it was impossible to allow further delays.[43] Bevin did, however, tell the British delegation to inform the Security Council that short-term relief for the Palestinian refugees was urgent and that the International Red Cross should be asked to work with the Red Crescent.[44] Finally, Cadogan raised the question of the Palestinian refugees at the Security Council on 2 August 1948. He addressed the issue of both Jewish displaced persons and Arab refugees despite information to the State Department from the British Foreign Office that instructions had been given to tone down the speech at the Security Council.[45] Nevertheless, Cadogan still asked that ECOSOC and other bodies find places other than Palestine for Jewish displaced persons.[46] He also called upon the Security Council to impress upon the mediator the gravity of the refugee issue and to consider the urgency of short-term relief, announcing Britain's £100,000 contribution as evidence of this.[47]

Aid: An extension of foreign policy by other means

The challenge facing London and Washington was to synchronize their positions in order to initiate a strategy towards the refugees which would be mutually beneficial to their interests in the region. While the US was opposed to British attempts to link Jewish displaced persons with Arab refugees at the Security Council, there was general agreement between the two allies on the need for some kind of joint action. This recognition of the necessity for refugee relief to reduce Arab resentment led to the steps that were taken towards creating a comprehensive aid package. It was reiterated by both that they coordinate their positions in order to avoid the perception among Arabs and Israelis that Britain championed one side and that the US championed the other.[48]

There was a genuine belief that, in the words of Jessup, the 'basic factors' influencing British policy towards Palestine 'are similar if not wholly identical' to those of the US.[49] It was also Jessup's view that the refugee problem was likely to become more acute in the future and that this would complicate negotiations for a political settlement.[50] Less than two weeks later, US Secretary of State George Marshall echoed this view and informed his UN delegation that Washington deemed the refugee issue central to the Palestine problem, as its alleviation would improve the chances of a peaceful settlement.[51] By August, significant relief plans were underway, and the mediator was expressing his desire to organize a large-scale programme to assist the refugees through a 'working fund'.[52]

However, it was one thing to agree on the need to provide humanitarian assistance and relief. It was quite another to provide the actual funding. During the period of the second truce, 18 July to 15 October, when an additional 100,000 Arabs were made refugees,[53] the US was concerned about the source of funding for a long-term programme because at that time there were no US public funds available.[54] Congressional approval would have been needed for Washington to release such funds. Britain initially released the paltry sum of £100,000 (approximately US$400,000) as a charitable donation for refugee relief. It was with disappointment that several days later Britain learned of a 'most unfortunate slip' by the Reuters news agency which announced that Britain was donating the sum of £100,000 towards relief for Arab *and Jewish* refugees. This mistake was repeated in several Arab newspapers and media outlets.[55] But it was solely to the Arab refugees that the aid had been directed, not to Jews.[56] Regardless, the US Ambassador to London Lewis Douglas was actually surprised that Britain 'came through' with the figure.[57] For its part, the US's Amcross made available US$250,000 in the form of clothing and medical supplies to the International Committee of the Red Cross. Church organizations also looked to assist both Arabs and Jews.[58] The State Department recommended that approaches be made to relevant agencies for relief while efforts also be made to obtain private donations.[59] The Arabian American Oil Company and the Trans Arabian Pipeline offered US$100,000 to assist the refugees.[60]

Having received dispatches from the region about the plight of the Palestinian refugees from diplomatic missions, by mid-August 1948 the

British Middle East Office (BMEO) in Cairo understood that the problem was beyond the means and capability of the Arab governments to handle on their own.[61] On 26 August, a meeting was convened between Harold Beeley of the Foreign Office's Eastern Department, Mr Wilkinson of the Refugee Department and Sir Raphael Cilento. The latter was making his way to the region to head the mediator's efforts for refugee relief. At the meeting, the nature of Britain's £100,000 contribution was discussed. The foreign secretary was considering if Britain should approach Commonwealth nations for food aid.[62] The Commonwealth was duly approached, and in a message to British high commissions in Canada, Australia, New Zealand and South Africa, it was argued that, apart from making a practical contribution to the humanitarian problem, it would demonstrate sympathy for the Arab peoples, countering disillusionment and ill-feeling towards the Western world in the process.[63] However, dispatches from missions in the region reported that despite increasing donations and assistance (Britain's £100,000, Australia sending a consignment of wheat, Belgium assisting Nazareth refugees, US charitable organizations sending US$100,000 and medicine and Switzerland sending milk and cheese), it was unlikely to last more than just a few days.[64] In Washington, it was suggested that the president use his power as commander-in-chief to direct the military to issue blankets, cloth, wheat and medicine; however, the move was referred to the attorney-general's office as it was unclear if the president had the authority to permit such action for relief during peace time.[65]

Following an appeal for supplies for the refugees facilitated by the mediator,[66] the State Department drafted an action plan that called for the raising of US$25 million by late spring 1949 with contributions from the IRO and the Children's Fund being credited to this amount. The plan stated that a substantial portion of this figure would have to be taken from private and voluntary sources. However, immediate steps to raise some funds were recommended because it was estimated that congressional appropriation would not have been made during the period when the aid was most needed.[67] This US involvement was pleasing to Britain. Forwarding a report compiled by Brigadier Gilbert Clayton on his visit to a refugee camp, John Troutbeck, head of the BMEO in Cairo, commented that the new US ambassador to Egypt was even publicizing his interest in the problem.[68]

Following on from an earlier State Department recommendation that vast sums be raised by late spring 1949, another draft State Department position paper recommended that the US together with Britain should provide the largest proportion of the assistance required by the refugees. Further, the new paper stated that such a move should be announced to the UN, stipulating that the US was prepared to present the assistance programme to Congress for approval upon its resumption in January 1949.[69] Among the State Department's other recommendations was that US$6 million should be utilized from the residual funds of the United Nations Relief and Rehabilitation Administration (UNRRA) and be given to UNICEF to form a programme under the coordination of the Acting Mediator Ralph Bunche. It was further recommended that in addition to the assistance of the World Health Organization (WHO), the IRO should also assist as much as its budgetary and constitutional limits would allow. Also, the acting mediator would receive a supplementary credit of US$1 million to obtain services of staff.[70] The paper also argued that a concrete programme should be presented to the General Assembly once reports by medical and relief experts had been provided. From preliminary estimates, it was calculated that such a programme would cost US$25 million and would have to be carried by Middle Eastern nations, Britain, the US and also nongovernmental and voluntary organizations.[71]

The role of the International Refugee Organization

The question of what role the IRO should play in refugee relief was a source of contention between Britain and the US. Initially, the US preferred IRO involvement. A State Department plan noted that more detailed preparation for refugees needed to be transmitted to the General Assembly and the mediator as well as the General Council of the IRO.[72] From a US perspective it made sense to include the IRO as it had the funds available and was constitutionally permitted to hand over US$5 million for relief.[73] On the surface, the disagreement over IRO involvement did not appear significant; however, it was a source of contrasting strategies. The IRO was set up to deal with refugees at the end of World War II with the intention of resettling or repatriating the war's one million refugees. The British position was that involving the IRO could risk the failure of the operation. The IRO was scheduled to cease functioning after 30 June 1950 and therefore the British did not want to burden it with more refugees. Also, the Arab refugee problem was, in the eyes of the British, a problem of disaster relief and not a World War II-related issue.[74] It was reported that Lewis Jones, the First Secretary at the US Embassy in London, agreed with some of the arguments presented to him by Foreign Office officials and would forward them to Washington. London argued, in addition to some of the points already raised above, that although it was possible that provisions in the IRO would allow for some support for the Palestinian refugees, it would be unwise to pursue this course prior to a ruling by the mediator.[75] Shockingly, Ralph Cilento of the Disaster Relief Organisation (DRO) had his own reason to oppose IRO involvement. The food and clothing provided by the IRO were vastly superior to that of the normal standards of the Middle East poor, as well as the extras such as fuel, tents and household utensils. Cilento argued that this could draw Arabs to the camps and prevent resettlement.[76] Britain's concern about potential IRO involvement compelled it to prevent the US from tabling their IRO proposal at the General Council and, if proposed, they were prepared to criticize it as constructively as possible.[77]

Britain was so adamant on this matter that the Foreign Office wrote to its UN delegation stressing the aforementioned reasons for opposing IRO involvement and stating that the delegation's task was to prevent the US from tabling their proposal at the General Assembly, despite claiming that it had, temporarily, at least, managed to persuade the US not to involve the IRO.[78] The strong stance Britain took on the question of IRO participation suggests that there were additional reasons why Britain did not want to involve the IRO. The first was that London was concerned that UN member states would think that they could get rid of the Arab refugee problem to a quasi-independent organization such as the IRO. Instead, Britain wanted UN member states to face up directly to their financial and other responsibilities for the Arab refugees.[79] More importantly, IRO involvement was particularly significant as it alluded to the question of resettlement. As a body which dealt with the resettlement of refugees from World War II, its involvement in the Palestinian refugee problem would also imply resettlement as a solution to the refugee problem.

The mediator's report called for 'the right of the Arab refugees to return to their homes in Jewish controlled territory' as well as repatriation, resettlement and rehabilitation under the supervision of the conciliation commission.[80] By attempting to limit IRO involvement in the relief operation, Britain was excluding an organization which specialized in refugee resettlement, thus hampering one of the components of solving the refugee problem. This was not because Britain thought that the majority of refugees would be repatriated. On the contrary, it was believed that the majority would need to be resettled.[81] At one point it was even conceded that when 'an agreed plan for a settlement' was closer to fruition, then the handling of the refugee problem by the IRO might be the best solution.[82]

However, the British did not want to undermine the report of the mediator which, as will be later demonstrated, they had hoped would provide the basis for a UN resolution on reaching a settlement on the Palestine question. Implicit in this was the concern that any action towards resettlement could hamper Arab goodwill, as the Arab states were demanding refugees be repatriated. Therefore, British policy was that relief for these refugees should be under the DRO, a body which Britain thought would later see its responsibilities expanded to include resettlement, as a result of the work of the conciliation commission which would seek a solution to the Palestine question and would then be put under the direct control of the secretary-general.[83]

Jessup was also of the opinion that the immediate return of refugees to Israel was impossible, and agreed with Israel that the matter should be dealt with as part of a future settlement.[84] However, Marshall disagreed, arguing instead that under the supervision of the mediator, a substantial number of refugees could return without harming Israel's internal security.[85] Even though Britain managed to prevent the US from pursuing IRO involvement, on 5 October, a US draft position paper on Arab refugees recommended inviting the IRO to render its fullest practical assistance within its budgetary and constitutional limits.[86] When British and US proposals of what would become General Assembly Resolution 212 were drafted, the IRO was indeed mentioned,[87] albeit only in the context of outside assistance and support.

Approximating the appropriation

Before drafting a UN resolution to provide aid for Palestinian refugees, there needed to be some kind of identification of how much was needed for congressional appropriation as well as a strategy in place to ensure its success. In discussions with British officials, it was explained that Congress would be more favourable to the refugee relief project if it were presented as a contribution to the political settlement, more than just relief. Therefore, the First Committee, the General Assembly committee concerned with political and security affairs, would be best suited for considering this aspect of the Palestine problem and would then provide a framework for the recommendations of the Third Committee, the General Assembly committee concerned with humanitarian affairs. While the British accepted the logic of this argument, it still felt that the matter should be presented to the Third Committee as an immediate emergency, as the US position might delay the provision of funds and bring the work of the emergency disaster relief effort to a standstill.[88] Arguably, the compartmentalized nature of the UN process whereby potential resolutions would be categorized on the basis of whether they were defined as economic, political or humanitarian problems, affected the handling of a refugee issue which had both political and humanitarian dimensions.

Meanwhile, the US was concerned that an IRO survey had predicted that US$38 million was required, with US$20 million immediately. However, they felt that to request UN member states to make a donation in addition to their UN contributions was unwise. At the same time, the US was concerned that voluntary contributions were also unsatisfactory. Therefore, the US wanted a definite appropriation for the administrative expenses of the DRO and for member states to make a contribution in accordance with the scale of their contributions to the UN budget. It was essential that other states contribute because Congress would not be convened until January, and it would take four months before a US contribution could be made. Such contributions would also help the cause of congressional funding. It was decided that further consultation with other delegations was required before a resolution could be drafted in order to ascertain how much Arab and Commonwealth governments would be expected to contribute.[89] The delay in congressional funding left Britain to make its own contribution of £2 million ahead of others towards refugee relief.[90]

Britain had initially believed that the UN would cover the costs of expanding disaster relief. One British proposal suggested that contributions be made from all UN member states on a pro rata basis. Alternatively, approaches could be made to 34 countries which were listed informally.[91] The response was lukewarm because of doubts over its feasibility. The State Department did not believe that countries without direct involvement in the region would significantly increase payment. The only real possibility to obtain funding, according to its view, was for governments with strong interests in the region to proffer voluntary contributions. Therefore, the State Department recommended that it should be left to Washington to announce its intention to seek an appropriation from Congress worth US$10 million. It was calculated that if Britain were to donate half that amount, together with UNICEF contributions, US$21 million would be raised.[92]

Soon the necessity of the relief effort became more urgent. From Tel Aviv, the US received word that out of approximately 400,000 refugees, it was estimated that the approaching winter could kill more than 100,000 who were without shelter. The implication was that unless there was a comprehensive programme and immediate action there would be 'horrifying losses'. It was argued that the mediator's staff was totally unsuited to handle emergency relief and resettlement.[93] US Undersecretary of State Robert Lovett wrote to Rusk at the UN that President Truman agreed that while a long-range project should preferably be the responsibility of the UN, if its member states appropriated the necessary funds, the US would still be confronted with an immediate emergency while waiting for a UN decision.[94]

Towards a UN resolution on refugee relief

One of the successes of British and US diplomacy was the passing of General Assembly Resolution 212. Despite the large gaps between the two allies that had emerged over the Palestine question, London and Washington were not only able to recognize the mutual benefit in a concerted relief effort for the refugees, but also, after much wrangling, they managed to draft and pass a resolution implementing such an aid programme. On 19 November 1948, the UN General Assembly voted in favour of Resolution 212. It called for assistance to the Palestinian refugees, citing the reports of the UN mediator and acting mediator calling the situation of the refugees critical.[95] The resolution, using the acting mediator's estimates, approximated that US$29.5 million would be needed to provide relief for 500,000 refugees over a nine-month period, plus an additional US$2.5 million for administrative and local operational expenses. The resolution also called for all member states to make voluntary contributions while authorizing the secretary-general to establish a special fund through which the contributions would be paid. The resolution invited the assistance of specialized agencies of the UN, UNICEF, the International Committee of the Red Cross, the League of Red Cross Societies, the IRO and other voluntary organizations.[96]

Although progress had been made in bridging the British and US positions to form a resolution for relief, further compromises were required. The details of the original British draft resolution were discussed by British officials in mid-October with a first draft being considered on 12 October.[97] However, it was a second draft of the resolution that was placed before the UN. The differences between the draft resolutions, although small, were significant. For example, the second draft requested up to US$7 million from the working capital fund and called for UN member states to assist. But it left out the word 'all' member states that had been included in the earlier draft. An amendment to the second draft recommended by the Foreign Office stipulated 'Arab' refugees in the resolution.[98] At the same time as Britain's second draft resolution, the US proposed its own draft resolution. It was similar to the British one in that it referenced the report of the late mediator who had been ambushed and assassinated by gunmen from Lehi, one of the armed revisionist Zionist underground groups, near Jerusalem on 18 September 1948,[99] which referred to the necessity of refugee relief and of raising US$30 million, but it only called for a US$5 million advance from the UN working capital fund. It did not call on the secretary-general to use the Disaster Relief Project Organization, but rather called on him to utilize appropriate voluntary governmental and UN agencies. While both resolutions called for organizations such as the WHO, the Food and Agriculture Agency of the United Nations (FAO), IRO and UNICEF to contribute supplies, specialist personnel and other services, the British resolution called for this to be under the framework of the DRO; the US draft called for it to be under 'the relief program herein established'.[100]

The debate at the Third Committee of the UN began on 20 October, halting its discussion on human rights to hear Acting Mediator Bunche and Sir Raphael Cilento, the director of social questions, speak on the situation of the refugees.[101] By this time, the second truce had been broken, and the fighting which would continue until the end of the year would produce an additional 200,000 to 230,000 refugees.[102] The drafting of what became a joint Anglo-American resolution was not without obstacles. The Soviet representative was dismissive, even speaking in favour of resuming talks on human rights which had just been discussed at the previous session. He also argued that if Palestinian refugees were to be discussed, so should all refugees.[103] Further Soviet disruption occurred throughout the committee's deliberations over the next few weeks. On one occasion, the Soviets blamed British and US oil monopolies for the refugee crisis and suggested that the Fifth Committee, the General Assembly committee for budgetary and administrative affairs, urgently consider the budgetary implications of the resolution.[104]

Britain saw the importance of getting US and Commonwealth support for the resolution in order to obtain most of the necessary funds, even though it was thought that Britain could force through the resolution without their support.[105] However, the Australian representative expressed doubts about the expediency of tabling the draft resolution without knowledge of what funds Western countries were able to contribute.[106] Later, these same countries, including the US, resisted the British attempt to bring a debate at committee level. However, Britain managed to obtain an understanding from the US delegate to the UN, Eleanor Roosevelt, that if Britain were to set the date to 29 October, the US would not oppose it.[107] The date was passed by 44 votes in favour to none against.[108] Britain noted that it had the support of the Arab nations, Latin America and the Scandinavian countries, but the US, France and the Commonwealth, countries more likely to supply funds, wanted further time to consider how they could provide practical help.[109]

After initially objecting to some of the wording in the draft resolution that pertained to the financing of the operation, the US delegation considered the phrasing of a new British draft of the resolution sufficient. It urged UN states to make initial and further contributions to ensure enough supplies and funds were available.[110] The US delegation noted, however, that the amount of member state contributions would be predicated on political factors, meaning contributions would only significantly come from the US and Britain. It was also believed that relief operations should be kept distinct from the proposed conciliation commission or any new conciliation vehicles that could be established, and that the US would take up the matter of appropriation with Congress as soon as it was practical to do so.[111]

The earlier apparent procrastination on the part of the US and Commonwealth nations led the Foreign Office to believe that those nations were not seriously addressing the problem.[112] However, in reality, it was not that the US was indifferent to the situation. It was reported that the US delegation did not want the issue debated before US elections on 2 November 1948. With US opposition to holding an early debate so strong, Roosevelt, in what the British deemed 'blackmail', threatened to refuse to serve on any subcommittee which would endanger US congressional support.[113]

The US insistence on delaying a debate was also because a US contribution would require consultation with congressional leaders, and it was considered impractical to attempt this at that time.[114] Britain was forced to concede to a delay on the debate. However, there was some movement towards the British position because Lovett acknowledged that the British draft proposal was a moral rather than a financial obligation for every UN member state. He also believed that only Britain, the US and the Arab states were likely to contribute financially. As such. Congress would not likely be pleased with an unrealistic budget.[115] Moreover, the British draft would probably win Third Committee support.[116]

An attempt was made by Britain and the US to merge their draft proposals, which consisted of amendments to the wording and phrasing of the resolution. The main British concern was for strong mention to be made to the DRO for coordinating and facilitating work. The

US did not object to this.[117] In turn, Britain reluctantly agreed to drop references to the scale of contributions which the US feared would create time-consuming and difficult negotiations.[118] Also Britain resigned itself to the need to drop references to UNRRA's recommendation for UNICEF funds, as a result of opposition from the US, the Dominions and Western European countries, in order to get approval for the US$30 million towards relief. The reference was about the UNRRA's Control Board and whether it had the right to tell UNICEF how to spend funds.[119] Roosevelt, at the Third Committee, emphasized that while the refugee problem had to be dealt with effectively and promptly, its connection with political problems should be kept in mind so that 'the final conclusion formed a sound and workable pattern'. Together with the British delegate, Roosevelt called for a director general of relief to be appointed with wide powers.[120]

Progress on the Anglo-American resolution was slow. On 3 November, the Foreign Office wrote to its delegation in Paris that it was disappointed that the resolution had been temporarily shelved pending further discussions at subcommittee level due to the Soviet position.[121] A British official commented that this came after Britain and the US, after some difficulty, had agreed upon a satisfactory draft resolution.[122] The Foreign Office outlined its position, stressing the importance of having a director general of relief rather than an advisory board as being the most effective method of ensuring action as well as securing a financial advance.[123] However, the Foreign Office conceded that if the US preferred an advisory board then they would support it.[124] At the committee, the US argued that there was no need for an advisory board; however, it stated that if there were to be one, it should consist of representatives of specialist agencies, a position not that different from the British, who did not want such a board to be directly involved in operational development, preferring it to have an advisory role only.[125]

On 5 and 6 November, the subcommittee met five times, and after rejecting all further amendments, it finally approved several paragraphs of the resolution with just minor changes pertaining to the US$29.5 million required and the approval of the secretary-general to ask for a US$5 million advance from the working capital fund of the UN.[126] It was also agreed that contributions should be on a voluntary basis.[127] Further progress was made on 8 November with the adoption of a paragraph that urged all member states to make voluntary contributions. This came only after many hours spent discussing and then rejecting what the British delegation deemed a 'well intentioned but impractical' Venezuelan amendment, as well as a Soviet amendment which sought to place the burden on UN states that had not suffered from German occupation during the war.[128] Earlier, on 6 November 1948, Lovett recommended to President Truman that the US delegation to the UN be permitted to announce the intentions of the US government to seek congressional appropriation for US$16 million. This was needed in order to stimulate contributions from other countries and obtain the US$5 million advance.[129] By 11 November, the resolution had passed the subcommittee, despite the US delegate delaying its passing by reserving his delegation's right to resurrect the question at an ad hoc Advisory Committee, a move he had earlier opposed. Britain was annoyed that the US delegate then walked out to catch a flight before the end of the discussion. The British delegation resolved to convince him that such a move would be a tactical blunder.[130] Just ahead of the UN vote on the refugee relief resolution, President Truman approved the proposed congressional appropriation of the US contribution of US$16 million.[131]

On 19 November, UN General Assembly Resolution 212 (III) was passed unanimously. In fact, the relatively smooth passing of the resolution during the final few days of the committee[132] even raised concern and speculation about the lack of Russian hostility. British officials hypothesized that the Soviets could be entering a second phase of 'Operation Palestine'. The first stage was the establishment of a Jewish state to obtain a foothold in the region. The second stage revolved around the Soviets looking to get credit for meeting Arab demands. There was also the view that the Russians saw the refugee problem as providing fertile ground for their propaganda via Soviet efforts at the UN.[133]

Not debating refugees: Drafting Resolution 194

On 11 December 1948, the UN General Assembly passed another resolution which pertained to Palestinian refugees.[134] Echoing the conclusions of the late mediator's report, Resolution 194 called for the refugees wishing to return to their homes and live at peace to be permitted to do so.[135] This resolution has had long-term implications for the conflict. However, the refugee problem was directly referenced only in article 11 of the resolution's 15 articles. It is worth quoting in full:

> [It] *Resolves* that the refugees wishing to return to their homes and live at peace with their neighbours should be permitted to do so at the earliest practicable date, and that compensation should be paid for the property of those choosing not to return and for loss of or damage to property which, under principles of international law or

in equity, should be made good by the Governments or authorities responsible ... Instructs the conciliation commission to facilitate the repatriation, resettlement and economic and social rehabilitation of the refugees and the payment of compensation, and to maintain close relations with the Director of the United Nations Relief for Palestine Refugees and, through him, with the appropriate organs and agencies of the UN.[136]

What is apparent in US–British debates and dialogues over the make-up of the resolution was a general lack of attention to the above article pertaining to the refugees. Instead, the focus was on the other articles of the resolution. These included the status and protection of Jerusalem and the holy places, as well as the economic development of the areas in question.[137]

The reason why there was so little attention to the refugees in British and US dialogue over the resolution is that in its original inception, the resolution sought to reaffirm the report of the late Mediator Count Bernadotte. The mediator's earlier interim report of June 1948 recommended the return of 200–300,000 Arab refugees to their homes and the inclusion of Jerusalem and the Negev into Arab territory.[138] Rejected by both Israel and the Arabs,[139] his position on reducing the size of the Jewish state, especially the loss of Jerusalem, attracted the odium of Lehi who, in addition to focusing their war efforts in the Jerusalem area, orchestrated a campaign against Bernadotte over the summer of 1948 which ultimately led to his assassination by Lehi gunmen on 17 September.[140] In Bernadotte's final report released posthumously two days after his death, one paragraph of the late mediator's 11 'specific conclusions' pertained to the refugees in addition to one paragraph of his seven 'basic premises'.[141] Just over a week before, the Israeli Cabinet had voted to not discuss the return of refugees until a peace settlement.[142] The basic premise of the final report stated that, 'The right of innocent people, uprooted from their homes by the present terror and ravages of war, to return to their homes, should be affirmed and made effective, with assurance of adequate compensation for the property of those who may choose not to return.' His specific conclusion called for:

> The right of the Arab refugees to return to their homes in Jewish-controlled territory at the earliest possible date ... [with] their 'repatriation, resettlement and economic and social' rehabilitation, and payment of adequate compensation for the property of those choosing not to return, should be supervised and assisted by the United Nations conciliation commission.[143]

Not only did the mediator call for a conciliation commission to be established, but he also, controversially, recommended that the Galilee be defined as Jewish territory with the Negev becoming Arab. This was in contrast to the UN partition plan of 1947 which put the Negev firmly in the territory of the proposed Jewish state but excluded west Galilee. He also argued that Haifa should become a free port and Jerusalem should be placed under UN control.[144]

In the actual drafting of the resolution, Britain and the US had to once more overcome significant obstacles in order to find common ground. As mentioned, the original focus of what was to become Resolution 194 was to affirm the conclusions of the Bernadotte Report. The debate surrounding the resolution started at the First Committee of the General Assembly on 15 October. Just two days later, as had happened during discussions on the other resolution, it was reported that President Truman wished to see the UN debate on the mediator's proposals deferred until after the elections and for the US delegation to avoid debate on the issue.[145]

The possibility that the resolution would be a basis for territorial adjustments as stipulated in the Bernadotte Report was soon dashed following Truman's speech of 24 October 1948 outlining the Democratic Party platform towards Palestine. 'We approve the claims of the State of Israel to the boundaries set forth in the UN resolution of 29 November and consider that modifications thereof should be made only if fully acceptable to the State of Israel.'[146] In other words, the US position was that the Northern Negev was Israel's, but any other border amendments should be discussed by the parties under the auspices of the conciliation commission, rather than the current session of the General Assembly.[147]

The US was unable to support the British delegation's position which would have given effect to the Bernadotte plan.[148] The British complained that instead of creating a conciliation commission to implement the Bernadotte proposals, the US had put forward a resolution to create a conciliation commission to facilitate negotiations itself; a complete departure from the 'agreed' Bernadotte proposals.[149] On 20 November, Phillip Jessup reiterated the US position, in what would become known as the 'Jessup Principle', by informing the First Committee that while the US agreed to the 'basic premise' of the Bernadotte plan, Israel was entitled to the territories assigned to it under the partition resolution of 29 November 1947. However, if Israel wanted more territory, it had to offer an appropriate exchange through negotiations aided by the conciliation commission.

On hearing this, the British said the speech was worse than they had expected it to be.[150] The US thought that the British position was too rigidly attached to the Bernadotte plan which was self-defeating because military operations and political conditions had changed.[151] It was communicated to the British that there was no way the US would modify its position, with Lovett frankly commenting that the US believed that its position was the right one.[152] A revised British draft of the resolution was presented in light of US amendments tabled the previous day.[153] 'Behind the scenes' bridging formulas were discussed[154] and by 30 November it was reported that Britain and the US had agreed on a revised British draft text.[155] Particular references to the Bernadotte plan's specific territorial proposals were dropped.[156] This did not mean that British officials were pleased with the outcome. It was reported that the following day British officials called the idea of not giving the conciliation commission specific instructions 'hopeless'.[157]

While little attention was focused on the refugee section of the draft resolution, there was still some reference to it. On 23 November, during discussion in the Political Committee, US representative Jessup proposed a change to the second paragraph of the British draft resolution in the section pertaining to refugees. Instead of the section making references to 'technical' questions of compensation for losses which were incurred during the fighting, Jessup proposed that the problem could be dealt with in detail by the parties themselves through the assistance of a claims commission.[158] The next day Britain declared that it could not accept this amendment.[159] On 30 November there were only minor amendments to the wording of the first paragraph pertaining to refugees, which were agreed to by both Britain and the US. These amendments now included reference to the 'principles of international law or in equity' when referring to compensation, as well as the absence of reference to property being lost to 'pillage', 'confiscation' or 'destruction' and an additional reference to the conciliation commission having close relations with UNRPR, the relief body set up by Resolution 212. There was now also a reference to the conclusions of the mediator on refugees as outlined in his final report. Crucially, the word 'Arab' was now omitted from references to the refugees.[160]

Meanwhile, it was reported that the nature of the resolution would give the conciliation commission a virtual 'free hand' to work out a settlement on Palestine.[161] No longer was it constrained by the parameters of the mediator's recommendations; just two days before the passing of the resolution, it was decided at the Political Committee of the UN to delete the first clause of the refugee section referring to the mediator's report. This was not only to free the conciliation commission's hand, but also because of the Arab insistence that no reference should be made to his report.[162] However, the phrasing of the mediator's proposal pertaining to Palestinian refugees remained largely intact.

That being said, the above discussions on the refugee paragraph were for the most part superficial in nature, and there was still relatively little attention devoted to the refugee question while devising the resolution. Perhaps Britain and the US underestimated the importance and ramifications of the repatriation/resettlement issue, although it had been mentioned during discussions about Resolution 212 over the role of the IRO as well as the comments of US officials such as Jessup and Dean Acheson acknowledging that the refugee issue would affect an overall settlement.[163]

The lack of discussion between the US and Britain over the paragraphs pertaining to Palestinian refugees suggests that the political aspect of the refugee problem and the question of resettlement and/or repatriation were given lesser priority than that of the issue of territory. However, it also indicates that Britain and the US preferred to defer the refugee question to the proposed conciliation commission, the vehicle which was being established to facilitate an Arab–Israeli understanding on all outstanding issues between them. Indeed, the pattern which emerges from the drafting of Resolution 194 is one of US reluctance to endorse the mediator's proposals in order to allow the parties flexibility in negotiations under the aegis of the conciliation commission. In the case of the refugees, it appears that Britain and the US did not consider the phraseology of the mediator's recommendation to be problematic. They viewed this as a sound basis for future discussions that demanded less attention. This was a fatal error because, as subsequent chapters will demonstrate, the lack of consideration to the wording of the refugee question in Resolution 194 would have a grave impact on future diplomatic efforts to solve the refugee problem.

Conclusion

Mutual interest brought Britain and the US together to take action in establishing mechanisms for solving the Palestinian refugee problem and providing a short-term initiative to alleviate their suffering. Both Britain and the US shared the view that a large-scale humanitarian gesture was necessary not only for humanitarian purposes but also to deflect Arab anger away from both countries. London and Washington were able to overcome considerable policy differences to draft UN General Assembly Resolution 212. This was quite an achievement, as the resolution provided US$29.5 million plus an additional US$2.5 million for administrative expenses for a humanitarian aid programme that would have the assistance of many specialized agencies.

Such an expensive operation could only be sustained on a temporary basis. It did not resolve the crucial issue of the fate of the over 700,000 refugees. Nor did Britain and the US successfully deal with the political ramifications of the refugee problem. These questions were just mentioned incidentally in UN General Assembly Resolution 194. This joint British and US initiative saw the creation of a conciliation commission, a body conceived by the late mediator in his posthumous report of 16 September 1948.[164] The resolution instructed the conciliation commission to 'facilitate' the repatriation, resettlement and rehabilitation of refugees, and also called for the payment of compensation.[165]

These references to the refugee problem were scarcely debated during the drafting stage of the resolution. Instead, the debate centred on the mediator's other recommendations, especially about territory and the status of Jerusalem. Both Britain and the US had either underestimated just how explosive the refugee question would be in future negotiations or they were content with the wording of the drafts of the resolution. Whichever the case, as the following chapters will reveal, the passages relating to refugees in the resolution proved to be a stumbling block for future negotiations, undermining the work of the conciliation commission and, with it, the attempts to find an Arab–Israeli understanding.

3
Diplomatic Deadlock: The Palestine Conciliation Commission and the Palestinian Refugee Problem (Part 1)

Introduction

In early 1949, Walter Eytan, the head of the Israeli diplomatic delegation at the Arab–Israeli armistice talks in Rhodes, reflected on the possibility of Arab–Israeli reconciliation. He was both sanguine and prophetic. Eytan recalled that initial animosity between the Israeli and Egyptian delegations had been, during the course of six weeks, gradually eroded. In one instance, Eytan recalled being shown photographs of his Egyptian counterpart's family. On another occasion, he sat by the bed-side of an Egyptian advisor who had fallen ill and comforted him.[1] On 24 February 1949, having signed the armistice, and now awaiting the commencement of further diplomacy by the PCC, Eytan recalled:

> We felt that night, and I am fairly sure the Egyptians did too, that we had not only brought the fighting phase to a formal end, but laid the foundations, if not of love and affection, at least of formal relations between our two countries.[2]

Eytan's optimism was premature. Further armistice talks were success-fully concluded between Israel and Lebanon (23 March 1949), Israel and Jordan (3 April 1949) and Israel and Syria (20 July 1949). Ralph Bunche, who facilitated these talks, was later awarded the Nobel Peace Prize, but there was no permanent settlement. There would be another three wars and multiple skirmishes before a negotiated settlement would be achieved between Israel and Egypt three decades later. It would be an additional 15 years before there was a peace treaty between Israel and

Jordan. A final settlement between Israel and Lebanon, Syria, Iraq and the Palestinians has been even more elusive. However, Eytan was correct in one regard. The year was one of opportunity. The fighting in Palestine was coming to an end and the international community was committed to finding a settlement to the Arab–Israeli conflict. Not only did this take the form of large-scale relief packages for the Arab refugees, but there were also schemes and ideas for resettlement and regeneration projects across the Middle East. On the diplomatic level, two main initiatives were launched under the UN umbrella. The first initiative, the aforementioned armistice talks, was successful (no Israel–Iraq armistice was achieved, however). The second initiative, the work of the PCC, the main focus of this chapter, was not successful.

In 1949, finding a solution to the Arab–Israeli conflict under the auspices of the UN was an imperative for both Britain and the US. Armistice talks were underway and the PCC had been mandated to 'assist the Governments and authorities concerned to achieve a final settlement of all questions outstanding between them'.[3] Anglo-American activities were centred primarily on the work of the PCC. The US was a member of the PCC (the other two members being France and Turkey); Britain was an active outsider offering advice and assistance. Concluding in July 1949, when the PCC's Lausanne Conference took a two-week recess, this chapter will look at how the Palestinian refugee problem impaired the success of the PCC's work. It will chart the PCC's attempts to overcome the problem and analyse why the PCC's efforts led to a stalemate at Lausanne.

While there have been several previous studies which refer to the activities of the PCC,[4] with the exception of Neil Caplan's 1993 volume[5] and the works of Michael R. Fischbach,[6] and most recently Jacob Tovy,[7] they have predominantly been carried out without the use of US and British archives. While Caplan does make use of archival material, the focus of his research is much broader, a history of Arab–Israeli negotiations, and does not focus primarily on either the refugee issue or US and British policy. Fischbach, who makes excellent use of British, US, UN and even Jordanian archives, is a study on Palestinian refugee property. Tovy's work is an excellent account of the formation of Israeli policy towards the refugee issue. Nevertheless, there is a lacuna in the scholarship from the perspective of the Great Powers as to why the PCC ultimately failed in its attempt to bring about an Arab–Israeli peace. The US was by far the dominant actor in the PCC. Therefore, the use of US documents and archival material is fundamental not only to understanding the actions of the PCC, but also for any proper analysis of its strategies, objectives, successes and, indeed, its failures. Similarly, although not a member of the PCC, Britain was a highly important external party to the process. Britain was also very influential in the Middle East, especially in Jordan, Iraq and to a lesser extent Egypt, all states subject to PCC engagement. Indeed, it was the British who offered advice to US officials as well as the states in the region, sometimes, as in the case of Israel's offer to Egypt to repatriate 230,000 refugees in return for the Gaza Strip, to the detriment of the PCC.

The PCC failed not because of a psychological reluctance on the part of the Arab states to negotiate with Israel,[8] or because the US supported the position of the Arab League[9] or due to the lack of US pressure on Israel.[10] Nor as some scholars have argued, was the make-up of the PCC to blame.[11] While the differences between the sides were monumental, American, British and UN documents also indicate that the PCC, backed by the US, pursued a flawed strategy. The PCC considered multilateral talks between Israel and the Arab states through the PCC preferable to direct bilateral talks between Israel and Jordan. It therefore represents a missed opportunity which could have led to more fruitful results. This option was sacrificed in order to pursue a much larger and comprehensive peace between Israel and all of the Arab states. However, with the prospect of higher gains came higher risks, and the odds were not in the PCC's favour. Later into its work, the PCC, desperate for a breakthrough, mistakenly believed that concessions had been achieved on the ground when in fact they had not. The PCC, Britain and the US came to believe that the key to breaking the impasse lay with an Israeli concession, which was unrealistic because it crossed Israeli red lines. Meanwhile, the PCC tried not only to get the Arab states to negotiate with one voice, but also to acknowledge that the resettlement of Palestinian refugees in their territory was inevitable. This chapter demonstrates that these were unrealistic strategies and contributed to the PCC's failure by 1 July.

The formation and composition of the PCC

The PCC was established by UN General Assembly Resolution 194, a resolution which was not supported by either Israel or the Arab states. It was originally conceived as a resolution that endorsed the conclusions of the report by the late Mediator Count Folke Bernadotte, but during the resolution's drafting stage, references to the report were dropped. This opened the PCC's terms of mediation beyond the confines of the specifics of the Bernadotte Report. Comprising of three UN member states, the PCC was commissioned to 'take steps to assist the

Governments and authorities concerned to achieve a final settlement of all questions outstanding between them'.[12] These outstanding questions included the status and protection of Jerusalem, the future of the Palestinian refugees and, though not mentioning it specifically, borders and territory.[13] However, it was the refugee issue which ultimately dominated the work of the PCC. The resolution called for the return to Israel of refugees who wished to live at peace with their neighbours with compensation paid to those choosing not to return. The resolution further stipulated that the PCC, to be headquartered in Jerusalem, was to facilitate the repatriation, resettlement and economic and social rehabilitation of the refugees.[14]

As General Assembly Resolution 194 was being passed, the five permanent members of the Security Council met to discuss the make-up of the PCC. Britain wanted the US, France, Turkey or China to be included, but was opposed to the participation of Australia or New Zealand, countries which had clashed with Britain during the composition of Resolution 194.[15] Neither the US nor the Soviet Union wanted a Great Power to be part of the Commission; however, Britain insisted on US participation. Since US influence would be central to any settlement, it was reasoned that the US should be directly involved in the process.[16] Sharett reported that it was the idea of the US to have one pro-Jewish and one pro-Arab representative as well as a Great Power.[17] France agreed with Britain that US participation was necessary and eventually so did China. Not wanting a second Anglo-Saxon nation on the Commission, the quintet appointed France. Turkey was the third appointee, much to Britain's pleasure. The Turkish Republic was a Muslim state which could help bridge differences between East and West. There was also an implicit hope that Britain could transmit its interests through the Turkish channel. Immediately after Turkey's appointment, Britain expressed to Ankara its desire to have the opportunity to discuss ideas for a settlement in Palestine.[18] The US considered the composition of the PCC to be 'fair' and 'workable', commenting that Turkey was the most moderate of all the friends of the Arabs. Although France had supported partition, it was viewed with suspicion by Israel because of its views on Jerusalem. For its part, the US was seen as being supportive of Israel.[19] Ilan Pappé makes the interesting observation that because the PCC did not include a British member, it marked an end to 'a period of more than thirty years of British mediation' and began a 'new era characterized by American diplomacy'.[20] While there is some validity in this assertion, in reality Britain was still very important in Middle East diplomacy having close ties to Egypt and Jordan, and its influence was required by Washington as was its financial support. London was often viewed as having an advisory and strategic coordination role.

Although initial reports were that Turkey had appointed Selim Sarper, an experienced diplomat and ambassador to the UN as its representative,[21] Hussein Yalcin was eventually appointed to the PCC. Britain greeted the appointment of the aging Yalcin[22] as the Turkish delegate with some enthusiasm. It was acknowledged that the veteran journalist did not have clear views or much knowledge of the Palestine problem. However, British officials noted positively that he had ideas on an Arab federation with Turkish military guarantees and held a positive view of the Greater Syria concept, which Britain interpreted as a sign of sympathy towards its client, King Abdullah of Jordan.[23] Yalcin had also been outspoken in his support for Britain's historical role in the region, noting that if Britain had been eliminated from the Middle East, the Orient would have been dominated by the Nazis.[24]

James McDonald, the US ambassador to Israel, viewed Yalcin's appointment in less favourable terms. McDonald recalled that Yalcin soon embarrassed himself and his colleagues by publishing an article that called for a Turkish–Syrian rapprochement at a time when he was supposed to be acting impartially.[25] Yalcin was just several months into his work at the PCC when the British ambassador in Beirut reported a conversation with the Turkish representative. Yalcin told him that before his new role, he had had a soft spot for the Jews, but now 'he was definitely [an] anti-Semite'.[26] Regardless, the US did not expect Yalcin to play a very active role.[27]

It was with horror that the British Foreign Office greeted the appointment of Joseph Keenan, the former chief prosecutor for the International Military Tribunal for the Far East, as head of the US delegation to the PCC. 'Mr Keenan is not merely a drunkard', one Foreign Office official reported, 'but is incompetent, quarrelsome and conceited. This is a most disgraceful appointment'.[28] This antagonism originated from Britain's experience with Keenan during the Japanese war crimes trials where he was found to be 'irresponsible', 'tactless', 'superficial in his judgment' and at times 'came out with public statements which have been embarrassing to us'.[29] News of Keenan's resignation, apparently for personal reasons,[30] no doubt brought relief to the Foreign Office. His replacement, Mark Ethridge,[31] was a Kansas-based newspaper editor and publisher.

The State Department wrote to Ethridge that its 'admiration' for his acceptance of the appointment was 'unbound'.[32] The Foreign Office was less effusive, but Ethridge's appointment was well received in Whitehall.

It was noted that although he saw things from a journalistic perspective, he was not known to have pro-Zionist leanings.[33] Nevertheless, the problems stemming from his newspaper background were identified. 'He does, however, tend to look at situations with a journalist's eye and perhaps to give the press on occasions more than is desirable.' He also had 'an eye towards the "sensational"',[34] and (most likely on the plus side) Britain's ambassador in Beirut noted that Ethridge 'throws a party properly'.[35]

The third member of the Commission's triumvirate was the French representative Claude de Boisanger,[36] a career diplomat with the rank of minister. He was greeted with enthusiasm by members of the British Foreign Office who described him as both 'friendly' and 'intelligent', 'reasonable' and 'cooperative'.[37] According to Pablo de Azcarate, the PCC's Principle Secretary,[38] he was also 'one of the more brilliant diplomats of the younger generation'.[39] However, some considered him 'typically French', meaning, apparently, that he enjoyed the night life, Paris, cars and other things that would lead some people to think him lazy, unforceful and indifferent.[40] From Geneva, a US official wrote of his first impressions of the PCC's make-up. 'The Turk has said very little, while the Frenchman talks incessantly', and they seemed more interested in financial and administrative matters with little interest in the actual job that needed to be done. In conclusion, the success of the PCC would, according the official, depend on the US representative.[41]

It has been contended that the PCC's membership was a contributing factor in its lack of success.[42] Many years later, Ethridge would concede his own unsuitability for the job. When asked about the PCC and whether a man whose career was outside government could be as effective as a career Foreign Service officer, Ethridge replied, 'No, I came to feel that it was a mistake to send special non-career people ... including me'.[43] However, this was an unfair assessment. Despite the fact that at first glance the members of the PCC appeared unsuited to the task, there were some strengths in its composition. Boisanger was a career diplomat with high ambitions, and it was a good sign that France had sent a serious and valued representative to the Commission. Meanwhile, the appointment of Ethridge as the US representative also had its strengths. He was close to President Truman who was suspicious of the State Department, which he once accused of making him look like a 'liar and double-crosser'.[44] As a State Department outsider and friend of the president, Ethridge was trusted by Truman. He was committed to the task, even making personal sacrifices by not seeing his family for long periods during which time his mother was on her deathbed.[45] Ethridge was also not totally inexperienced, having worked on fact-finding commissions for both the State Department and the UN in the Balkans and Greece between 1945 and 1947.[46]

It has also been argued that the participation of governments with strong interests in the Middle East was to the PCC's disadvantage because the members worked for the interests of their own respective governments rather than for the UN and the countries in need of conciliation. Earl Berger argues that the US sought to impose a settlement through the PCC based on Arab demands.[47] Saadia Touval argues that, while each nation desired peace, they pursued a peace consistent with their interests rather than peace in the abstract, especially the US attempt to gain credit from the Arabs for getting the Negev, and France improving relations with Syria by changing the Israeli–Syria boundary in Syria's favour.[48]

Were the member states of the PCC acting in their own countries' interests? Indeed they were. As Fischbach observes, the US seat on the PCC served to guarantee that the body never strayed too far from US policies in general and UN officials were naive to assume that representatives would act independently of their countries' interests.[49] However, the more pertinent question is whether this was the reason why the PCC failed. The reality is that the US was actually quite flexible in its approach. In fact, Dean Acheson had instructed Ethridge that the PCC should endeavour to find common ground for an agreement without preconceived ideas for a final settlement. Only in the case of an impasse, Acheson instructed, would there be a desire to put forward terms for an agreement, but even then they should be in consultation with other PCC members and the British.[50] It should also be recalled that the US was opposed to the British insistence that the Bernadotte plan be the basis for a settlement. US policy was based on the Jessup Principle. Rather than imposing an idea, it was a fluid concept allowing for territorial swaps based on the UN's 1947 Palestine partition resolution, but only if it was mutually agreed by the parties themselves.[51]

The early stages of the PCC: Talks with Israel and Jordan

Although the PCC was established in Geneva on 17 January 1949 and moved to Jerusalem's King David Hotel on 24 January[52] where there were reports of Israeli wiretapping,[53] its first full-scale meeting with Mark Ethridge in attendance did not take place until 3 February.[54] The absence of delegates and commissioners became a common occurrence.[55] In this case, the delay in the appointment of the new US representative led to speculation in Arab circles that it showed that the US was not interested in the work of the PCC, preferring to leave Arabs 'to [the] tender mercies [of the] Jews'.[56] However, in the following weeks, the PCC made a series of visits and consultations across the Middle East, speaking separately to Israel and the Arab states. Eventually these talks would bring the parties to the city of Lausanne by the shores of Lake Geneva in the French-speaking part of Switzerland. The PCC would pursue a multilateral approach to conciliation, attempting an agreement between Israel and the Arab states altogether, grouped as one bloc. This conference would last from April until September 1949.

Although Jerusalem was anticipated by the PCC to be their chief worry,[57] from the PCC's initial talks with Israel and the Arab states in February 1949, the Palestinian refugee issue proved to be the main obstacle. Talks started with a meeting between the PCC and Israeli Foreign Minister Moshe Sharett on 7 February. Sharett explicitly said that Israel wanted to negotiate separate treaties with the Arab states rather than participate in a general conference.[58] He also argued that the refugee issue could only be solved as part of an overall peace settlement. He cited his country's security concerns and the economic burden of a return. Furthermore, Sharett explained that there would not be a significant return of the refugees before, and possibly following, a settlement.[59]

Four days later the PCC held talks with Jordan's Prime Minister Tawfic Pasha Abu al-Huda. In a record of the conversation sent to the British Foreign Office, Tawfic Pasha expressed the hope that all refugees would be permitted to return to their homes in both Jewish and Arab areas of Palestine. Alternatively, if Israel refused, compensation could be paid preferably to the Jordan government in a lump sum in order to settle refugees on state domain, plus a settlement loan.[60]

The significance of Jordan's position was not just its willingness to forgo demands that the refugees return. It was Jordan which had emerged from the 1948 War in possession of East Jerusalem and the West Bank, the latter having been earmarked for a future Palestinian state. It was Jordan that according to the Bernadotte recommendations, should absorb the territory the UN partition resolution had allotted to the Palestinian Arabs.[61] Therefore, not only was Jordan the location of the majority of refugees, but it was also the state which had a vested interest in the future of the Palestinian Arabs not least because had Amman's claims over Palestine been fully realized during the 1948 War, it would have gained sovereignty over much of the Palestinian Arab population. Furthermore, if Jordan were now to maintain territorial aspirations towards Arab Palestine, implicit is dominion over its population, which would advance the possibility of such territorial acquisition.

This was in contrast to the other Arab states who, according to Ethridge, after having had discussions with Arab governments, feared the domestic repercussions of the refugees' presence as they were potential agitators that could become the core of irredentist movements that could threaten the existence of Arab governments.[62] Jordan's prime minister went on to tell the Commission that 'any body representing all the Arab states would not even agree internally let alone [with] Israel'. The Turkish representative then asked if Jordan was free to conclude a separate settlement with Israel. The response was that all that was essential was agreement with Israel, and that Amman was willing to disregard the objections of other Arab governments who had mishandled the issue throughout.[63]

According to the US account of the meeting, when asked if he preferred a separate or general peace conference with Israel, Tawfic Pasha replied that past experience showed that a separate peace conference would be more productive, and he did not think it necessary to have a general peace conference.[64] This meeting led the British Foreign Office to believe that King Abdullah had 'gone still farther in the direction of unilateral negotiations with the Jews'.[65]

Jordan's motivation for absorbing refugees was territorial acquisition and its position was that Israel should evacuate territories obtained after 14 May.[66] In other words the Arab parts of Palestine would be incorporated into Jordan, which also demanded a Mediterranean port such as Gaza. At this early stage, the PCC had been told by both Israel and Jordan, in terms which could not have been more certain, that they preferred bilateral negotiations and not a general peace conference and that their respective positions on refugees were not particularly distant. Yet the PCC did not facilitate or encourage direct bilateral talks at the time, preferring to pursue a multilateral process involving all Arab states.

Talking with one voice: The PCC's discussions with Arab states

Following the round of talks with Israel and Jordan, the PCC left for Cairo to begin its tour of Arab countries.[67] Despite it being reported that the Arab states, with the exception of Jordan, were expected to speak in one voice demanding the return of refugees to Israel, the PCC expressed optimism.[68] The Egyptians informed the Commission that the principle of refugee return was fundamental and that Israel had to allow the refugees to return before talks on a peace settlement could begin. Cairo then concluded that there could be no further progress until Jewish intentions were known, with Israel's position at

Rhodes where armistice negotiations were being held, an important indicator.[69] In Egypt, Yalcin, the Turkish representative, commented that politically it was difficult enough for the Egyptians to conduct talks with the Israelis at Rhodes, let alone have formal peace talks which might involve a public admission of defeat causing an embarrassing and dangerous situation with the public.[70] It was also reported that despite the Egyptian press being respectful towards the PCC, there was widespread pessimism over the Commission's chances for success. The pro-government *Al-Assas,* for example, doubted that Israel would accept reasonable recommendations, particularly in regards to the return of refugees.[71]

In Saudi Arabia, talks were held with Foreign Minister Amir Faisal, who told the PCC that he considered the refugee question as separate from the other problems the Commission had to deal with.[72] A similar message was received from Kaled El Azem, the Prime Minister of Syria, who said that the refugee question had to take priority and be solved in advance of a final deal.[73] Several days later, after talks with Ibn Saud and the regent of Iraq, Ethridge told the British Ambassador to Iraq, Sir Henry Mack, that he believed that with the exception of Jordan, the Arab nations had clearly agreed to adopt a common line.[74] He noticed that there had been minor changes in emphasis and attitude, but that they had all insisted that the refugee problem be solved in advance of any settlement meeting.[75] This observation proved correct. On 22 February 1949, Mack was given details of a meeting between Arab representatives (excluding Jordan) held in Cairo on 5 February where it was agreed to adopt a common attitude towards the PCC; proof must be given of Israel's good intentions in regards to the refugees before the Arab states would agree to negotiations. Mack was also given a memorandum from the Iraqi Foreign Ministry declaring that if Britain and the US were to support this position (which also demanded that Jerusalem should be considered Arab), talks with the Commission could be successful.[76]

After the PCC had returned from visiting the Arab states, Ethridge told Moshe Sharett that they had shown a 'genuine desire' for peace, but that their primary concern was the Arab refugees, and they hoped that Israel would indicate whether it accepted the principle of return as set out in General Assembly Resolution 194. Such a conciliatory gesture, Sharett was told, would help the Commission when meeting with the Arab states.[77] Sharett's response was noncommittal. He argued that if Israel indicated the concession it would make, the other side might still not cooperate and the extent to which Israel was ready to admit returning refugees depended on the spirit and provisions of the peace settlement. However, he did say that he would discuss the possibility of such a gesture, but settlement elsewhere was essential and Israel was unable to consider repatriation as the major solution to the problem, although some Arabs might return depending on the conditions of a peace settlement.[78]

The following day there were conversations between the PCC and Israeli Prime Minister David Ben-Gurion, who was also told by the Commission that an Israeli gesture in advance of talks would help facilitate a settlement. Ben-Gurion did not disagree outright, but instead he stressed the importance of Israel's security.[79] The PCC was unable to get an Israeli goodwill gesture in advance of their meeting with the Arab states in Beirut. Writing on 28 February, summing up his impressions following the PCC's tour of Arab capitals, Ethridge wrote that the 'Immediate key to peace negotiations if not to peace, is [the] refugee problem'.[80] Ethridge would find out that it was also its biggest obstacle.

Building a bloc at Beirut

Pablo de Azcarate, the Principle Secretary of the PCC, recalled that the idea of the Beirut conference came after returning to Jerusalem from talks with the Arab states. Moreover, the PCC decided action must be taken to persuade the Arab states not to insist on a prior solution to the refugee problem.[81] Azcarate's recollection of the timing and reasoning behind the conference's conception was not accurate. The PCC had already conceived the idea while still on its tour of Arab capitals. The idea of a preparatory Arab summit to discuss refugees was proposed to Iraqi Prime Minister Nuri al-Said as early as 19 February.[82] The Arab summit idea was soon repeated in talks with the Lebanese foreign minister on 23 February.[83] It was reported that the PCC, with the backing of the US, was seeking to get the Arab states to have a common policy prior to talks with Israel.[84] The Commission had also received advice against organizing such a conference. Two days after the PCC's visit to Lebanon, in a message referring to a meeting with members of the PCC on 21 February 1949, Sir Alec Kirkbride in Amman wrote to Eastern Department official Bernard Burrows informing him that Boisanger was mainly responsible for the Commission's scheme to get representatives of the Arab states together to formulate an agreed policy. Kirkbride expressed his doubts as to the wisdom of this method citing his past experiences of Arab League meetings.[85] However, the desire of Arab states to negotiate in a bloc was probably a reflection of their distrust of King Abdullah of

Jordan and his attempt to annex the non-Israeli area of Palestine which he had occupied after the 1948 War.[86]

Despite being advised not to pursue such a meeting by the British Foreign Office, the British minister in Amman, the British counsel general in Jerusalem and the Israeli government, the PCC went ahead anyway.[87] On 2 March, Bardett, the US counsel in Jerusalem, reported to the secretary of state that the governments of the Arab states had been invited to an exchange of views with the Commission.[88] Ironically, Ethridge, who on 7 March reported that Israel was conducting talks with Jordan on Jerusalem, later commented that if the Beirut summit were to fail, he could see no alternative other than to pursue direct bilateral negotiations between Israel and the Arab states.[89]

The first progress report of the PCC published on 15 March 1949 was optimistic about the possibility of a settlement. It stated that it had found the sides 'in an attitude of mind definitely favourable to peace'.[90] The ink of the report had barely time to dry when several days later, in anticipation of the 21 March meeting, the Council of the Arab League adopted a resolution demanding the right of the refugees to return and calling for Arab representatives to consult together before the Beirut meeting.[91] The summit had not yet started and the Arab position had already hardened. The general Arab position was supported by statements made by representatives of the Palestinian refugees who expressed that the desire of the majority of refugees was to return to their homes.[92]

At Beirut, the PCC met with each Arab delegation separately in an effort to counter rejectionist rhetoric.[93] However, this did little to change the nature of the impasse. Seven days into the conference, Ethridge reported back to the State Department on 28 March that the Arab states viewed the 700,000–800,000 refugees as both a political weapon to use against the Jews and a potential internal threat to stability.[94] He also stressed that his talks with the Arab governments had only confirmed his belief that if Israel were to make a conciliatory gesture towards the refugees, the PCC would be able to continue its work. Israel's failure to do this would prejudice the basis of a peace settlement.[95] Ethridge was no doubt deeply frustrated, complaining that the Commission was 'making bricks without straw and with, I fear, too little support from home, it is going on with its work'. Fearing that the failure of the Commission would inflame anti-American sentiment in the Middle East, in a despairing memorandum Ethridge wrote, 'I am frankly asking for help.'[96] Several days earlier it had been reported that Israel had submitted a memorandum to the PCC arguing that resettlement in Arab countries was in its view the best solution.[97]

Action was indeed taken after Ethridge's plea. Moshe Sharett was informed that President Truman thought it time for Israel to make a 'real contribution' to a political settlement. It was suggested that Israel could state publically that although the refugee problem was part of a political settlement, it was willing to repatriate one fifth of the population (800,000 was the number of refugees the US representatives were using). 'A statesmanlike move by Israel with respect to the refugees would make it possible for the President to continue his strong and warm support for Israel.'[98] In response, Sharett disputed the number of refugees, putting the number between 500,000 and 550,000 and then restated Israel's position that the refugee question had to be resolved in the context of a final peace advocating resettlement in particular.[99] Several days earlier a lengthy Israeli memorandum was written stating that it was necessary to repudiate the 'propaganda' that the refugees were driven from their homes by Jews. Estimating the number of refugees at around 530,000, the report rejected that repatriation could be achieved as expressed in UN Resolution 194. It recommended that the solution was in resettlement. It examined resettlement possibilities according to urban and rural refugees and listed potential possibilities for their resettlement in Arab countries such as Iraq, Syria and Jordan.[100]

Meanwhile, at the Beirut conference, the PCC saw it as their task to make the Arab governments realize that not all refugees would be repatriated and that they should help find homes for those who would be resettled outside of Israel.[101] Britain and the US used their regional legations to urge the Arabs to attend the conference and participate in a constructive manner.[102] At the end of the summit, Ethridge was able to make what he considered a breakthrough. In a final meeting with the Arab states, it was agreed that another exchange of views would be held between Arabs and Jews at another location.[103] In return, the PCC told the Arab delegates that it would focus its efforts on changing the Jewish attitude on the refugee issue.[104] Ethridge had reported the day before that the Arabs had made a real 'concession' by agreeing to go ahead with peace talks and that if Israel were to make a concession 'we'll be on our way'.[105]

This revealed a flaw in the thinking of Ethridge, which was shared by the State Department and the PCC. What the PCC achieved at Beirut was only to obtain the Arab states' agreement to attend a peace conference at which Israel had already agreed to be present. In other words, the Arabs had not dropped their precondition that the refugee issue had to be solved before they would negotiate directly. They only offered to attend another conference. The Arab states' demand that Israel repatriate refugees prior to negotiations was once again stated as soon as the Lausanne Conference commenced.

Crossing red lines

In the following months, the PCC initiated discussions at the Lausanne Conference, which commenced in April and recessed in July. Ahead of the conference, the PCC found itself facing a significant obstacle. Israel wanted to discuss the refugee issue only in the context of an overall settlement; however, the Arab states, except Jordan, were refusing even to talk until the return of refugees had been guaranteed. In order to overcome this impasse, the PCC brought the Arab states together in March for a conference in Beirut to persuade them to drop their precondition.[106] Meanwhile, the PCC also sought to obtain a gesture from Israel on the refugees, something they could use to encourage Arab cooperation. But how feasible was such a strategy? It appears that it was dangerously close to what both the State Department and the Foreign Office knew to be the red lines of both Israel and the Arab states. Herbert Parzen has argued that both the Arab states and the PCC appeared to assume that many refugees would be able to return to Israel and become law-abiding citizens, an assumption he calls 'ludicrous'.[107] In reality, the views of the PCC as well as Britain and the US, the primary states dictating PCC policy, were more nuanced, flexible and realistic. In fact, at a very early stage they did recognize that the return to Israel of large numbers of refugees was implausible.

Ethridge had identified that the PCC needed some kind of gesture from Israel, preferably related to the number of refugees Israel would be willing to repatriate.[108] Acheson's response was that the State Department was in full agreement.[109] Ethridge also felt that the Arab states would have to be told that not all refugees would go back and that homes must be found for these refugees to be resettled outside of Israel. Plans for resettlement would need to be proposed as well as methods to finance resettlement with indemnification from Israel to Arab countries for the value of individual Arab property inside Israel. Additionally, outside help through loans and contributions would be needed.[110]

However, this strategy contradicted the impressions of the majority of Foreign Office and State Department officials who had not anticipated an Israeli acquiescence on refugee repatriation to any significant level. As early as January, Alec Kirkbride had been told by Dr Beyard Dodge, the former president of the American University in Beirut, of the need to raise funds for resettlement taking as 'his point of departure the assumption that very few Arabs would be able to return to their homes'.[111] In February, the Foreign Office wrote to its mission in France that according to their information, the Israeli government was unlikely to accept repatriation for more than a 'fairly small proportion of the refugees...assuming, what is far from certain, that the refugees are willing to return to Israel'.[112]

Meanwhile, the Foreign Office had written to its missions in the Middle East inquiring about the economic possibilities (and political consequences) of resettling refugees in Iraq, Lebanon, Egypt, Syria, Jordan, Saudi Arabia and Sudan.[113] Furthermore, while dispatches from American legations in the Middle East forwarded on to Britain were certainly not optimistic about present opportunities for refugee resettlement in Arab countries, there was even more pessimism about refugees returning to Israel. The US representative in Amman, for example, even recommended that the problem had to be approached on the basis that no refugees would return to their homes in Israeli territory.[114] The US legation in Saudi Arabia wrote the following: 'There can be no question of returning large numbers of Arabs to Israeli territory. It is inevitable that they would be treated as second-class citizens ...A new large dissident minority in a Near Eastern state is certainly not something to be sought after'.[115]

The question of long-term refugee resettlement was considered by both Britain and the US, who tried to coordinate their findings and exchange views. The views of Britain had been informally requested by the US after the State Department had sent out questionnaires on the matter to their diplomatic missions in the Middle East. Some of the long-term ideas that were proposed included the development of Jordan Valley irrigation and resettlement in Iraq and Syria.[116] A memorandum by Dean Acheson forwarded to the Foreign Office by the US consul general in Jerusalem noted that a general solution must presuppose the retention by Israel of most of its territory now held and the willingness of Israel to permit the return of only a very small number of refugees.[117] While looking into the problematic task of resettlement, the chancery in Washington informed the Eastern Department of the Foreign Office that the US's focus on resettlement 'underline[s] more clearly the unlikelihood of any return of the refugees to Israeli territory', and that resettlement schemes should be presented as 'reconstruction projects', as the term 'resettlement' highlighted the extent of the Arab defeat.[118] Reports of Israel demolishing Arab property also convinced British officials of the impossibility of Arabs returning to their homes.[119]

Hugh Dow, the British Chargé d'Affaires in Israel, believed that the number of refugees Israel would be prepared to accept would be negligible. With the exception of a few wealthy proprietors, he did not believe that the majority of refugees would return to their homes anyway.[120] Bernard Burrows shared this view, arguing that Britain should work on the assumption that, 'In spite of the Conciliation Commission's efforts not more than a few thousand refugees will be admitted to Israel.'[121] On 30 March, the US Ambassador Stanton Griffiths met the minister of state in New York and argued that while he thought Israel should be forced to take in a small portion of refugees, he did not consider that they could absorb many and went on to criticize the reluctance of Arab states to employ Palestinian Arabs.[122]

The Israeli position that the refugee problem could only be solved in a final peace settlement and that resettlement was the proper solution was reiterated in talks with both Sharett and Ben-Gurion, who, despite their differences, were united in rejecting the pressure of an advanced gesture to repatriate refugees. Caplan argues that there was no evidence of disagreement between the Israel foreign minister and prime minister on this issue.[123] Despite British and US understanding that Israel would be very unlikely to allow many refugees to return, the US was formulating a policy that strayed dangerously close to, if not one that crossed, the Israeli red lines. It called for a limited return of refugees and an Israeli gesture, despite the knowledge that it would be difficult to obtain Israeli acquiescence on either. In a 15 March State Department policy paper, for example, released just six days before the start of the Beirut summit, it was stated that the US was urging Israel to implement 'the purposes' of the December Resolution (194) as a means to prepare for a *modus vivendi* with the Arab states; however, it was conceded that it was doubtful that the State of Israel would allow more than 'a handful' of refugees to return.[124]

The paper went on to estimate that as many as 600,000 refugees would have to be resettled in Arab states (the paper estimated 725,000 refugees in total).[125] With this in mind, it recommended that Israel be persuaded to accept the principle of repatriation of an agreed number or category of refugees gradually and to compensate those who would not return but had assets in Israel. It was also recommended that the refugees be resettled in other areas elsewhere in the region including Gaza and Lebanon. Another crucial recommendation in this paper was based on the assumption that Arab Palestine, or at least a large part of it, would be allotted to Jordan, with the permanent settlement of refugees in that area absorbing as many refugees as possible.[126]

Britain and the US were, therefore, not under the impression that Israel would adopt a large-scale repatriation policy. However, despite this view, the US began to pressure Israel into making a concession out of the fear that, unless it did so, negotiations would be stalled completely.[127] Ethridge, backed by the State Department, argued that Israel's red lines had to be pushed to their limit or else there would be an Arab refusal to negotiate. This would, in turn, jeopardize the resettlement of the majority of refugees in Arab countries through the schemes Britain and the US were planning. For example, the US secretary of state wrote that the:

> Unrealistic and intransigent attitudes of both Israel and Arab states re agreement to repatriation and resettlement, respectively, of Arab refugees has created problem of serious concern to USG and major obstacle to PCC's task of implementing Dec 11 res ... Dept considers it essential that strongest diplomatic approach be made to both sides.[128]

A memorandum from Dean Rusk, the Assistant Secretary of State for UN affairs, to Undersecretary of State James Webb, noted that it was becoming increasingly clear that a final settlement of the Palestine problem would rest on the ability to find a solution to the Palestinian refugee problem. While it was noted that a quarter of the total (700,000 was quoted) could be returned to their former homes in Israel and only a fraction could be resettled where they were presently located, the bulk would have to be resettled in Arab Palestine or neighbouring Arab states. In order to achieve this specific resettlement, projects had to be worked out and supported by EX-IM bank loans, international bank loans, private capital and other resources. This could be done through work and construction projects such as irrigation and drainage schemes.

As US national interests were considered at stake, it was recommended that George McGhee be appointed as a special assistant to the secretary of state with the rank of minister to mobilize the resources needed to deal with the problem.[129] On 13 April a meeting took place in London between Sir John Troutbeck of the BMEO, the Foreign Office, G. Lewis Jones, US ambassador to the United Kingdom and McGhee in his role of US Coordinator on Palestine Refugee Matters. Resettlement proposals including the Jordan Canal Plan, the Jezira Scheme in Syria and resettlement in Jordan as well as possibilities in Iraq were discussed.[130] It was stated that the British view was that Israel either repatriate or resettle the refugees. McGhee said that, having discussed the question with Ethridge, the repatriation of some refugees to Israel was of the utmost importance as a gesture to the Arabs. Ethridge put the number at 200,000.[131] The State Department was of the opinion that no progress could be made on resettlement until the political atmosphere improved. It was believed that this could only be achieved by Israel agreeing to the principle of repatriation and the Arabs to resettlement.[132]

On 22 April, just five days before the start of the Lausanne Conference, George McGhee wrote to the US secretary of state enclosing a number of papers on the Palestine refugee problem based on studies by departmental officers. Among the conclusions and recommendations included was an Israeli agreement for the repatriation of at least 200,000 refugees with particular attention to refugees formerly from Arab areas under Israeli control which were not assigned to the Jews in the UN partition resolution of 1947.[133] However, in notes prepared for a discussion with the president, McGhee reflected on the 200,000 number, arguing 'the real question is how far we go in putting pressure on the Israelis to repatriate [a] considerable number of refugees (at least 200,000), which Ethridge feels necessary for success of the Lausanne talks'. This option was considered in the context of the possibility of withholding a US$49 million loan to the Jewish state.[134]

In a note from the secretary of state in advance of a meeting with the Israeli ambassador, details were given about the refugee issue and the efforts of Ethridge and the PCC to pressure Israel into making a conciliatory gesture by accepting the principle of refugee repatriation. As a snub to the Israeli ambassador, it was recommended that the secretary of state should refrain from looking at an Israeli draft statement about Israel's entry to the UN, if possible, as the Israelis wanted to give the impression to the UN that it had been submitted to the US first.[135] The reason was that the US had noted that several members of the UN had expressed displeasure over Israel's position towards the Palestinian refugees and the State Department also wanted to demonstrate its support for Ethridge's position that Israel must make a conciliatory statement.[136] However, in Israel, it was believed that relations with Ethridge were important to its ties with the US and Israel therefore sought to avoid being blamed by him if talks in Lausanne were to fail.[137]

The commencement of the Lausanne Conference

Following the Beirut summit, the PCC set itself to work on preparations for the next conference scheduled for Lausanne in late April. In laying the groundwork for the conference, the PCC sought to obtain an

Israeli gesture on Palestinian refugees that had so far eluded them. The Commission had come out of the Beirut meeting under the impression that the Arab side had offered a concession by dropping their precondition to attend the Lausanne Conference. However, the PCC was unable to get an Israeli concession before the start of the Lausanne Conference. This was despite a meeting between Secretary of State Acheson and his Israeli counterpart Moshe Sharett. The Israeli foreign minister was told that the US believed that it was time for Israel to make a 'real' contribution to the political settlement of the 800,000 Arab refugees by repatriating a quarter of the refugees coming from areas under Israeli control but not allotted to the Jewish state under the partition plan.[138]

Despite being told that such a move would make it possible for the US to continue helping Israel's economic and political development, Sharett once more disputed the number of refugees. He also restated that returning refugees would pose a security threat, and repeated the Israeli position that the refugee issue could only be solved as part of a final peace settlement and that resettlement was the best solution.[139] In a meeting between the US ambassador to Israel James McDonald and David Ben-Gurion, the Israeli prime minister simply repeated Sharett's earlier points made in Washington, that repatriation should be part of an overall peace settlement and that it must wait until the Arabs were no longer threatening a resumption of hostilities. Ben-Gurion also added that Israel's answer on this point was 'unshakable'.[140] The previous day the Israeli prime minister refused to give an Israeli gesture on repatriation ahead of talks at Lausanne in talks with the PCC.[141] Israel had earlier given the PCC a memorandum, presumably the previously mentioned report that was drafted in March, stating that it would be easier to settle the refugees in Arab states and that in Israel there was virtually no Arab economy left.[142] Commenting on his assignment to the PCC, Mark Ethridge wrote to the US president exclaiming that 'this is by far the toughest assignment you have ever given to me'. He added that the Commission considered that the Arabs had made great concessions, but 'the Jews had made none so far'. This he put down to them being 'too close to the blood of their war and their narrow escape, as they regard it, from extinction'.[143]

The Lausanne Conference started on 27 April.[144] Ethridge openly acknowledged that the chief problem was the refugees.[145] Walter Eytan, the head of the Israeli delegation, would recall the conference as being a 'tragic farce'.[146] It was not just Israelis who were disillusioned at the Lausanne talks. Muhammad Nimr al-Hawwari, a representative of the Palestinian refugees, commented that 'the Arabs stalled and pro-crastinated…The Israelis wanted to use the pressing problem of the refugees in order to prod the Arab states into making peace with it', but for Israel and the Arab states, 'none of their residents would starve or be stranded in the wilderness'.[147] It is important to note that there was little Palestinian representation at Lausanne. The AHC had approached the PCC in Beirut and requested being recognized as representing Arab Palestine, only to be rejected. The AHC in turn boycotted by the PCC and the Palestinians were represented by a Jordan delegation representing land and property owners and businessmen, and later, a group representing refugees in Gaza as well as three delegations said to be representing the recently established Ramallah-based General Refugee Congress (later its name changed to the Palestine Arab Refugee Congress) that included representatives such as Aziz Shehadeh and Muhammad Nimr al-Hawwari, who were hostile towards delegations from the Arab states.[148]

The conference convened after the armistices between Israel and the Arab states had been signed with the exception of Syria. In contrast to the armistice talks in Rhodes, the Arab states were considered as a single entity in so much as there were negotiations between Israel and the Arab bloc and not individual states. In Rhodes, Israel and the Arabs states had been housed in different floors of the same hotel together with the acting mediator Ralph Bunche[149] and his staff. However, at Lausanne, the parties were housed in different locations.[150] This was an important point. At Rhodes, Bunche had deliberately made interaction between the sides unavoidable. Housed in separate locations in different parts of Lausanne, the sides were able to, and did indeed avoid each other.[151] This was contrary to the expectations of the Israelis. As early as 28 February, Re'uven Shiloah told James McDonald that in order to make progress in negotiations, a neutral atmosphere such as Geneva or Paris was required where delegates could meet privately and 'accidentally' outside of the public meeting.[152] The make-up of the delegation did not help this imperfect start. The British analysis of the composition of the Egyptian delegation, for example, concluded that its authority was limited and should be considered 'light weight'.[153] This was also noted in Israel. It was brought up at the Knesset that the Arab delegations at Lausanne lacked the 'proper credentials'.[154] It was reported several days before the conference that all meetings would be in private and there would be no formal agenda.[155] Furthermore, talks were held indirectly whereby the Israeli and Arab delegations did not meet directly or face-to-face, but rather through the PCC.[156] Nevertheless, Egypt's PCC representative, Abdel Moneim Mustafa Bey, previously met Israel official

Tuvia Arazi in New York in April 1949 ahead of the conference where he questioned the Israeli official if any goodwill towards the refugee issue would be shown at Lausanne.[157]

During these first few days at Lausanne, the PCC again approached the Israeli delegation for a gesture and told Israel that unless it changed its attitude, the Arab states would not discuss peace.[158] Israel made an offer to repatriate members of Arab families if their chief bread winner was currently residing in Israel.[159] But this was not considered enough, because the US secretary of state instructed consular offices in the Middle East to make diplomatic approaches to both sides, alongside PCC efforts, on the refugee issue owing to their 'unrealistic and intransigent' attitudes.[160]

By the early stages of the Lausanne talks, the PCC sought to get the parties to agree to a protocol linking the issue of boundaries and the refugee problem. This effort culminated, just one day after Israel had been admitted into the UN,[161] in the signing of the Lausanne Protocol on 12 May 1949.[162] The protocol provided the basis for which further talks at Lausanne could continue. The sides signed separate copies of a map of the 1947 partition plan (though not labelled as such) with the text of the protocol. This stated the intention of achieving the objectives of Resolution 194 regarding refugees, as well as territorial and other questions, with the map taken as a basis for talks with the PCC.[163] However, no further progress was made at Lausanne. Days before the protocol had been signed, it was reported that Mark Ethridge had resigned from his post,[164] although he would stay on until late June. Despite the signing of the protocol, there was little movement in the position of the Arab states during the rest of the Lausanne talks. Instead, on 18 May, the Arab states presented demands to the PCC that Israel cease seizing Palestinian lands, that Arab bank accounts (which was discussed in some detail under the auspices of the PCC) be unfrozen, that there should be repatriation of orange grove owners and their workers as well as the freeing of Waqf property.[165] On 27 May, it was noted in a *Times* editorial that the Arabs demanded an immediate return and that there would be no settlement until issues such as the refugees had been resolved.[166] Meanwhile, later in June, Abba Eban dismissed the protocol as 'waste produce'.[167]

The first crisis in US–Israeli relations

Ethridge had previously complained that he had not received enough support from the Truman administration. This was a criticism that has been supported by some scholars who have claimed that the US did not put enough pressure on Israel.[168] This poses the question as to why the US did not put more pressure on Israel in order to elicit a more flexible approach from Jerusalem, especially as Israel required US support for admittance into the UN as well for the approval of a US$49 million loan. In fact, the US did exert some pressure on Israel at Lausanne, which culminated in an official rebuke on 29 May. Truman sent a belated response to Ethridge's 11 April letter in which the latter had expressed the hopelessness of his task. Truman informed Ethridge that he had been disgusted at the way the Jews had approached the subject of refugees and had related this to the Israeli President Chaim Weizmann.[169]

However, this made little headway and, on 5 May, a week before the Lausanne Protocol was signed, Ethridge was still complaining because Israel had still not modified its position.[170] However, the US was reluctant to further increase pressure until Israel had been admitted into the UN. The secretary of state explained to the legation in Lausanne that the US had cosponsored the resolution to admit Israel because it would help bring about a Palestine settlement and was consistent with US policy. Failure by Israel to gain admittance, it was argued, would militate against both the Arab and Israeli sides moving towards a settlement.[171] This indicates that the US believed that using admission into the UN as leverage would have been counter-productive. However, after Israel was accepted into the UN on 11 May, the State Department now believed the time had come for Israel to produce a basis for a settlement. Dean Rusk, the Assistant Secretary of State, insisted that the Israeli delegation accept repatriation as a substantial element in solving the problem.[172]

On 20 May, Eytan informed Ethridge that by signing the Lausanne Protocol, Israel had made a concession and would do nothing more at present.[173] This prompted action from Washington. Rusk asked Ethridge to comment on a draft note to the Israeli ambassador in Washington which stated that Israel's present policy on refugees was not stimulating further discussion and noted that if Israel continued to reject the principles of Resolution 194 and the advice of the US government, the US would 'regretfully be forced to the conclusion that a revision of its attitude towards Israel has become unavoidable'.[174] This received a positive reply from Ethridge, who, while suggesting several amendments, viewed a note of this character as strengthening his position.[175]

Finally, Rusk, in a memorandum to the president, advocated that the Israeli government be informed forcefully that if it continued to reject America's advice, Washington's attitude towards Israel would be revised. Measures which might be taken included refusing Israeli requests for US technical advisors and training and withholding the approval of the

US$49 million loan.[176] It was further believed that the strategic threat of Arab perceptions of Israeli territorial expansionism would aggravate Arab charges against the US, and the ensuing conditions of instability and mutual suspicion would provide an atmosphere for Soviet regional penetration.[177] On 28 May, Rusk informed the US Embassy in Israel that the president had approved the ambassador to deliver the note to the Israeli prime minister. The note informed Israel that it should be in no doubt that the US:

> Relies upon it [the Israeli government] to take responsibility and positive action concerning Palestine refugees, and that, far from supporting excessive Israeli claims to further territory within Palestine, the US Govt believes that it is necessary for Israel to offer territorial compensation for territory which it expects to acquire beyond the boundaries of the Nov 29, 1947 res[sic] of the GA.

It was also relayed that a revision of US policy towards Israel would be the result if Israel chose to reject the principles of Resolution 194.[178] McDonald hand-delivered the message to David Ben-Gurion on 29 May. He recalled the Israeli prime minister's reaction. He said aloud, 'this will have to be answered. It is very serious and very stiff'.[179] Sharett also called the letter the 'stiffest ever delivered'.[180] But there were still limits to the amount of pressure the US exerted. Touval notes that the US did not appeal to public opinion as a means to influence Israel, plausibly arguing that such an appeal would have caused domestic opposition and would not necessarily have made the Arab position any more flexible. Applying too much pressure would also have constrained the mediator's freedom of action, as it was dependent on support from both sides.[181] Details of White House and State Department pressure on Israel to repatriate refugees as well as the Israeli reaction were, nevertheless, reported in the press.[182] The US also made sure that it was clear to Israel that it was disappointed with its position in Lausanne and this was made clear in subsequent meetings with Israeli officials.[183] Perhaps one reason why US pressure on Israel was limited was because the US saw Israel as an important potential ally in the region. For example, Britain's ambassador to Washington, after consultations with Acting Secretary of State Robert Lovett, said that the US believed that Israel would be the most dynamic, efficient and vigorous government in the Near East and would play an increasingly important regional role from every point of view, and as such, Britain and the US should avoid a policy which risked permanently estranging the Israelis.[184]

Over the next few months, there was an improvement in US–Israel relations. Ambassador McDonald commented that Washington reappraised the situation, but this time in more realistic terms, and threw off what he believed to be British influence.[185] However, it had not been just 'British influence' which influenced Washington to take a firmer stance against Israel. Ethridge, the head of the PCC and therefore at the forefront of the US's diplomatic efforts on the issue, advocated a tougher stance, and it cannot be a mere coincidence that after he resigned from the PCC in mid-June, US–Israeli relations improved.

There are of course limits to the extent to which a Great Power can influence the policy of a small state when that state deems it detrimental to its national interests. As Caplan aptly notes, the US's ability as a Great Power to make the parties change their policies was never as great as some had hoped.[186] Moreover, US pressure on Israel had succeeded somewhat as, in the following weeks, Eban stressed to the Israeli delegation in Lausanne that it was essential that Israel was not blamed for the collapse of the PCC and to 'shower them [with] constructive proposals'.[187] Israel put forward a proposal to the PCC to incorporate the Gaza Strip including its population into Israel. This went a long way in satisfying US concerns and was a significant factor that led to the improvement of American–Israeli relations.

Land for refugees: Israel's Gaza Proposal

Despite Israeli red lines of repatriating refugees, it put forward to the PCC its Gaza Proposal. This idea, to obtain the Gaza Strip along with its Arab population and refugees, had already been suggested to the PCC on several previous occasions as early as 18 April.[188] The Israeli Cabinet discussed the possibility on 3 May. Stressing the security benefits, Ben-Gurion supported the idea and managed to obtain backing from the majority of ministers, despite Sharett calling the move a catastrophe, as Israel had not matured significantly enough to absorb such a number of refugees.[189] From 28 May onwards, Israeli officials began speaking to the PCC about the proposal in a more concrete manner.[190] This was even put into writing by Eytan in a letter to the PCC elaborating the Israeli proposal.[191] Ambassador McDonald reported that the Israeli Cabinet had voted for the proposal with two abstentions, adding that, in private, Egypt had indicated its willingness to relinquish the Gaza Strip.[192] According to State Department figures, the proposal would mean that Israel would take in 230,000 Palestinian refugees.[193] However, despite the proposal, by mid-June it was reported that the Commission was back to where it had started six weeks earlier after further talks with Israeli representative Eytan were inconclusive.[194] Initially, the State Department was divided over the Gaza-for-refugees offer.[195] However, soon the US became more receptive to Israel's proposal. Writing to the Lausanne delegation, the acting secretary of state commented that the US would approve this plan as part of a final settlement provided Egypt consented and received territorial compensation if it so desired.[196]

The US was even optimistic of an Egyptian approval, noting that Israel would assume the refugee burden and that the territory was becoming a financial liability for Egypt in any case.[197] The US believed that the Gaza Strip proposal was a potential key to unlocking the whole problem and they encouraged Uriel Heyd, the Israeli Chargé d'Affaires, to help get the Egyptians and Israelis together.[198] In a memorandum to the US Embassy in Egypt, Washington stated that the proposal could form the basis of an important contribution to the final settlement of the Palestine problem.[199]

However, when the Israeli plan was revealed to Egypt and the Arab states, it was rejected. In fact, they called it a flagrant violation of the Lausanne Protocol signed on 12 May.[200] According to David P. Forsythe, the reason for its rejection was that not only Egypt but also Jordan had interests in the territory. The Gaza Strip, together with parts of the Negev, could serve as a Mediterranean outlet for Jordan. Egypt and Jordan had also made a verbal agreement not to give up the Gaza Strip without further consultations.[201] Egypt responded to the Israeli offer by calling it 'cheap barter', arguing that the first step should be to let the refugees in Gaza who wished to do so return to their homes, but made no suggestion about what should happen to the remainder.[202] Indeed, Israel had made it clear that the reintegration of the refugees in Gaza to Israel was subject to national security and economic feasibility.[203] The Egyptian ambassador's comments did not diminish the State Department's optimism. The secretary of state called for the US ambassador in Cairo to inquire about the Egyptian position on border rectification, connecting this to the refugee situation in Gaza and informing them of the low economic potential of Gaza for the refugees, as well as the problem that many refugees in Gaza might not want to return to Israel. In exchange for Gaza, the possibility of frontier rectification further south could be explored.[204]

There was another reason for Egypt's rejection – British involvement. The US had requested British support and hoped that Britain would influence Egypt's attitude.[205] In response, the Foreign Office advised its legation in Cairo to withhold any advice to the Egyptians over Israel's

Gaza offer except where the refugee issue was concerned, as this would put Cairo in a difficult position if they were to retain the Gaza Strip without agreeing to settle refugees.[206] Coincidently, Israel's proposal came just two weeks after a Foreign Office minute considered the future of the Gazan refugees. There was, it speculated, a 'very real danger' that neither Egypt nor Israel would be prepared to look after the refugees. A possible means of solving the problem was that Britain should suggest to Egypt or Jordan that Israel should take the Gaza Strip along with all the refugees. In return for this, as well as Western Galilee, Jaffa, Lydda and Ramleh, the Arabs should get an area in the Southern Negev placing the Auja–Beersheva–Hebron road in Arab hands. However, Britain's representatives in the Middle East advised against suggesting this idea.[207] So when news came of the Gaza Proposal, Britain was of the opinion that it was a bad bargain, and that the Arabs should not be asked to make further territorial concessions even in exchange for concessions elsewhere, especially as the plan was vague and Israel had made it clear that it was not willing to cede the Negev.[208] British sources also believed that Egypt had a psychological need to retain the Gaza Strip, as this territory was its only gain from the 1948 War.[209] With the offer rejected, Israel also hardened its position. At the Knesset, Sharett berated attempts to undermine Israel's national security and dismissed the idea of a limited return of refugees as a gesture.[210]

While the US looked positively on the Gaza Proposal, it would be a mistake to believe that this was deemed by Washington to be a sign of Israeli benevolence. The US began to argue that the proposal was proof that Israel could assume responsibility for 230,000 refugees. Raymond Hare, who temporarily replaced Mark Ethridge as the US representative to the PCC following the latter's resignation,[211] was instructed by Rusk to express disappointment to the Israeli government.[212] Wanting to coordinate policy with Britain, the US commented that the Gaza Proposal was an admission of Israel's ability to accept a substantial number of refugees.[213] As the subsequent chapter will show, this was a mistaken assumption. Nevertheless, Egypt rejected the offer, the Lausanne talks were entering a recess and negotiations between Arab and Jew had reached a stalemate. There would be little further progress in the following six months.

Conclusion

On 1 July, the Lausanne Conference took an 18-day recess. Officially, this was because the PCC had decided a break was needed in order to consider the possibility of linking the refugee issue with that of territory.[214] However, in reality, the conference had ground to a halt over the refugee question.[215] This was for the most part based on advice given by Ethridge to Acheson and it left the French representative Boisanger furious.[216] Regardless, negotiations stalled because of the divergence between the sides. The Arab states demanded that Israel agree to refugee repatriation as stipulated by Resolution 194 before face-to-face negotiations could begin. Israel refused to comply, insisting that such a concession would only be made in the context of a final settlement. This deadlock would last right through the PCC's work and diplomacy in the forthcoming years. The reason why the PCC failed to bridge the differences between the sides was not because of its make-up or personnel, which had both drawbacks and benefits. To a certain degree, the PCC's failure reflected the distance between the sides over the future of the Palestinian refugees. However, the PCC was quick to recognize that the refugee issue was the main source of disagreement between Arab and Jew. Where the PCC failed was in its tactics. Supported by the US, not only did it allow but it also encouraged the Arab states to negotiate as a bloc, despite receiving contrary advice from British officials and against the wishes of Israel and Jordan. This fatal mistake was the ultimate reason for the PCC's failure. Even US pressure on Israel in the form of an official rebuke and Israel's curious offer to acquire Gaza in return for settling refugees did not overcome the impasse at Lausanne, which was, ultimately, the PCC's own doing.

4
Economics over Politics: The Palestine Conciliation Commission and the Palestinian Refugee Problem (Part 2)

Introduction

The previous chapter examined the work of the PCC, a UN body charged with the task of finding an Arab–Israeli compromise and a path to peace. Specifically, its mission was to facilitate a solution to the outstanding issues of refugees, territory and Jerusalem. The chapter concluded on 1 July 1949 when the Lausanne Conference organized by the PCC took an 18-day recess. This chapter will chart the evolution of British and US attitudes towards the Lausanne talks and explain how both nations strategized ahead of the conference's resumption. It will then detail the actual talks at Lausanne and explain the circumstances for the establishment and activities of the ESM as well as its activities and the context for its interim report. This report became the basis for future diplomatic efforts and for the establishment of UNRWA, initially conceived as a vehicle to resettle and rehabilitate Arab refugees in their host countries.

The ESM was a supplementary body under the PCC and part of a US and British initiative to resettle Palestinian refugees in Arab countries through developing public works projects in the Middle East. Its establishment was under discussion as the PCC facilitated talks at Lausanne. However, despite the PCC's best efforts, little was achieved in the talks at Lausanne. Notwithstanding several offers and proposals, Israel's unwillingness to repatriate refugees in large numbers and Arab resistance to resettlement proved unbridgeable. In Anglo-American discussions, there was a significant difference in what the ESM's role should be, especially as talks at Lausanne had stalled. Britain and the US found their respective policies representing opposing sides of an inescapable dilemma.

Britain believed that the ESM should be a political body with a mandate to negotiate. The problem with this approach was that it risked losing the cooperation of both Israel and the Arab states. In order to avoid this, the US believed that the ESM should be purely apolitical, addressing the issue of refugee resettlement from an economic and technical perspective. With Arab–Israeli talks at a standstill, the US was under the illusion that the economic potential of refugee resettlement through ambitious works programmes could incentivize the Arab states to reverse their aversion to refugee resettlement. This chapter will argue that although the US strategy was adopted, it was flawed, naive and proved unsuccessful. Not only did it misjudge the extent of the division between the parties, but it also miscalculated the extent to which economic incentives could bring about political solutions. Despite its technical nature, the ESM was still treated with suspicion by all parties. Therefore, what emerged in the second half of 1949, just as it did in the previous six months, was the formation of an ill-conceived strategy primarily responsible for the Arab–Israeli diplomatic stalemate. It was already apparent that without a political breakthrough, international efforts by organizations such as UNRWA to solve the refugee problem through resettlement in Arab states would ultimately fail.

Untying the knot: Anglo-American discussions during the Lausanne recess

While the Lausanne Conference was in recess during the first half of July 1949, the challenge facing British, US and international diplomacy was to find a way to overcome the impasse that had developed during the previous months. The refugee issue proved to be the major obstacle. The Third Progress Report of the PCC made this clear. Written two weeks before the recess, it stated that the Commission had not succeeded in getting Israel to agree to the principle of repatriation which the Arab states demanded as a prerequisite to negotiations.[1] Israel's subsequent Gaza Proposal, a source of some optimism for the US,[2] had been rejected by the Arab states just prior to the recess. Nevertheless, during the adjournment, Abba Eban was still making additional inquiries to Washington about the offer's progress, leading US Ambassador to the UN Warren Austin to believe that Israel attached considerable importance to its Gaza Proposal.[3] The Foreign Office told the US ambassador to London that Britain could not go further in approaching Cairo about Israel's Gaza offer, as forcing it upon Egypt in isolation would prejudice Egypt's options in regards to other offers. The Foreign Office was referring specifically to Britain's own eight-point plan, detailed below. It felt that, if supported by the US, the plan offered the most hope for success and it would then give 'appropriate' support to gain its acceptance.[4]

Despite being rejected, the Gaza Proposal was a starting point for British and US ideas for diplomatic initiatives. Britain's initial proposal consisted of eight points, most notably the acceptance of the terms of the rejected Gaza Proposal whereby Israel would take the Gaza Strip together with its 200,000 plus refugees. However, Britain insisted that in such a scenario there would have to be safeguards to ensure that the returning refugees were protected and had access to any part of Israel. More importantly, Britain rejected the notion of linking territory and the acceptance of Arab refugees. Instead, it favoured a territory-for-territory approach. This meant that, if Israel were to obtain the Gaza Strip along with its refugees, the Jewish state would still have to compensate the Arabs with its own territory; a far cry from the original Israeli intention and a complete alteration to the offer in the original proposal. The Negev was mentioned as well as the possibility of other areas that had not been allocated to the Jewish state under the 1947 partition plan but had been gained by Israel in the 1948 War. Jordan or Egypt would also benefit with the creation of a land bridge between them, while Israel would be guaranteed access to the Red Sea.[5]

US Assistant Secretary of State for Near Eastern and African Affairs George McGhee, with some reservations, agreed with many of the British eight points. There was agreement with London regarding the additional conditions to the Gaza Proposal. Safeguards were indeed needed for incoming Arab refugees, as was territorial compensation for Egypt. Furthermore, Israel needed to give territorial compensation for areas obtained outside of the 1947 partition plan, a position consistent with the 'Jessup Principle'. If such compensation to Egypt and Jordan took the form of a land bridge in the Negev, as suggested by Britain, McGhee reasoned that Israel must in turn be given guarantees of both freedom and access to the Red Sea. The Arabs would be granted access to the Mediterranean through the ports of Gaza and Haifa. However, while in general agreement with Britain about territorial compromises, the State Department, adhering to the flexible nature of the Jessup Principle, warned that there was a danger in creating an impression that the US would not support any settlement which did not provide territorial compensation. If compensation was not desired, the State Department did not see why it should be insisted upon. Nor did it believe that Israel should be expected to repatriate any more than 250,000 refugees.[6]

McGhee also told British officials that it would be desirable for the PCC to take a more positive approach. He agreed that Israel's acceptance of the 230,000 refugees in the Gaza Strip was the most important objective, even more important than the exact nature of the territorial settlement. In fact, it was McGhee's contention that political obstacles could be overcome if the economic aspects were investigated. And if Israel and Egypt were to agree on the Gaza Plan, then a start could be made on the proposed survey group (which was to become the ESM, discussed later in this chapter), making way for territorial negotiations.[7] This became the basis of US and later PCC strategy. Recognizing the refugees as the main source of the Lausanne impasse, McGhee emphasized the need to survey the refugees and the economic problems stemming from hostilities. This would help facilitate an agreement by offering the assistance required for both repatriation and resettlement programmes. This initiative, McGhee argued, could be conducted without committing the US or the UN to any specific line of action. McGhee believed that any specific allocations of refugees on a geographical basis would take into consideration the technical analysis of this proposed survey group.[8] While McGhee's recognition of the primacy of the refugee problem was prescient, his hopes of finding a solution by using economic development as an inducement proved (as this thesis will show) overly optimistic, especially as a political agreement between the parties at Lausanne had not been achieved. The consequences were disastrous.

Changing of the guard

The previous chapter highlighted the circumstances surrounding the appointment of representatives to the PCC. While some scholars have questioned the wisdom of the appointees, it has also been argued that criticism of the appointment of Mark Ethridge was, for the most part, unjustified. However, in his study of the PCC, David P. Forsythe described the events surrounding the appointment of Paul A. Porter, the replacement of Ethridge who apparently left in disgust believing that his leverage over Israel had been eroded[9] as the US representative to the PCC, as one of the most bizarre episodes in the history of the organization.[10] It most certainly was. Ethridge had resigned from his post on 16 June 1949. He was temporarily replaced by Raymond A. Hare; however, the permanent replacement was not appointed until two days before the resumption of the Lausanne Conference. Paul Porter, a practicing lawyer, had no expertise on Palestine and did not follow events in the Middle East. When asked by President Truman to join the PCC, he declined. Porter's excuse was that he was needed in his law firm. Unwilling to take no for an answer, President Truman arranged permission from Porter's law firm for him to go to Lausanne. Porter now had no option but to accept the post. As he was preparing to leave, Porter was briefed by Ethridge who (mis)informed him that progress had been made. Porter flew to Switzerland believing that all he had to do was to put the finishing touches on a peace settlement.[11] As the previous chapter has clearly demonstrated, a final settlement was not even close. It is likely that the bizarre circumstance of Porter's appointment was a sign of desperation. There had been several candidates shortlisted for the position.[12] Philip Jessup, perhaps the most qualified and informed member of the State Department on the Palestinian refugee problem, was also considered for the post but Jessup was advised against it by Ethridge.[13]

Porter did not arrive on time for the restart of the Lausanne Conference.[14] According to the PCC's General Secretary Pablo Azcarate, as soon as he discovered the actual situation at Lausanne, Porter quickly adjusted his attitude to deal with the reality he faced.[15] Indeed, despite his lack of knowledge about Middle Eastern affairs, Porter was both capable and proactive. McGhee praised the new representative during a conversation with a senior official of the British Embassy in Washington. Recalling his work with Porter in Greece, McGhee commented that he displayed a good grasp of problems in a short time and predicted that at Lausanne he was likely to do a good job.[16]

Despite the unusual appointment process of its new representative, the US considered it 'essential' and in the 'national interest' to overcome the impasse at Lausanne. Recognizing the Palestinian refugee issue as the main problem, it was argued that failure would lead to starvation and hardship; developments on the ground were likely to be exploited by communist agitators.[17] As talks between Britain and the US continued into late July, the Foreign Office commented that even though there was general agreement between Britain and the US, it was unsatisfactory that several days after the resumption of the Lausanne Conference, the US still had not gone beyond its 'tentative thinking'.[18]

Nevertheless, British and US talks continued, and by this time, Britain stated that it was only entertaining the Gaza Proposal because it did not want to exclude any constructive suggestion. But in reality, Britain, which was lukewarm to the proposal in the first place, did not consider its chances for success very high. In fact, it believed that, if pushed, the proposal would have the reverse effect and deepen Arab resentment.[19]

By 20 July, two days after the start of the Lausanne Conference,[20] the US was told that Egypt had decided not even to discuss the Gaza Proposal.[21] And when an Egyptian representative did express an interest in discussing the proposal, it was noted that it was 'obvious' he was planning to summarily dismiss it.[22]

By the time Porter arrived in Lausanne, the US position was that in order to increase his authority and chances for success, the US would put pressure on Israel by using the future of its loan as leverage and would also consider ways that the US and the UN could help the repatriation and resettlement of refugees. To the Arabs, the US would emphasize its position that, although some refugees should be repatriated, they wanted Arab representatives to make constructive suggestions about resettlement.[23] Later, Boisanger, the French representative, would criticize the US approach, claiming that because the Arab states felt the US was pressing Israel, they were sitting back and awaiting concessions.[24]

The previous chapter argued that the strategy of pursuing a multilateral peace agreement instead of direct talks between Israel and individual Arab states was a major strategic error. This was especially true in the case of Jordan, which indicated a willingness to negotiate directly with Israel, and in the case of Syrian leader Husni Zaim, who had indicated willingness to resettle 250,000 refugees in return for vast territorial concessions (examined in Chapter 6). This strategic error continued throughout the entire process. However, the US believed that part of the reason for the earlier impasse was that the representatives had been authorized only to talk about limited aspects of the problem. In order to strengthen the PCC, the US diplomatic offices in Cairo, Tel Aviv, Beirut, Damascus and Amman were instructed to urge their host governments to give full authority to their delegations to discuss all issues under the PCC purview. They were also instructed to enter into negotiations with a positive attitude and new and constructive approaches.[25] For his part, Secretary of State Dean Acheson called on Israel and the Arab states to send delegations to Lausanne with 'full authority' to negotiate a settlement on all outstanding issues.[26] This had some impact. In talks with the Syrian prime minister several days later, US Minister in Syria James Keeley reported that Damascus was considering a significant reduction in the size of its delegation due to both the high maintenance costs and the unlikelihood of anything being achieved because of Israeli intransigence.[27] However, after further discussions, the Syrian prime minister agreed to strengthen the Syrian delegations and add more 'realists' to its composition.[28]

Too little too late: Israel's 100,000 offer

On the resumption of the Lausanne Conference, the PCC announced its mandate to solve the refugee problem and emphasized the necessity of making progress. It did this with the intention of drawing the Arab governments into serious negotiations.[29] Porter was not optimistic. He wrote to the secretary of state on 26 July of his preliminary impressions of his task. He noted that it had been the Muslim fast month of Ramadan, that the Israeli representative Re'uven Shiloah had not yet arrived and that the Egyptian delegation had been unavailable.[30] He said he was dubious about the prospect of any changes in the participants' attitudes following the recess. Porter added that after talks with colleagues, neither the PCC nor the delegates gave him grounds for optimism.[31]

Porter must have been unaware that the previous day Major General John H. Hillring, a former member of the US delegation to the UN and assistant secretary of state for occupied areas, had filed a report of his contacts with Israeli officials to the State Department (he had already reported his meetings to the president). In New York, the Israeli consul general had approached him and expressed his government's willingness to repatriate 100,000 refugees including the 20,000 already repatriated.[32] This was without demanding territorial compensation. The consul general further stipulated that this number was final and would only be proposed if it were satisfactory to the president and the US government.[33]

Three days later, in a meeting with US officials including Deputy Undersecretary of State Dean Rusk and George McGhee, Eliahu Elath, the Israeli Ambassador to Washington, repeated the offer.[34] Two reasons were given for the proposal. The first was to demonstrate Israel's cooperation with the US. The *Manchester Guardian* reported that Israel's position was a result of US pressure.[35] Indeed, two months previously, Israel had received a rebuke from President Truman and Israel was in the process of receiving an increased US$100 million loan. Israel reiterated its position that the solution to the refugee problem lay with their resettlement in Arab countries.[36] The second was to contribute to a solution to the Arab refugee question. Elath stated that this offer was being made despite the opinions of Israeli security and economic experts who considered such a move 'disastrous'.[37] There had also been considerable opposition to the offer in the Israeli Knesset.[38]

However, the offer was not well received by the State Department. McGhee inquired whether the 100,000 figure was rigid, given the need to tackle the problem of 750,000 refugees. He also wanted each party to accept some responsibility for absorbing refugees or else there would be a significant shortfall. Israel and the Arab states should solve the whole problem and not part of it. However, Elath responded that 100,000 was the maximum offer.[39] Despite these differences, the *Palestine Post* reported that Truman was pleased with it.[40] One British official noted he had heard that Abba Eban had received word from a source close to the White House that President Truman was satisfied with the figure.[41] Porter reported that Elath and Shiloah were also of this impression.[42] Acheson had to reassure his delegates in Lausanne that there was no difference between the president, the State Department, and the representatives at the conference in Lausanne and instructed them to inform the Israelis of this.[43] The message was relayed, although Shiloah reported that Porter seemed embarrassed while giving the message as it appeared that the president had commented that the 100,000 offer was progress.[44]

In Lausanne, Porter was approached by Shiloah, who told him that Israel was willing to discuss the refugee issue outside of the context of a final settlement. While not revealing a definitive number, Shiloah informed the US representative that Israel would commit itself to the repatriation of a specific number; however, the actual repatriation would not begin until an overall plan for resettlement and repatriation had been drawn up with evidence of real progress towards a final settlement.[45] Again, this failed to make an impression on Porter, who reported that he was not encouraged by Israel's position but would, regardless, attempt to build on it.[46] The US secretary of state was more optimistic, expressing to the US delegation his hope that recent approaches to the Middle East and the growing realization of the necessity for early action over refugees could produce results.[47] Meanwhile, it was reported that Porter had told the Arab delegations that they must give up the pretence that all refugees would ultimately go back to their former homes, a position Washington considered unrealistic.[48] Nevertheless, Porter informed Shiloah of his reluctance to announce the Israeli offer in fear that the Arabs would enounce it as too small and subsequently create another crisis or deadlock.[49]

In the Knesset, the Israeli proposal was condemned by Menachem Begin, the leader of the right wing Herut Party. Even Mapam, which supported the return of 'peace-loving Arabs', condemned the Israeli proposal as surrendering to US 'imperialism'. Also, the proposal did not have the support of the liberal Progressives nor the United Religious Front. Even within Ben-Gurion and Sharett's own Mapai Party there was considerable dissention.[50] Sharett put forward a watered down version of the proposal.[51] Speaking in the Knesset on 1 August, Sharett had to modify Jerusalem's position to that of public opinion, and called the return of refugees before a peace treaty national 'suicide' and qualified any such return, if a peace treaty were achieved, with limitations of large numbers based on Israel's economic considerations.[52] Indeed, when challenged, Sharett stated that 100,000 was the maximum offer, pointing at internal opposition to the proposal.[53]

The Lausanne Conference continues: Questions asked not answered

On 3 August, Re'uven Shiloah transmitted Israel's 100,000 offer to the PCC in an official capacity.[54] Believing Israel's offer unsatisfactory[55] and likely to receive an instant rejection, the PCC at first did not even forward Israel's offer to the Arab delegations. Instead, its members held a private meeting with Shiloah to persuade him to reconsider his position.[56] Despite one optimistic newspaper's leading article arguing that the deadlock had been broken with the Israeli offer and the prospect for talks was now promising,[57] the Arab delegations officially rejected it on 15 August.[58] In a meeting with the PCC, the Arab delegation argued that Resolution 194 called for Israel to repatriate one million refugees, but Israel was offering only 100,000.[59] However, the Israeli delegation reported from Lausanne that the Arab states had intended to inform the PCC that the Israeli offer was 'ridiculous'. However, if pressed, they would have countered that Israel should repatriate a total of 440,000 refugees.[60] However, this counter-offer was never forthcoming. Apparently, Stewart Rockwell, a member of the US delegation at Lausanne, found it so unrealistic he decided not to forward it to the Israelis.[61]

Porter, for his part, reported to the State Department that although the atmosphere was now more conciliatory, the basic positions had not changed. Porter was now increasingly convinced that no more progress could be made.[62] Identifying the refugee issue as a major obstacle, Porter nevertheless asked for State Department approval to spend the week ascertaining the different dimensions to the problem. He also wanted to press the PCC privately to consider suggesting its own solution to the outstanding points of contention and then submit to each delegation their conclusions as a working draft. Porter had set his sights high and wrote that within ten days he wanted a declaration by both sides indicating joint responsibility for finding a solution to the refugee problem. The declaration would also recognize the variables in statistics pertaining to the number of refugees while achieving an agreement that each side would accept refugees in accordance to each country's capacity and need for economic assistance. Further, he wanted to obtain a pledge from all parties that they would give due weight to the findings of the forthcoming survey group.[63] This policy was approved by Acheson on 11 August.[64] The US and Turkish representatives to the PCC agreed that if the sides were to reject these proposals, then it might consider presenting a compromise solution to the UN General Assembly.[65] This position was opposed by Boisanger, the French representative, who argued that the PCC should continue its conciliation role as it was, in his opinion, making progress.[66]

On 15 August, the same day as the Arab states formerly rejected Israel's offer to repatriate 100,000 refugees, the PCC gave the parties a series of substantive questions in writing.[67] One of the questions asked whether the delegations were prepared to sign an accord which would stipulate that the solution to the refugee problem should be sought through repatriation of refugees in Israeli-controlled areas and the resettlement in both Arab countries and a zone in Palestine not under Israeli control. Regarding the planned survey group, the parties were asked if they would take all measures to aid the implementation of solutions that the group might suggest. The questionnaire also asked the parties if, without committing their governments, they would be prepared to make a provisional estimate on the number of refugees their governments would accept along with the territorial adjustments each government wanted to make to the 12 May Protocol (see Chapter 3).[68] The Israeli and Arab responses to the PCC's questionnaire came two weeks later.[69] By this time, the survey group that would ultimately become the ESM had been established.

The responses to the PCC questionnaire were not positive. The Arab states referred to an earlier memorandum they had submitted on 23 May, which called for the return of refugees originally from the areas designated for the Arabs or internationalized under partition. In addition, the refugees from Jewish-allotted territory should receive compensation in the form of territory.[70] In other words, the Arab states wanted territorial compensation in addition to the return of refugees to Arab-allocated territory held by Israel. However, they did state that they would recommend to their governments that they help to implement any solutions the mission might propose.[71]

More positively, the Syrian and Jordanian delegations stated that in conjunction with the possible recommendations of the ESM, their governments would be willing to receive refugees that might not be repatriated.[72] Indeed, the recently overthrown Syrian leader Husni

Zaim had previously conveyed his interest in resettling approximately 250,000 refugees if he received territorial compensation in the Galilee. Meanwhile, Jordan had already indicated that after repatriation to Israel, it would be prepared to cooperate on the question of the refugees who remained.[73] The Egyptian delegation stated that its country was too densely populated to contemplate resettlement, but it was prepared to re-examine the question if its eastern frontier were to be readjusted. Therefore, 12,000 square kilometres of territory should be transferred from the Jewish state to Egypt. They also wanted to receive international, technical and financial aid. The Lebanese delegation declared that it was in the same position as Egypt; it was too densely populated.[74]

The Israeli response came on 31 August. It stated its willingness to sign the PCC's declaration as long as the solution was sought primarily in resettlement in Arab territories. While it would facilitate and consider ESM proposals, Israel would not bind itself to implementing a solution in advance. Israel also wanted international assistance to be extended to Jewish refugees from Arab-controlled areas of Palestine. The Israeli delegation reiterated its previous offer of 100,000 in response to the question of numbers.[75] Israel also stated that it would not make any territorial concessions beyond the armistice lines.[76]

Despite the stark reality that the Arab and Israeli positions did not represent a significant shift in policy, Rockwell tried to view the responses optimistically. He reasoned that the Arab responses, especially those of Syria and Jordan, indicated an acceptance of the principle of resettlement. Israel had also committed itself more formally to the principle of repatriation. Rockwell even went as far as to comment that the replies could be considered a political agreement on sharing responsibility for solving the refugee problem.[77] He predicted that Syria and Jordan would probably put into effect the survey group's recommendations for resettlement of refugees in their territory even if there was no territorial agreement and no substantial number of refugees returning to Israeli-controlled areas.[78]

This optimism was short lived. Not only was Zaim overthrown and executed, but the PCC tried, in vain, to create a declaration on refugees embodying the responses of Israel and the Arab states, incorporating both repatriation in Israel and resettlement in Arab states.[79] However, both Israel and the Arab states were unwilling to sign the declaration. Other PCC attempts to salvage the Lausanne Conference, whose activities were winding down as the ESM was gaining momentum, included a letter sent to the delegations which stated that the armistice agreements should not be considered as a final solution to the problems discussed at

Lausanne. Notes were then delivered to the delegations on 12 September which asked for a re-examination of policy. It stated that Israeli and Arab territorial demands exceeded the 12 May Protocol (the map of the UN partition resolution signed by Israel and the Arab states with a declaration that they would achieve the objectives of Resolution 194), and if governments did not make substantial modifications or new proposals to their positions, a final settlement would be very difficult or even impossible to achieve.[80]

By this time, the parties were waiting for the UN General Assembly to convene, and they wanted to examine how it would interpret the events at Lausanne.[81] Just as importantly, the ESM had already been established and the State Department was calling for its delegation at Lausanne to bring the talks to a close in order to add emphasis and importance to the work of the ESM and to avoid the possibility that continued talks would actually lead to the hardening of the parties' positions.[82] The PCC suspended its regular meetings and agreed to reconvene in New York on 19 October where it would resume talks with the parties and examine any new proposals submitted.[83] The Lausanne Conference had concluded. Now the US and Britain were placing their hopes for finding a solution to the refugee problem in the ESM, which would offer an economic solution to the refugee problem. Yet, as Washington and London would discover, without a political breakthrough, the ESM's potential effectiveness became diluted and did not yield the intended results.

It's the economy, stupid? The origins of the ESM

The role of the ESM was to examine the possibilities for work and development projects which would use Palestinian refugee labour to develop the economies of the Middle East and help facilitate the rehabilitation and resettlement of the refugees on a self-sustaining basis.[84] Funds for relief were running out for the Palestinian refugees,[85] and in order to ensure the self-sustenance of the refugees in the future, it was necessary to reduce dependency on outside relief. The establishment of the ESM was announced on 23 August 1949[86] before the Lausanne Conference had officially concluded. The following day, Gordon Clapp, not the State Department's first choice,[87] was appointed chairman. The UN secretary-general made the announcement which was followed by another broadcast, this time by Truman, to increase the prestige of the group.[88] The ESM convened on 8 September in Lausanne where, in addition to meeting the delegations of Egypt, Jordan, Israel and Lebanon, it received its terms of reference from the PCC.[89] Headquartered in Beirut, despite the objections of Israel, as it would deprive it of equal opportunity to engage the organization,[90] its work began on 11 September. Its members toured across the region with experts examining areas where the refugees were located, holding discussions with technical committees and establishing and considering measures to remedy the economic dislocation.[91]

The idea of economic development as a means to facilitate refugee resettlement had already gained currency earlier in the year. In February, Acheson had commented that the solution to the refugee problem was based on their absorption into neighbouring countries, especially Jordan, which would require large-scale projects including the irrigation of the Jordan Valley and the development of the Port of Aqaba.[92] Britain was also considering refugee resettlement in Jordan and Iraq, noting the need for the development of projects in each country.[93] Mark Ethridge, then still at the PCC, put forward the idea that the Arab states would be provided with experts, plans for resettlement possibilities with indemnification from Israel and outside loans and contributions.[94] Acheson responded positively to Ethridge's proposals. At first, he asked if Arab states might undertake plans for short-term work projects using refugee labour aided by financial support and the help of experts. This would enhance the productivity of the Arab states and also encourage them to have a more realistic view of the future for the refugees.[95] From this stemmed the idea to survey the region's need for economic development and to provide technical assistance.[96]

As part of a strategy to combat Soviet influence in Africa and Asia and maintain Britain as a Great Power by leading a Euro-African 'third world force',[97] Bevin told Acheson that after the Palestine issue had been resolved, he would like to focus on development schemes in Lake Victoria and Lake Tana as well as the Euphrates to create good living conditions for 5–6 million people. Bevin added that 40,000 refugees could be resettled on the Jordan slopes, 200–300,000 in Syria and the remainder in Jordan.[98] Britain was concerned about the 'loss' of China and did not want the same to happen to the Middle East. Therefore it wanted to 'marry' its development plans with the resettlement of the refugees, which London believed was a destabilizing factor in the region.[99] Noting that such schemes should not be initiated with UN involvement as it risked Soviet infiltration, some of the resettlement possibilities included projects in Jordan funded by an interest-free £1 million loan and a project in the Jordan Canal to resettle 100,000 refugees and the development of the Jezira in Syria to resettle a further 100,000. The possibility of resettlement in Iraq was also mentioned.[100]

It was reported that the 'McGhee Plan', the name sometimes used to describe the idea of the survey group in recognition of one of its most passionate advocates George McGhee, apparently calculated that the projects in Syria and Iraq would take upwards of 15 years.[101] In April 1949, McGhee, who had just visited the region, saw the areas for the potential schemes and was enthusiastic, but he stressed that the US should avoid unilateral responsibility and therefore he advocated a UN or PCC lead role.[102] He added that the 'resettlement of refugees *is* the Middle Eastern development program'.[103] Indeed, it was reported that the plan, 'concluded' by McGhee, was part of Truman's inaugural pledge to aid 'backward areas'.[104]

This was put into a more formal proposal in April when a plan of action was circulated. It argued that the political stalemate at Lausanne could be overcome by a joint British and US scheme which would establish an economic survey group to foster a regional development programme and work to overcome economic dislocation among refugees. It would do this by assisting refugee reintegration into the economic and political life of the region on a self-sustaining basis. It would also facilitate activities on economic development projects. Not only would this serve to rehabilitate the refugees, but it would also increase the economic potential of the region. The survey group would also recommend measures, examine the situation of the countries concerned and look into sources of financing and the means of carrying them out. At a later stage a more permanent agency, which would become UNRWA, would be created to carry out the programme.[105]

The US relayed to Britain that the survey group would be a venture under the PCC rather than a joint British and US effort so as not to undermine the authority of the PCC by assuming direct responsibilities.[106] Despite British objections to linking the operation too closely to the UN, Britain went along with the US position, as the 'most important single factor' was to 'ensure American participation and provision of American funds'.[107]

On 9 May, the State Department sent a report to Truman written a few days earlier which estimated that there were 700,000 refugees. Assuming that Israel would resettle 200,000, the report stated that the remainder must be absorbed within Arab states, especially Syria because Lebanon, Arab Palestine and Jordan lacked the economic capacity to resettle the refugees within their borders. Overall, the report calculated that resettlement and repatriation would cost a minimum of US$267,500,000 over three years.[108] On 27 May, the State Department drafted a resolution for the establishment of the survey group tasked with examining the economic circumstances of countries affected by the Palestine War and mandated to 'make recommendations' for 'development programs' to overcome economic 'dislocations' and 'reintegrate refugees' into the economic life of the host country. This would be done in collaboration with the countries concerned and look at existing plans and proposals made by governments in order to absorb refugees on a self-sustaining basis.[109] On 31 May 1949, the CIA drafted a report on the refugee issue claiming that the problem heightened instability in the already volatile region. It also stated that the answer was in resettlement in Arab countries rather than repatriation to Israel. Resettlement would be a mammoth task with international capital required for irrigation and land reclamation in the Arab world. Although the cost would be high, it was justifiable to the US taxpayer, as such a project would shore up the US strategically in the region.[110]

On 3 June, McGhee sent the Foreign Office a collection of working papers about refugee resettlement possibilities which had been prepared by various agencies of the US government and Britain throughout 1949.[111] Minute disagreements aside, Britain was in accord with the US over the need for technical advisers to be involved, although it disagreed with the US over its composition and suggested possible candidates.[112]

However, there was a significant stumbling block. At Lausanne, discussions were not progressing and were heading towards a deadlock. By early June, there was concern within the State Department over the delay in launching the survey group and implementing its terms of reference as it was believed that further congressional and UN action on the refugee issue would be based on its plans.[113] Despite the delay, there was eagerness within the State Department to launch the survey mission. Admitting the danger that both sides might stall at Lausanne while waiting for the survey group's recommendations, McGhee revealed that the US was considering launching the survey group even before the PCC had reached an agreement over refugees.[114] The outgoing US representative to the PCC, Mark Ethridge, warned against such rashness. He argued that no commitment should be made until it was clear that both Israel and the Arab states were in the process of reaching an agreement on territory, and that both refugee and territorial problems must be solved simultaneously.[115] Ethridge's advice went unheeded. The response to him was that positive progress needed to be made ahead of congressional and UN General Assembly meetings later in the year. Therefore, it hoped to activate the survey group so its activities would work concurrently with negotiations over territory.[116]

Nevertheless, the political deadlock at Lausanne prompted the US to seek the opinions of Britain about the feasibility of the survey group in early July. In talks, Lewis Jones of the US embassy read an extract of a letter from McGhee. It stated that if the political deadlock could not be overcome, an alternative plan to that of the survey group might have to be considered, perhaps with separate organizations for resettlement and the administration of relief work and projects not associated with development.[117] Britain did not share McGhee's pessimism. In fact, British officials responded that they were not convinced that the setting up of the survey group was as unpropitious as the State Department suggested. They cited the willingness of the Syrian and Jordanian governments to settle large numbers of refugees.[118]

Towards the end of the Lausanne recess, US policy was fully behind the need to establish the survey group despite the political deadlock. Fatefully, instead of the survey group being contingent on political progress in Lausanne or operating concurrently with negotiations, it was now being seen as a means to help facilitate progress, an economic answer to the political stalemate over the fate of refugees. On 13 July, McGhee stressed the importance of establishing the ESM as a means to offer:

> Hope to countries concerned for the assistance known to be required for any successful repatriation or resettlement program, and serve to divert their preoccupation from their present short-range objections to longer-range economic solutions to broader problems.[119]

Britain was in favour of appointing the survey group as soon as possible on the grounds that it would be more likely to encourage the sides to be more forthcoming in negotiations.[120] The decision for the survey group to go ahead despite the lack of progress in discussions would have a devastating effect not only on the ESM's work and conclusions, but also on the very idea of resettling refugees through works programmes. After the ESM had been established, and following discussions with Britain, the State Department believed that the chances of reaching a settlement by political means had been temporarily exhausted.[121] In August, the State Department compiled a briefing book entitled *The Palestine Refugee Problem* which focused on resettlement without much attention to compensation or repatriation, indicating that resettlement had become the main priority of the US.[122] Less than two months later, the Royal Institute of International Affairs at Chatham House published *Arab Refugees: A Survey of Resettlement Possibilities*, a study which appeared see repatriation as feasible for just 100,000 refugees, the number Israel earlier offered. Instead, it focused on resettlement opportunities in the Arab world.[123]

Rifts in US–British perceptions of the ESM

The Foreign Office had mixed thoughts on hearing from McGhee that he believed Britain's traditional imperial rival, France, should also be deputizing on the ESM. While Sir Hoyer-Millar, Britain's minister in Washington, thought it could be both useful and encouraging, the Foreign Office, however, thought it could leave the survey group 'top-heavy'.[124] By 26 July, the US stated that it was in full agreement with Britain on the desirability of an early establishment of the ESM and for a US member to be appointed within a 'few days'.[125] Apart from the personnel, Britain expressed similar sentiments.[126]

Sir Desmond Morton was Britain's nomination.[127] Having met him before in London, McGhee was familiar with Morton. Although Morton did not have a background in economics, as McGhee had hoped the nominee would possess, he did think they could cooperate, as long as Morton was not a 'prima donna'. It was McGhee's opinion that one of the failures of the PCC was that individual members considered them-selves representatives of their respective governments. In order to be successful, the survey group had to function as an international body with different parts of a machine cooperating loyally and subordinate to the head of the mission.[128] However, this was contrary to Britain's expectations of how the ESM should be organized and conduct its affairs.

Initially, the establishment of the ESM served US purposes. McGhee was able to respond to the assistant secretary of state for congressional relations to reassure him about his concerns that difficulties could arise in Congress for further funding of refugee relief if there was no evidence that the Arabs and Israelis were making progress. McGhee told him that an effort through the ESM was now being made to try to break the political impasse.[129] The US was able to take the position that relief allocations for refugees in 1950 should be considered by the General Assembly in the context of the ESM's report later in the year.[130] The British position by the end of August was that, provided the task of the survey group was established to make recommendations for the financing of development projects leading to resettlement, Britain could announce to the UN its willingness to participate in further interim relief measures.[131]

Technical or political? The two halves of a Gordian knot

British optimism about the work of the ESM was short lived and this soon soured Anglo-American cooperation. A significant source of disagreement was the character of the survey group. As noted previously, the US wanted to maintain the group under the context of the UN in order to avoid responsibility falling to the US or Britain. It wanted members of the group to act independently of their governments in order to reduce problems such as fragmentation and make it easier to enter countries without prejudice towards the group's effectiveness.[132] One Foreign Office official called this development a 'bombshell'.[133] Britain believed the solution to the refugee problem was not relief, but was within the framework of a territorial settlement,[134] and as such, Britain favoured the survey group forwarding its own plans for a settlement.[135] However, the US wanted the ESM to avoid political questions in its work.

It was also the US position that it was inadvisable to put to Israel or the Arab states any specific plans for a territorial settlement. This was because the chances of reaching a political settlement, according to the US, had temporarily been exhausted.[136] Instead the ESM should be a technical study, albeit on the economic issues of repatriation and resettlement.[137] A State Department aide d'memoir stated that, while a territorial settlement would hasten the disposition of the refugee problem, the US believed the problem could be dealt with on existing territorial delineations.[138] This was increasingly pressing, as the current relief programme was drawing to its close, making the need for an integrated programme to tackle economic dislocation an urgent priority.[139] However, in a fateful reversal of the ESM's very *raison d'être*, it was not only the territorial issue which needed to be avoided, according to the US, but also the use of the term 'resettlement'. Ahead of visits to Middle Eastern states, Clapp wrote to the US State Department that 'discussion with Arab States should be along lines of work projects...with less talk of re-settlement during first stages'.[140]

However, for Britain the ESM was supposed to be a body with political power and not just a technical study group. It was reported from Lausanne that Morton, the British representative, had been empowered by Bevin himself to suggest and develop political solutions for the problems of resettlement and repatriation.[141] Morton was concerned that the ESM had become just a technical body with members not acting as representatives of their respective governments[142] and he had to deny press reports that quoted him as saying that refugees would be settled in the countries where they were now resident.[143] Britain's concerns, as reported from Beirut, were that permanent resettlement would now be set aside by the ESM in order to find support from Arab governments for the temporary employment of refugees 'pending' their 'eventual repatriation or re-settlement'.[144] However, the work of the ESM, the Foreign Office argued, must be to get the Arab states to understand that the problem could only be solved through large-scale resettlement in addition to repatriation or else it would defeat its purpose.[145]

From Egypt, British officials warned that the views of the ESM and its approach to tasks would change as a result of discussions with Middle Eastern governments.[146] Morton stated that Britain was concerned about the direction the ESM was going because it believed that the body would consist of government representatives empowered to suggest and conclude political agreements with states based on repatriation and resettlement projects. The British Chargé d'Affaires in Amman expressed similar concerns. More importantly, so had Bevin.[147] By the end of September, tensions between London and Washington had reached such a level that the State Department expressed concern that Britain had neither informed their missions to support the ESM nor explained its objectives until US representations had been made to the government in London.[148]

A US official summed up the difference between the US and British view of the ESM as being 'technical vs political'. Britain, he argued, wanted to re-enter the Palestine conflict or share an initiative to settle the dispute. Therefore, Britain wanted to use the ESM as an instrument for this and did not understand the need to divorce the technical from the political aspects of the ESM.[149] Hugh Dow in Jerusalem believed the US position would not bring a solution to the problem any nearer. Israel, he stressed, intended to fill up its absorptive capacity with Jews. There needed to be an understanding about a territorial settlement before it could be decided how many refugees should go back to Israel. Regardless, both Jew and Arab were swayed by political not economic problems.[150] Although on 20 September it was conceded that Morton and the ESM were in concurrence, Britain's view was that the political and economic aspects of the refugee question were inextricably connected and it was impossible to deal with them separately.[151]

Suspicious intent: Arab and Israeli mistrust of the ESM

Despite ongoing tensions between Britain and the US over the work of the ESM, visits were made to Israel and the Arab states. However, the ESM was greeted with suspicion. In Israel, although it had been reported that virtually no one from the 'Prime Minister down wishes to see a single Arab brought back',[152] the government was slightly more enthusiastic about the ESM[153] than the Arab states were. The Israeli press was generally sceptical.[154] There were even reports that the security of British members of the group could not be guaranteed. Israeli security services warned that ex-terrorist groups might be tempted to demonstrate their disapproval of the British return to Palestine.[155] Clapp complained to the Israeli authorities and told the UN secretary-general that the ESM would not proceed to Israel until the safety of all ESM members was assured.[156] When the ESM did eventually arrive in Israel, it was received with 'excessive politeness'.[157] Morton was not impressed. He reported that the ESM was welcomed with long speeches by Israeli officials trying to prove that it was the only 'honest state in the world and had been treated disgracefully'.[158] During talks, it was reported that Israel now had doubts over its 100,000 offer, and that it would not pay compensation to dispossessed Arabs nor accept the 11 December UN Resolution. However, Israel would be interested in an economic rehabilitation scheme for the Middle East and would expect advice and technicians to help carry it out.[159] The *Manchester Guardian* and other newspapers reported that Clapp commented that he was disappointed with Israel's attitude.[160]

The reaction in the Arab world to the formation of the ESM was unenthusiastic. This was because the ESM was seen as a surreptitious attempt to get the Arab states to agree to resettlement before a political solution had been reached. The US told its missions in the region to attempt to extend maximum publicity and support for the survey group by emphasizing its technical objectives.[161] This was despite a comment from the US Embassy in Cairo that optimism for the ESM was based on the 'private admission' by Arab states that they would be willing to accept 'fairly large' numbers of refugees.[162] But crucially, in order to gain support, the issue of refugee repatriation and resettlement was avoided. Iraq was particularly uncooperative, expressing its unwillingness even to receive the ESM. The State Department enlisted Britain to use its influence to reverse Baghdad's position.[163] Britain instructed its missions in Iraq, Israel, Syria, Lebanon and Jordan to speak in favour of the ESM and urged them to cooperate.[164] Nevertheless, Iraq stated that it was unable to meet the ESM and both Clapp and Morton saw no reason why Iraq should be pressured any further.[165] Iraqi opposition was not the only case in point. The Lebanese foreign minister informed the British representative that no development projects would enable Lebanon to absorb more than a token number of refugees, possibly a few hundred.[166] The theme in the Lebanese press was that the ESM's real aim was to 'enable the Jews to obtain access to the resources of the Arab world'.[167] In turn, there was disappointment in Lebanon's reluctance to support or cooperate with the ESM and its reported desire to involve the Arab League.[168]

Morton reported his concern that, in light of hostility towards the ESM, the problem of permanent resettlement was being set aside in favour of the attempt to collaborate with governments in order to find temporary employment to replace direct relief for refugees.[169] While in Lebanon, Clapp said that he was not discouraged by the reception that the ESM had encountered, but he decided to delay a visit to Syria and first travel to Egypt instead,[170] where the ESM was told there was no room for refugees.[171] Syria was reported to be the main source of Arab opposition.[172] Representatives of Palestinian refugees themselves also declined to meet the ESM.[173]

When Syria later indicated its willingness to meet the ESM, it was on the condition that Damascus could decide whether or not to take in refugees; talks would be purely on technical matters and not prejudice the general political settlement of the Palestine question, including the right of return for Palestinian refugees.[174] The State Department was also disappointed over Saudi Arabia's initial refusal to meet the ESM,[175] although a meeting did take place in which the Saudi representative accused the ESM of trying to dispose of refugees by resettling them in Arab countries.[176]

After completing the first round of visits, Clapp wrote that they were conducted amid an atmosphere of suspicion that receiving the ESM would weaken the Arab position regarding resettlement and repatriation.[177] There were also domestic factors to be considered. Regarding Syria, for example, public opinion was against an accommodation on the refugee problem, and the minister of foreign affairs said that he would only allow the work of the ESM if it had no connection, direct or indirect, to refugee resettlement.[178]

In later talks, there were some optimistic signs after the Syrian minister for foreign affairs told the ESM that, while his government would never publicly allow the word 'resettlement', they would privately guarantee that if financial assistance would be provided to develop projects in Jezira or the Yarmuk marshes, the government would resettle as many refugees as were willing to go there.[179] Iraq also finally received the ESM.

On 14 October, Nuri Pasha al-Sa'id said that he agreed with ESM policy wholeheartedly and would do anything to help. He also invited the mission to return with its experts when it began to study long-term projects in Iraq.[180] However, Prime Minister Shakir al-Wadi said he doubted that the economic approach could be separated from the political problem, stressing the Arab–Israeli conflict required a boundary settlement.[181] Although Clapp maintained that resettlement would be the only viable solution to solving the Palestinian refugee problem, he also relayed his frustrations to McGhee, commenting that the term 'resettlement' was explosive in the countries he visited, and that the US should stop pressing concepts that the Arabs saw embodied within UN resolutions and that was seen to be an Israeli answer to the problem.[182]

Sir John Troutbeck, the head of the BMEO in Cairo, rightly wrote that the suspicion towards the ESM was because it consisted of foreign governments from 'partition' countries. Also, the ESM originated from the UN, and was considered sympathetic to Israel, and they suspected that it was an indirect attempt to get them to accept an unfavourable political settlement. Troutbeck also believed that the Arab states feared that the ESM wanted to integrate the region's economy which would then be dominated by Israel.[183] The exception to the trend of Arab hostility towards the ESM was Jordan.

Unlike other Arab states, Jordan was willing to resettle Palestinian refugees. Morton reported that King Abdullah had warmly welcomed the mission, even promising full cooperation for both temporary work and resettlement. Abdullah warned, however, that it would be a waste of time to try to convince Iraq, Lebanon or Egypt, although he thought Syria would possibly resettle some refugees in the Jezira.[184] Ultimately, the ESM's work, which continued until it submitted its interim report on 16 November, was marred by suspicions of its intentions by all parties. This was the inadvertent consequence of US and British strategy which sought to use the ESM as a vehicle to promote an economic solution to the refugee problem in order to overcome the political deadlock. Instead, it fuelled further mistrust and deadlock. Worse still, in order to make the work of the ESM acceptable, its report had to omit reference to the 'resettlement' of the Palestinian refugees, the very basis for its original conception.

The Clapp Report avoids the resettlement quagmire

Several days before the release of the ESM's interim report, the US secretary of state wrote that the report would 'not stress [the] connection between political and economic activities'. He also made a series of suggestions for the ESM. While arguing that recommendations should be directed towards a solution without being overly influenced by potential opposition, he felt it should make no mention of resettlement or repatriation. Except for the brief allusion to conciliation and the continuation of the PCC's work, everything else was about technical and economic relief and regional development.[185] Similarly, Morton reported that the ESM believed that no detailed references should be made to territorial settlement in the interim report but might be considered in the final report.[186] Later, in discussions between Britain and the US over the report, it was noted by one British official that the report did not mention how many refugees would be repatriated to Israel. The reason, it was explained, was that the ESM had purposely avoided the subject, but there would be plenty of opportunity to discuss it at the General Assembly.[187]

The Interim Report of the ESM was signed on 6 November 1949 and transmitted to the PCC on 16 November.[188] One of the recommendations of the ESM was the continuance of emergency relief through voluntary contributions at the UN until 1 April 1950 under the present system, with a reduction in the number of rations. Also, it called for a programme of public works to be planned and arranged to begin on 1 April 1949. This would coincide with the reduction of rations, and by 31 December 1950, no more rations would be supplied by the UN. Beginning in April 1950, this new agency would direct the programme of relief and public works. It would have full autonomy to make decisions in the sphere assigned to it, be located in the region and have the assets of the UNRPR turned over to it. The purpose of the public works and relief programme, it was stated, was to stop refugee demoralization; employment would widen alternatives to refugees, increase the productivity of the country's economy and reduce the need for relief and its associated costs. With regards to the number of refugees, the ESM admitted that the exact number was not known, but estimated the total number at 774,000. This figure included 31,000 Palestinian refugees in Israel and an additional 17,000 Jewish refugees internally displaced during the 1948 War, but classed as refugees by international relief agencies. Of the 774,000, 147,000 were self-supporting, leaving 627,000 in need of assistance. The report also called for US$48 million to be allocated for the new public works programme.[189]

It was hoped that the Clapp Report would provide the basis for refugee resettlement together with a relief and works programme that would also be the backbone of regional development enterprises under the UN umbrella. However, the Arab states were deeply suspicious of the ESM and its intentions for refugee resettlement. If resettlement had been emphasized, it would not have been well received by the Arab states, and possibly also the General Assembly. While it was reported that the ESM had proposed to defer the issue of permanent resettlement until its final report, the ESM's preliminary report would confine itself to relief projects limiting General Assembly voting to a large-scale relief and works programme.[190]

Conclusion

Chapter 3 demonstrated that Britain, the US and the PCC followed an ill-conceived strategy whereby an overall peace agreement was pursued between Israel and the Arab states grouped as one bloc. Ultimately, this hardened the positions of both Israel and the Arabs and led to a stalemate at the peace talks in Lausanne. Upon the conference's resumption, the same strategy was still pursued and the conference concluded without a settlement. Meanwhile, the idea of a survey group was conceived. Initially, it was intended to work in tandem with political negotiations or after tentative agreements had been made. It would work towards establishing public works projects to facilitate refugee rehabilitation, repatriation and resettlement, and then be supported by an economic plan of action. The US increasingly advocated the launching of a survey group to investigate projects that would not only be the economic backbone of a political solution but would also help regenerate the region. However, by the time the Lausanne Conference took a recess in July, the parties had reached a political stalemate. The US, concerned that if the ESM were to openly address political questions it would fail, wanted to focus purely on technical issues whereby the survey group would be an economic incentive for a political solution. This amounted to an attempt at an economic solution to the refugee problem as a means of overcoming the political deadlock. However, the problem with this position was represented by the British view that political issues needed to be addressed in order for the economic study to be feasible (especially in terms of territory because the final boundaries of the states had yet to be decided), and also the states had to agree on the principles of resettlement and repatriation in order for the ESM's proposals to be achieved. The ESM was greeted with suspicion in Arab capitals and, ultimately, the ESM's interim report did not even mention resettlement, although the resettlement of Palestinian refugees was the main reason for its formation. However, the report did pave the way for the establishment of a relief and works agency. As will be demonstrated in Chapter 7, this however, did not lead to the resettlement or rehabilitation of refugees nor make them independent of foreign aid, which was the original intention of US and British strategy.

5
Compensation: The Key to Break the Logjam?

Introduction

If one were to summarize the major obstacles to solving the Palestinian refugee problem between 1948 and 1951, they would come under the following headings: relief, resettlement, rehabilitation and repatriation. As 1949 came to a close, the contours, although not an agreed solution, of how best to solve these four problems became clear. Take, for example, the problem of relief. As Chapter 2 demonstrated, by the end of 1948, a multi-million dollar mechanism for immediate refugee relief had been established through UN General Assembly Resolution 212. By the end of 1949, this emergency relief programme had been extended for the following year, as recommended under General Assembly Resolution 302 (IV).[1]

In the case of rehabilitation and resettlement, the very same resolution called for the establishment of UNRWA as recommended by the report of the ESM.[2] This envisaged the rehabilitation and relief of Palestinian refugees through enterprising work and development projects in the region. As the ESM's Interim Report stated, such an organization was needed to increase the economic productivity of the areas Palestinian refugees populated while also increasing 'the practical alternatives available to refugees, and thereby encourage a more realistic view of the kind of future they want'.[3] The last phrase was a euphemism for the politically loaded term 'resettlement'. Thus, at least in theory, the mechanisms that offered relief, resettlement and rehabilitation were in place. While a mechanism for the repatriation of Palestinian refugees into Israel had yet to be formulated or agreed, Israel had given indications of a willingness to accept limited repatriation, although its offer to repatriate about 230,000 refugees in return for the Gaza Strip and repatriate 100,000 refugees without territorial compensation were both rejected.

However, linked to the issue of repatriation and resettlement was the question of compensation. Resolution 194 called for payment of compensation 'for the property of those choosing not to return and for loss of or damage to property'.[4] This was reaffirmed by Resolution 302 (IV) of December 1949 which recalled earlier UN resolutions on the Palestine question.[5] This chapter will focus on US and British policy towards the payment of compensation to Palestinian refugees as negotiated through the PCC, the primary instrument of Anglo-American diplomacy towards the Palestine question and the body charged with the task of facilitating an Arab–Israeli settlement.

Between 1949 and 1951, London and Washington believed that compensation was a possible means to break the impasse that had developed during earlier PCC reconciliation attempts. Furthermore, despite indications that the sides were willing to discuss compensation and show flexibility, without a peace agreement, even a tentative one, mechanisms and formulae to address how compensation could be initiated, financed and administered remained speculative. More importantly, the PCC, the organization entrusted by the US and indeed the international community to broker an agreement, was no longer seen as a legitimate body in the eyes of Arab and Israeli governments. Despite recognizing that the organization was inefficient, it was still used by the US to bring the parties together. This was a significant strategic blunder. As the PCC's efforts evaporated by the end of 1951, so did any potential agreement on compensation for the foreseeable future.

For lack of better alternatives: The PCC reconvenes

When looking at the question of compensation or any other matter up for negotiation under the PCC rubric, it must be recognized that discussions were made in the context of continued stalemate and stagnation. The sides did not negotiate directly, and for long periods, they were in disagreement as to how the negotiating process should even take place. Worse still, the PCC did not carry out its work with the full confidence of British and US officials. In fact, its continued existence into 1950 was due more to a perceived lack of credible alternatives than to any belief in its potential. This was certainly not a confidence boost to the PCC's work or its prestige. The opinions of the BMEO in Cairo illustrate the point. It argued that the PCC, or whatever body succeeded it, risked attracting ill will and possible 'Slav penetration', as well as inheriting the 'odium' already attached to the PCC. Ultimately, the BMEO argued that the PCC would disappear, 'taking its bruises with it'.[6]

When the PCC reconvened in New York on 19 October 1949 with Ely Palmer as the new US representative,[7] various newspapers ran stories that Israel had withdrawn from PCC talks and was planning to attempt direct talks instead.[8] Even though this was later denied by Israeli officials, it was reported that Israel had informed the PCC of its preference for direct talks and that indirect negotiations could be of no further use.[9] Over a week later, Israeli Prime Minister David Ben-Gurion told the Knesset that the continuation of the PCC was useless 'and even likely to be harmful'.[10]

In fact, the PCC was such an ineffective body that by the end of 1949, Britain and the US were considering its dissolution and replacement with a new 'Palestine Commission' led by an agent-general.[11] Later in August 1950, General Riley of the DRO and Acting Mediator Ralph Bunche suggested transferring the PCC's functions by expanding the armistice agreements to discuss border adjustment and the cessation from Israel to Jordan of territory adjacent to Hebron to settle refugees, particularly from the Gaza Strip. However, if such talks were to be discussed under the framework of the armistice agreements, then the PCC's future would have to be decided and Britain and the US would have to bear pressure on the parties.[12]

Ultimately, despite its animosity towards the PCC, the Foreign Office was not well disposed to the idea of tampering with the existing organization. This was not due to optimism or a belief in the PCC's work, quite the reverse. It was decided that the proposed changes would not have any positive effect and would risk precipitating another Palestine debate in the General Assembly, amid concerns that any new body would be deemed an agent of Anglo-American imperialism which would attract an unfavourable attitude of the parties towards the PCC.[13] Indeed, later in 1951, it was argued that any transference of the PCC's powers could lead to the US facing charges of American domination.[14] Therefore, what is significant in the debate over the future role of the PCC is that an important reason for its continuation was because the Great Powers wanted to avoid charges such as that of US domination. This was made expressly clear by McGhee, who informed the British that the US wished to avoid unilateral responsibility for the diplomatic process and therefore preferred to work under the UN and PCC.[15] This was despite the case that the PCC did not at anytime pursue a course of action that the US considered detrimental or out of synchronization to its policy, an example being Acheson's disagreement with the French PCC representative Boisanger on his attitudes towards compensation which were not subsequently pursued, detailed in the following section.

Despite the fact that it was the State Department which made the proposal to reform the PCC in the first place, George McGhee, the Assistant Secretary of State for Near Eastern and African Affairs, agreed with the British stance.[16] In regards to Bunche and Riley's later proposal, Britain was doubtful whether the scope of the Armistice Commission could be widened.[17] Citing their previous successes, a later Foreign Office minute conceded that a single mediator such as Bunche or Riley could be better positioned to find a settlement. However, the minute continued, both men were considered by the Arab states to be favourable to Israel.[18] It was also said that the solution to the Palestine problem lay in achieving goodwill between the sides rather than tinkering with mediation machinery.[19]

Thus the body mandated to examine the possibility of compensation lacked the legitimacy and confidence of Arabs and Israelis, and the Western powers who sought to broker an agreement. This would have negative consequences for US and British efforts to use compensation as a means to overcome the Palestinian refugee logjam and was therefore a major strategic blunder. Looking ahead to the work of the PCC as 1949 drew to a close, the US thought that the body should address the issue of blocked Palestinian accounts in Israel and family reunification using technical committees and fact-finding groups. However, Washington also advocated a study into refugee compensation, though at this stage it was limited to ascertaining the amount of compensation due rather than the payment procedure.[20] The reason for this US caution was because it wanted to avoid a situation where one or more of the parties would refuse to deal with or ignore the PCC altogether.[21]

Therefore, in the context of a lack of better alternatives, the PCC, now chaired by Ely Palmer, the third US representative in less than 12 months, resumed its meetings in Geneva on 28 January 1950.[22] Even before it examined the problem of compensation, its first task was one that it never quite solved; finding a method of procedure that all sides would agree to.[23] The irony of this process was that getting the sides to agree on a mutually amicable method of negotiation proved to be a mammoth task in itself, never mind the actual issues they sought to address. By March 1950, the procedure for negotiations had still not been confirmed, even though on 29 March it was decided that there would be joint committees chaired by the PCC.[24] Each committee would work under precise terms of reference and would either discuss or study questions which the PCC, in agreement with all the sides, had submitted for examination. Each committee could also study and discuss proposals made by the PCC. This method was intended to bridge the Arab desire for PCC mediation[25] and the Israeli insistence on direct negotiations.[26] As one US official quipped, the PCC was using the 'indirect approach to direct negotiations'.[27]

The PCC discusses compensation

According to its Sixth Progress Report for the period between December 1949 and May 1950, the PCC had consulted with the parties about the question of compensation and considered undertaking a preliminary evaluation of the property involved.[28] A PCC secretariat paper recommended establishing a small technical group which would survey and evaluate refugee property in Israel and study methods for repayment before making recommendations to the PCC.[29] Meanwhile, the French PCC representative, Claude de Boisanger, wanted Israel informed that refugee compensation could not be tied to a final peace settlement or to the payment of war damages, which was Israel's position in previous talks. Instead, Boisanger thought that Israel should pay a lump sum to a trustee who would establish a procedure for payments.[30]

On hearing of Boisanger's idea, Palmer erred on the side of caution. He feared that such an immediate proposal could endanger the success of the PCC at a later stage, but he conceded that it would be worthwhile for the PCC to set up limited machinery to study compensation. Once this body had obtained factual data, Palmer reasoned, the PCC would then be in a stronger position during later negotiations.[31] Returning to the subject several days later, Boisanger added that as a first step, the PCC should find out how many refugees actually wanted to return to Israel, while a study on compensation would be launched immediately. This, according to Boisanger, should then be followed by Israel paying a lump sum as a token of acceptance of the principle of refugee indemnity. This sum would be low enough for Israel to pay but high enough to make a good impression on the Arabs.[32]

US Secretary of State Dean Acheson supported the establishment of machinery to further study the problem. However, crucially, Acheson did not think it was an appropriate time to apply Boisanger's other ideas.[33] Although Washington was of the view that refugee property needed to be surveyed, additional initiatives might conflict with the Arab states. They might not be favourable to a lump sum payment because it could be construed as an attempt to undermine the possibility of refugee repatriation to their homes in Israel.[34] Furthermore, Israel, for its part, would probably not be able to offer a large enough sum to please the Arab states anyway. Therefore, Boisanger's ideas risked causing another impasse and could even harden Arab public opinion against Israel.[35] On 24 February 1950, during a PCC meeting, Boisanger finally accepted Washington's position.[36]

At another PCC meeting, held on 2 March, it was agreed to determine the extent of the damage, technical aspects of the compensation procedure and the mode of settlement claims.[37] It was noted that Israeli cooperation was needed if the PCC was to undertake a general study of the problem. However, Palmer, reflecting on Acheson's earlier instructions, suggested that the PCC wait to approach Israel until after a separate initiative for Israeli participation on a joint committee on Gaza had gained some momentum.[38] Unfortunately for the PCC, this delay in the study of compensation was in vain, as a breakthrough in getting the sides to agree to a new negotiating process did not materialize.

Despite the PCC informing Arab and Israeli delegates on 29 March of its new method for negotiations in the form of committee meetings[39] and Boisanger and Azcarate's 4 April departure to the Middle East,[40] success was not forthcoming in getting the sides to agree to its negotiating process. Even when the Arab League did come around to accepting the PCC's proposed method on 12 April, it was only on the condition that Israel accepted UN decisions on Palestine.[41] This was a reference to the Arab interpretation of Resolution 194 which Egyptian Foreign Minister Muhammad Salah al-Din Bey, on behalf of the Arab states, said demanded Israel accept.[42]

The Arab states understood the resolution as calling for refugee repatriation and this was a major reason for the diplomatic impasse between the sides in the previous year. Israel rejected the Arab position,[43] calling it 'bogus' because in information they had received from reliable sources including a Jordanian delegate to the Arab League, the Arab position was couched in terms that gave the impression of cooperation, but in reality was designed to make it impossible for Israel to reply positively.[44]

The PCC sent the parties a letter on 11 May. This time it clarified that the objectives of its earlier proposals were aimed at achieving a final settlement of the Palestine problem based on General Assembly Resolution 194, which the Arab states had referred to in their response. The letter also stated that various problems raised by such a settlement were interlinked and that some of the problems were of an urgent nature.[45] Again, this did not break the impasse. The PCC received from the Egyptian representative a text containing the common reply of all four Arab governments. It restated its previous reply.[46] Meanwhile, Israel stressed that the Arab demand for the unconditional return of refugees emanated from a desire that Israel would collapse economically, as would their preparations for a 'second round'[47] of war.

As the year progressed, there was little sign of any substantial change. On 12 June, Egyptian official Abdul Moneim Mustafa, backed by the Palestinian diplomat Ahmad Shuqayri who was representing Syria at the time, once again reiterated that only if Israel accepted unconditionally and categorically the return of refugees would they be willing to take part in discussions on refugees in mixed committees. It was added that after one and a half years the PCC had achieved very little.[48] So harsh was the Egyptian and Syrian position that the following day James Barco, Palmer's advisor who had earlier prolonged his service in Geneva, asked to return home to the US.[49] If there was any issue on which the Arab and Israeli side agreed, noted US Ambassador to Israel James McDonald, it was that the PCC was failing in its role.[50] Nevertheless, the US and Britain persisted in the strategic error of using the PCC to facilitate discussions, thus hampering the possibility of a breakthrough.

Tentative plans without implementation

Despite the continued deadlock at Geneva, Palmer still considered ideas for future mechanisms to deal with the refugee problem. Thinking about the Arab position, Palmer opined that no Arab statesman really wanted the refugees to return to Israel to become 'hewers of wood and carriers of water, as described in the bible'.[51] The reason for Arab calls for repatriation, Palmer reasoned, was because of the Arab states' emotional involvement in the issue and because they were legally looking to protect their stand on judicial aspects of the Palestine problem. He also thought that some states, especially Egypt, believed the refugees could become a useful fifth column inside Israel.[52] However, the main reason for Arab demands for repatriation was that the refugees had left something behind and if they went back they would be able to recover something of what they owned.

The refugees, Palmer ruminated, faced a Hobson's choice; they would either receive little from Arab governments if Israel were to pay a lump sum, or face the unlikelihood of receiving anything significant if they were to negotiate the value of their property with the Israeli government directly.[53] Palmer, therefore, called for an international commission comprising of representatives from the US, Britain, France and Israel, as well as one representative for the Arab states and another for the refugees themselves, plus others from small and neutral states.

The commission would act as a tribunal to assess claims for lost or damaged property and declare the value prior to April and May of 1948, and they would guarantee investigation into compensation if a claim were made within a reasonable time limit. In return for compensation, the claimant would sign a declaration to give up the right to return to Israel. Palmer believed that if 60 per cent of refugees accepted such an arrangement, talks with Arab states could begin about the resettlement of those who had signed the waiver in Syria, Jordan and Iraq under Truman's Point Four Programme, the president's January 1950 proposal in his Inaugural Address in which he called for economic aid and US technical knowledge for poorer nations.[54] Palmer believed that the number who would actually insist on returning would be within the region of 100,000, a number Israel had previously indicated it would accept.[55]

Meanwhile, in a note on compensation prepared by the PCC secretariat, it was stated that there could be two methods for appraising the value of property: estimation or an overall appraisal by a single body working under mixed principles.[56] The note stated that in accordance with Resolution 194, it was the Israeli government which had assumed 'definite obligations' towards the refugees. However, a preliminary study of the compensation issue was needed and a committee might be set up for this purpose consisting of a legal expert, a financial expert and an additional expert with knowledge of the land issues in Israel.[57] However, for such studies into compensation to be successful, Israel's acquiescence was required.

In June 1950, Palmer told a PCC meeting that while action was needed on compensation, Israel would only accept it in conjunction with the issue of war reparations. Nevertheless, the PCC should still inquire if Jerusalem would permit a survey to be conducted in Israeli territory to determine the amount of compensation needed to be paid.[58] However, since it was of paramount importance that nothing be done to make the Arab states refuse to participate in the PCC's mixed committees, Palmer argued that the PCC should not approach Israel until Washington had persuaded the Israeli government to make an announcement that would bring the Arab states to the committees.

Therefore, it was agreed that a letter would be sent to Israeli Foreign Minister Moshe Sharett requesting information, without alluding specifically to repatriation, on the Israeli government's position on compensation.[59] The Israeli response came over a month later with Sharett stating that the only context in which Israel would discuss compensation was through comprehensive peace negotiations and that there was no useful purpose in discussing compensation in isolation.[60] On 10 July, the PCC declared that it had failed to bring the sides together in Geneva and was returning to Jerusalem.[61] Thus, six months into its work in 1950, Washington and the PCC's plans for compensation as a means to solve the refugee problem had not only remained tentative, but had yet to be practically implemented.

Breakthrough? An Israeli compensation offer

On 31 August, during a PCC meeting held together with officials of UNRWA's advisory commission, Palmer stated that the question of most immediate urgency was that of compensation. Despite recalling meetings with Israeli Prime Minister David Ben-Gurion and Foreign Minister Sharett in which both adopted the 'traditional Israeli attitude' that compensation should only be discussed in the context of a final settlement,[62] Palmer felt 'sure' that it was possible to establish a 'firm basis' to settle the compensation question.[63] What followed in the subsequent months were talks between Washington, the PCC and Israeli leaders which attempted to break down this 'traditional' Israeli position and gain some flexibility, particularly over compensation. A key factor in limited Israeli flexibility was the concern from Israel as expressed by Eban that the breakdown of the PCC would adversely affect Israel's relations with the US as well as advice from Palmer that compensation was the antithesis of repatriation.[64]

Palmer complained to Washington that no Arab government appeared ready to envisage peace with Israel or, at the UN's request, discuss with Israel the question of resettlement, but they did realise the hopelessness of insisting on repatriation and the urgent need for assurance on compensation and support for resettlement.[65] Indeed, the PCC visited the Middle East in August 1950 but did not obtain any significant change of attitude by the states in the region. However, letters from Ambassador John Blandford, the US member of the UNRWA Advisory Committee, presented to the State Department a different message. Blandford wrote of what he considered a change in the attitude of Arab states towards resettlement when it was linked to the question of compensation in October 1950.[66] Perhaps this was a reference to the Arab League's plan to seek, through the UN, a final settlement of the Palestine Arab refugee problem on the basis of repatriation or voluntary resettlement in Arab lands with full compensation.[67]

This occurred in the context of the PCC drafting a report to the UN. The US had still not decided on a final position and was discussing it with Israeli officials.[68] This explains why towards the end of the year, talks between Israel, the PCC and the US did lead to a slight shift in Israel's position on compensation. Israeli officials Abba Eban and Gideon Rafael were again asked if Israel could consider the compensation question without it being part of an overall settlement. Eban replied that Israel could consider it as a first item, a forerunner to negotiations, with assurance that there would also be a settlement to other outstanding questions. Eban mentioned that the General Assembly could pass a resolution that might refer to compensation as being a matter to be discussed outside of an overall settlement and the need for the parties to negotiate for a settlement either directly or through the PCC.[69] Thus, by October 1950, Washington managed to obtain an indication of flexibility from Israel. Compensation could be the first item leading to an overall agreement rather than something that was only addressed during final agreement talks.

Britain was less enthusiastic about Israel's apparently new flexibility. London warned Washington that Israel might take the initiative on the issue of limited compensation but only to offer a 'take it or leave it approach',[70] and thought it questionable whether an Israeli payment to UNRWA's proposed reintegration fund,[71] an account available for projects for refugee reintegration, surveys and technical assistance, would be sufficient. Regardless, London also doubted whether Israel and the Arab states could reach an agreement on the total amount of compensation. Such an impasse on the amount of compensation would necessitate an impartial body to assess claims and counter-claims.[72] Knox Helm in Tel Aviv argued that Israel's financial circumstances ruled out the idea that the compensation offer could be substantial enough to satisfy the Arab states.[73] This problem was repeated in a report to the Foreign Office from Beirut that a token Israeli payment would not be regarded as large enough.[74]

US representative to UNRWA Blandford postulated that a more forthcoming Israeli approach to the compensation issue might contribute to the solution as indicated by the UNRWA concept of a reintegration fund.[75] On 28 November, Acheson conveyed the message that as Israel had contributed a token sum (US$50,000) to UNRWA and as UNRWA's future funding was being discussed, now was a good opportunity to obtain substantial financial support from Israel in the millions. Acheson added that such a donation could help as a payment of compensation and could be considered a pro tanto discharge of Israel's obligation, while refugees who took up resettlement would waive claims for compensation.[76]

The Israeli government indicated its willingness in principle to pay compensation for abandoned Arab property into the proposed UNRWA reintegration fund, subject to reservations of counter-claims, and to discussions with the UN on the constitution of the fund and the extent of Israel's contribution. This was indicated to mean that Jerusalem regarded this advance payment as a first stage towards peace with the Arab states, as the statement would be made without committing the Arabs.[77] Later, in a 13 December meeting, Israel said that it was willing to contribute US$2.8 million to a Palestinian reintegration programme if it were assured that it would be released from all individual compensation claims for abandoned land.[78] This Israeli position was announced by Sharett to the Knesset at the end of 1950 and was conditioned that the sums paid would be qualified upon evidence that the money would be for resettlement. Sharett warned that this offer would, like its 100,000 offer the previous year, not stand permanently. The only vocal opponent to this policy was Shmuel Katz of the Herut Party who argued that it could risk Israel obtaining responsibility for the refugee problem.[79]

Muddying the water

Although conditional and financially limited, Israel had made an offer of compensation. The US and the PCC were unable to convince Israel to make a gesture significant enough to bring about the basis for further discussions with the Arab states. Israel's conditional offer to make a one-off payment of compensation to UNRWA's new reintegration fund, as detailed above, was brought up at an UNRWA–PCC meeting. The PCC argued that as a gesture of goodwill, the Israeli offer should be made unconditionally.[80] The US secretary of state, despite considering the offer in its present form unacceptable, was not under the impression that Israel would make such an unconditional offer.[81] Nevertheless, he thought the offer could be negotiable. Possibly an agreement of procedure could be discussed whereby Arab claims would be cancelled as Israeli funds would be used to resettle individuals. It was even suggested that Palmer could then propose to the other PCC representatives that the offer should be held open and receive direct consideration in PCC–Israeli talks.

Furthermore, Israel should be urged to make a large contribution in good faith, and Palmer was told to try to induce an Israeli offer of more than US$5 million as a first instalment by linking compensation to resettlement in future talks.[82] It was certainly possible that Israel could make a better offer. King Abdullah had written a letter to Israeli Foreign

Minister Sharett requesting more information about the Israeli compensation payment. The king wrote that the offer appeared limited, but recalled that Israel had been prepared to go further in talks that Israeli officials had had with him.[83] Sharett indicated that Israel was indeed willing to go further when he replied that what he had said represented the official Israeli standpoint, but not necessarily what Israel was ultimately prepared to concede in negotiations.[84] What is telling here is that once again Israel, in direct talks with Arab states, had shown greater flexibility than it had in discussions through the PCC.

Palmer did not agree with Acheson's suggestions, quite the reverse. Not only did he argue that the PCC did not consider the Israeli offer a proper subject for negotiation, but he also remarked that any suggestion by the PCC to Israel to keep its offer open would make the original PCC suggestion, that Israel make a contribution as a goodwill gesture, pointless, ineffectual and prejudicial to the work of both the PCC and UNRWA.[85] Palmer explained that even though an Israeli assurance of US$5 million could prove to be an important contribution, the PCC and UNRWA's director and its Advisory Committee believed that the contribution might affect negotiations about refugee compensation rights.

Further still, the PCC and UNRWA believed that any Israeli contribution to the reintegration fund might seriously damage resettlement plans contemplated by UNRWA, which expected the Arab governments to accept resettlement gradually and to offer their cooperation. It was feared that this cooperation could only be granted if the refugees' rights to compensation were not affected.[86] While Palmer did think there was a basis to link compensation to reintegration, he did not believe this could be done prior to an agreement with Israel about the overall sum of money to be paid as well as the method of payment.[87] Palmer's position was shared by James M. Ludlow of the Office of United Nations Political and Security Affairs; however, Palmer had been instructed to reconsider the problem, as it was feared that Congress could oppose a large US contribution if Israel did not make a substantial contribution itself.[88]

What becomes apparent is that not only was the PCC an obstacle to Arab–Israeli discussions because it had been discredited and loathed by the sides, but also progress on such matters as compensation were further complicated by PCC attempts to play a role. Rather than the Israeli offer being a basis for potential reconciliation, it was put on the backburner to meet the PCC's negotiating framework. However, by the end of 1950, General Assembly Resolution 394 (V) was passed, giving the PCC its own body to investigate compensation.[89]

Despite renewed US and British talk of replacing the PCC and the eventual decision to keep the PCC alive,[90] backed up by a strongly worded resolution,[91] it was the Soviet Union, having been unsuccessful at the Ad Hoc Political Committee, that put forward a draft resolution calling for the PCC's abolition at the 325th UN plenary meeting on 14 December 1950.

The draft called for the termination of the PCC. It was rejected by 48 votes, with only five in favour and one abstention.[92] Following the rejection of several draft resolutions forwarded by Israel, Egypt and Egypt and Pakistan respectively, the four-power joint-resolution draft was discussed.[93] A contentious element of the four-power draft was its call for direct negotiations. Ultimately, it was a Chinese amendment calling for the parties to either seek negotiations with the PCC or directly, which formed the basis for an (eventual) agreement,[94] in the form of General Assembly Resolution 394 (V) passed on 14 December 1950.

The new resolution recalled the earlier one of 11 December 1948 which established the PCC. It noted with concern that an agreement between the parties for a final settlement had not been reached and that the resettlement, repatriation and rehabilitation of the refugees as well as compensation had not been affected. The resolution therefore called for the refugee question to be dealt with in an urgent manner and then urged the parties to seek 'agreement by negotiations either with the Conciliation Commission or directly, with a view to the final settlement of all questions outstanding between them'.[95] The resolution also directed the PCC to establish a new office, hereafter referred to as the Refugee Office, which would assess and make arrangements for compensation for refugees as well as consult parties for the protection of rights, properties and interests of the refugees.[96] However, much like other PCC-affiliated bodies, the Refugee Office did not make significant progress.

Anglo-American considerations and ruminations

During the period between 1950 and 1951, British, US and PCC officials had additional thoughts on the dynamics of the compensation issue. Sheringham of the Foreign Office's Eastern Department, noting the PCC's inability to make significant headway on compensation, advocated a limited Anglo-American approach in which Israel, following the signature of a general agreement with any Arab government, would make a firm offer of a definite sum over a certain period as an advance on what might finally be agreed was owed to individual refugees. If Israel were to make Jordan such an offer, Britain would recommend it to the kingdom. Britain would also propose that part of the money should be made available to the actual owners of property living in Jordan and part be given to UNRWA for the purpose of resettlement.[97] In order to put this forward to the State Department, details of PCC studies would be required. And while there was no wish to bypass the PCC, Britain felt that in practice, discreet US–British action for an Israeli–Jordanian settlement would be more likely to succeed. It was also noted that compensation would only have a limited effect unless payment was made for the purpose of resettlement and not just paid to wealthy landowners.[98] The other idea considered by Britain was to get Israel to indicate publically that in any negotiations with the Arabs, compensation would be discussed in amounts that were realistic in terms of available resources and political limits.[99]

In October 1950, the head of the Foreign Office's Eastern Department Geoffrey Furlonge argued that the sum that Israel should offer would have to be enough to make a substantial difference to the lives of refugees and help push forward conciliation. With this in mind, he wrote that he had read the minutes of the 27 August meeting between the advisory commission, the director of UNRWA and Sharett in Tel Aviv, where it was stated that the longer the situation lasted, the less likely it was that Israel would keep hold over financial reserves earmarked for compensation.[100] This concerned Furlonge, as he believed that cash was the best method of payment, leading to the problem of how Israel would find the necessary foreign exchange to honour any agreement. He noted that the US was not enthusiastic at the possibility of making a loan, and it was unlikely that the Export/Import bank would have been forthcoming. Possibly the US government could consider a direct loan or even a direct grant. It would also help if Israel were to match such aid with a contribution of its own. Possibly, it could be done through a combination of these alternatives.[101]

Several possibilities for making payment had been considered, including a loan to Israel by foreign sources, grant-in-aid from foreign sources to Israel which would be matched by parallel Israeli contributions, a contribution by Israel to regional development projects or a credit in Israeli pounds to Arab states which could be used for Israeli goods and services for development projects. It was also tentatively suggested that sums of over US$500 be paid to large landowners for the resettlement of refugees.[102] This latter contention was not totally opposed by the US. McGhee, in particular, had argued for further finance, stressing it was unlikely that there would be an Arab–Israeli understanding about compensation anytime soon.

McGhee stuck to his position that if the US was to end up paying for compensation, in the long term it would be better to do it directly than through refugee resettlement and by administering the funds either directly or through the UN. McGhee noted that US willingness to make funds available for resettlement could ease local tensions and make Arab states take the matter more seriously.[103] Although Israel and Germany had not yet officially agreed to German Reparations until 1952, Sharett had indicated to McGhee in March 1951 that the funds could be a source of funding for Palestinian refugee compensation, something that was later dismissed as a possibility.[104]

Throughout 1950, British and US officials considered how compensation could be administered. In July 1950, for example, it was thought that compensation could be channelled through UNRWA in the first instance. However, it was recognized that there was also some strength to the argument that landowners should be compensated first.[105] The two were contradictory because refugees utilizing UNRWA services were less likely to be large landowners. Most land belonged to a relatively small number of owners who would be the most influential in the Arab states they resided in and who would want a high proportion of the value of their properties.[106] For UNRWA to take over this issue would require it to broaden its scope and then diminish its chances of full cooperation with Arab states.[107] But the State Department thought it wrong to weigh compensation in favour of larger landowners.[108] There was also concern that such preferential treatment to a 'class which while fulminating against Zionism, has in the past sold land to the Jews' could lead to communist-inspired criticism.[109] Furlonge, writing in October 1950, suggested that there would need to be a compulsory investment of sums paid to large landowners for the resettlement of refugees or possibly a special reintegration fund, a concept which UNRWA was recommending.[110] Other possibilities included creating another agency that assessed claims and arranged for the distribution of such claims, possibly under the aegis of the PCC.[111] However, Israel's position had not advanced other than in its view that compensation should go to the reintegration fund.[112]

Pushing Israel towards a policy review

In talks with the British Foreign Office in March 1951, Ely Palmer's deputy, James Barco, believed that it would be dangerous to investigate the amount of compensation that Israel should pay before actually considering to whom to make the payments. Similarly, he mentioned a PCC proposal which suggested that it would be impossible to look into each individual claim.[113] Instead, argued Barco, there should be a survey of land records in Palestine followed by an examination into the value of Arab land in 1945. Then Israel would be presented with this amount and asked whether it would be willing to accept liability for the payment of this figure which would not factor in counter-compensation claims. Israel would make payment by receiving funds in the form of a loan which would then be subscribed to by members of the UN. Israel would then put the compensation money into a fund which would be controlled by the PCC.[114]

Responding to questions fielded by the head of Britain's Eastern Department Geoffrey Furlonge, Barco said that Israel's recent offer to make a contribution to the reintegration fund did not affect the reintegration programme. As Israel's obligation was to individual refugees and not to an organization, the amount which Israel should pay to individual refugees should be assessed pro rata in terms of the value of land previously owned by them in Israel. He admitted that the method of compensation payment might have to involve a proportion of the funds owed to large landowners being set aside for the resettlement of poorer refugees.[115] However, McGhee visited London in early April where he explicitly said that he did not favour Israel being given a loan. He thought it better to contribute directly to resettlement and obtain from refugees a 'quit claim' once they had been resettled.[116]

In early June 1951, Palmer had a meeting with Sharett and other Israeli officials including Re'uven Shiloah and David Horowitz. Sharett wanted to discuss the substance of talks that had been held in May between Shiloah and Barco during which several important suggestions were made.[117] They included discussions that a compensation agreement could pave the way for a settlement between Israel and the Arab states, and that by relating compensation to resettlement, it could avoid wasting the funds that would be paid while encouraging resettlement. Palmer questioned Sharett as to whether Israel would consider it advantageous to settle compensation by undertaking a large-scale financial obligation if it was guaranteed international assistance in a manner which would not affect Israel's economic future; however, Palmer added, it would mean that compensation would be solved outside of a peace settlement,[118] a long-held Israeli prerequisite.

Sharett posed a series of questions in response to Palmer's proposal. He inquired how compensation payments would be implemented, whether the funds would be used for reintegration and be made to a trustee or to Arab governments. After payment, he inquired, would Israel be acquitted of responsibility, and if the money paid did not meet the claims in full, would the refugees still expect to hold a claim against Israel? Palmer answered vaguely, replying that it was not possible to obtain answers until actual principles had been agreed. However, Palmer did say that procedures could be worked out to answer each question in collaboration with the new Refugee Office.[119]

Sharett was apparently dissatisfied because he noted several further issues. One was that the compensation proposals were different from the traditional view that compensation was an incentive to a peace settlement that could be used as a trump card in overall peace negotiations. The new PCC proposition risked creating a scenario where, he believed, despite compensation being paid, peace talks might still be postponed indefinitely. Although Sharett appeared displeased with Palmer's ideas, there were hints that he had sympathy for the position that compensation could be used as a means to remove the Arabs' main grievance, another indication that Israel, or at least Sharett, was moving away from the 'orthodox' view that compensation be discussed only in the context of a general settlement.[120]

Indeed, commenting on the above meeting, the State Department replied that an important element of peace between Israel and the Arabs was the abandonment of Israel's 'orthodox view' which they claimed had been tried by Israel for three years with no success.[121] The State Department conceded that the alternative, a unilateral initiative, was for Israel to decide because it would constitute a policy shift with profound repercussions inside Israel and the country's leaders would have to be convinced that such a reversal would be in Israel's interests. Therefore, while the US thought that an Israeli concession would help facilitate a peace deal, it was not willing to push Israel into a change of policy.[122]

Washington, however, was less enthusiastic about the suggestion that there should be international assistance to ensure Israel's economic growth was not hampered by compensation payments. It was concerned that US taxpayers could end up paying; this was not a solution to which the State Department was reconciled. Instead, the onus had to be on Israel to take the initiative in developing proposals for international finances as a long-term obligation. It was also stated that talks of this nature should continue informally and that the State Department could not give answers to Sharett's questions as they could imply either advocacy or moral commitment or both. Instead, the PCC could work out with Israel a study for a comprehensive scheme about these problems.[123]

Meanwhile, Israel agreed that it would cooperate with the Refugee Office, but made clear that it would not recognize the sum of compensation that the body would calculate as the liability of the Israeli government.[124] Again, despite indications of a change of Israeli policy, it was the PCC that had been delegated with the task of discussing compensation and already, even before the work of the Refugee Office had got started, Israel indicated that its calculations as to the value of refugee property would not be the basis for the payment of compensation. This was something Barco and Palmer later gave Sharett assurance of, that the Refugee Office would not be responsible for paying the entire amount calculated in its investigation and the value of refugee property, but rather this would be based on Israel's ability to pay.[125] The PCC's ability to facilitate Arab–Israeli discussions was being further impaired, finally leading to its demise.

Palmer's despair

A key turning point in the activities of the PCC in 1951 was Ely Palmer's despairing comments to the US secretary of state. This would precipitate action and a concerted, though ill-conceived diplomatic effort. Despite talks with Israel over compensation, as well as some interaction with Arab states, very little substance was achieved in political matters. In May 1951, Palmer wrote to the secretary of state of his deep frustrations with activities since January. He admitted that no progress had been made on resettlement, compensation, blocked assets or peace negotiations.

With only six months before the opening of the next General Assembly session, Palmer wanted instructions so that he could play a more vigorous leadership role.[126] He continued that repatriation was a 'dead letter' as far as the PCC was concerned, and on peace talks, there were no grounds under which the PCC could propose direct or indirect discussions in the absence of a State Department initiative. Noting that his assistant James Barco had informally discussed compensation with Shiloah, Palmer opined that Israel would have to make some kind of concession to the Arab states and suggested a realistic plan for compensation and the financing of a fund to help Israel make payments.

Palmer also suggested immediate direct negotiations under UN auspices between Israel and Jordan and Israel and Syria which would move talks with armistice arrangements into a formal peace. Palmer warned that if these were not achieved, the PCC risked being a failure.[127] Palmer wrote an additional note on the same day about the need for an understanding of the State Department's thinking, while stressing the urgency for an exchange of views 'without limitations or delays of correspondence'. He therefore recommended that James Barco return to the US to review the situation with the State Department.[128]

Responding to Palmer's message, Acheson explained that the course of action chosen by the PCC necessitated slow progress. Moreover, the settlement of the refugee problem took priority over peace negotiations. And with compensation and resettlement being the most important aspects of the refugee problem, it did indeed need to be worked out promptly. However, Palmer had to be patient because the details could not be finalized until Holger Andersen's arrival in May to head the Refugee Office. Progress was slow, the secretary of state reasoned, because talks with Israel over possible linkages between compensation and resettlement would have been undesirable without an estimate of how much Israel would actually have to pay. Without this information, negotiations would be impossible.[129] However, Acheson suggested that recent developments (the resumption of Israeli–Syrian Mixed Armistice Committees, the relative restraint of the Arab League's message on refugee resettlement and possible forthcoming congressional approval of economic assistance for Israel and Arab states) did in fact indicate the possibility that the PCC could proceed more actively.[130] This was, however, a significant mistake.

Towards another PCC conference

The holding of another conference was mistimed and not based on mutual grounds for agreement. It was also a badly prepared affair. Not surprisingly, it was unsuccessful. Indeed, Touval makes the apt claim that a contributing factor to the PCC's lack of success was its predilection for convening general conferences instead of tackling problems bilaterally.[131] The conference was born out of the secretary of state's belief that another concerted approach was necessary. This would take the form of mediation within a conference framework with Israel and the PCC on one hand and representatives of Arab states and the PCC on the other. Expanding his thinking on compensation, Acheson clarified that an agreement between Israel and the Arab states on the principal of compensation and its approximate amount would advance the possibilities for the ultimate payment of compensation. It would also create a disposition among UN members to help Israel to obtain financial means. If the PCC were able to get Israel to announce its agreement to practical proposals, while also getting the Arab states to accept the proposals, setting down the financial aspects would be less difficult. It could also be a talking point between the PCC and Arab states that if they were to lift restrictions on Israeli trade, it would be easier for Israel to make payments.[132] The State Department expanded this line of thinking again towards the end of July, especially after having received a note from the assistant secretary of state for UN affairs. He referred to the State Department's concern over the ineffectiveness of the PCC and the belief that the PCC should try one more attempt to carry out its mandate by proposing a conference before the 6th General Assembly meeting.[133]

Palmer was told by Acheson that at an early meeting of the PCC he should advocate new and more vigorous efforts. A conference should be suggested to discuss solutions to specific problems such as refugee compensation, repatriation, territorial adjustments, the release of blocked bank accounts and problems associated with Jerusalem. It was also suggested that the PCC put forward ideas on several items such as a multilateral non-aggression pact to reduce tension in the region. Other ideas included approaching the repatriation issue by selecting classes of refugees whose return would be beneficial to Israel's economy, and the return of those whose resumption of property control would alleviate some of the larger compensation claims. The State Department believed it would be highly beneficial if just one or more of these issues could be solved.[134] The PCC decided that instead of shuttling between Israel and the Arab states conveying messages and ideas, it would use the conference to arbitrate between the parties.[135]

Learning that the PCC was organizing a conference, UNRWA Director John Blandford complained that the PCC had violated General Assembly resolutions that required his organization to concur to any steps the PCC might take. Blandford was reported to have taken up the matter with UN Secretary-General Trygve Lie.[136] When Palmer later met Blandford, he was told that the conference was both ill-timed and badly conceived. Blandford warned that whatever problems the PCC conference might address, it would have disastrous consequences on one or more of the numerous projects that he was developing. Palmer opined that Blandford's opposition stemmed from his being unaware of the origin and background of the PCC's decision to host a conference.[137] This was unexpected as it appeared that Blandford, an American, was unaware that PCC policy had been discussed and was favoured by the State Department; this was a source of embarrassment to the US, as this lack of communication was displayed to a newly appointed French representative to the PCC.[138]

It was not only UNRWA that was concerned about the Paris Conference. News of the proposed conference was greeted with surprise in Israel.[139] The Arab League, although accepting its invite, demanded that there be no direct contact with Israeli officials at the conference.[140] When the conference began, it drew protests from Palestinian refugee camps in Lebanon and Syria.[141] Privately, Israeli leaders thought the proposed conference disquieting.[142] Britain also had serious misgivings. Not consulting Britain, though perhaps a deliberate snub, was an error on the part of the State Department. Britain only learned of the decision to invite Israel and the Arab states to a conference, for which the State Department was already making suggested proposals, after the French embassy, in confidence, gave the Foreign Office a copy of Acheson's 27 July letter to Palmer.[143]

Surprised about the hasty manner of the conference, the Foreign Office was concerned that a matter of such importance had been decided upon without the opportunity for Britain to put forward its views. After all, Britain was a party to the Tripartite Declaration[144] and had a treaty of alliance with Jordan. It also doubted that progress could be made unless the ground had been carefully laid beforehand.[145] The Foreign Office had serious misgivings and thought that more preparation was needed because, if the conference were to fail, the opposite impact to what was intended could be the result. British missions were therefore informed that while they should support any move designed to improve Arab–Israeli relations, they could not express such a view until they had more information. Subsequently, they were informed not to give the impression that there was a difference between Britain and the three powers (France, Turkey and the US) sponsoring the initiative.[146] Furlonge, of the Eastern Department, was in no doubt that the conference would fail, but hoped that lack of British support would not be blamed for it.[147]

A week before the start of the conference, the governments of the PCC wanted the presence of a British observer to avoid risking any indication that there was British opposition. However, Britain, spurned, replied that because it was not part of the PCC, it would have to be issued an invite before it could attend. The State Department's explanation for not consulting Britain was that, apparently, Britain had not received the relevant documents.[148] However, because of its doubts over the conference, Britain concluded that it did not wish to be too closely associated with it.[149] Therefore, Britain did not use its full influence to support this important diplomatic initiative. This reduced pressure on the participants to be flexible during negotiations.

The Paris Conference opened on 10 September[150] and continued until 19 November.[151] Much of the time was spent discussing the PCC's pattern of proposals. One proposal was for Israel to agree to pay compensation to refugees who had not been repatriated for their abandoned property at a figure which would be decided by the Refugee Office. A payment plan would take into consideration Israel's ability to pay and it would be established by a special committee of financial experts created by a UN trustee through whom payments of individual claims would be made. Another proposal was for the release of blocked accounts in Israel, Jordan, Syria, Lebanon and Egypt.[152]

However, the sides were barely able to discuss these proposals because the opening preamble to the proposals outlining the conference's aims became the subject of much debate and turned out to be the main sticking point between the sides. This preamble took up most of the time well into October.[153] Another letter was sent to both sides on 31 October, reiterating the PCC's position that the basis of negotiations was the affirmative response to the PCC's position that discussions should centre on their proposals.[154] The Arab states replied affirmatively to the letter. So did the Israelis, albeit reluctantly.[155]

Regarding the proposals pertaining to refugees, Israel's position was that the return of refugees was incompatible with the national life of Israel, and by taking in 200,000 Jews from Arab countries, it had made a significant contribution to the settlement of population movements that had resulted from the Palestine conflict. Israel did, however, indicate a willingness to settle the compensation question for property abandoned by refugees, and suggested an immediate evaluation through the PCC or another UN body which would factor in Israel's ability to pay. Israel added that its ability to pay compensation was affected by Arab economic measures, and by absorbing Jewish refugees from Arab countries whose property, especially in Iraq, had also been abandoned.[156] Indeed, following the 1948 Palestine War, the condition of Jews in Arab countries had deteriorated, leading to a mass immigration to Israel. According to Israeli immigration statistics, between 1948 and 1951 over 250,000 refugees from Arab countries immigrated to Israel out of a total of 687,624 immigrants.[157]

Israeli officials would often refer to Israel's need to absorb Jewish refugees when in discussions about Palestinian refugee repatriation. Their answer to the Palestinian refugee problem lay in absorption in Arab states. Such statements were exemplified by Ben-Gurion and Sharett in 1949. 'It is inconceivable', wrote the Israeli prime minister, 'that the Government of Israel should find itself able to undertake on hand and in the same breath the absorption of mass Jewish immigration and the reintegration of returning Arab refugees'.[158] Meanwhile, the Israeli foreign minister said that 'efforts can now be made...[for] integration in neighbouring Arab states'.[159]

However, Ben-Gurion's reference to 'mass Jewish immigration' did not single out Jews from Arab countries, indicating that he meant Jews from all corners of the world. Within Israeli political circles before 1951, some Israeli officials 'toyed' with the idea of exchanging Jewish property in the Arab world for Palestinian property.[160] Occasionally would Israeli officials specifically mention Jewish immigrants from Arab countries, intimating that an exchange of populations had taken place. In one instance in February 1949, in a very brief one-line summary of a conversation with US officials, Sharett had apparently said that Israel would be happy to receive Jews from Arab countries over the 'question of exchange of populations'. No further elaboration was given.[161] In March 1951, Eytan told the US representative to the PCC that because Israel had to rehabilitate 100,000 Jewish Iraqi refugees, this would have to be linked to its contribution of compensation to the Palestinian refugees.[162] Similarly, later in September 1951, an Israeli PCC delegate informed the PCC that he was authorized to state that Israel was willing to make a contribution to the resettlement of the Palestinian refugees, but such an arrangement had to be mutual, adding that Israel had taken in 200,000 Jewish refugees from Arab countries. Israel, the official added, was willing to discuss this issue with the Arab states with a view to finding a constructive overall solution to the refugee problem.[163]

The timing of the above statements, March and September 1951, indicates that there had been no specific arrangement for an exchange of populations in place by the end of the PCC's activities and this period of US diplomatic engagement. Indeed, as Chapter 6 will show, while the possibility of a population exchange between Israel and Iraq was considered, especially in 1949, this had not been negotiated between the parties and no official agreement had been reached. In Israeli discussions with US, British and PCC officials about the Palestinian refugee problem, specific references to Jews from Arab countries were sometimes made. However, the Israeli position should not be looked at as a policy calling for an exchange of populations as such, but rather as an overall policy of the 'ingathering of exiles' whereby Jewish immigration to Israel from across the world was welcome, particularly where Jews were in danger, including Iraq. However, Israeli officials would contend that its absorption of Jewish refugees affected its capacity to repatriate Palestinian refugees, and later to compensate them. This position was strengthened following the immigration to Israel of Iraqi Jews to which Israel could argue that by the end of 1951 a 'two way population movement' had been made.[164]

The Arab states replied to the PCC that no limit could be put on the number of returning refugees and that in making the proposal, the PCC was in contravention of Resolution 194. Further, it was stated that 'as long as Israel refused to allow the return of the refugees, there could be no peace in the Middle East'. The Arab states argued that the UN shared responsibility with Israel for paying for those not repatriated as well as for paying indemnities for damaged property. This should not be based on Israel's ability to pay. If Israel could not pay, the UN should. Compensation should be paid on the value of the property, with refugees represented at all stages and with machinery for appeals. The value of state domain should be evaluated by experts.[165] Talks did not progress much further and by 19 November, they ground to a halt.[166]

In the conclusion of its progress report following the end of the conference, the PCC was pessimistic:

> The present unwillingness of the parties fully to implement the General Assembly resolutions under which the Commission is operating, as well as the changes which have occurred in Palestine during the past three years, have made it impossible for the Commission to carry out its mandate, and this fact should be taken into consideration in any further approach to the Palestine problem.[167]

Despite the lack of success at Paris, the PCC's Progress Report did contain the Refugee Office's study into compensation. Although useful, the investigation was rushed. The Refugee Office had only been established several months before and faced pressure from the PCC, which wanted to include the study in its progress report. UNRWA, hoping that the Arab states might resettle refugees and see compensation as part of this possibility, also wanted the study to come out quickly. Meanwhile, the Refugee Office was pressured from the US which was concerned that compensation was a political and not a 'book-keeping' question and did not want to see a figure too high for Israel to pay.[168] Specifically, the Refugee Office assessed the value of abandoned property. It estimated that the value of abandoned Arab lands, based on 'Village Statistics 1945' issued by the government of Palestine, including Jerusalem, excluding uncultivable land, stood at 100,000,000 Palestine pounds for non-movable property, without account of potential development value.[169] The value of movable property was estimated between £P2,500,000 and £P21,570,000; calculations based on the percentage of the national income of Mandate Palestine gave several estimates for movable property at £P21,570,000, £P18,600,000 and £P19,100,000, depending on methodological approaches and sociological perspectives.[170] Yet, without a political baseline from which Israel and the Arab states could move forward, the study, although eliciting debate and criticism at Paris, could not become the basis for an agreement on compensation. Instead, it was the disappointing culmination of three years of British and US considerations on the question of compensation.

Conclusion

By the end of 1949, some British and US officials were calling for the dissolution of the PCC. London and Washington did not heed these calls. By 1950, the PCC had not only been unable to facilitate negotiations between Israel and the Arab states over the refugee impasse, but it was now a despised body. Therefore, its work on the compensation question between 1950 and 1951, correctly identified as a potential avenue to regain momentum in discussions of the Palestinian refugee problem, did little to bring the sides closer together. Although Britain and the US made significant progress in understanding the complexity of issues including Israel's ability to pay, administering a compensation scheme and the schism between compensating individual refugees and the need to fund reintegration for the general refugee population, this was despite the PCC's mediation efforts rather than because of them.

The only limited success of which the PCC could boast was its Refugee Office, which by the end of 1951 had made an assessment of the value of compensation claims. But even this was limited in its scope and did not have the confidence of the parties. However, the PCC's swansong was the ill-timed and unsuccessful Paris Conference. This would be the last effort that the PCC would make to broker peace. The PCC continues to exist as a UN body until the present day, but only on paper (there was just a brief and an unsuccessful attempt to reactivate it during the 1960s). Britain and the US should have abandoned the PCC by the end of 1949. Instead, they let it drag on until the Paris Conference where, even before the issues were discussed, the sides had reached a stalemate. All the discussions and debate about mechanisms and funding for compensation went up in smoke in a blaze which also consumed the PCC and three years of Anglo-American diplomacy.

6

The Refugee Factor in Direct Arab–Israeli Negotiations

Introduction

From 1949 to 1951, the main diplomatic initiative to bring about a solution to the Palestinian refugee crisis was conducted through the PCC. Previous chapters have detailed the work of this UN body. However, it would be incorrect to assume that the PCC was the only avenue for Arab–Israeli dialogue over the Palestinian refugee problem. During the 1949–51 period, there were also discreet bilateral discussions between Israel and several of her Arab neighbours. During his short time as Syrian leader, Husni Zaim expressed his intentions to meet Israeli leaders and to transfer territory in exchange for refugees. Talks also occurred between Israel and Jordan, and Israel and Egypt. While there were no direct talks between Israel and Iraq, there were proposals set out by Iraqi leaders to British and US officials.

Some progress was made. Sometimes these talks would occur on the sidelines of PCC-orchestrated forums, but sometimes they were in stand-alone meetings. However, ultimately these talks were unsuccessful. This chapter will argue that there was a lack of participation by the US and Britain who, although supportive of such discussions, were reluctant to be involved, preferring to support PCC-led efforts.

The contrast between secretive bilateral talks and the more open and indirect discussions which were organized by the PCC cannot be more pronounced. Throughout the period in question, the efforts of the PCC were marred by the problem of refugee resettlement, repatriation and relief. As the previous chapters have demonstrated, the Arab states demanded the repatriation of refugees to Israel, something Jerusalem refused to do on any significant scale. Jerusalem insisted that resettlement was the only viable option for the vast majority of refugees.

For most of the time, the PCC focused on overcoming the impasse on the refugee question. In stark contrast, the refugee problem featured very little in Israel's bilateral talks with Jordan and only slightly with Egypt, and it did not appear to be a significant obstacle. In the case of Husni Zaim's Syria, his attitude to the Palestinian refugee problem was almost a complete reversal of the collective policy of the Arab states at the PCC's Lausanne Conference. Not only was he willing to discuss the refugee problem in the context of a settlement, but he was also willing to absorb them in large numbers. In the case of Iraq, the idea of a population exchange between Jewish citizens of Iraq and Palestinian refugees was entertained as a basis for discussion.

By evaluating the refugee factor in Israel's bilateral talks with the aforementioned Arab states, this chapter suggests that the contrast between the Arab position during bilateral discussions and the Arab collective position when negotiating through the PCC meant that the refugee issue was not necessarily an insurmountable obstacle. It will also argue that the US and British decision to dedicate their efforts to PCC-orchestrated discussions instead of direct talks represented a missed opportunity, especially as the local parties showed more conciliatory attitudes towards solving the refugee issue in bilateral talks. Britain and the US showed less enthusiasm for direct talks than for negotiations facilitated by the PCC because they feared the consequences of their own involvement in bilateral talks. If they were to facilitate or even mediate bilateral discussions, Britain and the US would not only risk obtaining ownership of the problem, but would also have to face the possible consequences of failed negotiations or disappointed parties looking to apportion blame. Therefore, Britain and the US attempted to steer or merge bilateral talks into the broader work of the PCC, which sought an overall settlement between Israel and the Arab states as a bloc.

Avoiding ownership of the problem: British and US attitudes towards direct Arab–Israeli negotiations

Britain and the US were reluctant to engage in direct talks between Israel and the Arab states. In the case of Jordan, Israeli Prime Minister David Ben-Gurion recalled that 'we tried to negotiate with him [Abdullah], but the British interfered, and a bullet came and put an end to the business'.[1] However, this was not a factual assertion and represents an overestimation of Britain's attitude towards a bilateral agreement with Jordan. Britain's caution was not out of hostility towards Israel, but because of fear that Jordan would be isolated in the Arab world.[2]

London, therefore, did not openly encourage Abdullah to make peace with Israel but did not oppose him, and they even encouraged the US to look positively at Abdullah's efforts in this regard.[3] Indeed, Moshe Dayan recalled that during unofficial talks with King Abdullah exploring the possibility of a peace treaty in January 1949, the king had said that the British knew of his intentions and did not object.[4] According to Foreign Minister Bevin, Britain wanted to promote good relations between Israel and the Arab states as a way of achieving regional stability and had taken a back foot while the PCC was in action.[5] But already noting the failure of the PCC on the issue of refugees and Jerusalem on 20 April 1950, Bevin stated that King Abdullah had been the only Arab ruler who had shown 'realism' and 'willingness to come to terms with Israel'.[6] Nevertheless, the British maintained policy coordination with the US in order to refrain from involvement in bilateral talks and instead to encourage the multilateral channel initiated through nongovernmental organizations.

The US was reluctant to deal with the refugee problem in all its complexities on a bilateral basis and instead preferred to use intergovernmental organizations, especially the UN. This was initially a source of disagreement with Britain. In a meeting between Undersecretary of State McGhee and multiple British officials including John Troutbeck and Michael Wright, the latter expressed concern that aid delivered to the refugees was going through the UN, to which McGhee responded quite candidly that the US wished to avoid unilateral responsibility and therefore preferred to work under the UN and PCC.[7] The following month, the US relayed to Britain that the survey group, which became the ESM, would be a venture under the PCC rather than a joint British and US effort so as not to undermine the authority of the PCC.[8] This preference for using intergovernmental organizations for diplomacy was again reiterated in response to a British proposal which would:

> Imply the assumption of direct responsibility with respect to solution of the refugee problem by the United States in conjunction with the United Kingdom. This Government is not prepared to accept such direct responsibility for solution of refugee problem.[9]

This did not mean that the US was opposed to direct bilateral talks between Israel and the Arab states. On the contrary, in response to a claim by British Foreign Office official Bernard Burrows that the US had discouraged Jordan from direct talks with Israel, it was retorted that the State Department did in fact encourage direct talks with Israeli and

Arab officials, but only if they were to contribute to the PCC-organized discussion at Lausanne.[10] Only in a few instances was the US not in favour of direct talks,[11] but the policy was to encourage direct negotiations whenever possible.[12] This response demonstrated that the US was only in favour of direct talks if they contributed to the multilateral proceedings facilitated by the PCC rather than if they were an end in themselves. Furthermore, even when the US was in favour of Israel and the Arab states attempting direct bilateral negotiations outside of the PCC forum, the US was not willing to act as a facilitator or mediator. It is clear that the US favoured using UN channels to avoid assuming responsibility. For example, when the PCC's Lausanne Conference entered a recess in July 1949, Washington was adamant that in any direct talks between Israel and Egypt, the role of the US was that of a 'friend' and not that of a 'mediator' or a 'third party' to discussions. This was because the US believed third-party assistance should be provided by the PCC.[13] London soon also adopted a similar approach. In December 1949, Geoffrey Furlonge of the Foreign Office told the US that Britain was now maintaining a 'hands-off' attitude towards Israeli–Jordanian negotiations.[14] Perhaps one reason for Britain's position was the impact of an Israeli–Jordanian agreement on other Arab states. For example, in December 1949, following a report from Cairo of a meeting with Ismail Chirine, King Farouk's brother-in-law, the Foreign Office commented that it would be beneficial if he would establish direct contact with King Abdullah to facilitate a mutually beneficial position.[15]

One of the consequences of the stalemate of the 1949 PCC Lausanne Conference was a change in the British and American approach to direct bilateral peace negotiations. Previously, the PCC discouraged bilateral talks between Israel and the Arab states outside of its framework. However, this approach changed following the unsuccessful conclusion of the Lausanne talks and the PCC now no longer objected.[16] Neil Caplan has argued that the PCC's attitude to Israeli–Jordanian negotiations during the last months of 1949 and early 1950 was generally positive and that the Israelis sought PCC cooperation in avoiding anything that might jeopardize these talks. Also, the US, PCC and Israel hoped that the successful conclusion to talks with Jordan would help start direct bilateral talks with other Arab states at the 1950 PCC proceedings in Geneva.[17] But, on the other hand, direct talks could stall the work of the PCC. This was noted by the US Political and Security Affairs Department for the UN who argued that the role of the PCC was 'equivocal', noting that two of the parties (Israel and Jordan) were preoccupied with direct negotiations. It was, therefore, unlikely that they would be favourably disposed to receiving independent proposals from the PCC on basic issues.[18]

Regardless, it was one thing for the US and Britain to support direct bilateral talks and another for them to become involved in them. Furlonge noted that while Britain had a hands-off approach to Israeli–Jordanian talks while talks stalled on the issues of territory and a corridor, he wondered whether it would be desirable for greater US and British involvement.[19] Again, the US response was that while it encouraged direct talks, it should refrain from intervening in them.[20] Secretary of State Acheson did, however, believe that the PCC experience showed that Israeli negotiations with Arab states one by one would be more conducive to a successful outcome. He was also concerned that the 'economic' approach that UNRWA had taken to help the political process had been unsuccessful. Nevertheless, Acheson stressed that US intervention in Israeli–Jordanian talks was still considered undesirable.[21]

US policy was further elaborated by George McGhee in talks with Jordanian diplomat Dr Yusuf Haikal, in which he stated that through the PCC and the ESM, the US had sought to create the conditions that would bring about a settlement between Israel and the Arab states. The recommendations of the PCC in particular were designed to alleviate the burden of the refugees on the Arab states and to allow them to consider a final settlement without having to place so much emphasis on the refugee issue.[22]

When the PCC reconvened in January 1950, this policy did not appear to have borne fruit because Ely Palmer reported that at informal meetings among the Arab states, little or no change from the position of previous meetings had been made.

The Egyptian delegate ruled out direct negotiations (under the pretext that Israel did not exist), the Lebanese representative said that Lebanon's primary concern was the return of refugees and the Syrian delegate reiterated these positions, adding that the Arabs would not abandon their moral position for an empty agreement.[23]

Despite this, Palmer told Gideon Rafael, the Israeli representative, that he supported direct negotiations. Rafael then said that it would be welcome if the PCC helped promote direct talks and prepared studies on issues such as compensation. However, Rafael warned that if the PCC were to make proposals of its own, it might stiffen the Arab position in direct talks, and Israel hoped to conclude agreements with Jordan and Egypt (Moneim Mustafa had been designated to engage in such talks).[24]

Nevertheless, there was no further significant progress. The PCC's influence and prestige was in decline, and the US and British position of pushing direct Egyptian–Israeli discussion towards PCC-orchestrated diplomacy contributed to their failure.

Land for refugees: Zaim's Israeli overtures

On 30 March 1949, Husni Zaim, a Syrian officer of Kurdish extraction, seized power in Damascus. Zaim's coup led to anxiety within the British Foreign Office because of its possible effect on Jordan where opposition elements were fermenting difficulties for King Abdullah.[25] On the other hand, there was also concern that the king might use the confused atmosphere in Syria to further his aims and revive his Greater Syria ambition.[26] Israel also feared the coup may be the 'first step on the road to Greater Syria'. Suspicious of Zaim's intentions, Israeli official Eliyahu Sasson recommended doing anything possible to weaken his regime.[27] Meanwhile, Secretary of State Dean Acheson's memorandum to President Harry Truman of 25 April stated that British, French and US ministers had indicated their belief that there was no likelihood of Zaim being displaced in the near future.[28] This was a much too optimistic assessment. Zaim's reign was short lived and he was ousted by a military coup on 14 August of the same year. However, during Zaim's short tenure, there were significant overtures for a settlement with Israel consisting of a potential agreement on refugees linked to a territorial concession. Former intelligence operative Miles Copeland has alleged that there was involvement by the CIA in the Zaim coup because it was thought he would 'do something constructive' in relation to the Arab–Israeli issue. Copeland has argued that their belief had influenced the State Department, although it preferred not to have any details of the plot and ignored the involvement of action teams led by Major Stephen Meade in Zaim's takeover.[29]

Several days after Zaim became leader, Israeli–Syrian armistice negotiations began. Later, on 28 April, Zaim intimated to James Keeley, the US Minister in Syria, his interest in resettling 250,000 refugees in his country in return for substantial development aid and 'realistic' frontier adjustments. He also offered to enter into a prompt agreement with Israel through direct negotiations.[30]

Zaim's proposal came just one day after the start of the PCC's Lausanne Conference where the Arab states, negotiating as a bloc, demanded that Israel repatriate the refugees before a final peace settlement. However, the new Syrian attitude was soon reflected in discussions with the PCC's US Representative Mark Ethridge. He reported that the Syrian representative and Acting Secretary-General of the Syrian

Ministry for Foreign Affairs, Farid Zeineddine, had modified his position because before he 'would not consider anything but refugees first. He is now willing to discuss... in private conversations with me Syria's willingness to take up to 250,000 refugees providing Syria was compensated territorially'.[31] This was a considerable break from the official Arab position which insisted on repatriation prior to any agreement with Israel. McGhee recalled that he and the State Department were 'elated' by the offer and tried to 'pin him down'.[32] However, Israeli Prime Minister David Ben-Gurion refused to meet the Syrian dictator until after the conclusion of armistice talks, despite being urged to do so by both the US State Department and the UN Acting Mediator Ralph Bunche.[33]

Most of the talks and intimations between Israel and Syria during this period concerned the armistice negotiations rather than the refugee issue. Nevertheless, on hearing that Zaim wanted to meet Ben-Gurion, Secretary of State Acheson asked his ambassador to Israel to relay Zaim's request, as it would not only be important to the success of armistice talks, but also to the Lausanne discussions.[34] On learning of Zaim's proposal, Israeli Foreign Minister Moshe Sharett, believing that Zaim was more bold and far-sighted than other Arab leaders and represented an opportunity to break the united Arab front, was more enthusiastic than Ben-Gurion, who thought that Zaim's rule might not last long; Sharett indicated through Bunche that he was willing to meet Zaim himself before conclusions of the armistice talks.[35] However, the Syrian military ruler (later president) refused on the grounds that Sharett was of a too junior position.[36] Instead, it was proposed that Sharett meet Adil Arslan, the Syrian Foreign Minister, a proposal which Sharett accepted, although the Syrians ended up withdrawing this offer.[37] Keeley in Syria wrote that Zaim had repeatedly expressed his willingness to repatriate a quarter of a million refugees; Keeley was critical of Ben-Gurion's refusal to meet the Syrian leader, accusing Israel of demanding her 'pound of flesh'. Keeley argued that Ben-Gurion was proving to be 'no Venizelos' while Zaim was trying to measure up to the status of Mustafa Kemal Ataturk.[38]

This was not the end of the affair. Later in July, in a message to the US legation in Syria, the secretary of state called for Zaim to inform his delegation at Lausanne of its official willingness to cooperate in facilitating a solution to the refugee problem by accepting a substantial number of refugees.[39] This was in anticipation of a forthcoming Arab League Political Committee meeting in Beirut, and it was hoped that the changed Syrian position at Lausanne would prevent a hardening of the Arab attitude. In another memorandum from the US secretary of state, but this time to the US Embassy in Israel, it was stated that

Ben-Gurion's desire to meet Zaim should be acknowledged by the Israeli delegation in Lausanne. It was reasoned that this might have the effect of promoting an agreement between Israel and other states and that 'it may be desirable at a later date to encourage direct talks between high Israeli and Arab officials... to supplement discussions at Lausanne'.[40] Syria's delegation to Lausanne was reinforced,[41] and an Israeli official even commented that Israel had been receiving, through a third party, cryptic messages from Zaim expressing his wish for a lasting peace.[42]

Acheson's comment that a meeting between Ben-Gurion and Zaim would help the Lausanne Conference demonstrates the tactical mis-judgement of the US. Instead of reading the possibility of a direct meeting between the leaders of Israel and Syria as an opportunity for a bilateral agreement, Acheson sought to use the possibility of top-level negotiations between two heads of states to supplement lower level talks at the peace conference. It also reflected the US preference for mul-tilateral diplomacy and its focus on the PCC channel. Acheson failed to realize that it was precisely because of the forthcoming Arab League meeting and the grouping of Arab countries into one bloc by the PCC that Zaim would not reveal his position at Lausanne.[43]

Moreover, rivalries, suspicions and self-interest plagued the Arab states. As Walter Eytan, the former Israeli representative to the PCC, observed, when put together into a bloc, there was an atmosphere of intimidation and fear of being perceived as weak or treasonable.[44] Indeed, it was not progress at Lausanne which opened the possibility of Israeli–Syrian talks, but rather a breakthrough in bilateral armistice talks. As early as 13 May, Acheson considered Zaim's offer of particular impor-tance because it was Syria along with Jordan which could realistically absorb such a large number of refugees in a short time. It was considered an 'opportunity to be exploited', and Acheson hoped that Zaim would use his influence on other Arab states to adopt similar attitudes to assist the PCC to liquidate the refugee problem.[45] Therefore, while the US was enthusiastic about Zaim's offer, it did not see bilateral talks as an end in themselves. In fact, when the US delivered its rebuke to Israel on 29 May 1949 for its lack of flexibility in PCC-organized negotiations, it did not refer to Ben-Gurion's refusal to meet Zaim, but instead to Israel's con-duct during PCC negotiating efforts at Lausanne.[46] This demonstrates that it was through the PCC process that the US prioritized Arab–Israeli negotiations. However, Zaim's proposal showed that it was in direct dis-cussions with Israel that opportunities for breaking the refugee impasse were present. However, these opportunities were sacrificed for the sake of the failing PCC process.

On 6 August, after a breakthrough in armistice discussions had been reached, Eliyahu Sasson sent a letter to Muhsin al-Barazi, both Prime Minister and Foreign Minister of Syria, proposing direct and informal talks.[47] However, just under a week later in the early hours of 14 August, three armoured vehicles pulled up to Zaim's residence and a senior army officer shot his way through the building to abduct the president. Another squad was dispatched to al-Barazi's home and dragged him away. They were both quickly tried and executed.[48] During Zaim's short reign, a real window of opportunity existed to solve the Palestinian refugee crisis. However, the US failed to recognize and explore this possibility as a potential end in itself and instead prioritized the ailing PCC talks. Within a short time, the window was closed.

Israeli–Jordanian talks, November 1949 to March 1950

Scholars who have examined the Israeli–Jordanian talks have noted that serious negotiations lasted for about four to five months from November 1949 to February or March of 1950 over three stages.[49] Abdullah accepted Israel's 11 November offer for direct negotiations in a permanent settlement believing that other Arab countries would follow suit. 'They wanted us to take the lead in war … and now wish us to be the first to make peace', he was quoted as saying.[50] During the first stage, between November and December 1949, the parties attempted to reach a comprehensive settlement. This was unsuccessful and faltered over the issue of territory, particularly Jordan's desire for a land link to the Mediterranean, which in the first form meant the surrender of part of the Negev.[51]

Eventually negotiations boiled down to Jordanian access to the Mediterranean, and therefore the requirement of a land bridge from Jordan to a small coastal area just north of the Gaza Strip.[52] However, the main point of contention proved to be the width of the Jordanian corridor. Jordan demanded that the corridor be several kilometres while Israel was only willing to concede hundreds of metres as a maximum plus three kilometres, for a seafront area next to the Gaza Strip, much less than what Jordan wanted for a port.[53] This stalled negotiations. However, in January 1950, the Israelis were still holding out for a breakthrough.

The previous chapters have shown that the acceptance of refugee repatriation to Israel was a precondition put forward by the Arab states and was one of the major impediments to hopes for peace. What is curious is that substantive talks between Israel and Jordan were taking place despite this impasse that had developed under the auspices of the PCC. In a similar vein to Zaim's peace overtures, Britain and the US failed to capitalize on and be fully engaged in these bilateral discussions.

It cannot be asserted that the Palestinian refugees were not a factor in Israeli–Jordanian talks. To some extent, they were; however, the subject was only discussed on a sporadic and inconsistent basis and with only some references to refugee repatriation. In fact, the lack of focus on the refugee question in early bilateral talks between Israel and Jordan suggests that it was only of minor significance. Discussions were very cursory and inconsistent. For example, on 29 December, it was reported that Jordanian negotiators wanted to settle refugees on the access road being discussed.[54] Also in December 1949, Radio Ramallah reported that King Abdullah had told a large audience that he was seeking an agreement whereby property would be regained or compensated. If such compensation were not obtained, Abdullah announced that he himself would find an arrangement for a compensation payment.[55] However, in contrast, on 2 January 1949, Sir Alec Kirkbride in Amman reported of a meeting between King Abdullah, Moshe Dayan and Re'uven Shiloah held the previous day about points for potential negotiations. While territory, corridors, Jerusalem, prisoners and economic relations were mentioned, the refugees were not even discussed.[56]

However, later on 11 January 1949, it was reported that among the king's five points for an agreement with Israel was the right of Arab refugees to go back to their homes.[57] Also on 11 January 1950, Jordanian Minister Dr Yusuf Haikal postulated to State Department officials that one reason for the perceived stalemate was Israel's refusal to permit any refugees to return to their homes. But McGhee replied that he was unaware that the refugee question had even come up in Israeli–Jordanian discussions.[58] While admitting that he had not been informed of the scope of the talks, Haikal went on to comment that it was difficult for any of the Arab states to be reasonable with Israel when they thought about the homeless refugees.

Referring to Israel's 'promises' of compensation, he estimated refugee property to be worth US$12 billion, a sum Israel could not afford to pay.[59] And yet six days later in another round of discussion between Sasson, Dayan and Abdullah, the refugee issue did not come up at all.[60] Nor was it referred to in another meeting towards the end of January 1949.[61] However, the refugee issue was addressed in February 1950. After asking British experts to report on Jordan's economic situation and devise a five-year economic development plan, it was reported by a 'well-informed source' that Jordan would do something shortly for the Arab refugees and that King Abdullah was working 'faithfully' to solve the problem in the near term.[62]

Later, in March 1950, Abdullah reportedly told a group of Turkish students that the main impasse between his country and Israel were the Jordanian Mediterranean port on the connecting corridor and compensation for Palestinian refugees.[63] Indeed the stalemate was a result of the sea access Abdullah was demanding. As already noted, Israel only envisaged the strip to be 50–100 metres wide while King Abdullah wanted considerably more. However, it is possible that the refugee problem also played a role because Abdullah had apparently intended to resettle refugees on this kilometre-wide land bridge running through Israel.[64]

When talks began to stall during the second stage of negotiations in February 1950, Shiloah and Dayan, Abdullah's Israeli interlocutors, noted that some of the points for a future non-aggression pact such as giving permission to Arabs or their attorneys to enter Israel to deal with their property by settling or selling it, pertained to the refugees. There was also the issue of compensation in Jerusalem neighbourhoods.[65]

Nevertheless, the refugee issue appeared to be less of a priority for the king and his position was far more flexible than that of the collective Arab states. Perhaps the lack of concern for the refugee issue can be attributed to Abdullah's view expressed in another meeting with Israeli representatives, that the refugees were 'now no important problem and after peace will solve itself'.[66] In a draft of a non-aggression agreement between Israel and Jordan, which was being discussed in the negotiations, the refugee issue was not even mentioned.[67] Even in later discussions, Abdullah departed from the general Arab position at PCC talks that refugees must be repatriated before a final settlement. It was reported by a British official on 16 April that when Abdullah was outlining his requirements for a final settlement, he stressed that Jordan required a port on the Mediterranean, and while he also referred to the need for refugees to be given compensation and have their assets unfrozen, he had not appeared to link the two issues together.[68] Therefore, what emerges from these Israeli–Jordanian direct talks is that an opportunity for overcoming the Palestinian refugee obstacle had manifested itself.

While these discussions were taking place, the Israeli Ambassador to Washington, Eliahu Elath, requested the PCC meeting in Geneva be postponed pending the conclusion of a final agreement with Jordan. He feared the resumption of PCC talks with Arab states could hinder the progress of direct talks with Jordan, the logic being that when the Arab states got together, although they tended to adopt a unified position, it was generally more unyielding. The Israeli ambassador stated that agreement with Jordan had been reached on all major points with the exception of the width of the sea corridor.

The ambassador was, however, sanguine about the possibility of a breakthrough and once a settlement had been signed with one Arab state, it would be comparatively easy to negotiate a settlement with the others, especially Lebanon.[69] Elath estimated that negotiations would need a month and a half or possibly a little more to be brought to their successful conclusion.[70] However, the US did not delay the resumption of the PCC in Geneva,[71] thus undermining the potential for an Israeli–Jordanian breakthrough.

The second phase of the Israel–Jordanian negotiations was primarily concerned with Jerusalem and the third phase focused heavily on reaching a non-aggression pact between the two countries. When it was reported, incorrectly, that such a pact had been signed, King Abdullah reportedly said, 'We decided to seek a decent solution and have already concluded with the Jews an agreement authorizing refugees on the East and West sides of the Jordan to return to their homes.'[72] Thus, like Zaim in Syria before him, in public, or indeed with the rest of the Arab world watching him, Jordan's leader fell into line with the joint Arab negotiating position.

This poses the question as to why Britain and the US restricted their involvement in the Israeli–Jordanian dialogue. During these talks, Britain's Minister in Amman, Alec Kirkbride, played a constructive role. With the exception of McDonald and David Fitzlan, the US Chargé d'Affaires in Amman, the US did not believe that anything could be accomplished by urging along negotiations.[73]

In November 1949, Hugh Dow in Jerusalem argued that it was undesirable to intervene in Israeli–Jordanian discussions unless Britain was prepared to make its involvement effective, which it was not. He argued that British involvement 'lends colour' to Israel's allegation that if Britain wanted to it could make Arabs 'behave'.[74] Indeed, by early 1951, Britain believed that Israeli–Jordanian talks were unlikely to produce any more than a limited ad hoc solution to certain outstanding bilateral problems between them.[75] Even though it was reported earlier, in April 1950, that Jordan had joined the Arab League in its decision to expel any member signing a separate peace with Israel, Jerusalem stayed positive, believing Jordan had done this to obtain Arab support in its desire to incorporate Arab Palestine and possibly Gaza into the Hashemite Kingdom.[76]

Meanwhile, it was reported in *The Times* that Israel had reacted coldly to a proposal by Britain's opposition leader Winston Churchill that Britain should try to bring Israeli President Chaim Weizmann together with King Abdullah. The article stated that Britain was still considered by Israel an enemy, Israel had not accepted Jordanian claims on Arab Palestine and Israel had 'coldness' to outside mediation.[77] By 8 August 1950, Geoffrey Furlonge of the Foreign Office informed the US ambassador to London that Kirkbride had been instructed to urge the Jordanian government to cooperate with the PCC while also its chargé in Tel Aviv had been instructed to convince Israel that the PCC was the best vehicle to conduct negotiations with Jordan.[78] Again, pushing the sides towards the PCC was a misconceived strategy that hampered rather than helped progress.

Towards the latter part of 1949 when the PCC had suspended its activities, Israeli–Jordanian talks entered their most crucial stage. Israel was even concerned that the reconvening of the PCC in early 1950 might hamper progress in discussions. While the problem of the refugees was not totally absent from Israeli–Jordanian talks, it was only mentioned occasionally when talks stalled. Overall, the intricacies of the refugee problem were still not the major obstacle to progress in discussions. It appears that King Abdullah, in contrast to the other Arab leaders, believed that a settlement with Israel was the first priority which would lead to a solution of the refugee crisis, a position similar to that of Israel. However, the refugee problem was still a preoccupation for King Abdullah. He faced internal opposition to talks with Israel as well as isolation and ostracism by the Arab states who had constructed a unified stance on the refugee issue at the PCC.

Earlier, on 2 November 1949, the US Chargé in Jordan, David A. Fritzlan, reported that in conversations between himself and other foreign representatives, King Abdullah had said that without the restraint of the UN and Arab League, he could negotiate a satisfactory agreement with Israel.[79] Fritzlan argued that it was inevitable that the talks could not remain secret and would affect King Abdullah's precarious position among Palestinians who were unwilling to compromise on UN resolutions pertaining to territory and refugees while their support was needed to annex Arab Palestine.[80] Fritzlan did also add that he was strongly of the opinion that there were enlightened and progressive Palestinians who saw the annexation of Arab Palestine to Jordan as the only salvation for their country.[81] This was a view that had some degree of legitimacy. For example, on 8 March 1950, it was reported that the mayors of the West Bank cities of Nablus, Jenin and Tulkarim had decided to urge King

Abdullah to begin peace negotiations with Israel which would provide the return of some refugees and compensation to others.[82] But it must also be understood that he faced opposition from Palestinian quarters. However, by March 1950, as talks were coming to an end, it was commented that a remaining difficulty in negotiations was finding a formula which would placate opposition to a settlement from Palestinians who had become Jordanian citizens.[83] Not only was there opposition to King Abdullah's dealings with Israel from his Cabinet,[84] the king appeared to have felt the need to emphasize his commitment to the refugee issues in public declarations. Regardless, talks ground to a standstill and were not encouraged following leaks into the Arabic press. Such leaks led to an Arab League resolution on 1 April declaring that no member state could conclude a deal with Israel or they would be expelled from the league. However, a deal was finally made whereby the league would abandon public objections to Abdullah's annexation of the West Bank as long as it would not go ahead with a planned non-aggression pact with Israel.[85]

In a poignant episode just three weeks before King Abdullah's 20 July 1951 assassination by a Palestinian while on a visit to Jerusalem's Al Aqsa mosque, Palmer reported of a meeting between the king and Fisher of the PCC Political Office. 'Please help me ... I am an old man ... I don't want to die of a broken heart', Abdullah reportedly appealed; 'I am hated by my own son', he admitted. Abdullah expressed his deep desire for peace with Israel, but said he needed some concessions such as territorial adjustments in the 'triangle' or a corridor to the Gaza Strip. He also mentioned that he understood that wholesale repatriation or complete compensation was not possible, but instead called for refugees to be permitted to go back to Israel to settle their affairs, and if they could get the income of their property, it would make them less bitter.[86]

This explains King Abdullah's general attitude towards talks with Israel. His priority was border adjustments in a scenario where he would gain more territory and his much-coveted access to the Mediterranean. While there might have been some concern for the Palestinian refugees, this was secondary to his goal of expanding his kingdom. Nevertheless, Britain and the US prioritized the faltering PCC-facilitated talks rather than the bilateral Israeli–Jordanian negotiations which managed to avoid the refugee stalemate.

Secret Egyptian–Israeli talks

Despite the advantages that a settlement with Jordan would offer, Egypt was the first country which Israel approached when it decided to seek a bilateral peace treaty.[87] There was demand from both Israel and Egypt for third-party, particularly US, mediation. For example, the prospects of US mediation were discussed in June and July of 1949.[88] Later in December, when Israeli talks with Jordan were ongoing, it was reported that Shiloah had said that peace with Egypt was more important and he expressed his concern that there would be no progress unless the US brought the sides together.[89] Shiloah had also said that Egypt was 'Dear [to] my heart' and that General Riley was carrying a note from Sasson to Chirine.[90] Sharett held similar views to Shiloah. Earlier in June, he commented that peace with Egypt would lead to other Arab states following suit.[91]

However, this potential avenue for negotiations may not have been the appropriate channel because Hasan Yusuf Pasha, an aide of King Farouk, said that a Sasson–Chirine dialogue was not of the appropriate level. But he also inquired of the US exactly why it might not make itself a go-between, noting that boundary adjustment would be the only outstanding issue if the settlement on the refugees occurred.[92] Again as with Jordan, the PCC was the preference for American diplomacy. Before the 1950 PCC-facilitated talks in Geneva began, the US ambassador to Egypt noted that King Farouk had agreed to have a special representative there who would agree to enter direct, bilateral, informal top-secret negotiations if he were to be approached by the Israeli delegate.[93]

There were individual voices within the Foreign Office who thought it desirable to intervene in negotiations to help facilitate an agreement. After recalling that he had been approached by an Egyptian believed to have 'palace connections' seeking advice from Britain about the desirability of Egypt joining Jordan in talks with Israel (he was told it was better for the Egyptian government to approach the British government more formally), Furlonge said he was personally considering whether there should be more US–British involvement in the talks.

He noted that John Troutbeck of the BMEO in Cairo was of the view that the US–British policy of promoting economic and social development to promote political stability, an allusion to the work of the ESM and UNRWA, was 'putting cart before horse'. Furlonge further argued that the biggest issue affecting political stability was the Palestine situation, therefore it was necessary for the US and Britain to take a more active role in promoting a settlement. He particularly emphasized the need to guarantee frontiers, a contentious issue not least because of Britain's treaty obligations with Egypt and Jordan.[94]

The US response to Troutbeck's comments about economic and social development was that although this seemed to be a 'hen and egg' situation, this approach was necessary because no progress had been made on the political front through the PCC. Washington even admitted that in light of PCC experience, it was better for Israel to negotiate with Arab states individually.[95] However, the US was still reluctant to get involved in direct talks, stressing that it was concentrating on the economic approach to the Palestinian problem and was 'strongly' opposed to US participation to any guarantees.[96]

Another obstacle to the potential Israeli–Egyptian talks was leaks following a *Newsweek* article that reported that negotiations between the two countries were taking place. This was especially troubling, as the Egyptians had indicated that if approached by the Israeli delegate at the PCC, their delegate would be prepared to talk. The Egyptians were also concerned that Abd al-Rahman Hasan Azzam Pasha, the Secretary-General of the Arab League who was vehemently opposed to direct talks, would find out.[97]

Another significant setback to Egyptian–Israeli talks occurred following a report featured in the Israeli newspaper *Hador*, which stated that the Wafd government of Egyptian Prime Minister Mustafa al-Nahhas Pasha had decided to undertake direct talks with Israel, and Egypt's PCC Representative, Abdel Moneim Mustafa Bey, would negotiate with Sasson in Ankara. The Egyptian Ministry of Foreign Affairs denied this story in its entirety.[98] There were also rumours that a peace treaty between Israel and Egypt would be discussed with UN participation on 26 February.[99]

Despite the setback which the story caused, on 27 February 1950, Mustafa Bey did have a meeting with Abba Eban and Gideon Rafael in Lausanne where he told the Israeli officials that he had an open mind about direct talks and personally favoured a definitive settlement with Israel. However, he added that Israel would have to agree on principles beforehand. Eban believed that these principles amounted to a commitment over concessions it was willing to make.[100] In other words, Egypt was asking Israel to reveal potential concessions before negotiations would take place. Little in these preliminary discussions centred on the Palestinian refugees. Mustafa Bey argued that Egypt was most interested in a settlement on the Negev and that the Gaza Strip was actually of little importance in comparison.[101]

Meanwhile, opportunities for limited direct talks even emerged within a PCC-orchestrated initiative. On 23 February, the PCC proposed that Israel and Egypt form a mixed committee under PCC auspices to study several proposals about refugees in the Gaza Strip. These proposals were originally put forward by Egypt. They called for inhabitants of areas of the 'no man's land' in the north of the Gaza region to be allowed to return to their lands to cultivate them, and for refugees residing in the Gaza area but with land in the surrounding area to be allowed to cultivate that land. Regarding the refugee issue, Sharett, in preparation of the talks, suggested that in any talks over Gaza it should be highlighted that the idea that Israel could absorb over 200,000 refugees was a 'physical impossibility'.[102]

Another proposal was for the refugees in Gaza who were originally from the Beersheba area to be allowed, provisionally, to re-establish themselves there.[103] Little progress was made. While reaffirming its desire to discuss with Egypt the conclusion of a peace settlement, Israel responded that another body, the similarly named Egyptian–Israeli Mixed Armistice Commission (MAC), was the best place to discuss Egypt's proposals. The PCC did not agree and retorted that the Mixed Committee on Gaza would be useful.[104] Even so, Egypt did not allow much room for Israel or the PCC to manoeuvre. It insisted that Israel first explicitly accept its proposals. Little further was achieved, with the PCC informing Israel of Egypt's position and then explaining to Egypt that only after an exchange of views at committee level would it be possible for it to be determined how the proposals could be put into effect.[105]

Mustafa Bey did not see the Gaza Committee leading to direct talks and considered it as having little scope. However, he could not oppose it because it was an effort by the PCC to give effect to his own suggestions about the refugees.[106] Eban argued that the Egyptian assumption that the US would force Israel to make concessions and that time was not on Israel's side had been proven incorrect. Responding, Mustafa Bey did not attempt to refute Eban's argument, but instead said that Egypt would not give up the Negev. Mustafa Bey did refer to the refugees in the context of the Gaza Strip. He argued that Gaza and its refugees did not pose a problem for Egypt.[107] Again, this episode demonstrates that in bilateral discussions, the Palestinian refugee problem was less of an obstacle.

US Representative to the PCC Ely Palmer reported that Rafael believed that Egypt was concerned over the form negotiations would take and whether Egypt should have peace with Israel at all. He wanted pressure to be exerted primarily by the US and also by the PCC, whose Gaza Committee, incidentally, he did not think would contribute very much. Rafael was told by Palmer's assistant James Barco that the US had indeed pressed Mustafa Bey but without success. Also, Barco said that while the US was not willing to exert pressure on Egypt for direct talks, it would be willing to press both sides to agree to follow a reasonable procedure at the PCC.[108]

Following the failure of PCC initiatives in March 1950, Israel debated internally the possibility of launching a direct initiative with Egypt. However, Gideon Rafael and Abba Eban determined that from discussions with Mustafa Bey and the PCC, circumstances for even a partial settlement would not be forthcoming unless, of course, pressure was exerted by the US on Israel to revive the Gaza Plan of 1949, the Israeli proposal to take control of Gaza along with its 230,000 plus refugees. However, Jerusalem rejected the Gaza Plan's resurrection.[109]

In an undated memorandum,[110] but dispatched on 6 May, the First Secretary of the Embassy in Egypt, Philip W. Ireland, reported of talks he had with Colonel Ismail Chirine, brother-in-law of King Farouk. Chirine said that any proposal that Israel would take over the Gaza Strip along with its refugees was built on a false premise, as the refugees would actually leave the area either because of Israeli mistreatment or fear of such treatment. However, by allotting territory between the coast and the north of the desert such as Beersheba, the refugees might earn a living.[111] Chirine was critical of how the Arab states had handled the refugee issue, stating that whether or not the refugees would want to go back or if Israel would be willing to take them made no real difference; there was no room for them in Israel and the sooner Arab states realized this, the quicker good relations with Israel would be established.[112]

This contrasting view can be understood in the context of a divide in the Egyptian Foreign Ministry. An assistant to the secretary of the PCC told a British official that there was one school of thought that favoured an agreement and one that was intransigent.[113] Indeed, Mustafa Bey, who it was assumed was talking with the knowledge of Nahas Pasha, said that a settlement with Israel could be possible if Israel were reasonable, meaning withdrawal from the Gulf of Aqaba, 'settlements of the Negeb' and a sensible attitude towards the Gaza Strip. It appears, however, that Mustafa Bey lacked the trust necessary when he was advised to test the reaction of the Israelis at the MAC or through the PCC. Doing such a thing would put him at the Israelis' mercy.[114]

However, it was one thing for Britain to recognize divisions within the Egyptian Foreign Ministry, and another for it to actually encourage bilateral discussions with the moderate factions. Despite the overtures between Israel and Egypt for direct bilateral discussions, progress over the refugee question was limited to preliminary meetings, or expressions of intent to third parties such as Britain, the US and, at least on one occasion, to the Soviet Union.[115] However, these did not progress to significant bilateral discussions. Discussions between Israel and Egypt were limited to the mistrusted PCC forum where talks had stagnated, specifically on the question of refugees.

A potential Israeli–Iraqi population exchange and the US–British response

The 1948 War had a significant impact on the Jewish communities of the Middle East. On 16 May, two days after Israel declared its independence, the *New York Times* ran a headline that read 'Jews in Grave Danger in All Moslem Lands'.[116] In Egypt, the Prime Minister Mahmud al-Nuqrashi Pasha declared that all Jews were potential Zionists, and by the end of 1948, more than 600 Jews were arrested and had their property confiscated. Later, in June, 22 Jews were killed following bomb attacks in Cairo and there were further incidences of attacks and looting throughout the year; in Morocco there were incidences of fatal mob attacks in several towns killing scores; in Libya many Jews were murdered during an attack on Tripoli's Jewish quarter on 12 June 1948 which followed 18 murders of Jews in the days after Israel's independence and, like Egypt, there were bomb attacks against Jewish targets throughout the year; in Yemen, the extremely harsh conditions of the Jews were also further deteriorating; in Syria, after the partition resolution, 18 synagogues, five schools and a youth centre were destroyed in Aleppo precipitating 6,000 of the city's Jews to flee; violent attacks were also reported in Bahrain.[117]

When Britain and the US discussed regional development projects in the context of works and relief for Palestinian refugee resettlement, the potential for such projects in Iraq was often highlighted. This was at a time when the position of Jews in Iraq had become extremely tenuous. There had already been eruptions of anti-Jewish violence during the 1941 Rashid Ali Coup that had led to a pogrom after the revolt which left 178 Jews dead and hundreds of Jewish shops and homes destroyed.[118] The Iraqi Jews did not fare much better during the 1948 Palestine War. It had been reported to the US secretary of state that after the Deir Yasin massacre in April 1948, the possibility of anti-Jewish pogroms in Iraq should not be discounted.[119] As in Egypt, hundreds of Jews were arrested, tried in military courts and either fined or imprisoned and, in some cases, there were even public hangings.[120] Meanwhile, Secretary of State Marshall expressed his concern about Israel's attitude towards allowing Arab refugees to return to their homes, fearing that a refusal could create difficulties for the Jews residing in Arab states.[121] The condition of Jews in Iraq continued to worsen in the period after the 1948 War leading to the mass exodus of Iraq's Jewish community. In March 1950, the same day as the Jewish holiday of Purim that celebrated the deliverance of the Jewish people from the Kingdom of Persia as recorded in the biblical book of Esther, the Iraqi government adopted a law that permitted Jews to legally emigrate; many left for Israel.[122] By the end of 1951, Israel had received 123,371 immigrants from Iraq.[123] However, this flood of Jewish immigrants to Israel was made without a negotiated settlement between Israel and Iraq or as an understanding about the future of Palestinian refugees, something which US and especially British officials were considering particularly in 1949; an exchange of populations could be a basis for at least a partial solution to the Palestinian refugee problem.

The idea of a population exchange with Iraq being the epicentre of such a policy was not in itself new. Explorer and adviser to Ibn Saud, H. St. John Philby, put forward the plan to Zionist Chaim Weizmann in 1943 that in exchange for £ 20 million, Ibn Saud could be amenable to the transfer of Palestinian Arabs to Iraq and Syria.[124] Britain's Labour Party's December 1944 conference adopted a resolution that called for the voluntary transfer of populations.[125] In his memoirs, Hugh Dalton recalled that during the time of this conference he had studied the possibilities for land cultivation and irrigation in the Middle East and concluded that the development of these areas was where the Palestinian Arabs would be happier than in a Palestine where, Dalton argued, there must be a large immigration of Jews.[126] In light of the Labour Party programme and the horrors of the Holocaust, in November 1945, former president of the US Herbert Hoover proposed that Iraq could be developed through the resettlement of the Arabs of Palestine making way for Palestine to be populated with Jews.[127] This in itself was not a unique proposal from someone of Hoover's stature. As early as 1938, US President Roosevelt was proposing various plans and possibilities for the transferring of Palestinian Arabs to neighbouring states, something he raised with various US Zionist leaders and even British officials during the early war period.[128]

British officials were one step ahead of Washington in considering the possibility of a population exchange in the aftermath of the 1948 War. In August 1948, having noted that there were sufficient latent resources in Iraq and Syria to accommodate a larger population, the BMEO in Cairo wrote that, 'It seems possible that the solution may lie in their [Arab refugees] transference to Iraq and Syria.'[129] But on the other hand it was 'hard to believe that the great [Jewish] business houses of Cairo and Bagdad will willingly leave their prosperous concerns to take up a pioneer life in Palestine'.[130] Despite this earlier dismissal of the transfer idea, the unstable position of the Jews of Iraq made such an option a distinct possibility. Marshall's earlier comments were prescient because later in January 1949, summarizing the Iraqi view to Britain, Prime Minister Nuri Pasha argued that Arab refugees should be allowed to return to their homes with compensation, otherwise the 150,000–160,000 Jews in Iraq would be sent to Palestine.[131] A day later, Nuri Pasha al-Sa'id added that even though Iraq would suffer if Iraqi Jews were to be expelled, it would 'get over them'.[132] However, the following month, the Foreign Office instructed its ambassador in Iraq, Sir Henry Mack, to caution Nuri al-Sa'id against expelling the Jews because it would negatively affect the position of the Arab states.[133]

This was not just an isolated comment, as the following month US officials reported that Nuri had said that while Iraq had been able to protect its Jews, it would be helpless to prevent 'spontaneous action' if Israel did not demonstrate its goodwill with deeds and not words.[134] In February 1949, the US noted that on several occasions, Sharett had indicated that as part of a final settlement for Palestine, the position, treatment and future of Jewish minorities in Arab countries would have to be considered. It was added that there were 'indications' that Israel may propose the transfer of Jewish minorities in Arab countries and the permanent resettlement of Arab refugees in Arab states.[135] While it was noted that this fell beyond the remit of the PCC, US diplomats were asked to ascertain the attitudes of their respective governments towards the emigration of its Jewish community, the attitude of the Jewish community and the economic impact of the Jews emigrating.[136] Jefferson Patterson, the US Chargé in Egypt, doubted that many Jews in Egypt would want to go to Israel voluntarily and believed the economic consequences would be adverse.[137]

In May 1949, the US ambassador to Iraq had been informed that Baghdad would be prepared to agree to an exchange of Iraqi Jews for Palestinian refugees with the figure of 100,000 mentioned. Apart from that, there was no contribution which Iraq could make regarding a settlement to the refugee problem.[138] In July 1949, Nuri said that 300,000 Arab refugees would be settled on territory Israel should give up in excess of the partition resolution, but added that some refugees should be settled in Arab states, and if the settlement was reasonable, Iraq would allow the voluntary removal of Jews to Palestine under certain conditions. If not, then Iraq might be prepared to consider an exchange of populations of equal amount of Jew and Arab under the supervision of an international committee which would assess lost Arab property in Palestine and compensation for Jews in Iraq.[139] This came as Britain put forward a proposal whereby Iraqi Jews would be moved to Israel and compensated for their property and Iraq would take in 100,000 Palestinian refugees who would be installed in the property in Iraq.[140]

While there were plans for the resettlement of Palestinian refugees in Iraq, some of which were even detailed in the work of the ESM, it was another case entirely to link this with the position of Jews in Iraq. The aforementioned British proposal was by no means unanimously accepted as policy within Britain. On hearing of Nuri Pasha's threat to expel Iraqi Jews, it was noted by the Middle East secretariat of the Foreign Office that although the idea of expelling Jews should be discouraged, a 'reasonable proposal' for the exchange of populations could be recommended.[141] This warranted further thought, especially if the threat evolved into an arrangement whereby Iraqi Jews would receive full compensation. There would be 'something to commend' if the Arab refugees would be installed with property and the economic disadvantages would be reduced by bringing in Palestinian Arab townspeople.[142]

The BMEO in Cairo detailed the benefits and negatives of the population exchange idea under the nebulous concept that British interests in the region were for the 'normal' conditions of the Middle East to be restored. First, it was noted that if Jews from Iraq were to go to Israel, the other Arab countries would probably follow suit. The problem therefore had to be understood on a regional level. It was also noted that there would be no more Jews in Arab countries and few Arabs in Israel. Arguably, this could lead to the establishment of good relations. The example of Turkish–Greek relations after the 1924 population exchange was given.[143]

However, it was conceded that the difference was that the Greeks were 'down and out', a reference to the fact that Greece had been defeated and totally routed from Anatolia by Turkish nationalist forces during the Turkish War of Independence, 1919–23. It was also argued that Mapai and other parties in Israel had declared themselves in favour of the transfer of Jews from everywhere to their homeland,[144] a reference to the long-held Zionist policy of *aliya*, or Jewish immigration to the land of Israel. However, Knox Helm's talks with Ben-Gurion indicated that Israel was also seeking economic integration into the Middle East by using the Jews in the region as a means to further this policy. It was also noted that while Britain might discourage the idea of expelling Jews from Arab countries, it would probably happen anyway. And for a population exchange to be carried out, elaborate arrangements would have to be made and it was 'very doubtful' that the Arab administrations would be capable of this, leading to

Jewish hardship to which Israel might respond.[145] The idea that Arab townsmen could take the place of a Jew was likened to exchanging 'managing directors of I.C.I.' with 'small shopkeepers from Peckham', who might anyway be afforded second-class citizenship. Finally, the Foreign Office recommended against putting forward an exchange of populations.[146]

The Chancery of the British embassy of Baghdad criticized the idea on the grounds that such a scheme would virtually admit the Iraqi thesis that the Jews there did not have a right to be in Iraq. There was also potential for a voluntary departure of Jews from Iraq turning into a forced one, with Britain then being accused of promoting the expulsion of Jews. However, the idea was not ruled out entirely, as it was believed that 100,000 Palestinian Arab townsmen could be resettled. It was then stated that if the ESM came to Iraq, it would be discussed.[147]

Knox Helm in Tel Aviv argued that from the perspective of compensation, a population exchange would be complicated. He believed that in Israel, Iraqi Jews would have a harder time than in Iraq, and their reception in Israel would be halfway between the enthusiastic reception experienced by agricultural Jews from Yemen and the unenthusiastic experiences of those from North Africa.[148] Rounding up the different views from the field, Sheringham of the Foreign Office concluded that while nothing should be done to discourage an 'amicable' agreement between Israel and Iraq, Britain should not press the sides on the matter.[149]

Eventually, Iraq was persuaded to receive the ESM. The mission met Nuri Pasha on 14 October 1949, where he said that he agreed with the policy of the mission wholeheartedly and would do anything to help. He also invited the mission to return with its experts when it began to study long-term projects in Iraq.[150] The following day it was reported that Nuri had 'dwelled' on the theme of exchanging 100,000 Baghdad Jews as well as another 80,000 Iraqi Jews for urban Palestinian Arab refugees.[151] This was also reported in the Iraqi press.[152] This upset Nuri, who thought that the discussions were confidential and he had not expected details to be released.[153] Several days later, some Baghdad newspapers published a 'half-hearted denial'. However, the right wing press took up the matter with enthusiasm arguing that the Jews constituted a dangerous fifth column with the only downside of an exchange being that it would necessitate recognition of Israel. Apparently, Nuri had told Desmond Morton of the ESM that the Jews could take their wealth with them; however, Morton doubted that Nuri really meant this.[154] Around the same time, the British Minister of State Hector McNeil even briefly told

Abba Eban in New York that he believed exchange and transfer were the best solutions and that he would speak to the Iraqi prime minister.[155]

Journalist and Zionist sympathizer, Jon Kimche, wrote several articles about the transfer of Jews from Arab countries as a solution proposed by Britain, presumably the one made earlier in July. One reported of splits in the Foreign Office towards the scheme. The article implied that Morton was in support of the proposal and had backing from the Foreign Office's Permanent Chief Sir William Strang.[156] In another article the following month, Kimche reported that Britain had told the PCC that 200,000 Jews from Arab countries should be exchanged for Arab refugees, with a further 100,000 Arab refugees permitted to return to Israel.[157] Kimche's articles were not well received in Israel. Eytan questioned where Morton got his information from.[158] He then called Kimche's articles 'utterly irresponsible' and asked if someone could 'muzzle' him.[159]

Later in October, the Iraqi press reported that five Jewish notables and the chief rabbi in Iraq had called on the deputy prime minister and discussed the situation of Jews following rumours that the government intended to agree to an exchange after confiscating their property. The press also reported that Israel had asked Britain to intervene to stop the persecution of Iraqi Jews.[160] For its part, the US Embassy in Iraq did not believe that Nuri seriously entertained the idea and only meant it as a rhetorical gesture to the ESM. The embassy also believed that such a move would be disastrous and that it should discourage public discussions on such a project.[161] The subject of the Jews of Iraq (and other Arab countries) had been discussed in the Knesset, especially after March 1949 when Zionism had been outlawed in Iraq. The Israeli response to the Iraqi offer to exchange populations, after it was made public in October 1949, as stated by Elath and earlier by Sharett in talks with the US, was that Israel would be happy to have Iraqi Jews and was interested in saving their lives.[162] However, this fell well short of agreeing to a population exchange. Indeed, Ben-Gurion commented that 'all the talk about an exchange is strange. Clearly, if the Iraqi Jews are able to leave, we'll receive them and not ask questions about an exchange or no exchange.'[163] Sharett, at an Israeli Cabinet meeting, expressed his concern that such an exchange would mean an Israeli agreement to have Jews' property confiscated in return for Palestinian property confiscated by Israel. This would also mean that Israel would be responsible for Iraqi Jewish requests or demands for compensation.[164] According to Yehouda Shenhav, Israel was also concerned because it had estimated that there were only 200,000 Jews that would come to Israel and therefore feared that in the event of a population exchange, Israel would have to accept the surplus number of Palestinian refugees. Its policy was therefore that of 'constructive ambiguity'.[165] While no formal agreement came to fruition and had dissipated after the denaturalization law in Iraq of March 1950, over the following years the condition of Iraqi Jews deteriorated and led to a mass exodus with Israel being the main destination. This was coupled with a series of laws that confiscated Jewish property that followed the loss of Iraqi citizenship and their emigration. This included Law No. 5, Law for the Control and Administration of Property of Jews Who Have Forfeited Iraqi Nationality, passed on 10 March 1951, which sequestered the property of Jews who had been denaturalized, registered for emigration, but still waiting to leave Iraq. This law froze the property of an estimated 104,670 Jews. Meanwhile, another law passed on the same day, the Regulations for the Control and Administration of Property of Jews Who Have Been Deprived of Iraqi Nationality No. 3, outlined the procedures for the custodian general's office that was newly established to be in charge of the property of denationalized Jews.[166] The mass immigration of Jews to Iraq strengthened the Israeli argument for a 'two way population movement' and a stronger case against Palestinian refugee repatriation, especially towards the PCC's diplomatic attempts in the Paris Conference in 1951.[167] Acting Secretary of State James Webb called the Iraqi law to allow for the emigration of Jews a 'positive development' in preventing discrimination against Jews in Arab countries.[168] This, however, happened without a negotiated agreement either for normal relations between Israel and Iraq or for an understanding about the future of the Palestinian refugees who would remain displaced in their host countries.

Conclusion

Pelcovits argues that 'no one can read the diplomatic record without being convinced that commission representatives, led by the US discouraged Israel from pursuing parallel informal talks'. While there is some substance in this assertion, it is not totally accurate. What really emerges from the diplomatic record, especially US archival sources, and what this study highlights, is that Washington was not against direct bilateral informal talks as such, but rather tried to channel them to help the work of the PCC.[169]

However, in contrast to the proceedings at the PCC-orchestrated discussions between 1949 and 1951, the Palestinian refugee problem was less of an obstacle in moves towards direct bilateral talks between Israel and her Arab neighbours. During the PCC's multilateral talks, the Arab states not only refused to discuss terms for a final settlement with Israel, but they also refused to meet Israel directly unless there was first an agreement to repatriate the refugees. This stalemate was to plague the PCC's attempts and ultimately led to its failure. However, the refugee problem was not a significant factor in the bilateral interactions between Israel and the Arab states outside of the PCC.

Three explanations for this emerge. First, the refugee problem was not a primary Arab concern and was viewed as a trump card to exert diplomatic pressure on Israel and a collective position each state advocated to deflect possible criticism from rival states. Just as during the 1948 Palestine War, the real interest of the Arab states was territory which would have, inevitably, come with a sizable Palestinian Arab population. Second, the refugee issue was a genuine concern but was less of an obstacle in bilateral discussions because it was already being dealt with at length by the PCC. Third, they were discreetly open to the idea that a settlement with Israel could facilitate the solution to the refugee crisis. This would certainly appear to be the case with Husni Zaim and King Abdullah.

Husni Zaim of Syria was willing to resettle hundreds and thousands of refugees. King Abdullah of Jordan paid little attention to the refugee problem, giving priority to the territorial question and a peace settlement. Even in overtures to talks between Israel and Egypt, the refugee question appeared to be less of a factor. However, Britain, and especially the US, had a vested interest in facilitating the PCC talks. As a UN body, negotiations through the PCC allowed the US and Britain to encourage, mediate and facilitate peace talks and find an agreement on the issues outstanding between the sides, including refugees, without having to assume responsibility for generating possible ill-feeling in the case of failure. Unfortunately, the PCC channel proved ineffectual and stalled. Realizing this, the US and Britain encouraged direct talks, but resisted involvement, preferring these talks to be a means of overcoming the PCC stalemate rather than providing a solution in themselves. Ultimately, talks with Egypt barely got off the ground; Husni Zaim's regime in Syria was overthrown before talks could really get started; Israeli–Jordanian negotiations failed to overcome the question of territory; and the possibility of population exchanges between Israel and Iraq became an indelicate subject. All that was left was the US and British-supported PCC channel which continued to stagnate over the refugee problem.

7
The Birth of UNRWA: The Institutionalization of Failed Diplomacy

Introduction

UNRWA represented the culmination of three years of British, US and international diplomatic efforts to solve the Palestinian refugee problem. It was an unmitigated failure. UNRWA was established following the passing of General Assembly Resolution 302 (IV).[1] The resolution called for the body to direct works and reliefs programmes in coordination with local governments.[2] Not only would UNRWA take over the function of the UNRPR, established following Resolution 212, which called for a relief programme for the refugees, but it would also produce an annual report and work with the PCC.[3]

The idea of a relief and works agency was outlined in the Interim Report of the ESM which envisaged an agency to take charge of refugee relief and also facilitate direct programmes for public works.[4] The reasons for this were fourfold. First, to reverse the effects of refugee demoralisation and poverty associated with handouts. Second, to offer work opportunities for the refugees. Third, to contribute to the economic productivity of the countries hosting the refugees. Fourth, to 'encourage a more realistic view of the kind of future they want'.[5] The last point was an insinuation that the possibility of refugees returning to their homes in Israel was unrealistic. However, as this chapter will show, from its very inception, UNRWA was marred by many obstacles, and it was unable to live up to the ESM's vision and the intentions of British and US officials. In its First Annual Report, UNRWA's director recommended that his organization's works programme be continued but 'gradually transformed' into a programme that would focus on the 'improvement of the refugees' living conditions, 'current and future' and continue relief efforts to coincide with a reintegration project.[6] This

166

was a far cry from the resettlement of Palestinian refugees, which was the actual intention of London and Washington. In its Interim Report of 1950, UNRWA itself admitted that it was 'unable to approach the high targets for numbers set by the ESM and, up to that moment, most of its works projects must be classified as short-term'.[7] Nearly one year later the Second Annual UNRWA Report would further concede that the UN organization had 'failed to produce the effect hoped for by the report of the Economic Survey Mission'.[8]

UNRWA offered several reasons why it was unable to meet the ESM's targets. It stated that it did not get started as early as it had hoped. On top of this, the time it had taken to get both refugees and governments interested in works programmes was much longer than what had been anticipated. Also, there were no opportunities for works programmes in the Gaza Strip and the programme in Lebanon was limited. In Jordan, UNRWA was also unsuccessful in providing work for the refugees. To add to its woes, UNRWA suffered from an acute lack of funding and receipt of pledged contributions.[9]

This chapter will elaborate on the aforesaid reasons why UNRWA was unable to fulfil the aspirations of the ESM as seen through the eyes not only of UNRWA, but also of British and US officials. Specifically, it will argue that UNRWA failed in meeting the ESM's expectations because of the delays getting started. More importantly, it faced resistance from Arab states who believed that full cooperation with UNRWA would lead to refugee resettlement. This was a direct consequence of the failure to find a political settlement to the Palestine conflict, and highlights the fallacy of British and US strategy which mistakenly hoped that the economic possibilities of such resettlement and works programmes for Palestinian refugees could offset the political impasse in negotiations. Within its first year, Britain and the US had severe concerns about the work of the organization. This chapter will detail the debates between Washington and London over the future direction of UNRWA. This was a defining moment in the history of the works and relief agency as it marks a period in which the direction of UNRWA drifted from that of which it was originally intended.

The inception of the idea of a works and relief organization

As the ESM's Interim Report was being drafted, Britain and the US discussed the future establishment of an organization which would not only facilitate work and long-term development projects in the Middle East, but would also utilize the productivity of the Arab refugees.[10]

Ultimately, the establishment of such an organization would be recommended by the ESM's report and would lead to the creation of UNRWA. However, as the ESM engaged in its activities, the US and Britain discussed the nature of this new body, referred to as the Near East Development Institute (NEDI), which replaced the ill-titled Economic and Financial Development Institute of Near East (EFENDI) whose acronym, it was feared, could give offense to Arab sensibilities,[11] as well as the Near East Settlement and Development Authority (NESDA).[12] The State Department had already noted that the new organization may have to use economic terms because Arab states would want to divorce the activities of the ESM from a settlement over the Palestine War.[13] This assumingly meant avoiding the explosive term 'resettlement'. However, Washington still hoped that the Arab states would acknowledge a direct relationship between their responsibilities for the refugees and the potential projects highlighted by the ESM.[14]

One of the British concerns in setting up this new organization was the risk that Middle Eastern governments might see the body as compromising their authority and thus withhold their full collaboration.[15] This was a legitimate concern, especially as Chapter 4 showed that the Arab states looked upon the activities of the ESM with suspicion. While avoiding a direct call for the resettlement of refugees, the ESM report did contain a reference to a 'more realistic view of the kind of future' for the refugees. However, the report went on to state that the resettlement of refugees outside of Palestine was a political issue, thus drifting from the initial idea which had prompted the creation of the ESM, which was to investigate how refugees could be resettled in the region.[16]

The linkage between the works and relief agency and the settlement issue continued to be diluted in Resolution 302, which set the terms for UNRWA's establishment. Nowhere in UN Resolution 302 of December 1949 is the word 'resettlement' mentioned, despite it being the body which would facilitate the resettlement, rehabilitation and reintegration of Palestinian refugees.[17] This enabled the Arab states to separate cooperation with UNRWA from actually resettling Palestinian refugees in their territory.

The ESM Interim Report recommended the continuance of emergency relief through voluntary contributions until 1 April 1950. On that date, the programme for public works would begin and coincide with an effort to reduce the number of rations being distributed. It was hoped that by 31 December 1950 no more rations would be supplied. The ESM wanted the new agency to direct the programme of relief and public works and have full autonomy to make decisions in the sphere assigned to it. It would be located in the region and have the assets of the UNRPR, the organization in charge of relief which involved the participation of several international aid agencies, turned over to it.[18] However, not only was UNRWA unable to resettle refugees through long-term development programmes, but it was also unable to significantly reduce rations and refugee dependency on aid.

A late start

A major reason for the failure of UNRWA was its late start. The first official meeting of UNRWA's Advisory Committee took place in Beirut where UNRWA had set up its headquarters on the week beginning 17 April 1950. During its first months, UNRWA's task was to develop its organizational administration as well as its rules of procedure. These were especially necessary because not only was it launching a works programme, but it was also taking over the functions of UNRPR.[19] However, the Advisory Committee had met as early as 6 March. During the early stages of its work, UNRWA needed a working definition of a refugee. It was thus defined as 'a needy person, who, as a result of the war in Palestine, has lost his home and his means of livelihood'.[20]

The first concern of John Troutbeck of the BMEO was the arrangement UNRWA would make with Arab states. He worried that UN members might reconsider their financial contribution if it was realized that it was the Arab states who would be responsible for procuring and distributing supplies rather than international agencies. Troutbeck speculated as to whether Britain would be prepared to accept the 'inevitable' corruption and inefficiency that 'administration by the Arab government entails'. He came to the conclusion that this was the price which would have to be paid if responsibility were put on Arab governments.[21]

The US appeared to be less concerned about this prospect than Britain because Joseph Palmer, the Second Secretary at the US Embassy to London, was told that UNRWA's personnel number would be kept at a minimum in order to have local governments conduct as many operations as possible.[22] As talks and discussion about UNRWA's organization continued, Troutbeck wrote on 26 January 1950 that it would take weeks or perhaps months for UNRWA to get going, the effects of which would be disastrous.[23] Troutbeck's foresight proved correct and the late start of UNRWA's activities proved to be a major operational setback.

For Britain, there was also the pressing question of choosing its representative to the Advisory Committee. Although this was important, the picking of agency staff proved to be a lengthy and time-consuming process. Initially, Britain proposed Desmond Morton, its Representative to the ESM. However, it was reported that such an appointment would upset UN officials, chief among them Secretary-General Trygve Lie who Morton had criticized in an outspoken attack on the UN.[24] Morton had also commented that the PCC 'stinks' and that the PCC had betrayed the Arabs to the Jews.[25]

The Foreign Office did not want to rule out the possibility of Morton's appointment, who they believed would add continuity between UNRWA and the ESM. They also felt that the State Department would favour it because, apparently, Morton and Clapp worked well together.[26] While Israel did not like Morton, its approval was not needed because, London reasoned, UNRWA would function in Arab countries. Opposition by the UN Secretariat also had its benefits because Britain and the US did not want UNRWA to be dominated by the UN.[27] Many other candidates were considered to be the British representative to the Advisory Committee; among them were Sir Hugh Dow, Sir Ambrose Dundas, Sir Harold MacMichael and Air Marshall William Dickson. However, it was Sir Henry Knight, an experienced official who had served in many high-ranking advisory and acting governor positions in India, who became the preferred British candidate, but only in February 1950.[28]

The US was also eager to have the US member of the Advisory Committee named.[29] By 16 January, John B. Blandford Jr had been earmarked for the position as the 'Interested Bureaus' were agreed that he was the ideal choice. He had the support of Gordon Clapp, the principle author of the ESM report.[30] However, although he was chosen more quickly than the British representative, Blandford had just come back from Greece where he was the Deputy Chief of the Economic Cooperation Authority's Mission to Greece, and he was reluctant to take on another temporary job.[31]

Blandford accepted the post on condition that the dates set by the Clapp Report were regarded as targets and not as a programme.[32] Indeed, Blandford made it clear from the beginning that he did not believe it possible to meet the schedule in transferring the refugees from direct relief to productive works projects, arguing that the number of refugees receiving rations was already 200,000 above the target figure. This demand was seen by the British delegation to the UN as 'realistic' and something Britain would have to accept.[33]

There was general agreement between Britain and the US that the Advisory Committee should play a role in formulating and executing UNRWA policy.[34] Even though such matters were highly important, a great deal of time was spent in 1950 deliberating over who would be the director, as well as the nature of his role and the make-up of the Advisory Committee and its relationship with the director. By 18 January, Britain had concluded that it would be unprofitable to continue such discussions and that the best thing would be for the director and the Advisory Committee to come up with a modus operandi. The British still believed that the director should be a 'Chief Executive Officer' in the 'British' not the 'American' sense.

This meant that the director should not be a member of the Advisory Committee and should not be entitled as a right to attend its meetings; however, the UN secretary-general would be allowed to designate tasks to both the director and members of the Advisory Committee.[35] Desmond Morton argued that the Advisory Committee should resemble a board of directors of a corporation, while the director should resemble a general manager. The Advisory Committee would lay down their policies and the director would implement them. The State Department and Gordon Clapp believed that the director should have more power with the position akin to that of a managing director to his colleagues on the board.[36]

By now it was feared by British officials that it would take weeks or months for UNRWA to start its work and that such a delay would have disastrous consequences.[37] Implicit in this position was another reason why UNRWA was so slow to take off; a power struggle between the UN and UNRWA's contributing members. At this stage, it was postulated that the Advisory Committee would consist of contributing states and although the role of UNRWA's director was uncertain, he would be answerable to the UN secretary-general. However, it appeared that the director would be American, but with a US member also on the Advisory Committee, the Arab states might look at UNRWA with suspicion. Regardless, Britain was willing to take this risk if it meant a director would be appointed soon.[38]

The British were hoping that the director would be a Commonwealth citizen,[39] and the US preferred the director to be Canadian.[40] In fact, Acheson was adamant that the director of UNRWA should be drawn from a country other than the US, Britain, France or Turkey because the 'symmetry' of the organization would be destroyed. Acheson also worried that if the director were to be a US citizen, the US would not be able to find a suitable candidate for the US representative of the Advisory Committee. Acheson even requested that the UN secretary-general make no more approaches to US citizens for the role and instead expressed his support for a Canadian candidate.[41]

Over the following weeks, many candidates were discussed. After the UN secretary-general said that candidates General Howard Kennedy and General James H. Burns did not have the relevant experience for the position,[42] the Foreign Office speculated that the real reason was that the secretary-general was looking for someone with administrative and executive ability, as the candidate would be negotiating with Arab governments and working with the Advisory Committee which consisted of members with much knowledge of the region as well as political experience.[43] However, Kennedy, from Canada, did become the preferred candidate after he had been interviewed by 'all concerned'. But he was unable to take up his duties until as late as 1 April.[44]

UNRWA's lack of funds

In its explanation as to why it was unable to meet the objectives of the ESM, UNRWA's later and more comprehensive 1951 Annual Report stated that the 'foremost' reason was the 'constant uncertainty' over the 'availability of funds'.[45] It reported that of the US$54 million target for the period January 1950 to June 1951, only US$37 million was freely disposable to the agency. Even receipt of these funds was delayed, forcing UNRWA to borrow from the UN's working capital fund in order to meet its commitments.[46] The burden was especially acute for the relief programme because there was a general price rise in commodities owing to a world shortage of flour and poor prospects for the harvest in the area.[47]

These setbacks echo some of the complaints Blandford registered from the field at the time. For example, in June 1950, it was reported that the late launching of the organization and the lack of funds resulted in the delayed reduction in the number of rations, as well as the high cost of procurement.[48] The report even requested US$5 million be paid to bridge the gap between the figure foreseen by the ESM and the figure that had been promised to UNRWA.[49]

The initial breakdown of funding according to the ESM report was that the US should pay just under US$27.5 million, Britain US$13 million, France US$6 million, Arab states US$6 million and US$2.5 million should be sought from smaller states.[50] A source of disappointment for the US was the amount of British funding for UNRWA. The US did not think it could increase its request from Congress to more than US$27 million which would be above the 50 per cent matching formula for what was required (the US would provide 50 per cent of UNRWA's funding). However, Britain's suggested contribution, a lesser figure of

£2,250,000, due to the burdens of its economic recovery programme, would mean that UNRWA's funding would be US$47,300,000, short of the US$54,900,000 requested. Washington considered this disastrous.[51] The US informed Britain that its proposed contribution would make a bad impression on Congress and prejudice the US$27 million request the State Department had made. It would be perceived that Britain was only interested in remunerative investments in Iraq and Egypt rather than the 'unattractive' problem of the Palestinian refugees.[52]

The Foreign Office, however, did not accept that its investments in Jordan and Egypt were remunerative.[53] Nevertheless, it was actually sympathetic to the US position and wanted to contribute more to UNRWA. It was noted by the Foreign Office that the message from the Treasury appeared to be that Britain simply could not afford the full amount, and that an increase in funding would only be possible if UNRWA's work was considered more in Britain's interests than competing obligations.[54] Palmer even reported that Foreign Office official Michael Wright was upset that the British chancellor of the exchequer turned down the request for the increase in the size of Britain's contribution for the third time.[55] The Foreign Office and indeed Palmer decided to get Bevin involved to see if he could influence the chancellor's decision, a course of action McGhee agreed to.[56]

The secretary of state appealed to the chancellor to reconsider Britain's position citing the difficulty the State Department would have convincing Congress to offer their 'matching' proposal in light of the reduced British contribution.[57] The chancellor replied that Britain just could not afford an increase.[58] Nevertheless, the Foreign Office still had misgivings about the chancellor's decision, as there was real concern that Britain would suffer more in the region for any failure to solve the problem than either France or the US would.[59] The Foreign Office finally managed to secure additional funding with Bevin's involvement (an additional US$1 million), but the British contribution worked out as only 20 per cent of UNRWA's total income rather than the 25 per cent that the US had planned for.[60] The State Department was satisfied with this development, calling it 'almost as much as we could hope for', especially as the British contribution appeared to promise US$7 million in the first 12 months and an additional US$3.5 million in the remaining six months of the programme.[61] Still, the funding crisis did not dissipate. By May, it was reported that Britain would contribute an even larger figure of US$9 million. The French contribution was just US$2.8 million.[62]

Just as concerning for the US was the lack of funds from the French, as reports were pointing to a French budget that only earmarked 600 million francs for UNRWA, far short of its expected US$6 million.[63] The State Department, in May 1950, expressed the view that the French contribution only constituted one third of that of Britain's when it needed to be half.[64] Two of France's objections were the misuse of funds by the previous Palestine Refugee Committee as well as a lack of jobs for French nationals; France also wanted its contribution to be put in a special fund without conversion and to be used in Lebanon and Syria.[65] On 27 July, it was reported of France's intention to advance 500 million francs.[66] Blandford commented that of all the issues facing UNRWA, its finances were what troubled him the most.[67]

The importance of meeting the projected UNRWA budget was outlined by McGhee who explained it to Francis Wilcox, the Chief of Staff of the Senate Committee on Foreign Affairs. If the works programme did not succeed, then the UN would be forced to continue providing relief, and its cost would continue for a long time. Furthermore, the longer the refugees remained indigent, the more they would be prey to political subversion, especially as the State Department had become increasingly concerned about the presence of communist agitators.[68]

However, even Washington's contribution was not safe. George McGhee had to argue the case for the restoration of the full US contribution after the Appropriations Committee recommended reducing the figure by 10 per cent. He restated the aims of the UNRWA organization, stressing that if significant funds were not available, the cost of dealing with the refugee problem would be higher and communist agitation would become a real issue.[69] UNRWA's operations were marred by this financial uncertainty. It has already been noted that Britain and France's contribution was lower than what was expected, but to add to UNRWA's woes, the State Department asked Britain to pay an early instalment, as it was unable to get US legislation passed until the end of May, one month later than it had hoped.[70]

The resistance of Arab states to UNRWA

UNRWA also faced another major obstacle in fulfilling its tasks – a lack of cooperation from the Arab states whose full support was needed to wean refugees off handouts and into work. One of the first challenges facing UNRWA was to reduce the number of rations being distributed from 960,000 to 800,000 by May 1950, the first month of its operation. However, citing humanitarian reasons, UNRWA was unable to meet this requirement. It distributed 860,000 rations. This was 60,000 more than its set target. In fact, in its Annual Report, UNRWA stated that it did not envisage reducing rations to less than 855,000 by September 1950.[71] This was a significant failure in the early phase of its operations. UNRWA's task was to rehabilitate refugees inducing them away from handouts towards self-sufficiency. Furthermore, by the end of September 1950, the State Department was of the view that UNRWA should terminate its ration distribution in Israel and that Israel should take up the responsibility.[72] Indeed, included in UNRWA ration distribution were 30,000 Arab refugees in Israel, and Jerusalem had requested that UNRWA discontinue such efforts.[73] With Israel taking up the responsibility of ration distribution, what this meant was that the only country where refugee rehabilitation was taking place was in the country with the least number of refugees and the least need for UNRWA's services. Meanwhile, in UNRWA's 1950 Interim Report it was stated that:

> The motives of the new Agency were not completely understood and little active response toward the starting of works projects was evidenced outside Jordan until after the June meeting of the Arab League, which approved of co-operation by its members with the Agency in its programme, provided the projects undertaken did not interfere with the right of the refugee to avail himself of the terms of General Assembly resolution 194 (III) of December 1948, which provided for repatriation or compensation.[74]

What the said Arab League's position effectively meant was that its member states could cooperate with UNRWA but only insofar as it would not lead to the resettlement of Palestinian refugees. Thus, already in its first six months of existence, UNRWA was unable to meet its most fundamental mandate as a relief and works agency for the large-scale resettlement of Palestinian refugees.[75]

The Arab League's position reflected the policies of several Arab states. For example, Syria stated in July 1950 that it would only be willing to cooperate with UNRWA if its projects did not involve resettlement.[76] This was further reiterated in another meeting two weeks later where the Syrian prime minister stated that his country would not give any work to a refugee if it implied his permanent resettlement in Syrian territory. Only the Syrian government's health director believed that if refugees were employed in works beneficial to the Syrian economy at no cost to the exchequer, then UNRWA plans could be accepted, such as draining the Gharb marshes (which would require housing for refugees).[77]

Syria proved particularly difficult for UNRWA because, following a change of government in the country in June 1950, UNRWA had to conduct negotiations all over again.[78] Even in Jordan where there was some enthusiasm about the work of UNRWA from King Abdullah, by April 1950, it was commented that while everyone had heard about UNRWA's plans, they had not seen concrete action. However, McGhee was appreciative of Jordan's cooperative position and thought that the king's policy would be strengthened once the economic benefits of the programme had been felt.[79]

Prior to the June Arab League meeting, all Arab governments, with the exception of Jordan, were non-committal in meetings with UNRWA.[80] And even though Lebanon soon agreed to work with UNRWA on certain projects, it was adamant that no refugees could be resettled.[81] By the end of 1950, there was information that the Lebanese government was 'anxious' to get UNRWA out of the country with the possible exception of refugees of Lebanese origin.[82] Egypt, by August 1950, remained uncommitted, despite talks on works and settlement in Sinai.[83] In Iraq, the prime minister stated that UNRWA's work would be limited unless the UN would put into force Resolution 194 calling for the compensation and repatriation of Palestinian refugees.[84]

By the end of September, Egypt had said it would work with UNRWA in accordance with the Arab League decision that a general settlement to the Palestine problem be left open and that nothing should be done to prevent the refugees' compensation or repatriation, and Cairo was reluctant to take on financial responsibility beyond the proportion of what it gave to the UN.[85] However, it would not object to refugees in Gaza, where UNRWA would conclude that there was no opportunity for any considerable works programme,[86] leaving to find work in Arab countries.[87]

Britain's representative to UNRWA's Advisory Committee was sober in his analysis and reported in May 1950 that, 'All governments seem very suspicious that the Agency is a cover for USA imperialistic aims.'[88] Also, when Israel was asked if its offer to repatriate 100,000 refugees which it had made to the PCC in 1949 was still on the table, its reply was 'no'.[89] When UNRWA visited Saudi Arabia in May 1950, it was reported that nobody immediately greeted the delegation at the airport, a result of, apparently, 'conflicting information as to the arrival of the mission'. However, Prince Faisal did finally travel from Ta'if for dinner with the delegation.[90] Regardless, Faisal, in a consultation later with Aramco officials, was scathing in his criticism of the UN, calling it a tool of the major powers in the world, and warning that the Arabs were losing faith in Western states and that they would have to look to Russia if they could not obtain assistance from the Western powers.[91]

The exception to the hostility towards UNRWA was Jordan, where the organization's director, Howard Kennedy, was given lists by local officials for public works projects for UNRWA assistance.[92] When Syria did come around to appointing a committee to work with UNRWA, it was only for what it considered short-term projects such as highway construction and irrigation.[93] This meant that it was unwilling to cooperate in long-term schemes, as they could lead to resettlement.

The other source of opposition towards UNRWA was the refugees themselves. For example, following a tour of the region by the organization, it was reported in the weekly roundup of UNRWA's activities in May 1950, that there were strikes in camps in the Damascus and Sidon area by refugees refusing food rations and medication, and that they had closed their schools allegedly in protest at the implementation of the works projects as they were seen as a move away from repatriation.[94]

Britain now had little confidence that the Arab states would be induced to resettle refugees through UNRWA's activities. For example, the brief Knight was given by the Foreign Office noted that UNRWA had no intention of intervening in the matter of a political settlement between Israel and the Arab states, but could only express the private view that it was unrealistic to imagine a settlement would be reached whereby any 'appreciable' number of refugees would return to their homes in Israel.[95] London also believed that resettlement was only possible within the framework of the large-scale economic development of the area. This would have to be undertaken by the Arab states themselves, with UNRWA placing funds and technical knowledge at the disposal of Arab governments which it hoped would be utilized without the 'short-sighted' idea that national sovereignty was being undermined.[96]

The US State Department recommended that approaches be made to the Arab League to encourage its officials to initiate statistical and regional studies. It was also argued that more emphasis should be on schemes in Jordan looking to increase its absorptive capacity rather than on road development in already populated areas.[97] It was also hoped that Syria's good relations with UNRWA would enable continuing studies of resettlement projects to bear fruit.[98] Although UNRWA was failing, the US was finding the proverbial silver lining by using its contributions to the agency to show the Arab states that it was making large-scale financial contributions to the Arab world.

In many respects, the investment in UNRWA by the US was a means to maintain good relations with the Arab world. This is why the State Department recommended that US leaders make statements of friendship with the Arabs whenever the appropriate occasion arose, and for the vice president to publically express satisfaction with UNRWA and its goal of aiding refugees.[99]

Britain and the US debate UNRWA's future

In arguing the case for continued US funding of UNRWA, McGhee summed up the problem best. The UN, he pointed out, would be faced with the continuing problem of paying for relief if the works programme failed.[100] As UNRWA was set to draft its report in 1950, the State Department felt that it should recommend that UNRWA's life be expanded for an additional year from June 1951, and that direct relief should be authorized beyond the end of 1950.[101]

While the Foreign Office accepted that there was a strong case for continuing direct relief, it was noted that this meant there would be less funds for works projects. However, the Foreign Office feared that Britain would be unlikely to make a further substantial financial commitment.[102] While it was acknowledged that under Kennedy, UNRWA had a 'first class team' and had won the blessing and cooperation of Arab governments, it was noted that, with the exception of Jordan, there was little prospect that this would lead to resettlement.[103]

The next step, therefore, was for UNRWA to gain acceptance from regional governments for the initiation of work projects which would have the 'affect of resettlement' and economic development in general. With its life prolonged, it was reasoned that UNRWA could not only play a role in bringing about a solution to the refugee question, but also develop the region economically. On these grounds, it was argued the US position to extend its life should be supported.[104] Not even one year into its work UNRWA was broken. Instead of weaning refugees off aid through work and development, relief needed to be extended and the possibility for resettlement was fading. Even in Jordan, the viability of works projects was in doubt. In a meeting with Ely Palmer, the US Representative to the PCC and Sa'id Pasha al-Mufti, the Jordanian Prime Minister, Palmer said that technical studies had indicated that even after land reclamation and water had been secured, only 100,000 refugees could be resettled, leaving 500,000 dependent on foreign aid which would cease in June 1951.[105]

In September 1950, it was reported that the US, frustrated by UNRWA's slowness, was increasingly in favour of the UN handling relief, and the US (or for that matter anyone else) tackling work relief projects bilaterally with specific countries.[106] Britain responded that the previous

November it was the State Department which wanted UN involvement so as to avoid direct US responsibility for the refugees and to avoid ownership of the problem.

In a reversal of previously held positions, it was now London that doubted whether within the four months it would take to set up a mechanism for bilateral assistance that it would be any more successful in putting refugees to work, not to mention the problem that another organizational shift could cause further delays. Britain also argued that US financial contributions would still be essential for direct relief as relief works needed to be coordinated; it was better therefore to use one organization.[107]

Washington soon backtracked from this idea, and it was later reported that McGhee was considering a fund for South Asia and to a lesser extent for the Middle East, and that he had no intention of modifying the machinery of Palestinian relief.[108] Nevertheless, this debate resurfaced the following year. In April 1951, it was reported from Washington that the US was again interested in initiating a bilateral contribution to a resettlement scheme, and it was suggested by a British official in Washington that Britain could do the same in Jordan.[109] This was something about which Britain's legation in Jordan was enthusiastic, especially in terms of projects in the south of the country.[110] Knight, however, saw a danger in such state sponsorship. France might adopt Lebanon, the US Syria, and leave Britain with Jordan along with the responsibility of supporting its economy and the burden of feeding the 350,000 refugees which Jordan could not absorb.[111] It was therefore unsurprising that this idea was not pursued.

During the drafting process of the UNRWA report, the Foreign Office set out some 'basic facts'; few refugees would ever be able to return to their homes and the problem could therefore only be solved by settlement outside of Israel. This made the development of economic resources essential.[112] London further identified a growing tendency for Arab governments to recognize this fact, though they were resistant to admitting it in public, while many refugees were yet to recognize this, even in private. Therefore, UNRWA's objectives had to be the maintenance of the cooperative attitude of Arab leaders while also facilitating the provision of funds for the coming year. The PCC should state the aforementioned facts and UNRWA's report should not mention them so that Arab governments would continue to cooperate and work towards the provision of funds for the following year.[113]

Despite UNRWA's abysmal failure so early on in its existence, some in the State Department believed the body to be a success. For example, in a memorandum of conversation written on 13 September by Acting Secretary of State James Webb, it was noted that UNRWA had made 'considerable progress' citing the fact that the organization was now established in Beirut having passed its organizational stage and that its reception in the Middle East had been 'generally favourable', naming Jordan in particular.[114]

Following UNRWA's 1950 Report, Acheson wrote in a memorandum to the president that UNRWA's work had 'stimulated' thinking among Arab governments about the possibility of finding an economic solution to the refugee problem.[115] It was also added that the State Department considered the programme to be an important step towards solving the differences between Israel and the Arab states as it would look towards the removal of the refugee problem.[116] Blandford was apparently 'optimistic' about the possibility of linking compensation to resettlement,[117] which as Chapter 5 demonstrated, proved to be a false hope.

However, what Blandford importantly omitted in his analysis was the crucial caveat on resettlement which Arab states, apart from Jordan, gave to UNRWA (that the right of refugees to be repatriated should be maintained), and the fact that UNRWA was behind schedule and a long way from realizing the projects outlined in the ESM report. In fact, the term 'resettlement' was so loaded that, when compiling UNRWA's report, Britain recommended that the only reference to resettlement should be made to 'those who do not wish to return to their homes', a direct quote from Resolution 194.[118]

It was decided that a resolution in support of the UNRWA report be sponsored by Britain, the US, France, Turkey and Canada.[119] However, a significant failure was that it proved impossible to obtain financial commitments prior to action for the resolution to be adopted, meaning that the Ad Hoc Political Committee felt it needed to put forward the resolution without prior financial arrangements being agreed.[120] By 24 November, it was acknowledged that due to difficulties in obtaining financial support from other countries, the US might have to contribute a larger share than in the past, possibly between 50 and 60 per cent of the US$50 million recommended in the UNRWA report.[121] However, Truman was adamant that the US contribution should not be above 50 per cent.[122] It was only after an appeal for him to reconsider that Truman relented and allowed the US contribution to be raised to 60 per cent.[123]

On 2 December, UN Resolution 393 (V) was passed. It called for UNRWA to continue direct relief, estimating that, for the period 1 July 1951 to 30 June 1952, approximately US$20 million would be needed.

It stipulated that it would not prejudice paragraph 11 of General Assembly Resolution 194 (III) which pertained to the right of refugees to return to their homes in Israel, and that there should be reintegration of the refugees into the economic life of the Near East either by repatriation or resettlement. Therefore, UNRWA should establish a reintegration fund for projects requested by any government in the Near East and approved by the Agency for the permanent re-establishment of refugees followed by their removal from relief rations. It was now recommended that for the period 1 July 1951 to 30 June 1952, US$30 million should be contributed to the fund.[124]

UNRWA's declining fortunes

Despite new life being breathed into UNRWA through the adoption of UN Resolution 393 (V), the establishment of the reintegration fund and the determination of the US to make UNRWA work, UNRWA did not fare much better the following year. Its own Annual Report for 1951 illustrates the reality in sober, self-critical and unequivocal terms. Discussing works projects, the report stated that those already launched did 'not appreciably improve the absorptive capacity of the host countries' and did not 'directly benefit the refugees except by the payment of labourers' wages'. Also, employment in projects such as road building was only temporary and therefore could not meet the ESM's objectives of removing refugees from ration lists. Just as importantly, and indicative of the extent of UNRWA's failure, the report stated that, 'Sober appraisal must record that the works programme was costly to the Agency, as it cost five times more to keep a man at work than on relief.'[125] Meanwhile, UNRWA had to devote itself to public health and preventative medicine but, due to lack of funding, it struggled to meet the standards of the host nations' social welfare and educational projects. Indeed, UNRWA was becoming a welfare state within a number of states, and almost no refugees were employed on UNRWA works projects in any country by June 1951.[126]

In a February 1951 report by British official Sir Thomas Rapp who visited Beirut, it was acknowledged that UNRWA had yet to resettle a single refugee. While a reintegration plan was about to be born, it was still six months behind, and it had to be accepted by each country that they would also require survey work, adding a further delay before resettlement could occur.[127] One of the problems of reintegration was highlighted by the Jordanian Prime Minister Samir Pasha al-Rifa'i. Palestinian refugees in Jordan were now Jordanian citizens. This meant that it was difficult to ask Syria, a foreign country, to take in these refugees, a possible necessity because of Jordan's difficulties in reintegrating many of them. Furthermore, many refugees would not want to leave Jordan for Syria.[128]

UNRWA's finances were still in a state of chaos. While it was supposed to have around US$55 million for 1950–51, US$40 million was nearer to the actual figure. There were bad harvests and UN rules prevented the purchase of anything before there were funds to pay for it.[129] In one case, UNRWA needed 8,000 tons of Australian flour but did not have the means to pay for it, prompting one British official to hope that he could raise with Commonwealth prime ministers the issue of contributions to UNRWA at a forthcoming conference.[130] The US also announced that it was considering increasing its US$25 million pledge to Palestinian refugees.[131] Truman wrote to the US Appropriations Committee to request US$2 million for August and US$3 million for September, citing positive steps by the Arab League and the grave danger facing refugees due to a shortage of funds.[132] Soon the British Treasury agreed with a Foreign Office suggestion that Britain should raise its contribution to US$9 million, perhaps even US$10 million if the French and Canadians agreed to increase their contributions as well.[133]

Despite US financial support for UNRWA, which for the 1951–52 period was expected to be US$30 million, the US had become so concerned about anti-American sentiment in the Middle East that the previous year it had undertaken a programme intended to convince Arab states that its policy of impartiality was sincere.[134] In conversations with British officials, McGhee expressed his extreme disappointment that the refugee problem had still not been solved after two years and he was discouraged by UNRWA's inability to 'get ahead with the real job at hand' which raised the question of whether any UN body was capable of doing the job.[135] During this conversation, McGhee agreed with Knight that the refugee problem should be decentralized with the cooperation of Arab countries and with assurances to them, especially Syria, that help with resettlement would be provided until the problem was solved.[136]

The attitude of Arab states towards resettlement did not improve. Ibn Saud refused Britain's request to tell refugees that there was no hope of their returning to Palestine.[137] In Jordan, the government was determined to resettle the refugees; however, the country's resources prevented it from doing so.[138] Still, the Jordanian prime minister noted that resettlement projects in Jordan had not been implemented.[139] The Arab League also passed a resolution stating that it would release a memorandum which would call for a solution based on repatriation and compensation and demanded the increase of funds intended to alleviate the conditions of the refugees.[140] It was reported that UNRWA had not been promised proposals from Egypt about reintegration, and Syria was refusing to discuss reintegration without a formal written guarantee that finance for refugee reintegration would continue until all refugees had been dealt with.[141] Meanwhile, the Lebanese government was not impressed with the fixed US$30 million sum towards the establishment of the reintegration fund on the grounds that it was insufficient to deal with the needs of the refugees.[142] This point was repeated in Trygve Lie's visit to Beirut.[143]

In Egypt, Sinai was being explored for possible works projects. Gaza proved to be the most difficult place to find work for refugees as it did not have any considerable natural endowments.[144] However, in a sign of anti-British sensibilities, Chirine Bey expressed his suspicion that British experts in Sinai were really intelligence agents and therefore urged Blandford to recruit experts from smaller countries.[145] Even in Israel, the reintegration of refugees had still not been fully completed. In a visit in September 1951, Blandford responded to Sharett's request for reintegration assistance by arguing that Israel was receiving large-scale aid to reintegrate newcomers and should therefore deal with reintegrating its own refugees without calling on UN assistance.[146]

Finally, the Arab League agreed to cooperate with UNRWA's three-year reintegration programme on 24 October. There were conditions of course. Most notably that this would not prejudice the rights of the refugees, that the major financial burden should be on the UN and that full respect be paid to the sovereignty of the Arab states.[147] The expected cost of the three-year reintegration programme was predicted at US$200 million with an additional US$50 million for relief lasting until the end of June 1954.[148]

To make matters worse, UNRWA had to worry about a potential clash of jurisdictions with an organ of the PCC, the newly established Refugee Office. Instructed by Resolution 394 (V) to establish an office for the assessment of payments of compensation to the Palestinian refugees while safeguarding their rights, property and interests, the PCC established the Refugee Office in Beirut on 25 January 1951. Denmark's Holger Andersen was appointed Head of Office, but did not take up his duties until May.[149] Conflict of interest began to emerge between UNRWA and the PCC.

Based on 'unimpeachable sources', David P. Forsythe has argued that the conflict between the two UN bodies intensified after the Refugee

Office was established.[150] The State Department was obliged to explain its understanding of PCC and UNRWA jurisdictions. The PCC had responsibility for resettlement under Resolutions 194 (1948) and 394 (V) (1950); however, Resolution 393 (V) (1950) gave UNRWA sole responsibility for the new reintegration programme. While Acheson acknowledged that UNRWA may or may not have been the appropriate agency to assess claims of compensation *following* a political agreement, UNRWA could end up being the agency which would handle a large portion of compensation claims. The State Department was aware that the largest claims would come from wealthy refugees who were not dependent on UNRWA services and who might even object to UNRWA handling the compensation issue.[151]

Overall, during its first years of existence, UNRWA spectacularly failed to live up to its promise. It faced severe obstacles including a lack of funding and intransigence from Middle Eastern countries suspicious that the body sought to resettle refugees without a prior political agreement.

Conclusion

In theory, it was a good idea to establish an agency to facilitate the employment of Palestinian refugees through public works projects which would develop the economies and absorptive capacities of Arab states while also weaning refugees off rations. However, in practice, the idea was disastrous. The failure of UNRWA was not a result of lack of political will on the part of the US and Britain. Indeed, both countries recognized the political and economic consequences of UNRWA's failure. Even though Britain struggled to meet UNRWA's financial expectations, key officials were fully aware of the negative impact of this, and they pleaded their case to the Treasury. UNRWA's case was not helped by its slow start, especially as the number of destitute refugees increased by the tens of thousands on a yearly basis. It was unable to find long-term projects and it soon realized that even if some projects were followed through, many thousands of refugees would still not be resettled. However, the most important factor in UNRWA's failure was the lack of a political breakthrough which meant that the Arab states clung to their opposition to the resettlement of Palestinian refugees and were unwilling to give UNRWA their full cooperation. They suspected that if they were to cooperate fully, they would be faced with a de facto resettlement of refugees and would therefore lose a significant trump card in future negotiations.

Instead of phasing out relief and replacing it with work, by the end of 1950, UNRWA sought to continue relief together with a reintegration fund which itself would only be a programme directed towards the improvement of refugee living quarters and help in rehabilitation projects. This was a far cry from the regional transformation of the Middle East through the use of refugee labour envisaged by the ESM.

From this point onwards, UNRWA became a welfare organization, increasingly distanced from its original task which, although not openly stated, was the resettlement of Palestinian refugees. This was the disappointing result of three years of US, British and international peace efforts between 1948 and 1951. It has locked the Palestinian refugees and their descendants into a state of dependency which continues to exist to this very day.

Conclusion

In the period between 1948 and 1951 there was a concerted effort on the part of the international community, spearheaded by the US and Britain, to find a solution to the Palestinian refugee problem. Mutual self-interest drove the two powers to facilitate refugee relief efforts as well as a diplomatic solution. This necessity to launch such programmes led the two powers to overcome prior differences that had developed over the future of Palestine in the post-war period. President Truman supported Jewish immigration into Palestine as well as the partitioning of the country. Britain feared that such a policy would estrange the Arab states and was concerned about its own presence in Palestine where 100,000 British troops were stationed.

However, after the emergence of the Palestinian refugee problem which occurred during the 1948 Palestine War, both states recognized that the perpetuation of the refugee problem threatened the maintenance of Arab goodwill, and was potentially a source for Soviet encroachment into the region and Arab hostility towards the West. Quick to recognize the potential fallout, Britain and the US took decisive action. Overcoming differences in their respective drafts, they oversaw the successful passing of UN General Assembly Resolution 212. This was quite an achievement, as the resolution provided US$29.5 million plus an additional US$2.5 million for administrative expenses for a humanitarian aid programme. With a relief effort in place, Britain and the US could now turn their attention to the question of the future of the 700–800,000 refugees.

It was through the creation of a conciliation commission which was recommended by UN General Assembly Resolution 194 that the future of the refugee problem would be decided. It was here that a fundamental error was made and it marked the beginning of a network of

186

failures in Anglo-American diplomacy. The joint Anglo-American UN Resolution 194 was originally based on the efforts of the late mediator in his posthumous report of 16 September 1948.[1] Although during the drafting stage of the resolution many of the mediator's conclusions were dropped or rephrased, the one pertaining to refugees remained largely intact and called for the repatriation of refugees wishing to return to their homes as well as plans for resettlement, rehabilitation and compensation for those wishing not to do so.[2] This, despite Israel's rejection of the mediator's recommendations. Chapter 2 highlighted the fact that references to the refugee problem were scarcely debated when drafting Resolution 194, indicating that either Britain and the US had underestimated just how explosive the refugee question would be in future negotiations or that they were content with the resolution's wording. Regardless, this volume showed how this was a major stumbling block for future negotiations, and it undermined the work of the Conciliation Commission which faltered over the question of refugees. Thus, London and Washington's first error occurred even before talks had taken place; it lay in the very basis of the mediation and led to a chain of tactical blunders that would end in the failure of the diplomatic process.

In the first half of 1949, diplomatic efforts to solve the Arab–Israeli conflict got underway and were facilitated by the PCC chaired by representatives from the US, France and Turkey. Although Britain was not on the PCC, London played a major advisory role. The efforts of the PCC culminated in the Lausanne Conference which took place from April 1949. Previously, the PCC's efforts were fixed on getting the sides to agree to attend a joint conference. On 1 July, the Lausanne Conference took an 18-day recess. The conference had ground to a halt over the refugee question which proved to be the major issue that the PCC had to address. The Arab states demanded that Israel agree to refugee repatriation as stipulated by Resolution 194 even before discussions could begin. Israel refused on the basis of the security risk and insisted that this could only be made in the context of a final settlement. This deadlock would continue for the duration of the PCC's work. The reasons why the PCC failed to bridge this crucial difference between the sides were multiple. Neil Caplan, author of the excellent *Futile Diplomacy* series, has argued that the PCC was facing near insurmountable obstacles put up by the parties themselves and that criticism of the PCC's tactics of allowing the Arab states to negotiate as a bloc overlooks the possibility that the Arab states would have refused to participate at all.[3]

Indeed, to a certain degree the PCC's failure reflected the considerable distance between the sides over the future of the Palestinian refugees. However, this in itself is not an adequate explanation for the failure; successful conciliation and mediation by its very nature is supposed to bridge differences of intractable problems. As Chapter 3 illustrated, the PCC failed because of the lethal mixture of the distance between the parties and the tactics the PCC adopted. Supported by Washington, the PCC allowed the Arab states to negotiate as a bloc. This method was followed despite it receiving advice from British officials that such a tactic would have real disadvantages and if pressed, the Arab states would still participate. This fatal mistake, to allow the Arab states to negotiate as a bloc, was an important factor for the PCC's failure, during the period leading up to its recess in July 1949. However, when the Lausanne Conference resumed, lessons were not learned and the same strategy was adopted once again. Indeed, as Chapter 5 illustrated, despite London and Washington quickly realizing that the PCC was a despised and hated vehicle for mediation by the parties, they nevertheless continued using the PCC for negotiations for an additional two years. This led to a disastrous conference in Paris in 1951.

At the same time that the PCC was active in 1949, Britain and the US discussed the possibility of establishing a survey group which became the basis of the ESM. The premise behind the organization was that the majority of refugees would not be repatriated and instead would have to be resettled. This could be achieved by employing refugees to engage in public works projects which would not only resettle the refugees and make them self-dependent and off welfare rations, a costly enterprise for Britain and the US to maintain, but would also see the economic development of the region. Chapter 4 demonstrated that the US, concerned that if the ESM were openly to address political questions it would fail, wanted to focus purely on technical issues whereby the survey group would be an economic incentive for a political solution. This represents another failure on the part of Anglo-American diplomatic efforts; the assumption that an economic solution to the refugee problem could work as a means of overcoming the political deadlock. The problem with this position was represented by the British view that political issues needed to be addressed in order for the economic study to be feasible. However, in what was becoming a trend, the US view prevailed. The ESM was greeted with suspicion in Arab capitals and, ultimately, the ESM's Interim Report did not even mention the term 'resettlement', although the resettlement of Palestinian refugees was the main reason for its formation. But the report did pave the way for the establishment of a relief and works agency, UNRWA, another ill-fated body.

As Chapter 7 showed, the failure of UNRWA was not a result of lack of political will on the part of the US and Britain. Indeed, both countries recognized the political and economic consequences of UNRWA's failure. UNRWA suffered from an acute lack of finances. Its case was not helped by its slow start, especially as the number of destitute refugees increased in the tens of thousands on a yearly basis. Meanwhile, UNRWA was unable to find long-term projects and also realized that even if some projects were followed through, many thousands of refugees would still not be resettled.

However, the most important factor in UNRWA's failure was the lack of a political breakthrough, which meant that the Arab states clung to their position against the resettlement of Palestinian refugees and were unwilling to give UNRWA their full cooperation. They suspected that if they were to cooperate fully, they would be faced with a de facto resettlement of refugees and therefore lose a significant trump card in future negotiations. Instead of phasing out relief and replacing it with work, by the end of 1950, UNRWA sought to continue relief together with a reintegration fund which itself would only be a programme directed to the improvement of refugee living quarters and help in rehabilitation projects. This was a far cry from the British and US vision of regional transformation through the use of refugee labour. UNRWA became a welfare state within a number of sovereign states, unable to fulfil its original but unstated task of resettling Palestinian refugees.

Chapter 5 explained that by the end of 1949, some British and US officials were calling for the dissolution of the PCC, but policy makers in London and Washington did not heed these calls. By 1950, the PCC had not only been unable to facilitate negotiations between Israel and the Arab states over the refugee impasse, but it was now an impotent and despised body. Therefore, its work on the compensation question between 1950 and 1951, correctly identified as a potential avenue to regain momentum in discussions of the Palestinian refugee problem, did little to bring the sides closer together. Although Britain and the US made significant progress in understanding the complexity and dynamics of how compensation might work, political deadlock meant that it could not come to fruition. The PCC's final diplomatic push was the badly conceived Paris Conference of 1951 where the gap between the sides widened, as they could not even agree to the conference's opening preamble let alone any substantive issues. The problem with the British and the US decision to continue the work of the PCC is that third-party mediation requires the trust, confidence and respect of the participants. The PCC could claim none of these.

It therefore begs the question as to why London and Washington persisted in using the PCC. As a UN body, negotiations through the PCC allowed the US and Britain to encourage, mediate and facilitate peace talks without having to assume responsibility and ownership of the problem or possible ill feelings that might result from failure. They were also tempted by the opportunity to find one all-inclusive, mutually agreed settlement between the parties, rather than separate agreements between Israel and one or more Arab states. The US and Britain encouraged direct talks but resisted involvement for the afore-mentioned reasons, preferring these talks to be a means of overcoming the PCC stalemate rather than a solution in themselves.

What makes this failure tragic is that, as Chapter 6 highlighted, the Palestinian refugee problem was less of an obstacle in direct discussions and overtures between Israel and her Arab neighbours than is widely assumed. Husni Zaim of Syria was willing to resettle hundreds and thousands of refugees. King Abdullah of Jordan paid little attention to the refugee problem, giving priority to the territorial question and a peace settlement and showed willingness to resettle refugees in his kingdom. Even in overtures to talks between Israel and Egypt, the refugee question appeared to be less of a factor. Perhaps with effective third-party involvement, the bilateral talks may have progressed. Instead, they constituted an underexplored possibility. The tragedy of Anglo-American diplomacy was that in the years in question, there was a real opportunity for solving the Palestinian refugee problem. Yet, to this very day, it remains unsolved and continues to be a major obstacle to a comprehensive Arab–Israeli peace.

Notes

Introduction: The Palestinian Refugee Problem as an Impediment to Peace

1. Progress Report of the United Nations Mediator on Palestine, Submitted to the Secretary-General for Transmission to the Members of the United Nations, General Assembly Official Records: Third Session Supplement No. 11, 16 September 1948, A/648.
2. United Nations General Assembly, 194 (III). Palestine: Progress Report of the United Nations Mediator, 11 December 1948, A/RES/194 (III).
3. M. Shertok to A. Eban, 15 July 1948, Tel.MH710, Yehoshua Freundlich (ed), *Documents on the Foreign Policy of Israel* (hereafter *DFPI*), Vol. 1, 14 May–30 September 1948 (Jerusalem: Israel State Archives, 1982), p. 334.
4. Progress Report of the United Nations Mediator on Palestine, 16 September 1948, A/648; M. Shertok to Count Bernadotte (Tel Aviv), 1 August 1949, 93.03/94/11, *DFPI*, Vol. 1, pp. 441–4.
5. Ahmed Shukairy, 'The Palestinian Refugees', Excerpts from a Speech at the United Nations, 1958, in Walter Laqueur and Barry Rubin (eds), *The Arab–Israeli Reader: A Documentary History of the Middle East Conflict* (New York: Penguin, 1995), pp. 119–21.
6. Abba Eban, 'The Refugee Problem', Excerpts from a Speech, 17 November 1958, in Laqueur and Rubin (eds), *The Arab–Israeli Reader* (New York: Penguin, 1995), p. 138.
7. Article V: Transitional Period and Permanent Status Negotiations, Israel–PLO Declaration of Principles on Interim Self-Government Arrangements, 13 September 1993, in Laqueur and Rubin (eds), *The Arab–Israeli Reader*, pp. 599–601.
8. The proceedings and offers made at the Camp David Summit of 2000 have been much disputed by participants and scholars alike, especially over the question of Israel's offer to the Palestinian Authority. For firsthand accounts see, for example, Dennis Ross, *The Missing Peace: The Inside Story of the Fight for Middle East Peace* (New York: Farrer, 2005); Bill Clinton, *My Life: The Presidential Years* (New York: Doubleday, 2004); Madeleine Albright, *Madame Secretary* (New York: Hyperion, 2003); Mahmoud Abbas, 'Reports of the Camp David Summit, 9 September 2000', Excerpts Published in *The Journal of Palestine Studies*, Vol. XXX, No. 2 (Winter 2001), pp. 168–70; Gilead Sher, *The Israeli–Palestinian Peace Negotiations, 1999–2001* (London: Routledge, 2006); For the academic debate on the subject see, Jeremy Pressman, 'Visions in Collision – What Happened at Camp David and Taba', *International Security*, Vol. 28, No. 2 (Fall 2003), pp. 5–43; Shimon Shamir and Bruce Maddy-Weitzman (eds), *The Camp David Summit–What Went Wrong? Americans, Israelis, and Palestinians Analyze the Failure of the Boldest Attempt Ever to Resolve the Palestinian–Israeli Conflict* (Brighton: Sussex Academic Press, 2005); Robert Malley and Hussein Agha, 'Camp David: The

Tragedy of Errors', *New York Review of Books*, Vol. 48, No. 13, 9 August 2001; Benny Morris, 'Camp David and After: An Exchange 1. An Interview with Ehud Barak', *New York Review of Books*, Vol. 49, No. 11, 13 June 2002; Ahron Bregman, *Elusive Peace: How the Holy Land Defeated America* (New York: Penguin, 2005); Aaron David Miller, *Much Too Promised Land: America's Elusive Search for Arab–Israeli Peace* (New York: Random House, 2005); Itamar Rabinovich, *Waging Peace: Israel and the Arabs, 1948–2003* (Princeton: Princeton University Press, 2004).

9. Ross, *The Missing Peace*, pp. 719–20.
10. Ibid., pp. 720–5.
11. Legal Unit, Negotiations Support Unit to Dr Mahmoud Abbas, 2 January 2001, AlJazeera Transparency Unit, *The Palestine Papers*, http://www.ajtransparency.com/en/projects/thepalestinepapers/20121821232131550.html (Last visited 08 July 2012).
12. Text: Beirut Declaration, *BBC.co.uk*, 28 March, 2002, http://news.bbc.co.uk/1/hi/world/monitoring/media_reports/1899395.stm (Last visited 08 July 2012).
13. Ibid.
14. 'Israel to offer counterproposal to Arab peace initiative, Peres says', *USA Today*, 20 May 2007, http://www.usatoday.com/news/world/2007-05-20-mideast_N.htm (Last visited 08 July 2012).
15. Ruth Lapidoth, 'Israel and the Palestinians: Some Legal Issues', The Jerusalem Institute of Israel Studies, *The JUS Studies Series No. 94* (2003), pp. 48–9.
16. 'Jewish State Call Alarms Mideast Press', *BBC.com*, 15 November 2007, http://news.bbc.co.uk/1/hi/world/middle_east/7096108.stm (Last visited 19 February 2013).
17. NSU to Palestinian Drafting team, 'The Precondition of Recognizing Israel as a "Jewish State"', 13 November 2007, AlJazeera Transparency Unit, *The Palestine Papers*, http://www.ajtransparency.com/en/projects/thepalestinepapers/20121823145359921.html (Last visited 08 July 2012).
18. Colin Shindler, 'Can Israel Really Call Itself a "Jewish State"?' *The JC*, 11 October 2012.
19. Saeb Erekat, 'The Returning Issue of Palestine's Refugees', *The Guardian*, 10 December 2010, http://www.guardian.co.uk/commentisfree/2010/dec/10/israel-palestine-refugee-rights (Last visited 08 July 2012).
20. 'Abbas Calls for Return of Palestinian Refugees', *Jerusalem Post*, 23 September 2011.
21. Nur Masalha, *Expulsion of the Palestinians: The Concept of 'Transfer' in Zionist Political Thought, 1882–1948* (Washington, DC: Institute for Palestine Studies, 1992); David Hirst, *The Gun and the Olive Branch* (London: Faber and Faber, 2003); Walid Khalidi, *From Haven to Conquest: Zionism and the Palestinian Problem Until 1948* (Beirut: Institute for Palestine Studies, 1971); Ilan Pappé, *The Ethnic Cleansing of Palestine* (London: Oneworld Publications, 2007).
22. Masalha, *Expulsion of the Palestinians*.
23. Hirst, *The Gun and the Olive Branch*, pp. 253–4.
24. Benny Morris, *The Birth of the Palestinian Refugee Problem Revisited* (Cambridge: Cambridge University Press, 2004), p. 165.
25. Masalha, *Expulsion of the Palestinians*, pp. 177–9.

26. Morris, *The Birth Revisited*, pp. 164–5; This is slightly in contrast to Morris' earlier study in which he called Plan D 'a strategic-ideological anchor', Benny Morris, *The Birth of the Palestinian Refugee Problem* (Cambridge: Cambridge University Press, 1987) p. 63.

27. Avi Shlaim, *The Iron Wall: Israel and the Arab World* (London: Penguin, 2001), p. 31.

28. Ibid.

29. Yoav Gelber, *Palestine 1948: War, Escape and the Emergence of the Palestine Refugee Problem* (Brighton: Sussex Academic Press, 2001), p. 98.

30. Nadav Safran, *From War to War: The Arab–Israeli Confrontation, 1948–1967* (New York: Pegasus, 1969), pp. 34–5.

31. Joseph B. Schechtman, *The Arab Refugee Problem* (New York: Philosophical Library, 1952), p. 3.

32. Ibid., pp. 55–7.

33. Jon and David Kimche, *Both Sides of the Hill* (London: Secker & Warburg, 1960), p. 124.

34. Morris, *The Birth*, pp. 84–5.

35. Ibid., p. 67.

36. Erskine Childers, 'The Other Exodus', *The Spectator*, 12 May 1961, pp. 8–11.

37. Walid Khalidi, 'Why Did the Palestinians Leave Revisited', *Journal of Palestine Studies* Vol. XXXIV, No. 2 (Winter 2005), pp. 43–8.

38. Morris, *The Birth*, p. 290.

39. Deir Yassin was a village that was attacked by Zionist underground forces on 9 April 1948 in which over 100 residents were killed (the original figure quoted and taken up by the Arab media was 254 dead) including women and children with incidents of reported rape and looting. For scholarly accounts see, Gelber, *Palestine 1948*, pp. 307–18; Uri Milstein, *History of the War of Independence Vol. 4: Out of Crisis Came Decision* (New York: University Press of America, 1996); Walid Khalidi, *All That Remains: The Palestinian Villages Occupied and Depopulated by Israel in 1948* (Beirut: Institute for Palestine Studies, 1992); Khalidi, *From Haven to Conquest; Benny Morris, 'The Historiography of Deir Yassin'*, *Journal of Israeli History*, Vol. 24, No. 1, 2005, pp. 79–107.

40. Dan Kurzman, *Genesis 1948: The First Arab–Israeli War* (New York: Signet, 1972), p. 183.

41. Arthur Koestler, *Promise and Fulfilment: Palestine 1917–1949* (London: Macmillan, 1949), p. 160.

42. Aharon Cohen, *Israel and the Arab World* (London: W.H. Allen, 1970), pp. 458–60.

43. Ibid., pp. 460–2.

44. William R. Polk, David M. Stamler, and Edmund Asfour, *Backdrop to Tragedy: The Struggle for Palestine* (Boston: Beacon Press, 1957), p. 290.

45. Ibid., pp. 292–4.

46. Morris, *The Birth*, pp. 114–5.

47. Nafez Nazzal, *The Palestinian Exodus from Galilee 1948* (Beirut: The Institute for Palestine Studies, 1978), pp. 102–9.

48. Morris, *The Birth*, p. 123.

49. Rony E. Gabbay, *A Political Study of the Arab–Jewish Conflict* (Geneve: Librairie E. Droz, 1959), pp. 83–4.

50. Hirst, *The Gun and the Olive Branch*, p. 264.
51. Morris, *The Birth*, pp. 287–8.
52. Shabtai Teveth, 'The Palestine Arab Refugee Problem and Its Origins: Review Article', *Middle Eastern Studies*, Vol. 26, No. 2, (April 1990), p. 214–9.
53. Efraim Karsh, 1948, 'Israel and the Palestinians: Annotated Text', *Commentary*, May 2008, http://www.commentarymagazine.com/viewarticle.cfm/1948--israel--and-the-palestinians--annotated-text-11373?search=1 (Last visited 31 October 2008).
54. Ibid.
55. Morris, *The Birth*.
56. Gabbay, *A Political Study of the Arab–Jewish Conflict*, p. 54; Schechtman, *The Arab Refugee Problem*, p. 3.
57. Teveth, 'The Palestine Arab Refugee Problem and Its Origins', pp. 219–20; Also see Shabtai Teveth, 'Charging Israel with Original Sin', *Commentary*, Vol. 88, No. 3, (September 1989), pp. 28–30.
58. Avi Shlaim, 'The Debate About 1948', *International Journal of Middle East Studies*, Vol. 27, No. 3, (1995), p. 288.
59. Avi Shlaim, *Collusion across the Jordan: King Abdullah, the Zionist Movement, and the Partition of Palestine* (Oxford: Clarendon Press, 1988).
60. Ilan Pappe, *Britain and the Arab–Israeli Conflict, 1948–51* (Basingstoke: MacMillan, 1988).
61. Benny Morris, 'Politics by Other Means', *The New Republic*, 22 March 2004.
62. Efraim Karsh, 'Rewriting Israel's History', *Middle East Quarterly*, Vol. 3, No. 2, (June 1996), pp. 23–6; 'Falsifying the Record: Benny Morris, David Ben-Gurion, and the "transfer" idea', *Israel Affairs*, Vol. 4, No. 2 (1997), pp. 47–71; Efraim Karsh, *Fabricating Israeli History: The 'New Historians'* (London: Frank Cass, 2000), pp. 37–68.
63. Morris, *The Birth Revisited*, pp. 4–5.
64. Nur Masalha, 'A Critique of Benny Morris', *Journal of Palestine Studies*, Vol. 21, No. 1(1991).
65. Anita Shapira, *Land and Power: The Zionist Resort to Force, 1881–1948* (New York: Oxford University Press, 1992), pp. 285–6; Shabtai Teveth, 'The Evolution of "Transfer"' in *Zionist Thinking, Occasional Papers*, Vol. 107. Moshe Dayan Center for Middle Eastern and African Studies, Shiloah Institute, Tel Aviv University, 1989.
66. Morris, *The Birth Revisited*, pp. 5–6, 39–65.
67. Issa Khalaf, *Politics in Palestine* (Albany: State University of New York Press, 1991), p. 202.
68. Ibid., p. 205.
69. Fortnightly Intelligence Newsletter No. 60, issued by HQ British Troops in Palestine and Transjordan for the period 1–14 March 1947, 17 March 1947, National Archives (hereafter NA) War Office (hereafter WO) 275/64.
70. 3.7 Airborne Field Security Section: Report No. 20 for the Week Ending 18 March 1947, NA, WO 275/79; Part 1: Middle East Affairs, No. 102 (Based on Information Received up to 2,000 hours 12 March 1947), 14 March 1947, NA, WO 275/120.
71. Fortnightly Intelligence Newsletter No. 53, issued by HQ British Troops in Palestine and Transjordan for the period 11–24 October 1947, 24 October

1947, NA, WO 275/64; CID Headquarters, Jerusalem (Catling) to Chief Secretary, 11 October 1947, NA Colonial Office (hereafter CO) 537/3956.
72. 3.7 Airborne Field Security Section: Report 19 for the Week Ending 11 March 1947, NA, WO 275/79.
73. Fortnightly Intelligence Newsletter No. 55, issued by HQ British Troops in Palestine and Transjordan for the period 8–21 November 1947, 22 November 1947, NA, WO 275/64.
74. W.A.C. Mathieson, London to J. E. Cable, 3 December 1947, NA, CO 537/3956.
75. Fortnightly Intelligence Newsletter No. 58, issued by HQ British Troops in Palestine and Transjordan for the period 18 December 1947–1 January1948, 1 January 1948, NA, WO 275/64.
76. Amman (Kirkbride) to Foreign Office, 15 January 1948, NA, Foreign Office (hereafter FO) 37168365 E720/G; H.M. Minister, Amman to Secretary of State, London, 25 April 1948, NA, FO 816/118.
77. Report, Amman January 28, 1948 in British Legation (Amman) to Eastern Department, Foreign Office, 30 January 1948, NA, FO 816/116 S/1014/48.
78. Mr Broadmead (Damascus) to Foreign Office, 16 January 1948, NA, FO 371/68365 E706.
79. Fortnightly Intelligence Newsletter No. 60, issued by HQ British Troops in Palestine for the period 2,359 hrs 14 January – 2,359 hrs 28 January 1948, 30 January 1948, NA, WO 261/573; NA, WO 275/64; the Nashishibis were a prominent Palestinian Arab family and rivals of the Husseinis who dominated the leadership of Arab institutions in Palestine.
80. High Commissioner for Palestine to Secretary of State, My Telegram No. 174: Weekly Intelligence Appreciation, 1 February 1948, NA, FO 816/116.
81. H.H. Minister, Amman to Secretary of State, London, 16 April 1948, NA, FO 816/117.
82. Jerusalem High Commission to Amman, 1 May 1948, NA, FO 816/118 S/1074/48 2/5748 18.40.
83. Secretary of State, London to H.M. Minister, Amman, 28 April 1948, NA, FO 816/118.
84. Fortnightly Intelligence Newsletter No. 67, issued by HQ British Troops in Palestine for the period 2359 hrs 19 April – 2359 hrs 3 May 1948, 6 May 1948, NA, WO 275/64.
85. Council General Marriott (Haifa) to Foreign Office, 16 April 1948, NA, FO 37168505 E6429.
86. From C in C MELF to War Office, 11 May 1948, NA, CO 357/3867.
87. Ibid., 3 May 1948, NA, CO 357/3867.
88. Ibid., 4 May 1948, NA, CO 357/3867.
89. General Sir A. Cunningham (Palestine) to Secretary of State for the Colonies, 8 May 1948, NA, CO 537/3869.
90. Ibid.
91. From C in C MELF to War Office, 7 May 1948, NA, CO 357/3867.
92. General Sir A. Cunningham (Palestine) to Secretary of State for the Colonies, 1 May 1948, FO, CO 537/3869.
93. Morris, *The Birth*, pp. 287–8.

94. United Nations Conciliation Commission for Palestine: Final Report of the United Nations Economic Survey Mission for the Middle East, (hereafter UNCCP: ESM Final Report), 28 December 1949, A/AC.25.6.
95. S.G. Thicknesse, *Arab Refugees: A Survey of Resettlement Possibilities* (London: Royal Institute of International Affairs, 1949), p. 6.
96. General Progress Report and Supplementary Report of the United Nations Conciliation Commission for Palestine, Covering the period from 11 December 1949 to 23 October 1950 (hereafter UNPCC Eighth Progress Report), 23 October 1950, A/1367/Rev.1.
97. *New York Times*, 5 August 1949.
98. 'Palestine Arab Refugees' 11 August 1949, enclosed in Sir D. Norton (Treasury) to Mr Sheringham (Foreign Office) 12 August 1949, NA, FO 371/75436 E9984.
99. United Kingdom Delegation to the United Nations, New York, to Foreign Office, 12 August 1949, NA, FO 371/75436 E10083.
100. Foreign Office to United Kingdom Delegation, New York, 2 September 1949, NA, FO 371/75436 E10083.
101. Palestine Refugees: Policy Paper Prepared in the Department of State, Washington, 14 March 1949, *Foreign Relations of the United States (hereafter FRUS)*, pp. 828–9.
102. Palestinian Refugee Problem: Conclusions annex 1 to Memorandum by the Coordinator on Palestine Refugee Matters (McGhee) to the Secretary of State, Washington, 22 April 1949, *FRUS*, 1949, Vol. VI, pp. 934–5; Memorandum of Conversation, Prepared Presumably by the First Secretary of Embassy in the United Kingdom (Jones), London, 13 April 1949, *FRUS*, 1949, Vol. VI, p. 906.

1 The Palestine Factor in Anglo-American Post-War Middle Eastern Policy, 1945–48

1. Palestine (Government Policy), *Hansard*, HC Deb, 25 February 1947, Vol. 433, cc1901–2007.
2. Ibid.; *New York Times*, 27 February 1947; *New York Times*, 26 February 1947.
3. *The Times*, 15 February 1947.
4. Ibid., 24 April 1947.
5. Ibid., 27 December 1946.
6. Alan Bullock, *Ernest Bevin: Foreign Secretary, 1945–1951* (London: Heineman, 1983), p. 164.
7. *Palestine Post*, 14 December 1944; Hugh Dalton, *The Fateful Years: Memoirs, 1931–1945* (London: Frederick Muller, 1957), pp. 425–7.
8. Richard Crossman, *A Nation Reborn: The Israel of Weizmann, Bevin and Ben-Gurion* (London: Hamish Hamilton, 1960), p. 69.
9. Bullock, *Ernest Bevin*, pp. 166–9.
10. Ibid., pp. 181–2; Crossman, *A Nation Reborn*, p. 69; Walter Laqueur, *The History of Zionism* (New York: Tauris Parke, 2003), p. 565.
11. Appendix: Joint Memorandum by the Secretary of State for Foreign Affairs and the Secretary of State for the Colonies, 6 February 1947, NA, Cabinet (hereafter CAB) 129/16 C.P. (47) 49.
12. Ibid.

13. Conclusions of a Meeting of the Cabinet held in the Prime Minister's Room, House of Commons, SW1, 7 February 1947, pp. 118–20, NA, CAB 128/9 C.M. (47), Cabinet 18 (47); 'Alan Cunningham, Palestine-The Last Days of the Mandate', *International Affairs*, Vol. 24, No. 4 (October 1948), p. 485.

14. See for example, Martin Jones, *Failure in Palestine: British and the United States Policy after the Second World War* (London: Mansell, 1986); Youssef Chaitani, *Dissension among Allies: Ernest Bevin's Palestine Policy between Whitehall and the White House, 1945–1947* (London: Saqi, 2002); Miriam Joyce Haron, *Anglo-American Relations and the Question of Palestine, 1945–47* (New York: Fordham University, 1979); Ritchie Ovendale, *Britain, The United States, and the End of the Palestine Mandate, 1942–1948* (London: Royal Historical Society, 1989); Amikam Nachmani, *Great Power Discord in Palestine: The Anglo-American Committee of Inquiry into the Problem of European Jewry and Palestine, 1945–46* (London: Frank Cass, 1987).

15. There have been several studies written on President Truman's Palestine policy and his support for Jewish displaced persons to enter the country. See for example, Michael J. Cohen, *Truman and Israel* (Berkely: University of California Press, 1990), pp. 109–22; Donald Neff, *Fallen Pillars: U.S. Policy Towards Palestine and Israel since 1945* (Washington, DC: Institute For Palestine Studies, 2002), pp. 25–54; Allis Radosh and Ronald Radosh, *A Safe Haven: Harry S. Truman and the Founding of Israel* (New York: Harper, 2009); Evan M. Wilson, *Decision on Palestine: How the U.S. Came to Recognize Israel* (Stanford: Stanford University Press, 1979), pp. 57–68.

16. Michael J. Cohen, *Fighting World War Three from the Middle East: Allied Contingency Plans, 1945–54* (London: Frank Cass, 1997), pp. 70–4; Also see Nicholas Owen, 'Britain and Decolonialisation: The Labour Governments and the Middle East, 1945–51', in Michael J. Cohen and Martin Kolinsky (eds), *Demise of the British Empire in the Middle East* (London: Frank Cass), p. 5.

17. John Kent, *British Imperial Strategy and the Origins of the Cold War 1944–49* (Leicester: Leicester University Press, 1993), p. 79.

18. Cohen, *Fighting World War Three from the Middle East*, p. 74.

19. Ibid., pp. 77–8.

20. Chiefs of Staff Committee, Palestine – Implications of Withdrawal: Report by the Chiefs of Staff, 27 October 1947, NA, CAB 134/526 repeated from DEFE 5/6/223; For further information on the strategic importance of Palestine in British defence planning, see Chiefs of Staff Committee, Palestine: Military Implications of Withdrawal: Report by the Joint Planning Staff, 20 October 1947, NA, DEFE 6/4/135; Annex 1: Palestine: Military Implications of Withdrawal; Annex: Palestine – Strategic Requirements, Draft Report by the Chiefs of Staff, Chiefs of Staff Committee, Palestine – Strategic Requirements: Report by the Chiefs of Staff, 5 January 1947, NA, DEFE 6/1/1.

21. Cohen, *Fighting World War Three from the Middle East*, p. 63; Also see Chaitani, *Dissension Among Allies*, p. 20.

22. W.M. Roger Louis, *The British Empire in the Middle East* (Oxford: Clarendon, 1984), p. 106.

23. Owen, 'Britain and Decolonialisation: The Labour Governments and the Middle East', pp. 5–6.

24. Cohen, *Fighting World War Three from the Middle East*, pp. 63–4.
25. David R. Devereux, *The Formulation of British Defence Policy Towards the Middle East, 1948–56* (London: MacMillan, 1990), p. 57.
26. Memorandum by the Chief of the Division of Near East Affairs (Merriam), Washington, 4 January 1946, *FRUS*, 1946, *The Near East and Africa*, Vol. VII, pp. 6–7.
27. Palestine, CM 18 (47), 7 February 1947, NA, CAB 195/5; Conclusions of a Meeting of the Cabinet Held at 10 Downing Street: Cabinet 22 (47), 14 February 1947, NA, CAB 128/9.
28. 6th Conclusions, Minute 3: Confidential Annex, CM (47), 15 January 1947, NA, CAB 128/11.
29. Ovendale, *Britain, The United States*, pp. 11–12.
30. UK Delegation (New York) to Foreign Office, 6 November 1947, NA, FO 371/61887 E10431.
31. For literature on the Grand Mufti's pro-Nazi activities see, Klaus Gensicke, *The Mufti of Jerusalem and the Nazis: The Berlin Years* (London: Vallentine Mitchell, 2011); Moshe Pearlman, *Mufti of Jerusalem: The Story of Haj Amin el Husseini* (London: Victor Gollancz, 1947); Zvi Elpeleg, *The Grand Mufti: Haj Amin al-Hussaini, Founder of the Palestinian National Movement* (London: Frank Cass, 1993); Philip Mattar, *The Mufti of Jerusalem: Al-Hajj Amin al-Husayni and the Palestinian National Movement* (New York: Columbia University Press, 1988).
32. Owen, 'Britain and Decolonialisation: The Labour Governments and the Middle East, 1946–51' , pp. 154–5.
33. John Kent, 'Britain and the Egyptian Problem, 1945–48', in Cohen and Kolinsky (eds), *Demise of the British Empire*, p. 154.
34. For example, Efraim Karsh, *Palestine Betrayed* (New Haven: Yale University Press, 2010), p. 84; Roger Lewis, *The British Empire in the Middle East*, (Oxford: Clarendon, 1984), p. 467; Howard M. Sachar, *Europe Leaves the Middle East, 1936–1954* (New York: Alfred A. Knopf, 1972), pp. 486–7.
35. *Manchester Guardian*, 16 January 1946.
36. Jones, *Failure in Palestine*, p. 186.
37. Memorandum of Conversation, by the Acting Secretary of State, 22 November 1946, *FRUS*, 1946, Vol. VII, pp. 723–4.
38. Norman Rose, *'A Senseless, Squalid War' Voices from Palestine, 1945–1948* (London: The Bodley Head, 2009), p. 140.
39. Jerusalem (Cunningham) to Colonial Office, 16 February 1947, NA, CO 537/2333.
40. Michael J. Cohen, *Palestine to Israel: From Mandate to Independence* (London: Frank Cass, 1988), pp. 231–2.
41. Ibid.
42. Nicholas Bethell, *The Palestine Triangle: The Struggle between the British, the Jews and the Arabs, 1935–48* (London: Futura, 1980), pp. 288–9.
43. For an analysis of the history, ideology and anti-British activities of the Zionist underground see, Joseph Heller, *The Stern Gang: Ideology, Politics, and Terror, 1940–1949* (London: Frank Cass, 1994); John Bowyer Bell, *Terror Out of Zion: Irgun Zvai Leumi, LEHI, and the Palestine Underground, 1929–1949* (New York: St. Martin's Press, 1977).

44. Elizabeth Monroe, *Britain's Moment in the Middle East* (London: Chatto & Windus, 1981), pp. 165–6; Wm Roger Louis, 'British Imperialism and the End of the Palestine Mandate', in Wm Roger Louis and Robert W. Stookey (eds), *The End of the Palestine Mandate* (London: I.B. Tauris, 1986), p. 10.
45. Monroe, *Britain's Moment in the Middle East*, p. 166.
46. In Greece, civil war had been waged intermittently since liberation in 1944. Britain was facing a fuel crisis which was putting a strain on the country's export programme. This was at a time when the American loan was approaching exhaustion. However, it was not just Britain's financial burdens which precipitated her withdrawal from the region. Bevin did not believe that Greece was a sound investment of economic resources because he had little faith that Greece would invest in reconstruction programmes to isolate the communists. Further, the continued presence of British forces could confront insurrections similar to those in Palestine. See Robert Frazier, 'Did Britain Start the Cold War? Bevin and the Truman Doctrine', *The Historical Journal*, Vol. 27, No. 3 (1984), p. 715; Lewis, *The British Empire in the Middle East*, pp. 95–6.
47. Bruce Robellet Kuniholm, *The Origins of the Cold War in the Near East* (Princeton: Princeton University Press, 1980), p. 406; Monroe, *Britain's Moment in the Middle East*, p. 158.
48. Rose, *A Senseless, Squalid War*, p. 141.
49. Kent, *British Imperial Strategy*, p. 134; Cohen, *Palestine to Israel*, p. 235.
50. Cohen, *Fighting World War Three from the Middle East*, p. 2; Dean Acheson, *Present at Creation: My Years in the State Department* (London: Hamish Hamilton, 1969), p. 195.
51. Edward F. Willett, 'Report, Dialectical Materialism and Russian Objectives', 14 January 1946, pp. 30, 41–2, President's Secretary's File, Truman Papers, Truman Presidential Library and Archive, Online Documents available at www.trumanlibrary.org (hereafter TPLA).
52. Memorandum, 'Analysis of Stalin's Address to Moscow Constituency', February 1946. Harry S. Truman Administration File, Elsey Papers, TPLA.
53. Telegram, George Kennan to George Marshall, 12 February 1946, Harry S. Truman Administration File, Elsey Papers, Truman Library, TPLA; A later memorandum in March put Soviet policy down to both Marxism and its Tsarist past. See Memorandum, 'Background of Soviet Foreign Policy', 14 March 1946. Harry S. Truman Administration File, Elsey Papers, TPLA.
54. Telegram, George Kennan to George Marshall ['Long Telegram'], 22 February 1946. Harry S. Truman Administration File, Elsey Papers, TPLA.
55. X, 'The Sources of Soviet Conduct', *Foreign Affairs*, Vol. 24. No. 4 (July 1947); in later years, Kennan has maintained that in writing the X telegram his vision of containment was a limited one and specifically concerned Greece; Turkey was not facing an internal communist threat, see George Kennan, *Memoirs 1925–1950* (New York: Pantheon Books, 1967), pp. 316–7.
56. 'Memorandum: Soviet Foreign Policy in the Middle East', April 1946, Harry S. Truman Administration File, Elsey Papers, TPLA.
57. Acheson, *Present at Creation*, p. 195.
58. Report, 'American Relations With The Soviet Union' by Clark Clifford ['Clifford-Elsey Report'], 24 September 1946. Conway Files, Truman Papers, TPLA; Gaddis, *The Long Peace*, p. 33; Daniel Yergin, *Shattered Peace: The*

Origins of the Cold War and the National Security State (Boston: Houghton Mifflin Company, 1977), pp. 241–5; Campbell Craig and Fredrik Logevall, *America's Cold War: The Politics of Insecurity* (Cambridge: Harvard University Press, 2009), p. 77.

59. Yergin, *Shattered Peace*, p. 245.
60. Cohen, *Fighting World War Three from the Middle East*, p. 2.
61. Barry Rubin, *The Great Powers in the Middle East 1941–1947: The Road to the Cold War* (London: Frank Cass, 1980), p. 6.
62. Memo, Joint Chiefs of Staff to Harry S. Truman, 26 July 1946, Subject File, Clifford Papers, TPLA.
63. Ronald E. Powaski, *The Cold War: The United States and the Soviet Union, 1917–1991* (Oxford: Oxford University Press, 1997), p. 70.
64. Walter Lafeber, *America, Russia and the Cold War* (New York: John Wiley and Sons, 1967), pp. 36–7; Richard Crockatt, *The Fifty Years War: The United States and the Soviet Union in World Politics, 1941–1991* (London: Routledge, 1995), p. 73.
65. Lafeber, *America, Russia and the Cold War*, p. 37.
66. Ibid., p. 52.
67. Robert Frazier, *Anglo-American Relations with Greece: The Coming of the Cold War* (Baskingstoke: Macmillan, 1991), pp. 715–6.
68. Rubin, *The Great Powers in the Middle East*, pp. 4–5.
69. Lafeber, *America, Russia and the Cold War*, p. 53.
70. Oral History Interview with Clark M. Clifford, Washington, DC, 19 April 1971, by Jerry N. Hess, p. 143, http://www.trumanlibrary.org/oralhist/cliford3.htm#142 (Last visited 15 April 2011).
71. Stephen E. Ambrose and Douglas G. Brinkley, *Rise to Globalism: American Foreign Policy since 1938* (New York: Penguin, 1997), p. 79.
72. Address of the President to Congress, Recommending Assistance to Greece and Turkey, 12 March 1947, TPLA.
73. Ibid.
74. Ibid.
75. Memorandum Prepared in the Department of State, Washington, 30 January 1945, *FRUS*, 1945, Vol. VIII, p. 683.
76. Report by the Coordinating Committee of the Department of State, Washington, 2 May, *FRUS*, 1945, Vol. VIII, pp. 34–7.
77. The American Director of Economic Relations in the Middle East (Landis) to President Roosevelt, Washington, 17 January 1945, *FRUS*, 1945, Vol. VIII, p. 682.
78. Memorandum by the Director of the Office of Near Eastern and African Affairs (Murray) to the Acting Secretary of State, Washington, 20 March 1945, *FRUS*, 1945, Vol. VIII, pp. 694–5.
79. Letter from President Roosevelt to King Ibn Saud, 5 April, 1945, The Avalon Project, http://avalon.law.yale.edu/20th_century/decad161.asp (Last visited 20 July 2012).
80. The Chargé in Iraq (Moose) to the Secretary of State, 22 August 1945, *FRUS*, 1945, Vol. VIII, pp. 725–6.
81. Memorandum by the Director of the Office of Near Eastern and African Affairs (Henderson) to the Secretary of State, Washington, 24 August 1945, *FRUS*, 1945, Vol. VIII, pp. 729–30.

82. Memorandum by the Chief of the Division of Near Eastern Affairs (Merriam) to the Under Secretary of State (Acheson), Washington, 8 May 1946, *FRUS*, 1946, Vol. VII, pp. 597–9.

83. Earl G. Harrison, *The Plight of the Displaced Jews in Europe: A Report to President Truman* (New York: Reprinted by United Jewish Appeal for Refugees, 1945).

84. Zvi Ganin, *Truman, American Jewry, and Israel 1945–1948* (New York: Holmes & Meier, 1979), p. 39; Miriam Joyce Haron, *Palestine and the Anglo-American Connection, 1945–1950* (New York: Peter Lang, 1986), p. 28.

85. Anglo-American Committee of Inquiry, Report to the United States Government and His Majesty's Government in the United Kingdom, Lausanne, Switzerland, 20 April 1946, The Avalon Project, http://avalon.law.yale.edu/subject_menus/angtoc.asp (Last visited 17 July 2012); For first-hand accounts by members of the committee see Richard Crossman, *Palestine Mission: A Personal Account* (London: Hamish Hamilton, 1947); Bartley C. Crum, *Behind the Silken Curtain: A Personal Account of Anglo-American Diplomacy in Palestine and the Middle East* (New York: Simon & Schuster, 1947).

86. Press Release Issues by the White House, 2 July 1946, *FRUS*, 1946, Vol. VII, p. 642.

87. Steven L. Spiegel, *The Other Arab-Israeli Conflict: Making America's Middle East Policy from Truman to Reagan* (Chicago: The University of Chicago Press, 1985), p. 24.

88. Peter L. Hahn, *Caught in the Middle East* (Chapel Hill: University of North Carolina Press, 2004), p. 33.

89. Quoted in Michael J. Cohen, *Palestine and the Great Powers, 1945–1948* (Princeton: Princeton University Press, 1982), p. 167.

90. Louis, 'British Imperialism and the End of the Palestine Mandate', pp. 2–3.

91. Haron, *Palestine and the Anglo-American*, p. 33.

92. *Manchester Guardian*, 9 July 1946.

93. Anglo-US Report – Military Implications: Report by the Chiefs of Staff, 10 July 1946, NA, CAB 129/11, C.P. (46) 267.

94. *Manchester Guardian*, 2 June 1946.

95. President Truman to the British Prime Minister (Attlee), Washington, 14 June 1946, *FRUS*, 1946, Vol. VII, p. 626.

96. *Manchester Guardian*, 3 July 1946.

97. The British Prime Minister (Attlee) to President Truman, London, 14 June 1946, *FRUS*, 1946, Vol. VII, p. 627.

98. *Manchester Guardian*, 25 February 1947.

99. The Acting Secretary of State to the Embassy in the United Kingdom, Washington, 22 August 1947, *FRUS*, 1947, Vol. V, p. 1140; *New York Times*, 23 August 1947.

100. *The Times*, 19 July 1947.

101. See for example the screenplay of Ben Hecht, *A Flag Is Born* (New York: American League for a Free Palestine, 1946), a play which toured across US cities and starred a 22-year-old Marlon Brando.

102. Lewis, *The British Empire in the Middle East 1945–1951*, p 466; *The Times*, 15 August 1946.

103. The Secretary of State to the British Secretary of State for Foreign Affairs (Bevin), Washington, 7 August 1947, *FRUS*, 1947, Vol. V, pp. 1136–7; *The Times*, 15 August 1947.
104. New York (Beeley) to I.P. Garran, Foreign Office, 11 October 1947, NA, FO 371/61948 E9685.
105. 6th Conclusions, Minute 4: Confidential Annex, 15 January 1947, NA, CAB/128/11, C.M. (47).
106. Ibid.
107. *New York Times*, 3 June 1947.
108. United Nations Special Committee on Palestine: Report to the General Assembly, Vol. 1, New York, 4 September 1947, UN A/364.
109. Palestine: The Autumn Session of the General Assembly, Undated, NA, FO 371/61948 E8126.
110. Ibid.
111. Ibid.
112. United Nations Special Committee on Palestine: Report to the General Assembly, Vol. 1, New York, 4 September 1947, A/364.
113. United Nations General Assembly Resolution 181 (II). Future government of Palestine, 29 November 1947, A/RES/181(II).
114. UK Delegation, New York to Foreign Office, 6 November 1947, NA, FO 371/61887 E10431.
115. New York (Sinclair) to Paul S. Falla, UK Delegation to United Nations, New York, 22 October 1947, NA, FO 371/61793.
116. Secretary of State to the Undersecretary of State, London, 25 November 1947, *FRUS*, 1947, Vol. V, pp. 1287–9.
117. Crossman, *A Nation Reborn*, p. 70.
118. Ibid., pp. 70–1.
119. Colin Shindler, *Israel and the European Left: Between Solidarity and Delegitimization* (New York: Continuum, 2012), pp. 140–1; Joshua Rubenstein and Vladimir P. Naumov (eds), *Stalin's Secret Pogrom: The Postwar Inquisition of the Jewish Anti-Fascist Committee* (New Haven: Yale University Press, 2005); Joel Cang, *The Silent Millions: A History of Jews in the Soviet Union* (London: Rapp & Whiting, 1969), pp. 225–8.
120. Arnold A. Offner, *Another Such Victory: President Truman and the Cold War, 1945–1953* (Stanford: Stanford University Press, 2002), pp. 284–5.
121. Ibid., p. 287.
122. Arnold Kramer, 'Soviet Motives in the Partition of Palestine, 1947–48', *Journal of Palestine Studies*, Vol. 2, No. 2 (Winter 1972), p. 111.
123. Ibid., p. 112; Shindler, *Israel and the European Left*, p. 132; Joseph Schechtman, 'The USSR, Zionism and Israel', in Lionel Kochan (ed.) *The Jews in Soviet Russia since 1917* (London: Oxford University Press, 1970), p. 115. A secondary but noteworthy factor is the possibility that Moscow was trying to win support from the Marxist branch of the Zionist movement which in turn attempted to gain a foothold in the government of Israel, see Martin Ebon, 'Communist Tactics in Palestine', *The Middle East Journal*, Vol. 2, No. 3 (July 1948), p. 263.
124. New York to Foreign Office, 16 October 1947, NA, FO 371/61791 E9673; New York (Falla) to Eastern Department, Foreign Office (Burrows), 29 October 1947, NA, FO 371/61886 E10353.

125. For an early prediction that the Soviets would change its position on Zionism see, Eliahu Ben-Horion, 'The Soviet Wooing of Palestine,' *Harper's Magazine*, Vol. 188, April 1944, p. 414.
126. FO Minutes (Beeley), 14 August 1947, NA, FO 371/61948 E7622.
127. Baghdad (Rusk) to Foreign Office, 12 September 1947, NA, FO 371/61878 E8462.
128. Commonwealth Relations Office to Canada, Australia, New Zealand, South Africa, 20 September 1947, NA, FO 371/61879 E8750.
129. Memorandum of Conversation, by the Undersecretary of State (Lovett), Washington, 15 October 1947, *FRUS*, 1947, Vol. V, pp. 1181–4.
130. Palestine: Memorandum by the Secretary of State for Foreign Affairs, 18 September 1947, NA, CAB 129/21.
131. Bethell, *The Palestine Triangle*, p. 346.
132. FO Minutes (Beeley): The Palestine Committee enclosed in Harold Beeley, New York to I.P. Garran, Foreign Office, 11 October 1947, NA, FO 371/61948 E9685.
133. Ibid.
134. FO Minutes (Garren): The Political Consequences for His Majesty's Government of a Solution of the Palestine Question Unfavourable to the Arabs, 8 April 1947, NA, FO 371/61874 E2932.
135. Ibid.
136. Ibid.
137. Ibid.
138. Secretary of State Colonies to Palestine (O.A.G.) 18 September 1947, NA, FO 371/61878 E8346; also see Palestine (O.A.G.) to Secretary of State Colonies, 16 September 1947.
139. Possible Compromise Settlements For Palestine, enclosed in Eastern Department minutes 14 October 1947, NA, FO 371/61885 E10108.
140. Ad Hoc Committee on the Palestine Question, Second Meeting, 26 September 1947, Lake Success, New York, UN (R1/1).
141. Beirut to Foreign Office, 2 October 1947, NA, FO 371/61880 E9146.
142. Speech to Be Delivered by The Right Honourable Arthur Creech-Jones M.P. in the Ad Hoc Committee on the Palestinian Question on Thursday 16th October, 1947, NA, FO 371/61883.
143. Ad Hoc Committee on the Palestine Question, Twenty-fifth Meeting, Lake Success, New York, 20 November 1947, UN (R1/1).
144. Michael J. Cohen, 'Truman and Palestine, 1945–1948: Revisionism, Politics and Diplomacy', *Modern Judaism*, Vol. 2, No. 1 (February 1982), pp. 10–1; Even though Truman denied lobbying other states to vote in favour of partition, American Zionists rallied groups of influential Americans, some of whom were Congressmen, to persuade countries such as Haiti, China, Liberia, the Philippines, Ethiopia and Greece to vote in favour. See Roosevelt, Kermit, 'The Partition of Palestine: A Lesson in Pressure Politics', *Middle East Journal*, Vol. 2, No. 1 (1948), pp. 14–15.
145. For example see John Snetsinger, *Truman, the Jewish Vote, and the Creation of Israel* (Stanford: Hoover Institution Press, 1974); Neff, *Fallen Pillars*, pp. 28–9; In contrast Michael J. Cohen argues that Truman was advised that he could harvest the best of both worlds, win Jewish support in policies that would also be in the national interest, see Cohen, *Palestine and the*

Great Powers, 1945–1948, pp. 47–8. Cohen also argues that Truman felt that he was being 'imposed upon' by lobbying groups, see Cohen, *Truman and Israel*, p. 60.

146. *New York Times*, 7 October 1946; *Manchester Guardian*, 2 August 1946; Ibid., 26 February 1947.
147. Paul C. Merkley, *The Politics of Christian Zionism 1891–1949* (London: Frank Cass, 1998), pp. 163–6; Michael B. Oren, *Power, Faith, and Fantasy: America in the Middle East, 1776 to the Present* (New York: W.W. Norton & Company, 2007), pp. 500–2.
148. Spiegel, *The Other Arab–Israeli Conflict*, p. 19.
149. Correspondence between Harry S. Truman and Eddie Jacobson, 8 October 1947, President' Secretary's Files, Truman Papers, TPLA.
150. Ibid., 27 February 1948, Correspondence File, Jacobson Papers, TPLA.
151. Evan M. Wilson, 'The Palestine papers, 1943–1947', *Journal of Palestine Studies*, Vol. 2, No. 4 (Summer 1973), pp. 45–6.
152. Position on Palestine: Excerpts from the Minutes of the Sixth Meeting of the United States Delegation to the Second Session of the General Assembly, New York, 15 September 1949, *FRUS*, 1949. *The Near East, South Asia, and Africa*, Vol. VI, p. 1147.
153. Ibid., p. 1148.
154. Ibid., p. 1149.
155. Ibid., pp. 1149–50; Dean Rusk recalled that he had a similar concern, Dean Rusk, *As I Saw It* (New York: W.W. Norton, 1990), pp. 145–6.
156. Spiegel, *The Other Arab–Israeli Conflict*, p. 26.
157. Ibid.
158. Robert D. Kaplan. *The Arabists: The Romance of an American Elite* (New York: The Free Press, 1993), pp. 94–105.
159. Director of the Office for Near Eastern and African Affairs (Henderson) to the Secretary of State, Washington, 22 September 1947, *FRUS*, 1947, Vol. V, pp. 1153–4; This was again reiterated to Undersecretary of State two months later five days before the UN vote on partition, see Director of the Office for Near Eastern and African Affairs (Henderson) to the Undersecretary of State (Lovett), Washington, 24 November 1947, *FRUS*, 1947, Vol. V, pp. 1281–2.
160. Ibid.: Certain Considerations against Advocacy by the US of the Majority Plan.
161. Acheson, *Present at the Creation*, pp. 169–70.
162. King Abdul Aziz Ibn Saud to President Truman (Transmitted on 30 October 1947), *FRUS*, p. 1212.
163. Radosh and Radosh, *A Safe Haven*, pp. 252–4.
164. The basis of what became known as the Truman Doctrine emanated from the President's speech of 12 March 1947, which requested congressional support for urgent requests from Greece for financial and economic assistance, and also for aid to Turkey, see Address of the President to Congress, Recommending Assistance to Greece and Turkey, 12 March 1947, TPLA.
165. Cohen, *Truman and Israel*, p. 27.
166. 'An Exclusive Interview with Clark Clifford', *American Heritage*, Vol. 28, No. 3, April 1977, p. 9.

167. Memorandum by Major General John H. Hilldring to the Acting United States Representative at the United Nations (Johnson), New York, 24 September 1947, *FRUS*, 1947, Vol. V, pp. 1162–3.
168. Harry S. Truman, *Memoirs, Vol. 2: Years of Trial and Hope* (New York: Doubleday, 1956), pp. 162–4.
169. Michael Ottolenghi, 'Harry Truman's Recognition of Israel', *The Historical Journal*, Vol. 47, No. 4 (2004), p. 967.
170. Ibid., pp. 971–2, 973–4.
171. Truman, *Memoirs*, Vol. 2, p. 157.
172. Bruce J. Evensen, 'Truman, Palestine and the Cold War', *Middle Eastern Studies*, Vol. 28, No. 1 (1992), p. 135.
173. For a comprehensive analysis of the role of the press in shaping Truman's Palestine policy see, Bruce J. Evensen, *Truman, Palestine and the Press: Shaping Conventional Wisdom at the Beginning of the Cold War* (New York: Greenwood Press, 1992).
174. Evensen, 'Truman, Palestine and the Cold War', p. 135.
175. Ibid., pp. 132–3, 135–41.

2 Friends Reunited? Britain and the US Respond to the Palestinian Refugee Problem

1. United Nations General Assembly Resolution 212 (III): Assistance to Palestine Refugees, A/RES/212 (III), 19 November 1948.
2. Ibid.
3. United Nations General Assembly, 194 (III). Palestine: Progress Report of the United Nations Mediator, 11 December 1948, A/RES/194 (III).
4. Musa Alami, head of the London-based Arab Office, wrote, 'The British were the prime causers of the disaster, and on them lies its responsibility.' See, Musa Alami, 'The Lesson of Palestine', *The Middle East Journal*, Vol. 4, No. 4 (October 1949), p. 374; Musa Alami, 'Letters to the Editor', *The Times*, 6 January 1950.
5. Fortnightly Intelligence Newsletter No. 67, issued by HQ British Troops in Palestine for the period 2,359 hrs 19 April–2,359 hrs 3 May 1948, 6 May 1948, NA, WO 275/64.
6. Morris, *The Birth Revisited*, pp. 202–3.
7. The Plight of Arab Refugees inside and outside Palestine: Text of Talks Given in English from the Arab Broadcasting Station at Ramallah, 29 July 1948, NA, FO 371/68578 E10440.
8. Haifa (Lippincott) to Secretary of State, 27 April 1948, United States National Archives (Hereafter USNA), 867N.01/-4-2648.
9. Cairo (Patterson) to Secretary of State, 15 August 1948, USNA, 867N.48/8-1548; Patterson also believed that the gesture would combat the belief that the US was only helping suffering Jews.
10. *Manchester Guardian*, 2 December 1947.
11. Damascus (Broadmeand) to Foreign Office, 28 July 1948, NA, FO 371/68576 E10175.

12. British Middle East Office, Cairo, to Foreign Office, 3 August 1948, NA, FO 371/68578 E10456; Repeated in British Middle East Office, Cairo, to Foreign Office, 3 August 1948, NA, FO 371/68579 E10693.
13. United Nations Security Council, Text of Suggestions Presented by the United Nations Mediator on Palestine to the Two Parties on 28 June 1948, S/863.
14. Morris, *The Birth Revisited*, pp. 317–8.
15. Ibid., p. 319.
16. Ibid., p. 320.
17. Ibid., pp. 319–20.
18. Ibid., p. 320.
19. Ibid., p. 323.
20. Ibid., pp. 414–5, 448.
21. Alami, *The Times*, 19 July 1948.
22. United Kingdom Delegation to the United Nations to Foreign Office, 22 July 1948, NA, FO 371/68575 E9928.
23. Ibid., Secretary of State to H.M. Minister, Amman, 24 July 1948, NA, FO 816/139.
24. London (Douglas) to Secretary of State, 24 July 1948, USNA, 501.BB Palestine/7-2448.
25. Memorandum of Conversation, by the Undersecretary of State (Lovett), 21 May 1948, *FRUS*, 1948, Vol. V, p. 1020.
26. Report by Major Hackett-Paine on the Refugee Problem in the Samaria District of Palestine, Consulate General, Jerusalem, to Foreign Office, NA, FO 371/68677 E11504.
27. Ibid.
28. London (Douglas) to Secretary of State, 2 August 1948, USNA, 501.BB Palestine/8-248.
29. New York (Jessup) to Secretary of State, 3 August 1948, USNA, 501.BB Palestine/8-348.
30. Memorandum by Mr Robert M. McLintock to the Director of the Office of United Nations Affairs (Rusk), 1 July 1948, *FRUS*, 1948, Vol. V, p. 1173.
31. New York (Jessup) to Secretary of State, 18 July 1948, USNA, 501.BB Palestine/7-1849.
32. Secretary of State to H.M. Chargé d'Affaires, Amman, 29 July 1948, NA, FO, 816/139.
33. Ibid.
34. London (Douglas) to the Secretary of State, 27 July1948, USNA, 501.BB Palestine/7-2748.
35. Ibid.
36. Hahn, *Caught in the Middle East*, p. 33.
37. Secretary of State to H.M. Chargé d'Affaires, Amman (Addressed to UKDEL New York Telegram No. 3160 of 27 July) 28 July 1948, NA, FO 816/139.
38. Alami, *The Times*, 29 July 1948.
39. New York (Jessup) to the Secretary of State, 28 July 1948, USNA, 501.BB Palestine/7-2848; also see New York to Foreign Office, 28 July 1948, NA, FO 371/68576 E10148.
40. Ibid.

41. Ibid.
42. Ibid.
43. Secretary of State to H.M. Minister, Amman, 31 July 1948, FO 816/139; Also see London (Douglas) to Secretary of State, 29 July 1948, USNA, 501.BB Palestine/7-2948. The US was informed of the reasons why Britain wanted no further delay. Britain wanted to show the Arab states that the UK and the UN were aware of the problem, to make the problem public, to emphasize to the mediator to take account of the refugee problem and to show that the UN was not hostile to Arab interests.
44. Foreign Office to United Kingdom Delegation, United Nations (Undated), NA, FO 371/68576 E10148.
45. See FN 1 in *FRUS*, 1948, Vol. V, p. 1262.
46. *Palestine Post*, 3 August 1948.
47. Alami, *The Times*, 3 August 1948; *New York Times*, 3 August 1948; *Manchester Guardian*, 3 August 1948.
48. New York (Jessup) to the Secretary of State, 28 July 1948, USNA, 501.BB Palestine/7-2848; also see New York to Foreign Office, 28 July 1948, NA, FO 371/68576 E10148; London (Douglas) to Secretary of State, 2 August 1948, USNA, 501.BB Palestine/8-248.
49. New York (Jessup) to Secretary of State, 1 July 1948, USNA, 501.BB Palestine/7-148; also see New York (Jessup) to the Secretary of State, 28 July 1948, USNA, 501.BB Palestine/7-2848.
50. New York (Jessup) to Secretary of State, 21 July 1948, USNA, 501.BB Palestine/7-2148.
51. The Secretary of State to the Embassy in the United Kingdom, 14 August 1948, *FRUS*, 1948, Vol. V, pp. 1310–12.
52. Amman (Stabler) to Secretary of State, 2 August 1948, USNA, 501.BB Palestine/8-248.
53. Morris, *The Birth Revisited*, p. 448.
54. The Secretary of State to the Embassy in the United Kingdom, 14 August 1948, *FRUS*, 1948, Vol. V, pp. 1310–12.
55. Cairo to Foreign Office, 2 August 1948, NA, FO 816/139.
56. Several months later, the Foreign Office would again be disappointed with the media's coverage of Britain's contributions. This time it was the BBC's failure to mention Britain's £1 million contribution to the Palestinian refugees when broadcasting news about a House of Commons debate on the refugee issue, Foreign Office Minutes, and Mr Baker White to Mr Mayhew, 11 November, 1948, NA, FO 371/68682 E14689.
57. London (Douglas) to Secretary of State, 4 August 1948, USNA, 501.BB Palestine/8-348.
58. The Secretary of State to the Embassy in the United Kingdom, 14 August 1948, *FRUS*, 1948, Vol. V, pp. 1310–12; Secretary of State (Marshall) to USUN (New York), 11 August 1948, USNA, 501.BB Palestine/8-348.
59. Memorandum by the Department of State to President Truman, Undated (drafted 18 August), *FRUS*, 1948, Vol. V, pp. 1324–6.
60. WM F. Moore, Arabian American Oil Company, BE. Hill, the Trans Arabian pipeline to George V. Marshall, Secretary of State, 17 August 1949, USNA, 501.BB Palestine/8-1748.

61. British Middle East Office, Cairo, to Foreign Office, 16 August 1948, NA, FO 371/68677 E10844.
62. FO Minutes (Beeley) 16 August 1948, NA, FO Minutes (Burrows) 17 August 1948, NA, FO 371/68677 E11361.
63. Commonwealth Relations Office, Foreign Affairs and UN Department to UK High Commissioner in Canada, Acting UK High Commissioner in Australia, UK High Commissioner in New Zealand, UK High Commissioner in the Union of South Africa, 3 September 1948, NA, FO 371/68678 E11813.
64. British Middle East Office, Cairo, to Foreign Office, 4 September 1948, NA, FO 371/68678 E11767.
65. The Acting Secretary of State to the United States Delegation at Paris, 18 October 1948, *FRUS*, 1948, Vol. V, p. 1491.
66. Alami, *The Times*, 17 August 1948; Bernadotte, in his suggestions to the Security Council, had already called for the Palestinian refugees 'to return to their homes without restriction and to regain possession of their property', United Nations Security Council: Text of Suggestions Presented by the United Nations Mediator on Palestine to the Two Parties on 28 June 1948, S/863.
67. Memorandum Prepared in the Department of State: Plan of Action on Arab Refugee Problem, 31 August 1948, *FRUS*, 1948, Vol. V, pp. 1364–5.
68. British Middle East Office, Cairo, (Troutbeck) to Foreign Office, 2 September 1948, NA, FO 371/68678 E11730.
69. Draft Position Paper on Relief for Near Eastern Refugees, 5 October 1948, *FRUS, 1948*, Vol. V, pp. 1454–5.
70. Ibid., pp. 1454–7.
71. Ibid.
72. Memorandum Prepared by the Department of State: Plan of Action on Arab Refugee Problem, 31 August 1948, *FRUS*, 1948, Vol. V, pp. 1364–5.
73. FO Minute (Boothby), 7 September 1949, NA, FO 371/68678 E11879.
74. Ibid.; FO Minute (Rundall), 18 September 1948, NA, FO 371/68678 E11879.
75. FO Minute (Boothby), 7 September 1948, NA, FO 371/68678 E11920.
76. Beirut (Evans) to Foreign Office, 2 October 1948, NA, FO 371/68679 E12900.
77. Foreign Office to Geneva, 11 September 1948, NA, FO 371/68678 E11920.
78. Foreign Office to United Nations General Assembly, Paris (United Kingdom Delegation), 25 September 1948, NA, FO 371/68678 E11879.
79. Foreign Office to United Nations General Assembly, Paris (United Kingdom Delegation), 25 September 1948, NA, FO 371/68678 E11879.
80. Progress Report of the United Nations Mediator on Palestine, 16 September 1948, A/648.
81. Foreign Office to United Nations General Assembly, Paris (United Kingdom Delegation), 25 September 1948, NA, FO 371/68678 E11879.
82. FO Minute (Boothby), 7 September 1948, NA, FO 371/68678 E11920.
83. Foreign Office to United Nations General Assembly, Paris (United Kingdom Delegation), 25 September 1948, NA, FO 371/68678 E11879.
84. New York (Jessup) to Secretary of State, 3 August 1948, USNA, 501.BB Palestine/8-348.
85. Secretary of State (Marshall) to New York, 14 August 1948, USNA, 501.BB Palestine/8-348.

86. Draft Position Paper on Relief for Near Eastern Refugees, 5 October 1948, *FRUS*, 1948, Vol. V, pp. 1454–5.
87. Paris (Marshall) to Secretary of State, 20 October 1948, USNA, 501.BB Palestine/10-2048 HH; United Kingdom Draft Resolution on Palestinian Refugees, NA, FO 371/68680 E13254.
88. FO Minute (Beeley), 5 October 1948, NA, FO 371/68679 E12980.
89. Ibid.
90. United Nations General Assembly, Paris (UK Delegation, Mayhew), to Foreign Office, 8 October 1948, NA, FO 371/68680 E13390.
91. United Nations General Assembly, Paris (UK Delegation), to Foreign Office, 6 October 1948, NA, FO 371/68679 E13033; United Nations General Assembly, Paris (UK Delegation), to Foreign Office, 6 October 1948, NA, FO 371/68679 E13082.
92. Draft Position Paper on Relief for Near Eastern Refugees, 5 October 1948, *FRUS*, 1948, Vol. V, pp. 1455–7; It was reported by the British delegation to the UN that the US believed a number of countries should contribute 'slightly larger' than their pro rata contribution, United Nations General Assembly, Paris (UK Delegation) to Foreign Office, 19 October 1948, NA, FO 371/68680 E13254.
93. Tel Aviv (McDonald) to Secretary of State, 17 October 1948, USNA, 501.BB Palestine/10-1748; The Special Representative of the United States in Israel (McDonald) to President Truman, Tel Aviv, 17 October 1948, *FRUS*, 1948, Vol. V, pp. 1486–7.
94. The Acting Secretary of State to the United States Delegation at Paris, 23 October 1948, *FRUS*, 1948, Vol. V, pp. 1506–7.
95. United Nations General Assembly Resolution 212 (III): Assistance to Palestine Refugees, A/RES/212 (III), 19 November 1948; For the acting mediator's report see, Progress Report of the United Nations Acting Mediator on Palestine Submitted to the Secretary-General for Transmission to the Members of the United Nations, Supplement No. 11A, General Assembly Official Records: Third Session, 18 October 1948, A/689, A/689/Corr.1 and A/689/Add.1.
96. Progress Report of the United Nations Mediator on Palestine, 16 September 1948, A/648.
97. 'Assembly Resolution on Arab Refugees', in United Nations General Assembly, Paris (UK Delegation), to Foreign Office, 12 October 1948, FO 371/68680 E13254.
98. United Nations General Assembly, Paris (UK Delegation), to Foreign Office, 19 October 1948, NA, FO 371/68680 E13543.
99. Alami, *The Times*, 18 September 1948.
100. United Nations General Assembly, Paris (UK Delegation), to Foreign Office, 19 October 1948, NA, FO 371/68680 E13543; Paris to Secretary of State (Marshall) 20 October 1948, USNA, 501.BB Palestine/10-2048.
101. Alami, *The Times*, 21 October 1948; 108th Meeting of the UNGA Third Committee, 21 October 1948, United Nations General Assembly Official Records, Third Committee, pp. 194–9.
102. Morris, *The Birth Revisited*, p. 492.
103. United Nations General Assembly, Paris (UK Delegation), to Foreign Office, 21 October 1948, NA, FO 371/68681 E13612; 109th Meeting of

the UNGA Third Committee, 21 October 1948, United nations General Assembly Official Records, Third Committee, p. 209.

104. The committee actually adopted these Soviet proposals, with the new subcommittee meeting on November 2; United Nations General Assembly, Paris (UK Delegation) to Foreign Office, 31 October 1948, NA, FO 371/68681 E14028; Paris (Marshall) to Secretary of State, 30 October 1948, USNA, 501.BB Palestine/10-3048; for the Soviet representative's comments see 118th Meeting of the UNGA Third Committee, 30 October 1948, United Nations General Assembly Official Records, Third Committee, pp. 299–302.

105. FO Minute (Rundall) 22 October 1948, NA, FO 371/68681/E13611.

106. United Nations General Assembly, Paris (United Kingdom Delegation), to Foreign Office, 20 October 1948, NA, FO 371/68680 E13547.

107. United Nations General Assembly, Paris (United Kingdom Delegation), to Foreign Office, 21 October 1948, NA, FO 371/68681 E13611.

108. United Nations General Assembly, Paris (United Kingdom Delegation), to Foreign Office, 21 October 1948, FO 371/68681 E13655; 109th Meeting of the UNGA Third Committee, 21 October 1948, United Nations General Assembly Official Records, Third Committee, p. 211.

109. United Nations General Assembly, Paris (UK Delegation), to Foreign Office, 21 October 1948, NA, FO 371/68681 E13611.

110. The Acting Secretary of State to the United States Delegation at Paris, 23 October 1948, *FRUS*, 1948, Vol. V, pp. 1509–11.

111. Ibid.

112. Foreign Office to United Nations General Assembly, Paris (United Kingdom Delegation), 22 October 1948, NA, FO 371/68681 E13729.

113. United Nations General Assembly, Paris (United Kingdom Delegation), to Foreign Office, 22 October 1948, FO 371/68681 E13831. Also see United Nations General Assembly, Paris (United Kingdom Delegation), to Foreign Office, 23 October 1948, NA, FO 371/68681 E13702.

114. Acting Secretary of State to Paris, October 27, 1948, USNA, 501.BB Palestine/10-2648.

115. Ibid.

116. Ibid.

117. Foreign Office to United Kingdom General Assembly, Paris (UK Delegation), 28 October 1948, NA, FO 371/68681 E13878; Paris to Secretary of State, 28 October 1948, USNA, 501.BB Palestine/10-2848; Paris to Secretary of State, 29 October 1948, USNA, 501.BB Palestine/10-2948.

118. Paris to Secretary of State, 29 October 1948, USNA, 501.BB Palestine/10-2948; Acting Secretary of State to Paris, October 27 1948, USNA, 501.BB Palestine/10-2648.

119. FO Minute (Smith) 26 October 1948; Kingdom General Assembly, Paris (UK Delegation), to Foreign Office, 25 October 1948, NA, FO 371/68681 E13820.

120. Kingdom General Assembly, Paris (UK Delegation), to Foreign Office, 29 October 1948, NA, FO 371/68681 E13983; 117th Meeting of the UNGA Third Committee, 29 October 1948, United Nations General Assembly Official Records, Third Committee, pp. 279–82.

121. United Kingdom General Assembly Paris, (UK Delegation), to Foreign Office, 31 October 1948; Foreign Office to United Kingdom General Assembly, Paris (UK Delegation), 3 November 1948, FO 371/68681

E14028; 118th Meeting of the UNGA Third Committee, 30 October 1948, United Nations General Assembly Official Records, Third Committee, pp. 301–3.

122. FO Minute (Beith), 2 November 1948, NA, FO 371/68681 E14028.
123. Foreign Office to United Kingdom General Assembly, Paris (UK Delegation), 3 November 1948, NA, FO 371/68681 E14028.
124. Ibid.
125. United Nations General Assembly, Paris (UK Delegation), to Foreign Office, 3 November 1948, NA, FO 371/68681 E14150.
126. United Nations General Assembly, Paris (UK Delegation), to Foreign Office, 6 November 1948, NA, FO 371/68682 E14316.
127. United Nations General Assembly, Paris (UK Delegation), to Foreign Office, 6 November 1948, NA, FO 371/68682 E14319.
128. United Nations General Assembly, Paris (UK Delegation), to Foreign Office, 8 November 1948, NA, FO 371/68682 E14392.
129. Memorandum by the Acting Secretary of State (Lovett) to President Truman, 6 November 1948, *FRUS*, 1948, Vol. V, pp. 1554–5; Lovett himself had received this recommendation, see Mr Satterthwaite and NEA to Undersecretary of State (Lovett), 22 October 1948, USNA, 501.BB Palestine/10-2248. It was not until November 29 that the US delegation was authorized to officially state that the president would seek funding from Congress, The Secretary of State (Marshall) to the United States Delegation at Paris, 29 November 1948, *FRUS*, 1948, Vol. V, p. 1635.
130. FO Minute (Beith), 12 November 1948; United Nations General Assembly, Paris (UK Delegation), to Foreign Office, 11 November 1948, NA, FO 371/68682 E14493.
131. Acting Secretary of State to Paris, 13 November 1948, USNA, 501.BB Palestine/11-1348.
132. United Nations General Assembly, Paris (UK Delegation), to Foreign Office, 14 November 1948, NA, FO 371/68682 E14589; FO Minute (Boothby), 8 November 1948; FO Minute (Boothby), 10 November 1948, NA, FO 371/68682 E14690. The final draft of the resolution was passed by 42 votes to none with 4 abstentions, 136th Meeting of the UNGA Third Committee, 13 November 1948, United Nations General Assembly Official Records, Third Committee, p. 495.
133. FO Minute (Beith), 8 November 1948; FO Minute, 9 November 1948; FO Minute (Watson), 17 November 1948, NA, FO 371/68682 E14690.
134. *New York Times*, 12 December 1948.
135. United Nations General Assembly, 194 (III). Palestine: Progress Report of the United Nations Mediator, 11 December 1948, A/RES/194 (III).
136. Ibid.
137. Ibid.
138. United Nations Security Council: Text of Suggestions Presented by the United Nations Mediator on Palestine to the Two Parties, 28 June 1948, S/863.
139. The Arab states saw the proposals as a reaffirmation of partition and Israel on the basis that the fighting would determine the borders, see Benny Morris, *Righteous Victims: A History of the Zionist–Arab Conflict, 1881–2001*

(New York: Vintage Books, 2001), p. 237; Pappé, *Britain and the Arab–Israeli Conflict*, pp. 143–53.

140. See, Cary David Stanger, 'A Haunting Legacy: The Assassination of Count Bernadotte', *Middle East Journal*, Vol. 42, No. 2 (Spring 1988), pp. 260–72; Heller, *Stern Gang: Ideology, Politics, and Terror*, pp. 239–55; Bell, *Terror Out of Zion*, pp. 335–40; It was also a message to the international community that the UN could not interfere in Israeli affairs, Kurzman, *Genesis 1948*, p. 622; Bernadotte was also considered a pawn of Britain, Bell, *Terror Out of Zion*, p. 330; Yitzhak Shamir, *Summing Up: An Autobiography* (London: Weidenfeld and Nicolson, 1994), pp. 74–76.

141. Progress Report of the United Nations Mediator on Palestine, 16 September 1948, A/648.

142. Morris, *The Birth Revisited*, pp. 330–1.

143. Progress Report of the United Nations Mediator on Palestine, 16 September 1948, A/648.

144. Ibid., 'Seven Basic Premises' and 'Specific Conclusions'; *New York Times*, 21 September 1948; for the partition resolution see United Nations General Assembly, Resolution 181 (II). Future Government of Palestine, 29 November 1948, A/RES/181(II).

145. The Acting Secretary of State to the Secretary of State, Washington, 18 October 1948, *FRUS*, 1948, Vol. V, pp. 1489–90.

146. Statement by Truman on Israel, 24 October 1948, http://www .jewishvirtuallibrary.org/jsource/US-Israel/truman_Israel1.html (Last visited 8 June 2011).

147. The Secretary of State to the Acting Secretary of State, Paris, 25 October 1948, *FRUS*, 1948, Vol. V, pp. 1514–5.

148. Foreign Office to Cairo, 19 November 1948, NA, FO 371/68595 E14457.

149. United Nations General Assembly Paris (United Kingdom Delegation) to Foreign Office, 16 November 1948, NA, FO 371/68596 E14756; FO Minute (Wright), 16 November 1948, NA, FO 371/68598 E15041/G.

150. Foreign Office to United Nations General Assembly, Paris (United Kingdom Delegation), 22 November 1948, NA, FO 371/68598 E14954; *New York Times*, 21 November 1948.

151. Acting Secretary of State to Paris, 22 November 1948, USNA, 501.BB Palestine/11-2248; Washington (Franks) to Foreign Office, 23 November 1948, NA, FO 371/68598 E15079.

152. Washington (Franks) to Foreign Office, 23 November 1948, NA, FO 371/68598 E15079.

153. *Manchester Guardian*, 25 November 1948.

154. London (Douglas) to Secretary of State, 24 November 1948, USNA, 501.BB Palestine/11-2448; United Nations General Assembly, Paris (United Kingdom Delegation) to Foreign Office, 23 November 1948, NA, FO 371/68598 E15086.

155. The Acting Chairman of the United States Delegation at Paris (Dulles) to the Secretary of State, 30 November 1948, *FRUS*, 1948, Vol. V, pp. 1636–8; United Nations General Assembly Paris (United Kingdom Delegation) to Foreign Office, 30 November 1948, NA, FO 371/68600 E15334.

156. Alami, *The Times*, 1 December 1948; *New York Times*, 1 December 1948.
157. *New York Times*, 3 December 1948.
158. United Nations General Assembly, Paris (United Kingdom Delegation), to Foreign Office, 24 November 1948, NA, FO 371/68599 E15108; 209th Meeting of the UNGA First Committee, 24 November 1948, United Nations General Assembly Official Records, First Committee, p. 728; Similar notions were briefly reiterated by Jessup in the 214th Meeting of the UNGA First Committee, 26 November 1948, United Nations General Assembly Official Records, First Committee, p. 780.
159. United Nations General Assembly, Paris (United Kingdom Delegation), to Foreign Office, 26 November 1948, NA, FO 371/68599 E15200; 212th Meeting of the UNGA Third Committee, 25 November 1948, United Nations General Assembly Official Records, First Committee, p. 726; *New York Times*, 25 November 1948.
160. Paris (Dulles) to Secretary of State, 30 November 1948, USNA, 501.BB Palestine/11-3048. An earlier redraft dropped 'not resulting from military necessity' when referring to destroyed property and compensation. See First Version of United States amendments to the United Kingdom Resolution on Palestine, 19 November 1948, NA, FO 371/68600 E15281.
161. *New York Times*, 4 December 1948.
162. The Acting Chairman of the United States Delegation at Paris (Dulles) to the Acting Secretary of State, 9 December 1948, *FRUS*, 1948, Vol. V, pp. 1656–7; Alami, *The Times*, 6 December 1948.
163. New York (Jessup) to Secretary of State, 21 July 1948, USNA, 501.BB Palestine/7-2148; The Secretary of State to the Embassy in the United Kingdom, 14 August 1948, *FRUS*, 1948, Vol. V, No. 2, pp. 1310–12.
164. Progress Report of the United Nations Mediator on Palestine, 16 September 1948, A/648.
165. United Nations General Assembly, 194 (III). Palestine: Progress Report of the United Nations Mediator, 11 December 1948, A/RES/194 (III).

3   Diplomatic Deadlock: The Palestine Conciliation Commission and the Palestinian Refugee Problem (Part 1)

1. Walter Eytan, *The First Ten Years: A Diplomatic History of Israel*, (London: Weidenfeld and Nicolson, 1958), p. 29.
2. Ibid., pp. 29–30.
3. Article 5, United Nations General Assembly, 194 (III). Palestine: Progress Report of the United Nations Mediator, 11 December 1948, A/RES/194 (III).
4. David P. Forsythe, *United Nations Peacemaking: The Conciliation Commission for Palestine* (Baltimore: Johns Hopkins University Press); Gabbay, *A Political Study of the Arab–Jewish Conflict*; Malcolm Kerr, *The Elusive Peace in the Middle East* (Albany: State University of New York Press, 1975); Nathan A. Pelcovitz, *The Long Armistice; UN Peacekeeping and the Arab–Israeli Conflict, 1948–1960* (Boulder: Westview Press, 1993); Don Peretz, *Israel and the Palestine Arabs* (Washington, DC: The Middle East Institute, 1959); Saadia

Touval, *The Peace Brokers: Mediators in the Arab–Israeli Conflict, 1948–1979* (Princeton: Princeton University Press, 1982).

5. Neil Caplan, *Futile Diplomacy Volume Three: The United Nations, The Great Powers, and the Middle East, 1948–1954* (London: Frank Cass, 1997). Several other studies have used primary sources to look at the work of the PCC, but they are more limited in scope. See Ilan Pappé, *The Making of the Arab–Israeli Conflict, 1947–51* (London: I.B. Tauris, 1994), pp. 196–7; Candice Karp, *Missed Opportunities: US Diplomatic Failures and the Arab–Israeli Conflict, 1947–1967* (Claremont: Regina Books, 2005).

6. Michael R. Fischbach, *Records of Dispossession: Palestinian Refugees and the Arab–Israel Conflict* (New York: Columbia University Press, 2003).

7. Jacob Tovy, *Israel and the Palestinian Refugee Issue: The Formation of a Policy, 1948–1956* (London: Routledge, 2014).

8. Safran, *From War to War*, pp. 39–40.

9. Earl Berger, *The Covenant and the Sword: Arab–Israeli Relations 1948–56* (London: Routledge & Kegan Paul, 1965), pp. 44–5.

10. Fred J. Khouri, 'United Nations Peace Efforts', in Kerr (ed) *The Elusive Peace in the Middle East*, pp. 36–7.

11. Touval, *The Peace Brokers*, pp. 89–90.

12. United Nations General Assembly, 194 (III). Palestine: Progress Report of the United Nations Mediator, 11 December 1948, A/RES/194 (III).

13. Ibid.

14. Ibid.

15. Foreign Office to the United Nations General Assembly (UK Delegation), 8 December 1948, NA, FO 371/68602 E15620.

16. Forsythe, *United Nations Peacemaking*, p. 29; United Nations General Assembly (UK Delegation) to Foreign Office, 12 December 1948, NA, FO 371/68602 E15735.

17. M. Sharett to Paris (Eytan), 6 December 1948, Coded Tel: U870, *DFPI*, Vol. 2 (October 1948–April 1949), p. 269.

18. Ankara (Kelly) to Monsieur Necmeddin Sadak, Ankara, 16 December 1948, NA, FO 371/75346 E32.

19. The Acting Chairman of the United States Delegation at Paris (Dulles) to the Acting Secretary of State, Paris, 12 December 1948, *FRUS*, 1948, Vol. V, pp. 1663–4; Sharett felt 'terribly let down' by the US over the PCC's composition, seeing France and Turkey as being too pro-Arab, see Paris (Sharett) to Washington (Elath), 13 December 1948, *DFPI*, Vol. 2, p. 292.

20. Pappé, *The Making of the Arab–Israeli Conflict*, pp. 196–7.

21. Division of Near East Affairs (Satterthwaite) to Lovett, 22 December 1948, USNA, 501.BB Palestine/12-2248.

22. Yalcin was nearly 80 at the time of appointment.

23. Ankara (Kelly) to Foreign Office, 5 January 1949, NA, FO 371/75346 E207.

24. *Palestine Post*, 18 January 1949.

25. James G. McDonald, *My Mission in Israel, 1948–51* (London: Victor Gollancz Ltd, 1951), p. 161.

26. Beirut (Houstoun Boswall) to Foreign Office, 2 April 1949, NA, FO 371/75349 E4281.

27. Secretary of State to Dean Rusk, 28 January 1949, USNA, 501.BB Palestine/1-2849.
28. FO Minute, 31 December 1948, NA, FO 371/75346 E166/G.
29. FO Minute (P. Paris), 29 December 1948, NA, FO 371/75346 E166/G.
30. *Palestine Post*, 16 January 1949.
31. *New York Times*, 24 January 1949; *The Times*, 25 January 1949.
32. Harding Bancroft (Department of State) to Mark Ethridge, 26 January 1949, USNA, 501.BB Palestine/1-2549.
33. FO Minute (Peck) 25 January 1949, NA, FO 371/75346 E1011.
34. Ibid.
35. Beirut (Houstoun Boswall) to Foreign Office, 26 January 1949, NA, FO 371/75346 E1269.
36. *Palestine Post*, 30 December 1948.
37. Foreign Office to Jerusalem, 2 January 1949, NA, FO 371/75346 E33; British Middle East Office, Cairo (Troutbeck) to Foreign Office, 20 January 1949, NA, FO 371/75346 E147.
38. Azcarate himself was not above criticism. Mark Ethridge referred to the Secretariat as not being politically minded and more inefficient than the Balkan Commission, Department of State (Rusk) to USUN, New York (Ross), 11 February 1949, USNA, 501.BB Palestine/2-1149.
39. Pablo de Azcarate, *Mission in Palestine*, 1948–1952 (Washington, DC: The Middle East Institute, 1966), p. 135.
40. Forsythe, *United Nations Peacemaking*, p. 37.
41. Geneva (Hickerson) to Department of State (Rusk), 18 January 1949, USNA, 501.BB Palestine/1-1849.
42. Touval, *The Peace Brokers*, pp. 89–90; In Chapter 5 of Michael E. Jansen's 1970 study *The United States and the Palestinian People*, it is argued that important US officials – James McDonald in Tel Aviv and Mark Ethridge – were Zionist sympathizers and that they affected Washington's position, see Michael E. Jansen, *The United States and the Palestinian People* (Beirut: Institute for Palestine Studies, 1970), pp. 106, 111; also see Khouri, 'United Nations Peace Efforts', pp. 33–4.
43. Oral History Interview with Mark F. Ethridge, by Richard D. McKinzie, Moncure, North Carolina, 4 June 1974, http://www.trumanlibrary.org/oralhist/ethridge.htm (Last visited 20 April 2009).
44. Harry S. Truman, Diary Entry, 20 March 1948, *Off the Record: The Private Papers of Harry S. Truman* (Columbia: University of Missouri Press, 1980), p. 127.
45. She passed on 23 March 1949, Dean Rusk to the Secretary of State, 24 March 1949, USNA, 501.BB Palestine/3-2449 CS EM; 'Obituary: Mrs William Etheridge', *New York Times*, 25 March 1949.
46. Oral History Interview with Mark F. Ethridge.
47. Berger, *The Covenant and the Sword*, pp. 41–2.
48. Touval, *The Peace Brokers*, p. 88.
49. Fischbach, *Records of Dispossession*, p. 84.
50. Department of State (Acheson) to Jerusalem (Ethridge), 25 February 1949 (also repeated to Embassy in London), USNA, 501.BB Palestine/2-2549.
51. *New York Times*, 21 November 1948.

52. *Palestine Post*, 24 January 1949; Azcarate, *Mission in Palestine*, pp. 139–40; The American Minister in Bern, John Carter Vincent, represented the US in Geneva in the absence of an official American representative, Bern (Vincent) to Secretary of State, 18 January 1949, USNA, 501.BB Palestine/1-1849.
53. *Palestine Post*, 25 January 1949.
54. *Palestine Post*, 4 February 1949.
55. *The Times*, 18 May 1949.
56. London (Holmes) to Secretary of State, 24 January 1949, USNA, 501.BB Palestine/1-2449.
57. Tel Aviv (Sharett) to New York (Eban), 9–10 February 1949, *DFPI*, Vol. 2, pp. 422–3.
58. The Consul at Jerusalem (Burdett) to the Secretary of State, Jerusalem, 8 February 1949, USNA, 501.BB Palestine/2-849.
59. Ibid.
60. Amman (Kirkbride) to Foreign Office, 12 February 1949, NA, FO 371/75347 E2073; also see Meeting with Transjordan, Jerusalem, holy places, refugees – United Nations Conciliation Commission for Palestine (UNCCP) – Summary Record, 11 February 1949, A/AC.25/SR/G/2.
61. Progress Report of the United Nations Mediator on Palestine, 16 September 1948, A/648.
62. Lebanon (Pinkerton) to the Secretary of State, 28 March 1949, USNA, 501.BB Palestine/3-2849.
63. Amman (Kirkbride) to Foreign Office, 12 February 1949, NA, FO 371/75347 E2073; Meeting with Transjordan, Jerusalem, holy places, refugees – UNCCP – Summary Record, 11 February 1949, A/AC.25/SR/G/2.
64. Jerusalem (Burdett) to Secretary of State, 12 February 1949, USNA, 501.BB Palestine/2-1249.
65. FO Minute (Beith), 15 February 1949, NA, FO 371/75347 E2073.
66. Amman (Kirkbride) to Foreign Office, 12 February 1949, FO 371/75347 E2073; Meeting with Transjordan, Jerusalem, holy places, refugees – UNCCP – Summary Record, 11 February 1949, A/AC.25/SR/G/2.
67. *New York Times*, 13 February 1949.
68. *The Times*, 14 February 1949.
69. Egypt (Patterson) to the Secretary of State, 15 February 1949, USNA, 501.BB Palestine/2-1549.
70. Egypt (Patterson) to the Secretary of State, 16 February 1949, USNA, 501.BB Palestine/2-1649.
71. The Chargé in Egypt (Patterson) to the Secretary of State, 25 February 1949, USNA, 501.BB Palestine/2-2549.
72. UNCCP: Summary Record of a Meeting between Conciliation Commission and His Highness Amir Feysal, Minister of Foreign Affairs of Saudi Arabia, 16 February 1949, A/AC.25/SR/G/6; *Palestine Post*, 17 February 1949.
73. UNCCP: Summary Record of a Meeting between Conciliation Commission and His Excellency, Kaled El Azem, Prime Minister and Minister of Foreign Affairs of Syria, 21 February 1949, A/AC.25/SR/G/11; Azem had already expressed similar sentiments to the US ambassador to Syria 12 days prior, see Damascus (Keeley) to Secretary of State, 10 February 1949, USNA, 501.BB Palestine/2-949.

74. Baghdad (Mack) to Foreign Office, 21 February 1949, NA, FO 371/75347 E2416; For details of the meeting with Ibn Saud and the regent of Iraq see, Baghdad (Dorse) to Secretary of State, 19 February 1949, USNA, 501.BB Palestine/2-1949.
75. Ibid.
76. Two memorandums from Baghdad (Mack) to Foreign Office, 22 February 1949, NA, FO 371/75348 E2472.
77. The Consul at Jerusalem (Burdett) to the Secretary of State, 26 February 1949, USNA, 501.BB Palestine/2-2649.
78. Ibid.; Meeting with Members of the Conciliation Commission, Tel Aviv, 24 February 1949, *DFPI*, Vol. 2, pp. 444–6.
79. The Consul at Jerusalem (Burdett) to the Secretary of State, Jerusalem, 28 February 1949, USNA, 501.BB Palestine/2-2849.
80. Ibid.; *Palestine Post*, 4 March 1949.
81. Azcarate, *Mission in Palestine*, pp. 147–8.
82. UNCCP: Summary Record of a Meeting between Conciliation Commission and His Excellency, Nuri al-Said, Prime Minister of Iraq, 19 February 1949, A/AC.25/SR/G/9.
83. UNCCP: Summary Record of a Meeting between Conciliation Commission and His Excellency, Hamed Frangie, Minister for Foreign Affairs of Lebanon, 23 February 1949, A/AC.25/SR/G/12.
84. *Palestine Post*, 28 February 1949.
85. Amman (Kirkbride) to Foreign Office (Burrows), 22 February 1949, NA, FO 371/75348 E2977.
86. Herbert Parzen, 'The Arab Refugees – Their Origins and Projection into a Problem (1948–1952)', *Jewish Social Studies*, Vol. 31, No. 4 (October 1969), p. 306.
87. McDonald, *My Mission in Israel*, 1948–51, p. 163; Forsythe, *United Nations Peacemaking*, p. 43.
88. The Consul at Jerusalem (Burdett) to the Secretary of State, 2 March 1949, 501.BB Palestine/3-249.
89. Jerusalem (Burdett) to the Secretary of State, 14 March 1949, USNA, 501.BB Palestine/3-1449; Jerusalem (Burdett) to the Secretary of State, 7 March 1949, USNA, 501.BB Palestine/3-1449.
90. United Nations Conciliation Commission For Palestine: First Progress Report, 15 March 1949, A/819.
91. *Palestine Post*, 18 March 1949.
92. *New York Times*, 25 March 1949.
93. Forsythe, *United Nations Peacemaking*, p. 43; It was not just Arab states who attended the Beirut summit. Palestinian Arab organizations such as the Gaza government and the Committee of Arab Refugees from Nazareth and Haifa were also present.
94. Lebanon (Pinkerton) to the Secretary of State, 28 March 1949, USNA, 501.BB Palestine/3-2849.
95. Ibid.
96. Ibid.
97. *Manchester Guardian*, 26 March 1949; *The Times*, 26 March 1949.
98. Memorandum of Conversation, by the Secretary of State, 5 April 1949, *FRUS*, 1949, Vol. VI, pp. 890–4.

99. Ibid.
100. Memorandum on the Refugee Problem, Tel Aviv, 16 March 1949, *DFPI*, Vol. 2, pp. 502–10.
101. Neil Caplan, *The Lausanne Conference, 1949: A Case Study in Middle East Peacemaking* (Tel Aviv University: The Moshe Dayan Center for Middle Eastern and African Studies, 1993), pp. 28–9; Jerusalem (Burdett) to the Secretary of State, Jerusalem, 28 February 1949, USNA, 501.BB Palestine/2-2849.
102. Caplan, *The Lausanne Conference, 1949*, p. 29.
103. *Palestine Post*, 6 April 1949; Lebanon (Pinkerton) to Secretary of State, 5 April 1949, USNA, 501.BB Palestine/4-549; this was with the exception of Iraq, who refused to join the agreement.
104. UNCCP: Summary Record of a Meeting between the Conciliation Commission and the Representatives of the Arab States, 5 April 1949, SR/BM/12.
105. Beirut (Pinkerton) to Secretary of State, 4 April 1949, USNA, 501.BB Palestine/4-449.
106. Azcarate, *Mission in Palestine*, p. 148.
107. Parzen, 'The Arab Refugees', p. 305.
108. Jerusalem (Burdett) to the Secretary of State, Jerusalem, 28 February 1949, USNA, 501.BB Palestine/2-2849.
109. Secretary of State (Acheson) to The Council at Jerusalem (Burdett), 9 March 1949, USNA, 501.BB Palestine/2-2849.
110. Jerusalem (Burdett) to the Secretary of State, Jerusalem, 28 February 1949, USNA, 501.BB Palestine/2-2849.
111. British Legation, Amman (Kirkbride) to Eastern Department, Foreign Office (Burrows), 14 January 1949, NA, FO 371/75417 E1195.
112. Foreign Office to Paris, 3 March 1949, NA, FO 371/75418 E1792.
113. Ibid.; Foreign Office to Baghdad and to Beirut, Cairo, Damascus, Amman, Jedda, Khartoum, 18 February 1949.
114. Telegram from American Representative, Amman, to Washington, 3 February 1949 enclosed in FO Minute (Burrows), 10 February 1949, NA, FO 371/75418 E2020. The report from the US Embassy in Baghdad held a dissenting view arguing that every effort should be made to repatriate refugees in accordance to GAUN Resolution of Dec 11. Telegram from American Embassy, Baghdad, to Washington, 5 February 1949.
115. Dispatch from American Legation, Jidda, 22 January 1949 enclosed in FO Minute (Burrows), 10 February 1949, NA, FO 371/75418 E2020.
116. FO Minute (Burrows), 16 February 1949, NA, FO 371/75419 E2390.
117. State Department to Foreign Office, 11 February 1949 FO 371/75420 E2921; another similar memorandum was sent from the American Consulate General in Jerusalem to the US Secretary of State, and also sent to the PCC, concluding that the solution should be based on the absorption of refugees in Arab countries, 5 February 1949, NA, FO 371/75420 E2921.
118. Chancery, Washington, to Eastern Department, Foreign Office, 16 February 1949, NA, FO 371/75419 E2463.
119. Cairo (Campbell) to Foreign Office, 2 March 1949, NA, FO 371/75420 E2883.
120. Jerusalem (Dow) to Foreign Office, 4 March 1949, NA, FO 371/75420 E2927.
121. FO Minute (Burrows), 2 March 1949, NA, FO 371/75420 E3000.

122. New York to Foreign Office, 30 March 1949, NA, FO 371/75423 E4313.
123. Caplan, *Futile Diplomacy*, Vol. 3, pp. 68–9.
124. Policy Paper Prepared in the Department of State, 15 March 1949, *FRUS*, 1949, Vol. VI, pp. 830–1.
125. Ibid., p. 831.
126. Ibid., pp. 841–2.
127. The Secretary of State to Certain Diplomatic and Consular Offices, 29 April 1949, *FRUS*, 1949, Vol. VI, p. 959; Memorandum Prepared Presumably in the Office of the Coordinator on Palestine Refugee Matters (McGhee), 2 May 1949, *FRUS*, 1949, Vol. VI, p. 964.
128. Ibid.
129. Memorandum by the Assistant Secretary of State for United Nations Affairs (Rusk) to the Under Secretary of State (Webb), 3 March 1949, *FRUS*, 1949, Vol. VI, pp. 788–9.
130. These schemes are analysed in detail in Chapter 4.
131. Memorandum of Conversation, Prepared Presumably by the First Secretary of Embassy in the United Kingdom (Jones), London, 13 April 1949, *FRUS*, 1949, Vol. VI, pp. 906–8; Resettlement of Arab Refugees: Record of a Meeting Held at the Foreign Office, 13 April 1949, NA, FO 371/75424 E4692.
132. Foreign Office to Cairo, 5 May 1949, NA, FO 371/75426 E5660.
133. See Annex 1: Palestine Refugee Problem Conclusions, Annex 2: Palestine Refugees, Policy Recommendations, in Memorandum by the Coordinator on Palestine Refugee Matters (McGhee) to the Secretary of State, Washington, 22 April 1949, *FRUS*, 1949, Vol. VI, pp. 934–43. This paper contained several annexes of proposals and conclusions of papers and meetings. For example, Annex 3 is the Proposed Plan of Action of Resettlement of Arab Refugees: Record of a Meeting Held at the Foreign Office, 13 April 1949, NA, FO 371/75424 E4692.
134. Memorandum Prepared Presumably in the Office of the Coordinator on Palestine Refugee Matters (McGhee), 2 May 1949, *FRUS*, 1949, Vol. VI, pp. 964–5.
135. Memorandum by the Director of the Office of Near Eastern and African Affairs (Satterthwaite) to the Secretary of State, Washington, 4 May 1949, *FRUS*, 1949, Vol. VI, pp. 973–4.
136. Ibid.
137. Tel Aviv (Sharett) to Lausanne (Eytan), 28 April 1949, Israel State Archives (hereafter ISA), LS1/61; it was in fact later reported by Eban that US officials were 'apprehensive to degree of panic' that the talks would fail, see New York (Eban) to Tel Aviv (Sharett), 27 April 1949, *DFPI*, Vol. 2, p. 594.
138. Memorandum of Conversation, by the Secretary of State, 5 April 1949, *FRUS*, 1949, Vol. VI, pp. 890–4.
139. Ibid.
140. Israel (McDonald) to Secretary of State, 8 April 1949, USNA, 501.BB Palestine/4-849.
141. Tel Aviv (Eytan) to New York (Sharett), 7 April 1949, *DFPI*, Vol. 2, p. 562.
142. *Palestine Post*, 6 April 1949.
143. Jerusalem (Ethridge) to President Truman, 11 April 1949, USNA, 501.BB Palestine/4-1149.

144. *New York Times*, 28 April 1949.
145. *The Times*, 28 April 1949.
146. Eytan, *The First Ten Years*, p. 51.
147. Muhammad Nimr al-Hawwari, as quoted by Caplan, *Lausanne Conference*, pp. 121–2.
148. Gabbay, *A Political Study of the Arab-Jewish Conflict*, pp. 265–6; Fischbach, *Records of Dispossession*, p. 91
149. It was speculated by Israel's President Chaim Weizmann that Bunche was going to be the US's representative following Keenan's resignation and his services would be retained by the PCC because of his invaluable experience. *Palestine Post*, 13 December 1948.
150. Eytan, *The First Ten Years*, pp. 50–1.
151. There were still some direct informal contacts made between Israeli and Arab officials, although not endorsed by the US. See for example, Lausanne (Eytan) to Tel Aviv (Sharett), 3 May 1949, *DFPI*, Vol. 4 (Jerusalem: Israel State Archives, 1986), pp. 10–14; Lausanne (Sasson) to Tel Aviv (Sharett), 1 June 1949, *DFPI*, Vol. 4, p. 86; Lausanne (Sasson) to Tel Aviv (Sharett), 2 June 1949, *DFPI*, Vol. 4, p. 89; Pappé, *The Making of the Arab–Israeli Conflict*, pp. 203–43; Shlaim, *Collusion across the Jordan*, pp. 476–88. Morris notes there was a discussion between Sasson and a member of the Palestinian delegation at Lausanne who requested that Israel repatriate 400,000 refugees, see Morris, *The Birth Revisited*, pp. 549–88.
152. Shiloah's comments were in the context of a critique of the PCC's decision to headquarter in Jerusalem, where he believed the Arab states would not come because of King Abdullah's jurisdiction and the intense political atmosphere and publicity. He suggested that while the PCC could base itself in Jerusalem, talks should be held elsewhere. See Tel Aviv (McDonald) to Secretary of State, 1 March 1949, USNA, 501.BB Palestine/3-149.
153. Cairo (Campbell) to Foreign Office, 27 April 1949, NA, FO 371/75350 E5286.
154. Tel Aviv (Sharett) to Eytan (Lausanne), 16 June 1949, ISA, LS64/40.
155. *The Times*, 25 April 1949.
156. See paragraph 6, United Nations Conciliation Commission for Palestine: Third Progress Report, (hereafter UNCCP: Third Progress Report) 21 June 1949, A/927.
157. New York (Arazi) to Sasson, 20 April 1949, *DFPI*, Vol. 2, p. 583.
158. *Palestine Post*, 29 April 1949.
159. Forsythe, *United Nations Peacemaking*, pp. 48–9.
160. The Secretary of State to Certain Diplomatic and Consular Office, 29 April 1949, *FRUS*, 1949, Vol. VI, p. 959.
161. *New York Times*, 12 May 1949.
162. Ibid., 13 May 1949; *Manchester Guardian*, 13 May 1949.
163. See for example Lausanne (Ethridge) to Secretary of State, 12 May 1949, USNA, 501.BB Palestine/5-1249; for the actual texts of the protocol, see United Nations Conciliation Commission for Palestine: Summary Record of a Meeting between Conciliation Commission and the Delegation of Israel, 12 May 1949, A/AC.25/SR/LM/8; UNCCP: Summary Record of a Meeting between Conciliation Commission and the Delegations of the Arab States, 12 May 1949, A/AC.25/SR/LM/9.

164. *Palestine Post*, 10 May 1949; however, Ethridge had requested to be relieved as early as 19 April because an associate of his had also been called for public duty and Etheridge did not believe both could be away from Louisville, Jerusalem (Ethridge) to Secretary of State, 19 April 1949, USNA, 501.BB Palestine/4-1949.
165. Fischbach, *Records of Dispossession*, p. 95.
166. Leader, *The Times*, 27 May 1949.
167. New York (Eban) to Lausanne (Eytan), 15 June 1949, ISA, NA14.
168. Khouri, 'United Nations Peace Efforts', pp. 36–7.
169. The President to Jerusalem (Ethridge), 29 April 1948, USNA, 501.BB Palestine/4-2949.
170. Bern (Ethridge) to Secretary of State, 5 May 1949, USNA, 501.BB Palestine/5-449.
171. The Secretary of State to the Legation in Switzerland, 12 May 1949, *FRUS*, 1949, Vol. VI, pp, 1004–5; this policy was also relayed to Israel's ambassador, see The Secretary of State to the Israeli Ambassador (Elath), Washington, 18 May 1949, *FRUS*, 1949, Vol. VI, p. 1021.
172. Ibid.
173. Switzerland (Vincent) to Secretary of State, 20 May 1949, USNA, 501.BB Palestine/5-2049.
174. The Acting Secretary of State to the Legation in Switzerland, Washington, 24 May 1949, *FRUS*, 1949, Vol. VI, pp. 1051–2.
175. Lausanne (Ethridge) to Secretary of State, 26 May 1949, USNA, 501.BB Palestine/5-2649.
176. Memorandum by the Acting Secretary of State to the President, 27 May 1949, *FRUS*, 1949, Vol. VI, pp. 1060–3.
177. Ibid.
178. The Acting Secretary of State to the Embassy in Israel, Washington, 28 May 1949, *FRUS*, 1949, Vol. VI, pp. 1072–4; J. G. McDonald to D. Ben-Gurion, Tel Aviv, 29 May 1949, *DFPI*, Vol. 4, pp. 75–77.
179. McDonald, *My Mission in Israel*, pp. 165–6; Ben-Gurion's response, on 8 June, was that it was inconceivable that Israel should absorb mass Jewish immigrants while reintegrating returning Arab refugees due to national security and economic feasibility. See The Government of Israel to the Government of the United States, 8 June 1949, *FRUS*, 1949, Vol. VI, pp. 1102–6; M. Sharett to J.G. McDonald, Tel Aviv, 8 June 1949, *DFPI*, Vol. 4, pp. 107–11.
180. Tel Aviv (Sharett) to Lausanne (Eytan), 29 June 1949, ISA, LS39/39.
181. Touval, *The Peace Brokers*, pp. 102–3.
182. *Palestine Post*, 9 June 1949; *New York Times*, 16 June 1949; *Washington Post*, 13 June 1949.
183. For example see Lausanne (Eytan) to Tel Aviv (Sharett), 23 June 1949, *DFPI*, Vol. 4, pp. 154–5; Aide-Memoire by the Government of the United States, Washington, 24 June 1949, *DFPI*, Vol. 4, pp. 173–176.
184. Washington (Franks) to Foreign Office, 13 January 1949, NA, FO 371/75334 E614; The Acting Secretary of State to the Embassy in the United Kingdom, Washington, 13 January 1949, *FRUS*, 1949, Vol. VI, pp. 658–61.
185. McDonald, *My Mission in Israel*, p. 168; it is worth noting that Ethridge complained that McDonald was not using his influence to underline Truman

and the State Department's position, Lausanne (Ethridge) to Secretary of State, 2 June 1949, USNA, 501.BB Palestine/6-249.

186. Caplan, *Futile Diplomacy*, Vol. 3, p. 270.

187. New York (Eban) to Lausanne (Eytan), 23 June 1949, ISA, NA10.

188. Lausanne (Ethridge) to Secretary of State, 2 June 1949, USNA, 501.BB Palestine/6-249; George McGhee recalled that it was mentioned by Ben-Gurion to Ethridge on 18 April, see George McGhee, *Envoy to the Middle World: Adventures in Diplomacy* (New York: Harper & Row), p. 36.

189. Morris, *The Birth Revisited*, p. 564.

190. Switzerland (Vincent) to the Secretary of State, 28 May 1949, USNA, 501.BB Palestine/5-2849.

191. UNCCP: Letter Dated 29 May 1949 Addressed by Mr Walter Eytan. Head of the Delegation of Israel, to the Chairman of the Conciliation Commission, 30 May 1949, A/AC/IS.19.

192. Tel Aviv (McDonald) to Secretary of State, 31 May 1949, USNA, 501.BB Palestine/5-3149.

193. *New York Times*, 4 June 1949; United States Participation in the United Nations: Report by the President to the Congress for the Year 1949, Department of State Publication 3765, Washington, DC: Government Printing Office, 1950, Cited in Forsythe, *United Nations Peacemaking*, p. 54.

194. *New York Times*, 14 June 1949.

195. New York (Eban) to Lausanne (Eytan), 20 June 1949, ISA, NA16.

196. The Acting Secretary of State to the Legation in Switzerland, 4 June 1949, *FRUS*, 1949, Vol. VI, pp. 1090–1.

197. Ibid.

198. Memorandum of Conversation, by the Deputy Under Secretary of State (Rusk), 25 June 1949, *FRUS*, 1949, Vol. VI, pp. 1177–8.

199. The Secretary of State to the Embassy in Egypt, 28 June 1949, *FRUS*, 1949, Vol. VI, p. 1191.

200. Gabbay, *A Political Study of the Arab-Jewish Conflict*, p. 245.

201. Forsythe, *United Nations Peacemaking*, p. 54.

202. The Acting Secretary of State to the Embassy in Egypt, 11 June 1949, *FRUS*, 1949, Vol. VI, p. 1116.

203. Karp, *Missed Opportunities*, p. 81

204. Ibid., pp. 1116–7.

205. The State Department (Acheson) to London, 25 June 1949, NA, FO 371/75430 E7983.

206. The Foreign Office to Cairo, 29 June 1949, NA, FO 371/75430 E7983.

207. FO Minute (Beith), 11 May 1949, NA, FO 371/75333 E6696/G.

208. FO Minute (Jackson) 16 June 1949, NA, FO 371/75333 E7648/G.

209. Morris, *The Birth*, p. 273; Pappé, *The Making of the Arab–Israeli Conflict*, p. 216.

210. Statement to the Knesset by Foreign Minister Sharett, 15 June 1949, Meron Mdzini (ed.), *Israel's Foreign Relations: Selected Documents, 1947–1974, Volume 1* (Jerusalem: Ministry for Foreign Affairs, 1976), pp. 373–5.

211. The *Manchester Guardian* reported his resignation as early as May, see *Manchester Guardian*, 10 May 1949; however, it was not until the end of June that he left his post.

212. The Acting Secretary of State to the Legation in Switzerland, Washington, 20 June 1949, *FRUS*, 1949, Vol. VI, pp. 1161–2.
213. The Secretary of State to the Embassy in the United Kingdom, 26 June 1949, *FRUS*, 1949, Vol. VI, pp. 1179–80.
214. United Nations Conciliation Commission for Palestine: Fourth Progress Report For the period 9 June to 15 September 1949 inclusive (hereafter UNCCP: Fourth Progress Report), 22 September 1949 A/992; The State Department had stated that it considered it desirable to find a simultaneous solution to both the refugee and territorial questions, Department of State to American Legation, Bern (For Lausanne), 7 June 1949, USNA, 501.BB Palestine/6-249.
215. Department of State to American Embassy, Paris, 21 June 1949, USNA, 501.BB Palestine/6-249.
216. Lausanne (Eytan) to New York (Eban), 15 June 1949, *DFPI*, Vol. 4, pp. 132–3.

4 Economics over Politics: The Palestine Conciliation Commission and the Palestinian Refugee Problem (Part 2)

1. UNCCP: Third Progress Report, 21 June 1949, A/927.
2. Neil Caplan, *Futile Diplomacy, Vol. 3*, pp. 90–2.
3. New York (Austin) to Secretary of State, 6 July 1948, USNA, 501.BB Palestine/7-649.
4. London (Douglas) to Secretary of State, 15 July 1949, USNA, 501.BB Palestine/7-1549.
5. FO Minute, 9 July 1949; Foreign Office to Washington, 12 July 1949, NA, FO 371/75350 E8393; The Secretary of State to the Embassy in the United Kingdom, 13 July 1949, *FRUS*, 1949, Vol. VI, pp. 1223–4.
6. The US also inquired how much of the Negev Britain thought should be transferred to the Arabs, The Secretary of State to the Embassy in the United Kingdom, 13 July 1949 *FRUS*, 1949, Vol. VI, pp. 1223–4; while accepting Britain's rejection of asymmetry between refugees and territory, McGhee argued that the PCC should not insist that Egypt obtain compensation for the Gaza Strip. Territorial compensation should only be negotiated if the Arabs demanded it, Washington (Hoyer Millar) to Foreign Office, 14 July 1949, NA, FO 371/75350 E8636.
7. Ibid.
8. Memorandum by the Assistant Secretary of State for Near Eastern and African Affairs (McGhee) to the Secretary of State, 13 July 1949, *FRUS*, 1949, Vol. VI, pp 1218–21.
9. Candice Karp, *Missed Opportunities: US Diplomatic Failures and the Arab–Israeli Conflict 1947–1967* (Claremont: Regina Books, 2005), p. 85.
10. Forsythe, *United Nations Peacekeeping*, p. 55.
11. Ibid.
12. Memorandum to Secretary of State attached in Summary: United States Support of the Palestine Conciliation Commission and Establishment of an Economic Survey Mission, 13 July 1949, USNA, 501.BB Palestine/7-1349; Arthur H. Compton to George McGhee, 13 July 1949, USNA, 501.BB Palestine/7-1349.

13. Geneva (Troutman) to Secretary of State, 15 June 1949, USNA, 501.BB Palestine/6-1549; Department of State to American Embassy, Paris, 15 June 1949, USNA, 501.BB Palestine/6-1549.
14. Lausanne (Rockwell) to Secretary of State, 18 July 1949, USNA, 501.BB Palestine/7-1849.
15. Azcarate, *Mission in Palestine*, p. 154.
16. Washington (Hoyer Millar) to Foreign Office, 18 July 1949, NA, FO 371/75350 E8796.
17. Near East Affairs (McGhee) to Secretary of State, 11 July 1949, USNA, 501.BB Palestine/7-1149.
18. Foreign Office to Washington, 23 July 1949, NA, FO 371/75350 E8789; London (Douglas) to Secretary of State, July 26, 1949, USNA, 501.BB Palestine/7-2649.
19. Foreign Office to Washington, 23 July 1949, NA, FO 371/75350 E8789; London (Douglas) to Secretary of State, 26 July 1949, USNA, 501.BB Palestine/7-2649.
20. *New York Times*, 19 July 1949; *Manchester Guardian*, 19 July 1949.
21. Mr Stewart R. Rockwell, Lausanne, to the Secretary of State, 20 July 1949, *FRUS*, 1949, Vol. VI, pp. 1238–9.
22. The Secretary of State to the Delegation in Switzerland, 22 July 1949, *FRUS*, 1949, Vol. VI, pp. 1243–4.
23. Memorandum by the Assistant Secretary of State for Near Eastern and African Affairs (McGhee) to the Secretary of State, 19 July 1949, *FRUS*, 1949, Vol. VI, pp.1235–7.
24. Bern (Rockwell) to Secretary of State, 23 July 1949, USNA, 501.BB Palestine/7-2249.
25. The Secretary of State to Certain Diplomatic Offices, 16 July 1949, *FRUS*, 1949, Vol. VI, pp. 1230–1.
26. *New York Times*, 21 July 1949.
27. The Minister in Syria (Keeley) to the Secretary of State, 18 July 1949, *FRUS*, 1949, Vol. VI, pp. 1234–5.
28. Ibid.
29. Forsythe, *United Nations Peacekeeping*, pp. 56–7.
30. Lausanne (Porter) to Secretary of State, 26 July 1949, USNA, 501.BB Palestine/7-2649.
31. Ibid.
32. Major General John H. Hilldring to the Secretary of State, 25 July 1949, *FRUS*, 1949, Vol. VI, pp. 1249–52.
33. Ibid.; Israel's offer stipulated that the Palestinian refugees would not be allowed back to their homes but to specified areas in accordance to Israel's economic development plans. See, Jansen, *The United States and the Palestinian People*, p. 112.
34. Memorandum of Conversation, by the Deputy Under Secretary of State (Rusk) 28 July 1949, *FRUS*, 1949, Vol. VI, pp. 1261–4.
35. *Manchester Guardian*, 1 August 1949; Also see Gabbay, *A Political Study of the Arab–Jewish Conflict*, p. 255; Pappé, *The Making of the Arab–Israeli Conflict*, p. 230.
36. *The Times*, 2 August 1949; *Manchester Guardian*, 2 August 1949; *Palestine Post*, 2 August 1949; *New York Times*, 3 August 1949.

37. Memorandum of Conversation, by the Deputy Under Secretary of State (Rusk), 28 July 1949, *FRUS*, 1949, Vol. VI, pp. 1261–4.
38. *Palestine Post*, 3 August 1949; *The Times*, 3 August 1949; *Manchester Guardian*, 3 August 1949.
39. Memorandum of Conversation, by the Deputy Under Secretary of State (Rusk) 28 July 1949, *FRUS*, 1948, Vol. V, pp. 1261–4; Washington (Elath) to Tel Aviv (Sharett), 28 July 1949, *DFPI*, Vol. 4, pp. 262–3.
40. *Palestine Post*, 8 August 1949, cited 80,000 as the figure; Shiloah had apparently told Porter something along similar lines, Lausanne (Porter) to Secretary of State, 4 August 1949, USNA, 501.BB Palestine/8-349.
41. FO Minute (Chadwick), 12 August 1949, NA, FO 371/75436 E9982; this individual close to Truman was probably David Niles, the Administrative Assistant to the President, as he is mentioned in an Israeli correspondence before the formal offer was made. See Tel Aviv (Sharett) to Washington (Elath), 21 July 1949, *DFPI*, Vol. 4, pp. 237–8.
42. Lausanne (Porter) to Secretary of State, 5 August 1949, USNA, 501.BB Palestine/8-549.
43. The Secretary of State to the United Sates Delegation at Lausanne, 9 August 1949, *FRUS*, 1949, Vol. VI, p. 1291; Department of State to US Delegation, PCC, 11August 1949, USNA, 501.BB Palestine/8-1149; Washington (Elath) to Tel Aviv (Sharett), 11 August 1949, *DFPI*, Vol. 4, p. 320; Washington (Elath) to Tel Aviv (Sharett), 18 August 1949, *DFPI*, Vol. 4, pp. 368–9.
44. Lausanne (Shiloah) to Tel Aviv (Sharett), 30 August 1949, ISA, SL102/115.
45. Lausanne (Porter) to Secretary of State, 18 July 1949, USNA, 501.BB Palestine/7-1849.
46. Ibid.
47. The Secretary of State to the United States Delegation at Lausanne, 28 July 1949, *FRUS*, 1949, Vol. VI, p. 1267.
48. *Palestine Post*, 1 August 1949.
49. Lausanne (Shiloah) to Eban (New York), 31 July 1949, ISA, LA20/213.
50. Peretz, *Israel and the Palestine Arabs*, pp. 45–8.
51. Shlaim, *The Iron Wall*, p. 591; Morris, *The Birth Revisited*, p. 573.
52. Peretz, *Israel and the Palestine Arabs*, pp. 49–50.
53. Caplan, *Futile Diplomacy, Vol. 3*, p. 108; Gabbay, *Political Study of the Arab–Jewish Conflict*, p. 256; Shlaim, *Collusion across the Jordan*, p. 473; Pappé, *The Making of the Arab–Israeli Conflict*, p. 215.
54. UNCCP: Summary of a Meeting between the Conciliation Commission and the Delegation of Israel, 3 August 1949, A/AC.25/SR/LM/30.
55. UNCCP: Fourth Progress Report, 22 September 1949 A/992.
56. Lausanne (Porter) to Secretary of State, 5 August 1949, USNA, 501.BB Palestine/8-549; Caplan, *Futile Diplomacy, Vol. 3*, p. 108; Gabbay, *Political Study of the Arab–Jewish Conflict*, p. 257.
57. 'Hope at Lausanne', *Manchester Guardian*, 3 August 1949.
58. *The Times*, 11 August 1949; Forsythe, *United Nations Peacekeeping*, p. 57; UNCCP: Fourth Progress Report, 22 September 1949 A/992.
59. Lausanne (Rockwell) to Secretary of State, 16 August 1949, USNA, 501.BB Palestine/8-1649.
60. Lausanne (Shiloah) to Tel Aviv (Sharett), 12 August 1949, ISA SL99/79.

61. Caplan, *Futile Diplomacy, Vol. 3*, p. 109; Gabbay, *Political Study of the Arab–Jewish Conflict*, p. 257.
62. Lausanne (Porter) to Secretary of State, 5 August 1949, USNA, 501.BB Palestine/8-549.
63. Ibid.
64. The Secretary of State to the United States Delegation at Lausanne, 11 August 1949, *FRUS*, 1949, Vol. VI, pp. 1297–8.
65. Mr Stewart W. Rockwell, Lausanne, to the Secretary of State, 11 August 1949, *FRUS*, 1949, Vol. VI, pp. 1299–301.
66. Ibid.
67. UNCCP: Fourth Progress Report, 22 September 1949 A/992; Mr Stewart W. Rockwell, Lausanne, to the Secretary of State, 15 August 1949, *FRUS*, 1949, Vol. VI, pp. 1313–4.
68. Mr. Stewart W. Rockwell, Lausanne, to the Secretary of State, 15 August 1949, *FRUS*, 1949, Vol. VI, pp. 1313–4; UNCCP: Summary Record of a Meeting between the Conciliation Commission and the Delegations of the Arab States, 15 August 1949, A/AC.25/SR/LM/32; UNCCP: Summary Record of a Meeting between the Conciliation Commission and the Delegation of Israel, 15 August 1949, A/AC.25/SR/LM/31.
69. Forsythe, *United Nations Peacekeeping*, p. 60.
70. UNCCP: Arab response to UNCCP questionnaire of 15 August 1949 – Letter and memo to UNCCP from Arab delegations (Lausanne Conference), 29 August 1949, A/AC.25/AR/17; UNCCP: Fourth Progress Report), 22 September 1949 A/992.
71. Ibid.; the importance of international guarantees for the fair treatment of refugees repatriated to Israel was also stressed.
72. Ibid.; *Palestine Post*, 29 August 1949; *Manchester Guardian*, 31 August 1949.
73. Amman (Stabler) to Secretary of State, 20 July 1949, USNA, 501.BB Palestine/7-2049.
74. UNCCP: Arab response to UNCCP questionnaire of 15 August 1949 – Letter and memorandum to UNCCP from Arab delegations (Lausanne Conference), 29 August 1949, A/AC.25/AR/17; UNCCP: Fourth Progress Report, 22 September 1949 A/992; *Palestine Post*, 29 August 1949; *Manchester Guardian*, 31 August 1949.
75. Ibid.; also see Mr Stewart W. Rockwell to the Secretary of State, Lausanne, 2 September 1949, *FRUS*, 1949, Vol. VI, pp. 1349–50; UNCCP – Resettlement of refugees – Letter from Israel, 1 September 1949, A/AC.25/IS.36; Lausanne (Shiloah) to C. de Boisanger, 31 August 1949, *DFPI*, Vol. 4, pp. 417–20; *Palestine Post*, 2 September 1949.
76. *New York Times*, 2 September 1949.
77. Mr Stewart W. Rockwell, Lausanne, to the Secretary of State, 2 September 1949, *FRUS*, 1949, Vol. VI, pp. 1354–5. Rockwell was pessimistic about the subject of territory because the Arab states were demanding more than what the partition resolution had assigned and were unable to agree among themselves on a common territorial position so they 'threw everything into the pot, apparently leaving it to the PCC or GA to decide what pieces should be pulled out or given to them'.
78. Ibid.

79. See Document 9: PCC Draft Declaration Embodying Apparent Consensus Reach Regarding an Approach to Resolving the Refugee Question, 5 September 1949, in Caplan, *Futile Diplomacy, Vol. 3*, pp. 296–7.
80. Forsythe, *United Nations Peacekeeping*, pp. 62–3; Mr Stewart W. Rockwell, Lausanne, to the Secretary of State, 14 September 1949, *FRUS*, 1949, Vol. 6, pp. 1387–8.
81. Forsythe, *United Nations Peacekeeping*, p. 63.
82. Caplan, *Futile Diplomacy, Vol. 3*, p. 120; The Secretary of State to the United States Delegation at Lausanne, 8 September 1949, Rockwell was pessimistic, p. 1369.
83. *New York Times*, 1 September 1949; *New York Times*, 16 September 1949; UNCCP: Fourth Progress Report, 22 September 1949 A/992.
84. UNCCP: ESM Final Report, 28 December 1949, A/AC.25.6: Appendix 1: First Interim Report of the United Nations Economic Survey Mission for the Middle East, (hereafter UNCCP: ESM Interim Report), 16 November 1949, A/AC.25.6; a similar version can be found in United Kingdom Delegation, New York, to Foreign Office, 25 August 1949, NA, FO 371/75436 E10315.
85. *The Times*, 30 August 1949.
86. *Manchester Guardian*, 24 August 1949.
87. General Lucius Clay was the first choice. However, Truman argued that Clay needed time to recover after 'four years of hell', a reference to his activities in post-war Germany overseeing the Berlin airlift and his subsequent retirement in May 1949; President Truman to Secretary of State, 28 July 1949, USNA, 501.BB Palestine/7-2849. Having met Clapp on 6 September, Abba Eban commented that his sympathies with Israel's position were 'undeniable'. See New York (Eban) to Tel Aviv (Sharett), 7 September 1949, *DFPI*, Vol. 4, pp. 442–3.
88. Memorandum by the Acting Secretary of State to the President, 24 August 1949, *FRUS*, 1949, Vol. VI, p. 1327; Washington (Franks) to Foreign Office, 24 August 1949, NA, FO 371/75436 E 10276; Washington (Hoyer Millar) to Foreign Office, 2 August 1949, NA, FO 371/75435 E9412.
89. Ibid.
90. Lausanne (Rockwell) to Secretary of State, 2 September 1949, USNA, 501.BB Palestine/9-249.
91. *The Times*, 12 September 1949; *New York Times*, 12 September 1949.
92. Department of State (Acheson) to London, 11 February 1949, NA, FO 371/75420 E2921.
93. Baghdad (Mack) to Foreign Office, 4 March 1949, NA, FO 371/75420 E2923; Amman (Kirkbride) to Foreign Office, 4 March 1949, NA, FO 371/75420 E2974.
94. Jerusalem (Burdett) to the Secretary of State, 28 February 1949, USNA, 501.BB Palestine/2-2849.
95. Secretary of State to the Consulate General at Jerusalem, 9 March 1949, *FRUS*, 1949, Vol. VI, pp. 805–7.
96. The Minister in Lebanon (Pinkerton) to the Secretary of State, 22 March 1949, *FRUS*, 1949, Vol. VI, pp. 857–9.
97. Cohen, *Fighting World War Three from the Middle East*, p. 63.

98. The Secretary of State to the Embassy in the United Kingdom, 5 April 1949, *FRUS*, 1949, Vol. VI, pp. 897–8.
99. Memorandum of Conversation, Prepared Presumably by the First Secretary of Embassy in the United Kingdom (Jones), 13 April 1949, *FRUS*, 1949, Vol. VI, pp. 906–8.
100. Memorandum of Conversation, Prepared Presumably by the First Secretary of Embassy in the United Kingdom (Jones), 13 April 1949, *FRUS*, 1949, Vol. VI, pp. 906–8; Resettlement of Arab Refugees: Record of a Meeting Held at the Foreign Office on 13 April 1949, NA, FO 371/ 75424 E4810.
101. *Palestine Post*, 23 May 1949.
102. FO Minute (Beith): Notes on a Preliminary Meeting with Mr McGhee and Mr Lewis Jones, 13 April 1949, NA, FO 371/75424 E4810.
103. Memorandum of Conversation, Prepared Presumably by the First Secretary of Embassy in the United Kingdom (Jones), 13 April 1949, *FRUS*, 1949, Vol. VI, pp. 906–8.
104. *Palestine Post*, 26 April 1949.
105. Annex 3: Palestine Refugee Problem, Proposed Plan of Action, in Memorandum by the Coordinator on Palestine Refugee Matters (McGhee) to the Secretary of State, 22 April 1949, *FRUS*, 1949, Vol. VI, pp. 939–41.
106. The Department of State to the British Embassy, 10 May 1949, *FRUS*, 1949, Vol. VI, pp. 990–2; Washington (Franks) to Foreign Office, 11 May 1949, NA, FO 371/75426 E5969.
107. FO Minute (Beith) 14 May 1949, NA, FO 371/75426 E5970.
108. Memorandum by the Secretary of State to the President: Annex 1, Memorandum on the Palestine Refugee Problem, 4 May, *FRUS*, 1949, Vol. VI, pp. 984–5.
109. The Acting Secretary of State to the Legation in Switzerland, 27 May 1949, *FRUS*, 1949, Vol. VI, pp. 1064–5; Foreign Office to BMEO (Cairo) 8 June 1929, NA, FO 371/75427 E6644.
110. Fischbach, *Records of Dispossession*, pp. 88–90.
111. Special Assistant to the Secretary of State (McGhee) to British Embassy, Washington (Bromley), 3 June 1949, NA, FO 371/75424 E5001.
112. FO Minute (Waterlow), 8 June 1949; Foreign Office to Washington, 16 June 1949, NA, FO 371/75429 E7345.
113. The Acting Secretary of State to the United States Delegation at Lausanne, 9 June 1949, Vol. VI, pp. 1108–9.
114. Hoyer Millar (Washington) to Foreign Office, 14 July 1949, NA, FO 371/75350 E8636.
115. Mark F. Ethridge, Lausanne, to the Secretary of State, 2 June 1949, Vol. VI, pp. 1086–7; according to an article written by Jon Kimche in October 1949, the representatives to the PCC before Porter (Ethridge and Hare) were told by President Truman that it was necessary to have a political peace agreement before McGhee's proposals for a development agency to facilitate work and aid. In August, Porter managed to convince Truman to reverse his decision. Truman agreed as long as the development agency was watered down into a survey mission, *Palestine Post*, 10 October 1949.

116. Department of State to American Legation, Bern (For Lausanne), 7 June 1949, USNA, 501.BB Palestine/6-249.
117. FO Minutes, 6 July 1949, NA, FO 371/75432 E8542.
118. Ibid.
119. Memorandum by the Assistant Secretary of State for Near Eastern and African Affairs (McGhee) to the Secretary of State, Washington, 13 July 1949, 1949, Vol. VI, p. 1219.
120. Foreign Office to Washington, 16 July 1949, NA, FO 371/75350 E8636.
121. Washington (Franks) to Foreign Office, 14 September 1949, NA, FO 371/75438 E11156.
122. Fischbach, *Records of Dispossession*, p. 90.
123. Thicknesse, *Arab Refugees*, p. 28.
124. Washington (Hoyer Millar) to Foreign Office, 18 July 1949; Foreign Office to Washington, 21 July 1949, NA, FO 371/75433 E8797.
125. Secretary of State Acheson to Embassy, London, 26 July 1949, USNA, 501.BB Palestine/7-2649.
126. London (Douglas) to Secretary of State, 6 August 1949, USNA, 501.BB Palestine/8-549.
127. Dr John Murray, an economic adviser to the British Middle East Office in Cairo had earlier suggested: 'Whoever is appointed...should be familiar with the Middle East, strong enough to help keep the Americans and the French and Turks in line, and capable of drafting the Survey Group's report.' FO Minute (Maitland), 13 June 1949, NA, FO 371/75430 E7626; *The Times*, 3 September 1949.
128. Washington (Hoyer Millar) to Foreign Office (Wright), 22 July 1949, NA, FO 371/75435 E9401; Memorandum: Survey Group, 1 August 1949, USNA, 501.BB Palestine/8-149.
129. Memorandum for the Foreign Secretary of State for Near Eastern and African Affairs (McGhee) to the Assistant Secretary of State for Congressional Relations (Gross), 3 September 1949, *FRUS*, 1949, Vol. VI, pp. 1357–8.
130. The Secretary of State, Washington to the United States Mission at the United Nations, 27 August 1949, Vol. VI, p. 1334.
131. Foreign Office to Washington, 30 August 1949, NA, FO 371/75437 E10651.
132. The Department to London, 4 August 1949, NA, FO 371/75435 E9412.
133. Ibid.; FO Minute (Beith), 30 July 1949; The Department (Acheson) to London, 26 July 1949, NA, FO 371/75435 E9402.
134. Foreign Office to Washington, 30 August 1949, NA, FO 371/75437 E10651.
135. The British Embassy to the Department of State, Undated, *FRUS*, 1949, Vol. VI, pp. 1342–4; From Foreign Office to Washington, 30 August 1949, NA, FO 371/75437 E10651; Britain's proposed settlement was a version of its eight-point proposal discussed earlier in this chapter. This version can be found in Enclosure: Proposed Basis of Settlement between Israel and the Arab States, *FRUS*, 1949, Vol. VI, pp. 1345–6.
136. Aide-Memoire (To the British Embassy), Washington, 13 September 1949, USNA, 501.BB Palestine (E)/9-1349.
137. Secretary of State (Acheson) to American Embassy, London, 15 September 1949, USNA, 501.BB Palestine (E)/9-1249 CS/W.
138. Washington (Franks) to Foreign Office, 13 September 1949, NA, FO 371/75438 E11156; Washington (Franks) to Foreign Office, 14

September 1949, NA, FO 371/75438 E11179; Aide-Memoire (to the British Embassy), Washington, 13 September 1949, USNA, 501.BB Palestine (E)/9-1349.

139. Ibid.; this was not dissimilar to the British position, although Britain stressed the importance of the territorial aspect of the conflict. Britain did not want to continue relief without being certain that resettlement was on the way. Foreign Office to Washington, 30 August 1949, NA, FO 371/75437 E10651.

140. In Tel Aviv, however, Clapp said he would speak about compensation and resettlement, Washington (Franks) to Foreign Office, 23 September 1949, NA, FO 371/75439 E11563.

141. Lausanne (Rockwell) to Secretary of State, 8 September 1949, USNA, 501.BB Palestine (E)/9-849; *Palestine Post*, 12 September 1949.

142. Ibid.

143. *Palestine Post*, 15 September 1949.

144. Beirut (Bailey) to Foreign Office, 16 September 1949, NA, FO 371/75439 E11297.

145. Foreign Office to Beirut, 22 September 1949, NA, FO 371/75439 E11297.

146. Alexandria (Chapman Andrews) to Foreign Office, 26 September 1949, NA, FO 371/75440 E11667.

147. Secretary of State (Acheson) to American Embassy, London, 21 September 1949, USNA, 501.BB Palestine (E)/9-2149.

148. Ibid.

149. London (Holmes) to Secretary of State, 24 September 1949, USNA, 501.BB Palestine/9-2449.

150. British Consulate General, Jerusalem (Dow) to Foreign Office (Burrows), 23 September 1949, NA, FO 371/75440 E11869.

151. FO Minute (Sheringham): Economic Survey Mission, 20 September 1949, NA, FO 371/75438 E11179.

152. Tel Aviv (Ford) to Secretary of State, 20 August 1949, USNA, 501.BB Palestine/8-2049.

153. For instance, Shiloah assumed the official Israeli attitude would be a positive one, although qualified, see Lausanne (Shiloah to Tel Aviv (Sharett), 23 August 1949, ISA SL09/65

154. *Palestine Post*, 28 August 1949.

155. Tel Aviv (Helm) to Foreign Office, 27 September 1949, NA, FO 371/75440 E11678; two newspaper offices also received warnings that the lives of the UN individuals were in danger, *Palestine Post*, 7 October 1949; New York (Austin) to Secretary of State, 4 October 1949, USNA, 501.BB Palestine (E)/10-449.

156. Beirut (Houstoun-Boswell) to Foreign Office, 30 September 1949, FO 371/75440 E11916; The Minister in Lebanon (Pinkerton) to the Secretary of State, Beirut, 1 October 1949, 1949, Vol. VI, p. 1416.

157. Beirut (Houstoun-Boswell) to Foreign Office, 13 October 1949, NA, FO 371/75443 E12411.

158. Ibid.

159. Ibid.; The Minister in Lebanon (Pinkerton) to the Secretary of State, 13 October 1949, FRUS, 1949, Vol. VI, p. 1425.

160. American Embassy, London (Holmes) to Secretary of State, 18 October 1949, USNA, 501.BB Palestine (E)/10-1449; *Manchester Guardian*, 11 October 1949; *The Times*, 11 October 1949.
161. The Secretary of State to Certain Diplomatic Offices, 3 September 1949, 1949, Vol. VI, pp. 1358–9.
162. American Embassy, Cairo (Patterson) to Secretary of State,4 September 1949, USNA, 501.BB Palestine/8-2449.
163. Washington (Franks) to Foreign Office, 13 September 1949; Foreign Office to Baghdad, 14 September 1949, NA, FO 371/75438 E11150; The Secretary of State, Washington, to the Embassy of the United Kingdom, 13 September 1949, *FRUS*, 1949, Vol. VI, p. 1382.
164. From Foreign Office to Cairo, 15 September 1949; From Foreign Office to Tel Aviv, 14 September 1949, NA, FO 371/75438 E11150; it was instructed to tell the Iraqi government that whatever the political and territorial settlement and the number of refugees Israel would accept, there was bound to be a hard core of refugees the Arab states would have to cope with.
165. Beirut (Baily) to Foreign Office, 14 September 1949, NA, FO 371/75438 E11202. Later, Nuri Pasha of Iraq said that with conditions he was willing to receive members of the ESM, Baghdad (Trevelyn) to Foreign Office, 21 September 1949, NA, FO 371/75439 E11456.
166. Beirut (Baily) to Foreign Office, 9 September 1949, NA, FO 371/75438 E10987.
167. Beirut (Baily) to Foreign Office, 9 September 1949, NA, FO 371/75438 E11003.
168. The Secretary of State, Washington, to the Legation in Lebanon, 15 September 1949, *FRUS*, 1949, Vol. VI, p. 1389.
169. Beirut (Baily) to Foreign Office, 16 September 1949, NA, FO 371/75439 E 11297.
170. The Minister in Lebanon (Pinkerton) to the Secretary of State, 19 September 1949, *FRUS*, 1949, Vol. VI, p. 1393.
171. *Manchester Guardian*, 26 September 1949; *Palestine Post*, 26 September 1949.
172. *Manchester Guardian*, 10 September 1949.
173. *Palestine Post*, 12 September 1949.
174. Damascus (Man) to Foreign Office, 21 September 1949, NA, FO 371/75439 E11479.
175. The Acting Secretary of State to the Embassy in Saudi Arabia, Washington, 29 September 1949. *FRUS*, 1949, Vol. VI, p. 1414; also see Jedda (Scott-Fox) to Foreign Office, 27 September 1949, NA, FO 371/75440 E11740.
176. The Chargé in Saudi Arabia (Hill) to the Secretary of State, 12 October 1949, *FRUS*, 1949, Vol. VI, p. 1424.
177. The Minister in Lebanon (Pinkerton) to the Secretary of State, 1 October 1949, *FRUS*, 1949, Vol. VI, p. 1415.
178. Damascus (Broadmead) to Foreign Office, 30 September 1949, NA, FO 371/75441 E11922.
179. Tel Aviv (Helm) to Foreign Office, 10 October 1949, NA, FO 371/75442 E12248; in the official UN account, the Syrian foreign minister expressed interest in long-term projects but not temporary works projects, see United

Nations Economic Survey Mission for the Middle East: Notes on a Meeting with Officials of the Government of Syria, Held in Damascus on 9 October 1949 at 10:30AM enclosed in American Legation, Beirut, (Clapp) to George McGhee, 17 October 1949, USNA, 501.BB Palestine/10-1349.

180. Beirut (Houstoun-Boswell) to Foreign Office, 17 October 1949, NA, FO 371/75444 E12637; Baghdad (Dorsz) to Secretary of State, 15 October 1949, USNA, 501.BB Palestine (E)/10-1549.

181. Beirut (Pinkerton) to Secretary of State, 17 October 1949, USNA, 501.BB Palestine (E)/10-1749.

182. Fischbach, *Records of Dispossession*, pp. 103–4.

183. British Middle East Office, Cairo (Troutbeck) to Foreign Office, 19 September 1949, NA, FO 371/75439 E11425.

184. Damascus (Broadmead) to Foreign Office, 28 September 1949, NA, FO 371/75440 E11785; The Minister in Lebanon (Pinkerton) to the Secretary of State, 1 October 1949, *FRUS*, 1949, Vol. VI, p. 1416; Amman (Fritzlan) to Secretary of State, 1 October 1949, USNA, 501.BB Palestine/10-149.

185. The Secretary of State to the Legation in Lebanon, 2 November 1949, *FRUS*, 1949, Vol. VI, pp. 1463–5.

186. Foreign Office to Beirut, 12 October 1949, NA, FO 371/75441 E11933.

187. Memorandum of Conversation, by the Second Secretary of the Embassy in the United Kingdom (Root), 9 November 1949, *FRUS*, 1949, Vol. VI, pp. 1479–80.

188. Editorial note, *FRUS*, 1949, Vol. VI, p. 1472; *Palestine Post*, 18 November 1949.

189. UNCCP: ESM Interim Report, 16 November 1949, A/AC.25.6. *New York Times*, 18 November 1949; *The Observer*, 20 November 1949.

190. Memorandum by the Assistant Chief of the Division of Near Eastern Affairs (Wilkins) to the Assistant Secretary of State for Near Eastern and African Affairs (McGhee), Washington, 27 September 1949, *FRUS*, 1949, Vol. VI, pp. 1407–8.

5   Compensation: The Key to Break the Logjam?

1. United Nations General Assembly Resolution 302 (IV). Assistance to Palestinian Refugees, 8 December 1949 A/RES/302 (IV).

2. Ibid.

3. UNCCP: ESM Interim Report, 16 November 1949, A/AC.25.6.

4. United Nations General Assembly Resolution 194 (III), Palestine: Progress Report of the United Nations Mediator, 11 December 1948, A/Res/194.

5. United Nations General Assembly Resolution 302 (IV). Assistance to Palestinian Refugees, 8 December 1949, A/RES/302 (IV).

6. Mr Crawford (British Middle East Office, Cairo) to Foreign Office, 20 October 1949, NA, FO 371/75444 E12724.

7. Paul Porter had resigned. His replacement, Ely Eliot Palmer, was a native of Providence, Rhode Island and a graduate of Brown, Sorbonne and George Washington Universities. He had held various diplomatic posts and had been stationed at Jerusalem, Beirut and was a former ambassador to Afghanistan. See Joseph Palmer (American Embassy, London) to Bernard

Burrows (Foreign Office, London), 4 November 1949, NA, FO 371/75446 E13248.

8. *Daily Mail*, 29 October 1949; *Daily Express*, 29 October 1949; *The Times*, 29 October 1949; *Manchester Guardian*, 29 October 1949.
9. *Manchester Guardian*, 1 November 1949.
10. Sir. K. Helm (Tel Aviv) to Foreign Office, 9 November 1949, NA, FO 371/75354 E13575.
11. Beirut (Houstoun-Boswell) to Foreign Office, 18 October 1949, NA, FO 371/75444 E12666. It is noted that Britain did not want to be part of the Palestine Commission because it would attach an 'odium' to it like the one the PCC had, see Beirut (Houstoun-Boswell) to Foreign Office, 6 October 1949, NA, FO 371/75444 E12666; Draft for Consideration ESM: Proposal for Long-Term Commission and Working Draft Resolution on Palestine, 26 October 1949, NA, FO 371/75445 E13041.
12. UK Delegation, United Nations (New York) to Foreign Office, 3 August 1950, NA, FO 371/82196 EE10110/38.
13. FO Minute (Sheringham), 25 October 1949, FO 371/75444 E12666; NA, FO Minute (Burrows), 31 October 1949, FO 371/75445 E13239; Foreign Office to Washington, 1 November 1949, NA, FO 371/75445 E13259; Memorandum of Conversation: Economic Survey Mission (Wilkins), 1 November 1949, USNA, 501.BB Palestine (E)/11-149 CS/P; London (Douglas) to Secretary of State, 3 November 1949, USNA 501.BB Palestine (E)/11-349.
14. The United States Representative to the United Nations (Austin) to the Department of State, 29 November, *FRUS*, 1951, Vol. 5, pp. 944–5.
15. Memorandum of Conversation, Prepared Presumably by the First Secretary of Embassy in the United Kingdom (Jones), 13 April 1949, *FRUS*, 1949, Vol. VI, pp. 906–8; FO Minute (Beith): Notes on a Preliminary Meeting with Mr McGhee and Mr. Lewis Jones, 13 April 1949, NA, FO 371/75424 E4810.
16. Record of discussion between Mr Michael Wright and members of the State Department (Communicated by the State Department), 14 November 1949, NA, FO 371/75356 E147821. Also in NA, FO 371/75056 E13986/G; Washington (Franks) to Foreign Office, 18 November 1949, NA, FO 371/75056 E13986/G.
17. Foreign Office to Washington, 23 August 1950, NA, FO 371/82196 EE10110/38.
18. FO Minute (P.R. Oliver): The Palestine Conciliation Commission and Prospects of a Lasting Palestine Settlement, 17 August 1950, NA, FO 371/82196 EE10110/41.
19. FO Minute (Furlonge): Future of the Palestine Conciliation Commission, 23 August 1950, NA, FO 371/82196 EE10110/42.
20. Memorandum by Messrs. John W. Halderman and James W. Barco of the Office of the United Nations Political and Security Affairs, 3 January 1950, *FRUS*, 1950, Vol. V, pp. 661–4.
21. Ibid.
22. *Manchester Guardian*, 29 January 1950.
23. United Nations Conciliation Commission for Palestine: Sixth Progress Report for the period 9 December to 8 May 1950 inclusive (hereafter UNCCP: Sixth Progress Report), 29 May 1950, A/1255.

24. Ibid.
25. Ibid.; it has been argued that the Arab states wanted a UN-imposed solution to avoid appearing to have surrendered rights to Israel, see Khouri 'United Nations Peace Efforts', pp. 8–14; Touval, *The Peace Brokers*, p. 79; Pelcovits, *The Long Armistice*, p. 18.
26. The United States Representative on the Palestine Conciliation Commission (Palmer) to the Secretary of State, 9 March 1950, *FRUS*, 1950, Vol. V, pp. 794–6.
27. Washington (Jones) to Harding F. Bancroft, Director, Office of United Nations Political Affairs, Washington, 27 February 1950, USNA, 357.AC/2–2750 CS/CVE.
28. UNCCP: Sixth Progress Report, 29 May 1950, A/1255.
29. UNCCP – The question of Compensation – Working paper of the Secretariat, 25 January 1950, A/AC.25/W/33.
30. Geneva (Palmer) to Secretary of State, 28 January 1950, USNA, 357.AC/1–2850.
31. Geneva (Palmer) to Secretary of State, 28 January 1950, USNA, 357.AC/1-2850.
32. Geneva (Palmer) to Secretary of State, 31 January 1950, USNA, 357.AC/1-3150.
33. The Secretary of State to the United States Delegation to the Palestine Conciliation Commission, at Geneva, 7 February 1950, *FRUS*, 1950, Vol. V, pp. 728–9.
34. Ibid.
35. Ibid.
36. UNCCP: Summary Record of the One Hundred and Twenty-Ninth Meeting, 24 February 1950, A/AC.25/SR.129.
37. UNCCP: Summary Record for the One Hundred and Thirty-Second Meeting, 2 March 1950, SR/132.
38. Ibid.
39. Commission's modus operandi/Meeting with Arab delegations – UNCCP – Summary record, March 29, 1950, A/AC.25/SR/GM/4; Commission's modus operandi/Meeting with Israel – UNCCP – Summary record, March 29, 1950, A/AC.25/SR/GM/5.
40. FO Minute (Furlonge), 6 April 1950, NA, FO 371/82195 EE10110/6; *New York Times*, 18 April 1950.
41. *The Times*, 13 April 1950; *Manchester Guardian*, 13 April 1950.
42. The Ambassador in Egypt (Caffery) to the Secretary of State, 14 April 1950, *FRUS*, 1950, Vol. V, pp. 858–9; Geneva to Secretary of State, 17 April 1950, USNA, 357.AC/4-1750; Washington (Franks) to Foreign Office, 17 April 1950, NA, FO 371/82195 EE10110/13. It was earlier reported that in Egypt, the Arab League had approved a proposal that Arab delegates could sit on purely technical commissions on the condition that 'the Jews' formally accept the UN decision on Palestine and the Lausanne Protocol, see Cairo (Campbell) to Foreign Office, 13 April 1950, NA, FO 371/82195 EE10110/7.
43. *Manchester Guardian*, 14 April 1950.
44. The United States Representative on the Palestine Conciliation Commission (Palmer) to the Secretary of State, 22 April 1950, *FRUS*, 1950, Vol. V, p. 867.

45. UNPCC Eighth Progress Report, 23 October 1950, A/1367/Rev.1. UNCCP – Note to Israel, 11 May 1950, A/AC.25/IS.49; UNCCP mixed committees, request to nominate representatives – Note from the UNCCP to the Arab governments (in French), 11 May 1950, A/AC.25/AR/29.
46. Ibid.
47. The Ambassador in Israel (McDonald) to the Secretary of State, 20 June 1950, *FRUS*, 1950, Vol. V, p. 935.
48. The United States Representative on the Palestine Conciliation Commission (Palmer) to the Secretary of State, 13 June 1950, *FRUS*, 1950, Vol. V, pp. 928–30; Establishment of mixed committee on refugees – UNCCP meeting with Arab delegations – Summary record, 12 June 1950, A/AC.25/SR/GM/6.
49. Mr. Bancroft (UNP) to Mr William Ketner, 14 June 1950, USNA, 357.AC/6-1450.
50. The Ambassador in Israel (McDonald) to the Secretary of State, 20 June 1950, *FRUS*, 1950, Vol. V, p. 935.
51. Memorandum: The Palestinian Refugee Problem (Palmer) enclosed in Palmer to Raymond A. Hare (State Department), 7 February 1950, USNA, 357.AC/2-750.
52. Ibid.
53. Ibid.
54. Harry S. Truman, *Inaugural Address*, 20 January 1949, http://www.trumanlibrary.org/calendar/viewpapers.php?pid=1030 (Last visited 26 July 2011).
55. Memorandum: The Palestinian Refugee Problem (Palmer) enclosed in Palmer to Raymond A. Hare (State Department), 7 February 1950, USNA, 357.AC/2-750; Palmer worried that if the amount of compensation reached US$300 million, Israel would not be willing or able to pay the sum and alluded to future loans.
56. Palestine Conciliation Commission for Palestine, Note: On Compensation for the Property of Refugees who Decide Not to Return to Their Homes (Working Document Prepared by the Secretariat), 22 April 1950, ACC.25/4/43.
57. Ibid.
58. UNCCP: Summary Record for the One Hundred and Sixty-Third Meeting, 7 June 1950, ACC.25/SR/163.
59. Ibid.
60. Geneva (Palmer) to Secretary of State, 15 July 1950, USNA, 357.AC/7-1550; Tel Aviv (Sharett) to Geneva (Boisanger), 9 July 1950, *DFPI*, Vol. 5, pp. 428–9.
61. *Manchester Guardian*, 11 July 1950.
62. See The United States Representative on the Palestine Conciliation Commission (Palmer) to the Secretary of State, Jerusalem, 21 August 1950, *FRUS*, 1950, Vol. V, pp. 875–6; The United States Representative on the Palestine Conciliation Commission (Palmer) to the Secretary of State, Jerusalem, 31 August 1950, *FRUS*, 1950, Vol. V, pp. 989–90.
63. UNCCP: Summary Record for the One Hundred and Eightieth Meeting, 31 August 1950, A/CC.25/SR/180; Meeting: M. Sharett – Members of the United Nations Conciliation Commission for Palestine, Tel Aviv, 17 August 1950, *DFPI*, Vol. 5, pp. 470–9.

64. Washington (Eban) to Tel Aviv (Sharett), 31 August 1950, *DFPI*, Vol. 5, p. 513.
65. Geneva (Palmer) to Secretary of State, 9 September 1950, USNA, 357.AC/9-950.
66. UNP Mr Ludow to UNE Mr Tomlinson, 22 September 1950, 357.USNA, AC/9-2250 CS/Y.
67. *New York Times*, 18 August 1950.
68. Memorandum by the Acting Assistant Secretary of State for Near Eastern, South Asian and African Affairs (berry), to the Secretary of State, 21 September 1950, *FRUS*, 1950, Vol. V, p. 1016.
69. Memorandum of Conversation, by Mr Wells Stabler, 9 October 1950, *FRUS*, 1950, Vol. V, pp. 1025–6.
70. Memorandum of Conversation, Compensation by Israel for Arab Refugees, 2 November 1950, USNA, 786.00/11-250.
71. The recommendations for a fund to be available for projects of refugee reintegration, surveys and technical assistance was at this time being discussed and later featured in UNRWA's interim reports and served as a basis for UNGA Resolution 393 (V) of 2 December 1950. For the report recommendations, see United Nations Assistance to Palestinian Refugees: Interim Report of the Director of the United Nations Relief and Works Agency for Palestinian Refugees in the Near East, General Assembly Official Records: Fifth Session Supplements No. 19, 6 October 1950, A/1451/Rev.1.
72. Foreign Office to New York, 5 November 1950, NA, FO 371/82257 EE18213/13; also see FO Minute (Furlonge), 4 November 1950, NA, FO 371/82257 EE18213/14.
73. Tel Aviv (Helm) to G.W. Furlonge, Eastern Department, Foreign Office, 14 November 1950, NA, FO 371/82557 EE18213/18A.
74. Beirut (Houstoun-Boswell) to G.W. Furlonge, Eastern Department, Foreign Office, 30 November 1950, NA, FO 371/82257 EE18213/24.
75. Memorandum of Conversation, by Wells Stabler, 26 October 1950, *FRUS*, 1950, Vol. V, pp. 1036–7.
76. The Secretary of State to the Embassy in Israel, Washington, 28 November 1950, *FRUS*, 1950, Vol. V, p. 1063.
77. Tel Aviv Helm) to Foreign Office, 1 November 1950, NA, FO 371/82257 EE18213/13.
78. Marseille (Palmer) to Secretary of State, 15 January 1951, USNA, 357.AC/1-1551.
79. Peretz, *Israel and the Palestine Arabs*, pp. 198–9.
80. The United States Representative on the Palestine Conciliation Commission (Palmer) to the Secretary of State, 27 January 1951, *FRUS*, 1951, Vol. V, 564–5.
81. Secretary of State (Acheson) to American Consul, Jerusalem (Palmer), 19 February 1951, USNA, 357.AC/2-1951.
82. Ibid.
83. Tel Aviv (Helm) to Foreign Office, 9 February 1951, NA, FO 371/91410 EE1826/12.
84. Ibid.
85. Jerusalem (Palmer) to Secretary of State, 6 March 1951, USNA, 357.AC/3-651.

86. Ibid.
87. Ibid.
88. Memorandum by James M. Ludlow of the Office of the United Nations Political and Security Affairs to the Assistant Secretary of State for United Nations Affairs (Hickerson), Washington, 14 March 1951, *FRUS*, 1951, Vol. V, p. 593.
89. United Nations General Assembly Resolution 394 (V). 14 December 1950, A/RES/394 (V).
90. For discussions during 1950 about the possible abolition of the PCC and possible alternatives, see Memorandum of Conversation, by Mr John W. Halderman of the Office of United Nations Political and Security Affairs, 11 July 1950, *FRUS*, 1950, Vol. V, pp. 949–50; UK Delegation, United Nations (New York) to Foreign Office, 3 August 1950, NA, FO 371/82196 EE10110/38; Foreign Office to Washington, 23 August 1950, NA, FO 371/82196 EE10110/38; FO Minute (P.R. Oliver): The Palestine Conciliation Commission and Prospects of a Lasting Palestine Settlement, 17 August 1950, NA, FO 371/82196 EE10110/41; Washington (Franks) to Foreign Office, 30 August 1950, NA, FO 371/82196 EE10110/47; Tel Aviv (Chadwick) to Foreign Office, 4 September 1950, NA, FO 371/82196 EE10110/50.
91. Washington (Franks) to Foreign Office, 11 October 1950, NA, FO 371/82197 EE10110/64; McGhee and Sandifer to Secretary of State, 25 October 1950, USNA, 357-AC/10-2550.
92. United Nations, Official Records of the General Assembly Fifth Session Plenary Meetings, New York, 19 September to 15 December, pp. 667–8; UK Delegation New York (Jebb) to Foreign Office, 15 December 1950, NA, FO 371/82197 EE10110/74.
93. See United Nations, Official Records of the General Assembly Fifth Session, Ad Hoc Political Committee, New York, 30 September to 14 December, pp. 443–68.
94. Ibid., pp. 456, 463–7.
95. United Nations General Assembly Resolution 394 (V), 14 December 1950, A/Res/394 (V).
96. Ibid.
97. FO Minute (Sheringham), 15 June 1950, NA, FO 371/82257 EE1823/3.
98. Ibid.
99. London (Douglas) to Secretary of State, 21 June 1950, USNA, 357.AC/6-2150.
100. Foreign Office (Furlonge) to Tel Aviv (Helm), 23 October 1950, NA, FO 371/82257 EE18213/7.
101. Ibid.
102. Memorandum of Conversation, Compensation by Israel for Arab Refugees, 2 November 1950; Personal Note for Mr Waldo: Compensation for Arab refugees, 2 November 1950, USNA, 786.00/11-250.
103. Memorandum of Conversation by the Assistant Secretary of State for Near Eastern, South Asian and African Affairs (McGhee), to the Secretary of State, 17 April 1951, *FRUS*, 1951, Vol. V, pp. 642–5.
104. Fischbach, *Records of Dispossession*, pp. 187–91.
105. Foreign Office to Washington, 12 July 1950, NA, FO 371/82196 EE10110/26.

106. Foreign Office to New York, 5 November 1950, NA, FO 371/82257 EE18213/13; also see FO Minute (Furlonge), 4 November 1950, NA, FO 371/82257 EE18213/14.
107. Ibid.
108. Washington (Franks) to Foreign Office, 18 July 1950, NA, FO 371/82196 EE10110/30.
109. Jerusalem (Judd) to Foreign Office, 20 July 1950, NA, FO 371/82196 EE10110/31.
110. Foreign Office (Furlonge) to Tel Aviv (Helm), 23 October 1950, NA, FO 371/82257 EE18213/7.
111. Foreign Office to New York, 5 November 1950, NA, FO 371/82257 EE18213/13; also see FO Minute (Furlonge), 4 November 1950, NA, FO 371/82257 EE18213/14.
112. New York (Jebb) to Foreign Office, 15 November 1950, NA, FO 371/82257 EE18213/17.
113. Memorandum of Conversation: Visit of Mr Barco (Brinson), 22 March 1951, NA, FO 371/91410 EE1826/23.
114. Ibid.
115. Ibid.
116. Memorandum of Informal United States–United Kingdom Discussions, in Connection With the Visit to London of The Honorable George C. McGhee, 2–3 April, 2 April 1951, *FRUS*, 1951, Vol. V, pp. 612–4.
117. Jerusalem (Palmer) to Secretary of State, 9 May 1951, USNA, 357.AC/5-951.
118. Ibid.; Jerusalem (Palmer) to Secretary of State, 7 June 1951, USNA, 357.AC/6-75; Tel Aviv (Comay) to New York (Lourie), 7 June 1951, *DFPI*, Vol. 6, pp. 364–7.
119. Ibid.
120. Ibid. It is worth noting that Sharett expressed his concern about Israeli public opinion to compensation for those it had only recently fought against.
121. 121 The Secretary of State to the United States Representative on the Palestine Conciliation Commission (Palmer), at Jerusalem, 12 June 1951, *FRUS*, 1951, Vol. V, p. 725.
122. Ibid.
123. Ibid.
124. British Legation, Tel Aviv (Helm) to G.W. Furlonge, Eastern Department, Foreign Office, 14 June 1951, NA, FO 371/91410 EE1826/26.
125. Fischbach, *Records of Dispossession*, p. 115.
126. Jerusalem (Palmer) to Secretary of State, 9 May 1951, USNA, 357.AC/5-951.
127. Ibid.
128. Ibid.
129. The Secretary of State to the United States Representative on the Palestine Conciliation Commission (Palmer), at Jerusalem, 12 June 1951, *FRUS*, 1951, Vol. V, pp. 714–17.
130. Ibid.
131. Touval, *The Peace Brokers*, pp. 94–6.
132. The Secretary of State to the United States Representative on the Palestine Conciliation Commission (Palmer), at Jerusalem, 7 July 1951, *FRUS*, 1951, Vol. V, pp. 753–6.

133. Memorandum by the Assistant Secretary of State for United Nations Affairs (Hickerson) and Assistant Secretary of State for Near Eastern, South Asian and African Affairs (McGhee), to the Secretary of State, 26 July 1951, *FRUS*, 1951, Vol. V, pp. 797–8.
134. The Secretary of State to the United States Representative on the Palestine Conciliation Commission (Palmer), at Geneva, 27 July 1951, *FRUS*, 1951, Vol. V, pp. 799–801.
135. *Manchester Guardian*, 9 September 1951.
136. Jerusalem (Palmer) to Secretary of State, 21 August 1951, USNA, 357.AC/8-2151.
137. Paris (Palmer) to Secretary of State, 30 August 1951, USNA, 357.AC/83051.
138. The United States Representative on the Palestine Conciliation Commission (Palmer) to the Secretary of State, 24 August 1951, *FRUS*, 1951, Vol. V, pp. 840–1.
139. *The Times*, 13 August 1951.
140. *The Times*, 30 August 1951; *New York Times*, 11 September 1951; *New York Times*, 14 August, 1951; Caplan, *Futile Diplomacy, Vol. 3*, p. 168; Forsythe, *United Nations Peacemaking*, p. 89.
141. *New York Times*, 15 September 1951.
142. Caplan, *Futile Diplomacy, Vol. 3*, p. 168.
143. FO Minute (Bowker), 9 August 1951, FO 371/91365 EE 1071/9.
144. The Tripartite Declaration was a joint American, British and French communiqué which opposed the use and threat of force in the region and pledged to limit arms sales to the region to prevent an arms build up and ensure arms purchases in the region would not be for acts of aggression. For its text see, *Tripartite Declaration Regarding the Armistice Borders: Statement by the Governments of the United States, the United Kingdom, and France*, 25 May 1950, http://unispal.un.org/UNISPAL. NSF/0/3EF2BAA011AD818385256C4C0076E724 (Last visited 13 June 2010).
145. Foreign Office to Amman, 10 August 1951, NA, FO 371/91365 EE1071/10.
146. Foreign Office to Amman, 11 August 1951, NA, FO 371/91365 EE1071/10.
147. Foreign Office (Furlonge) to Washington (Burrows), 30 August 1951, NA, FO 371/91365 EE1071/14.
148. Washington (Burrows) to Foreign Office (Furlonge), 24 September 1951, NA, FO 371/91366 EE1071/39.
149. FO Minute (P.R. Oliver): Palestine Conciliation Commission to be Held in Paris on the 10th September, 1951, 7 September 1951, NA, FO 371/91365 EE1071/30.
150. *The Times*, 11 September 1951.
151. For a comprehensive account of the Paris Conference see, Caplan, *Futile Diplomacy, Vol. 3*, pp. 162–211; Azcarate, *Mission to Palestine*, pp. 174–8; Forsythe, *United Nations Peacemaking*, pp. 86–93.
152. The United States Representative on the Palestine Conciliation Commission (Palmer) to the Secretary of State, 18 September 1951, FRUS, 1951, Vol. 5, pp. 864–69; UNCCP: Summary Record of a Meeting Between the Conciliation Commission and the Delegations of Israel, Paris, 21 September 1951, A/AC.25/SR/PM/5; UNPCC Tenth Progress Report, 20 November 1951 A/1985.

153. Ibid.; The United States Representative on the Palestine Conciliation Commission (Palmer) to the Secretary of State, 24 October 1951, *FRUS*, 1951, Vol. V, pp. 918–9.
154. Paris (Palmer) to Secretary of State, 31 October 1951, USNA, 357.AC/10-3151; UNCCP – Comprehensive proposals to Israel and Arab States – Letter to Israel/Egypt/Jordan/Lebanon/Syria, 31 October 1951, A/AC.25/IS.76.
155. UNPCC Tenth Progress Report, 20 November 1951 A/1985.
156. Ibid.
157. Central Bureau of Statistics, *Statistical Abstract of Israel 2012*, No. 63, Table 4.4: Immigrants, by Period of Immigration, Country of Birth and Last Country of Residence.
158. The Government of Israel to the Government of the United States, 8 June 1949, *FRUS*, 1949, Vol. VI, pp. 1102–6.
159. The Consul at Jerusalem (Burdett) to the Secretary of State, 8 February 1949, *FRUS*, 1949, Vol. VI, pp. 735–8.
160. Michael R. Fischbach, *Jewish Property Claims against Arab Countries* (New York: Columbia University Press, 2008), pp. 116–8.
161. The Consul at Jerusalem (Burdett) to the Secretary of State, 26 February 1949, *FRUS*, 1949, Vol. VI, pp. 772–4.
162. Tel Aviv (Eytan) to Tel Aviv (Palmer), 29 March 1951, *DFPI*, Vol. 6, pp. 196–7.
163. The United States Representative on the Palestine Conciliation Commission (Palmer) to the Secretary of State, 21 September 1951, *FRUS*, 1951, Vol. V, pp. 873–5.
164. Peretz, *Israel and the Palestine Arabs*, p. 76.
165. UNPCC Tenth Progress Report, 20 November 1951 A/1985.
166. *New York Times*, 22 November 1951.
167. Ibid.
168. Fischbach, *Records of Disposession*, pp. 115–6.
169. United Nations Conciliation Commission for Palestine: Tenth Progress Report, 20 November 1951 A/1985, Annex A: Evaluation of Abandoned Arab Property in Israel.
170. Ibid. For a detailed account of the methodology of the study and its calculations and the data used see Fischbach, *Records of Disposession*, pp. 114–30.

6   The Refugee Factor in Direct Arab–Israeli Negotiations

1. Shlaim, *The Iron Wall*, p. 68.
2. Barry Rubin, *The Arab States and the Palestine Conflict* (Syracuse: Syracuse University Press, 1981), pp. 209, 208.
3. Shlaim, *Iron Wall*, pp. 315–6.
4. Moshe Dayan, *Story of My Life* (New York: William Morrow, 1976), p. 136.
5. The Arab States and Israel: Memorandum by the Foreign Secretary, 20 April 1950, NA, CAB/129/39 C.P. (50) 78.
6. Ibid.
7. Memorandum of Conversation, Prepared Presumably by the First Secretary of Embassy in the United Kingdom (Jones), 13 April 1949, *FRUS*, 1949, Vol. VI, pp. 906–8; FO Minute (Beith): Notes on a Preliminary Meeting

with Mr McGhee and Mr Lewis Jones, 13 April 1949, NA, FO 371/75424 E4810.

8. The Department of State to the British Embassy, 10 May 1949, *FRUS*, 1949, Vol. VI, pp. 990–2; Washington (Franks) to Foreign Office, 11 May 1949, NA, FO 371/75426 E5969.

9. The Department of State to the British Embassy, Aide-Memoire, Undated, *FRUS*, 1949, Vol. VI, pp. 990–1.

10. The Secretary of State to the Embassy in the United Kingdom, 30 August 1949, *FRUS*, 1949, Vol. VI, pp. 1338–9.

11. For example see Tel Aviv (Eytan) to New York (Eban), 31 July 1949, *DFPI*, Vol. 4, p. 271.

12. The Secretary of State to the Embassy in the United Kingdom, 30 August 1949, *FRUS*, 1949, Vol. VI, pp. 1338–9.

13. The Secretary of State to the United States Representative at the United Nations (Austin), 8 July 1948, *FRUS*, 1948, Vol. V, p. 1213.

14. The Chargé in the United Kingdom (Holmes) to the Secretary of State, 22 December 1949, *FRUS*, 1949, Vol. VI, p. 1556.

15. Cairo (Campbell) to Foreign Office, 8 December 1949, NA, FO 371/75345 E14718.

16. Itamar Rabinovich, *The Road Not Taken: Early Arab–Israeli Negotiations* (Oxford: Oxford University Press, 1991), pp. 114–5.

17. Caplan, *Futile Diplomacy, Vol. 3*; however, Caplan also notes that when Israeli–Jordanian talks faltered, some sought to encourage Abdullah to consider redirecting negotiations to the wider framework of the PCC.

18. Memorandum by Messrs. John W. Halderman and James W. Barco of the Office of the United Nations Political and Security Affairs, 3 January 1949, *FRUS*, 1949, Vol. VI, p. 662.

19. The Chargé in the United Kingdom (Holmes) to the Secretary of State, 3 January 1950, *FRUS*, 1950, Vol. V, pp. 665–6.

20. FN, *FRUS*, 1950, Vol. V, p. 666.

21. Secretary of State to the Embassy in the United Kingdom, 20 January 1950, *FRUS*, 1950, Vol. V, p. 699.

22. Memorandum of Conversation, by Mr Stuart W. Rockwell of the Office of African and Near Eastern Affairs, 24 January 1950, *FRUS*, 1950, Vol. V, p. 700.

23. Geneva (Palmer) to Secretary of State, 28 January 1950, USNA, 357.AC/1-2850.

24. Ibid., pp. 707–8; this was denied by Egypt after the Israeli *Hador* newspaper reported it and further stated that at the PCC Egypt was working for the repatriation of refugees and to safeguard their property. See, Ambassador in Egypt (Caffery) to the Secretary of State, 29 January 1950, *FRUS*, 1950, Vol. V, p. 709.

25. Sir Alec Kirkbride, *From the Wings: Amman Memoirs, 1947–51* (London: Franks Cass, 1976), pp. 94–6.

26. Ibid.

27. Paris (Sasson) to New York (Sharett), 4 April 1949, *DFPI*, Vol. 2, pp. 547–9.

28. Memorandum by the Secretary of State to the President, Washington, 25 April 1949, *FRUS*, 1949, Vol. VI, pp. 1630–1.

29. Miles Copeland, *The Game of Nations: The Amorality of Power Politics* (Birkenhead: Wilmer Brothers, 1969), pp. 41–3.

30. Footnote 3 in *FRUS*, 1949, Vol. VI, p. 962; this offer was repeated on several occasions in the days following, see Minister in Syria (Keeley) to the Secretary of State, Damascus, 2 May 1949, *FRUS*, 1949, Vol. VI, pp. 965–6; The Minister in Syria (Keeley) to the Secretary of State, Damascus, 5 May 1949, *FRUS*, 1949, Vol. VI, p. 980.
31. Bern (Vincent) to Secretary of State, Bern, 9 May 1949, USNA, 501.BB Palestine/5-949.
32. McGee, *Envoy to the Middle World*, p. 36.
33. The United States Representative to the United Nations (Austin) to the Secretary of State, New York, 13 May 1949, *FRUS*, 1949, Vol. VI, p. 1007.
34. The Secretary of State to the Embassy in Israel, Tel Aviv, 9 May 1949, *FRUS*, 1949, Vol. VI, p. 990.
35. Avi Shlaim, 'Husni Za'im and the Plan to Resettle Palestinian Refugees in Syria', *Journal of Palestine Studies*, Vol. 15, No. 4 (Summer 1986), p. 75.
36. Rabinovich, *The Road Not Taken*, pp. 75–6.
37. Gabriel Sheffer, *Moshe Sharett: Biography of a Political Moderate* (Oxford: Clarendon Press, 1996), p. 473.
38. Damascus (Keeley) to Secretary of State, 19 May 1949, USNA, 501.BB Palestine/5-1949; the similarities between Zaim's reign and Kemal Ataturk's Westernization programme in Turkey were indeed striking. During his four and a half months in power, Zaim let it be known of his disapproval of traditional Arab dress and headgear. Literate women were given the right to vote, the use of traditional titles such as 'bey' or 'pasha' were banned and the process of breaking up religious endowments began while Sharia was being replaced with modern civil, criminal and commercial codes, see Patrick Seale, *The Struggle for Syria: A Study of Post War Arab Politics, 1948–58* (New Haven: Yale University Press, 1987), p. 58. The allusion refers to the Greek and Turkish statesmen who signed the 1923 Treaty of Lausanne following the war between the two nations which was effectively Turkey's war of independence. What followed was a population exchange in which 500,000 Muslim Greeks were transferred to Turkey while some 2 million Greek Orthodox Turks were evacuated to Greece.
39. The Secretary of State to the Legation in Syria, Washington, 22 July 1949, *FRUS*, 1949, Vol. VI, pp. 1245–6.
40. The Secretary of State to the Embassy in Israel, Washington, 26 July 1949, *FRUS*, 1949, Vol. VI, pp. 1256–6.
41. Secretary of State (Acheson) to Damascus, 27 July 1949, USNA, 501.BB Palestine/7-2149.
42. Bern (Rockwell) to Secretary of State, 22 July 1949, USNA, 501.BB Palestine/7-2249.
43. The Secretary of State to the Legation in Syria, Washington, 22 July 1949, *FRUS*, 1949, Vol. VI, pp. 1245–6.
44. Eytan, *The First Ten Years*, p. 50.
45. 45 The Secretary of State to the Legation in Syria, Washington, 13 May 1949, *FRUS*, 1949, Vol. VI, p. 1007.
46. The Acting Secretary of State to the Embassy in Israel, Washington, 28 May 1949, *FRUS*, 1949, Vol. VI, pp. 1072–4.

47. Rabinovich, *The Road Not Taken*, p. 79.
48. *The Times*, 15 August 1949.
49. Rabinovich, *The Road Not Taken*, p. 119; Shlaim, *Iron Wall*, pp. 62–8; Mordechai Gazit, 'The Israel–Jordan Peace Negotiations (1949–51): King Abdullah's Lonely Efforts', *Journal of Contemporary History*, Vol. 23, No. 3 (July 1988), p. 415.
50. Rubin, *The Arab States and the Palestine Conflict*, p. 209; this was conveyed to the US representative in Amman, see New York (Eban) to W. Eytan, 21 November 1949, *DFPI*, Vol. 4, p. 638.
51. Rabinovich, *The Road Not Taken*, pp. 124–5; Gazit, The Israel–Jordan Peace Negotiations, p. 415. Gazit writes that the first phase of talks lasted to January 1950.
52. Ibid.
53. Shlaim, *Iron Wall*, pp. 63–4; Rubin, *The Arab States and the Palestine Conflict*, p. 210; Mordechai Gazit argues that Israel believed Jordanian sovereignty of this area was out of the question, see Gazit, The Israel–Jordan Peace Negotiations, p. 415.
54. Tel Aviv (Sharett) to New York (Eban), 29 December 1949, *DFPI*, Vol. 4, p. 765.
55. *Palestine Post*, 23 December 1949.
56. Amman (Kirkbride) to Foreign Office, 2 January 1949, NA, FO 371/75330 E6.
57. Mr Wells Stabler to The Secretary of State, Amman, 11 January 1949, *FRUS*, 1949, Vol. VI, p. 644.
58. Memorandum of Conversation, by the Assistant Secretary of State for Near Eastern Affairs (McGhee), 11 January 1950, *FRUS*, 1950, Vol. V, p. 680.
59. Ibid., pp. 681–2; McGhee replied that the sum seemed particularly high to which it was then revealed that Dr Haikal had included Arab-owned desert areas which had unproductive soil.
60. The Chargé to the United Kingdom (Homes) to the Secretary of State, London, 19 January 1949, *FRUS*, 1949, Vol. VI, pp. 684–5.
61. Amman (Kirkbride) to Foreign Office, 31 January 1949, NA, FO 371/75337 E1482.
62. *Palestine Post*, 27 February 1950.
63. Ibid., 7 March 1950.
64. Rabinovich, *The Road Not Taken*, p. 129.
65. Ibid., pp. 134–5.
66. Tel Aviv (McDonald) to Secretary of State, 3 February 1949, USNA, S67N.01/2-349.
67. Drafts of a Non-Aggression Agreement between Israel and Jordan, 28 February 1950, *DFPI*, Vol. 5, pp. 146–52.
68. Amman (Kirkbride) to Foreign Office, 16 April 1949, NA, FO 371/75349 E4847.
69. Memorandum of Conversation, by the Directors of the Office of African and Near Eastern Affairs (Berry), 9 January 1950, *FRUS*, 1950, Vol. V, pp. 674–5.
70. Ibid., pp. 675–6; conversely, the prime minister of Jordan expressed his doubt that direct negotiations with the Israelis would take place and their reaching a settlement, The Chargé in Jordan (Fritzlan) to the Secretary of State, 9 January 1950, *FRUS*, 1950, Vol. V, p. 677.

71. The Department of State (Acheson) to Geneva (Palmer), 16 January 1950, USNA, 357.AC/1-1650.
72. *Palestine Post*, 17 March 1950.
73. Rubin, *The Arab States and the Palestine Conflict*, p. 210, Gazit, The Israel–Jordan Peace Negotiations, pp. 418–9. Gazit writes that similarly Sharett was concerned that US involvement could be interpreted as Jewish pressure.
74. Jerusalem (Dow) to Foreign Office, 11 November 1949, NA, FO 371/75354 E13695.
75. Political Problems of the Middle East: Memorandum by the Secretary of State for Foreign Affairs, 29 March 1951, NA, CAB/129/45 C.P. (51) 94.
76. Tel Aviv to Secretary of State, 'Joint Week A #14 (From SANA)', 10 April 1950, USNA, 784A.00(W)/4-1050.
77. *The Times*, 29 April 1950.
78. London (Douglas) to Secretary of State, 8 August 1950, USNA, 357.AC/8-850.
79. The Chargé in Jordan (Fritzlan) to the Secretary of State, Amman, 2 November 1949, *FRUS*, 1949, Vol. VI, pp. 1461–2.
80. Ibid.; The Chargé in Jordan (Fritzlan) to the Secretary of State, Amman, 4 November 1949, *FRUS*, 1949, Vol. VI, pp. 1468–9.
81. FN, *FRUS*, 1949, Vol. VI, p. 1486.
82. *Palestine Post*, 8 March 1950.
83. Ibid., 1 March 1950.
84. The United States Representative on the Palestine Conciliation Commission (Palmer) to the Secretary of State, 9 September 1950, *FRUS*, 1950, Vol. V, pp. 992–3; Jerusalem (Palmer) to Secretary of State, 10 August 1950, USNA, 357.AC/8-1050.
85. Caplan, *Futile Diplomacy, Vol. 3*, pp. 131–2; Shlaim, *Collusion across the Jordan*, pp. 550–60; Rabinovich, *The Road Not Taken*, p. 140; Bruce Maddy-Weitzmann, *The Crystallization of the Arab State System* (Syracuse: Syracuse University Press, 1993), pp. 133–5.
86. Jerusalem (Palmer) to Secretary of State, 28 June 1951, USNA, 357.AC/6-2851.
87. Rabinovich, *The Road Not Taken*, p. 184.
88. See for example, New York (Eban) to Tel Aviv (Sharett), 4 July 1949, *DFPI*, Vol. 4, p. 204; Lausanne (Eytan) to Tel Aviv (Sharett), 30 June 1949, *DFPI*, Vol. 4, pp. 186–9. Interestingly, Eytan commented that he did not think US mediation was a good idea, fearing among other things that the Egyptians might ask for an agreement along the Bernadotte lines, meaning Israel could lose territory in the Negev or around that region. This was a risk, as he thought the US mediation would almost certainly guarantee success. Soon it became apparent that Egypt was equally reluctant to enter direct talks at this stage much to the embarrassment of Washington, see Washington (Elath) to Tel Aviv (Sharett), 25 July 1949, *DFPI*, Vol. 4, pp. 247–8.
89. Tel Aviv (McDonald) to Secretary of State, 7 December 1949, USNA, 867N.00/12–749.
90. Ibid.
91. Tel Aviv (Sharett) to Lausanne (Eytan), 15 June 1949, ISA LS82/107.

92. The Ambassador in Israel (McDonald) to Secretary of State, 7 December 1949, *FRUS*, 1949, Vol. VI, p. 1554.
93. The Ambassador in Egypt (Caffery) to the Secretary of State, 2 January 1950, *FRUS*, 1950, Vol. V, p. 658.
94. The Chargé in the United Kingdom (Holmes) to the Secretary of State, 18 January 1950, *FRUS*, 1950, Vol. V, pp. 697–8.
95. Ibid.; The Secretary of State to the Embassy in the United Kingdom, 20 January 1950, *FRUS*, 1950, Vol. V, p. 699.
96. The Secretary of State to the Embassy in the United Kingdom, 20 January 1950, *FRUS*, 1950, Vol. V, p. 699.
97. The Ambassador in Egypt (Caffery) to the Secretary of State, 4 January 1950, *FRUS*, 1950, Vol. V, pp. 666–7.
98. Ibid., 29 January 1950, *FRUS*, 1950, Vol. V, p. 709.
99. Gabbay, *A Political Study of the Arab–Jewish Conflict*, pp. 320–1.
100. 100 Palmer (Geneva) to Secretary of State, 28 February 1950, USNA, 357.AC/2-2850.
101. Ibid.
102. Tel Aviv (Sharett) to Geneva (Eban), 27 February 1950, *DFPI*, Vol. 5, p. 143.
103. UNCCP: Sixth Progress Report, 29 May 1950, A/1255.
104. Ibid.; for the correspondence between the Israeli delegation and the Commission see UNPCC: Joint committee on Gaza refugees – Exchange of letters between UNCCP and Israel, 28 March 1950, A/AC.25/IS.46.
105. UNCCP: Sixth Progress Report, 29 May 1950, A/1255.
106. 106 Palmer (Geneva) to Secretary of State, 28 February 1950, USNA, 357.AC/2-2850. Mustafa Bey also said he would give thought to the idea of a non-aggression pact, and when the principles were to be met, it would not matter if negotiations were held directly or with the PCC.
107. Rabinovich, *The Road Not Taken*, pp. 185–6.
108. Palmer (Geneva) to Secretary of State, 7 March 1950, USNA, uncoded.
109. Rabinovich, *The Road Not Taken*, pp. 187–90. Rabinovich notes that Eban and Rafael argued that they were only proposing a limited discussion on Gaza and its refugees. Nevertheless, Sharett argued the Gaza refugees were a matter for the future.
110. There is a reference to an approach by Chirine about a settlement with Israel in a Foreign Office minute which recalls the approach being made in December 1949; however, a conversation with Chirine is also recalled for March, see FO Minute, 30 March 1950; Mr Chapman Andrews to Mr Wright, Foreign Office, 24 March 1950, NA, FO 371/82198 EE 10111/1G.
111. Memorandum of Conversation, by the First Secretary of the Embassy in Egypt (Ireland), *FRUS*, 1950, Vol. V, pp. 884–7.
112. Ibid.
113. Geneva (Beith) to Mr Sheringham, Foreign Office, 28 February 1950, NA, FO 371/82195 EE10110/3.
114. FO Minute, 30 March 1950; Mr Chapman Andrews to Mr Wright, Foreign Office, 24 March 1950, NA, FO 371/82198 EE 10111/1G.
115. David Ben-Gurion recalled that during the summer of 1950, Israel proposed to the Soviet Union that representatives of Israel and Egypt should

be invited to peace talks, but there was no reply. Ben-Gurion offered to talk about Arab refugees, limitations on arms, a non-aggression pact, border rectifications and widening armistice demarcation lines, see David Ben-Gurion, *My Talks with Arab Leaders* (New York: The Third Press, 1973), p. 269.

116. *New York Times*, 16 May 1948, cited in Martin Gilbert, *In Ishmael's House: A History of Jews in Muslim Lands* (New Haven: Yale University Press, 2010), p. 217.
117. Gilbert, *In Ishmael's House*, pp. 218–33, 211–4; see also Rubin, *The Arab States and the Palestine Conflict*, pp. 201–2; Hayyim Cohen, *The Jews of the Middle East, 1860–1972* (New York: Wiley and Kerter, 1973), pp. 33–4; Maurice Roumani, *The Jews of Libya: Coexistence, Persecution and Rehabilitation* (Brighton: Sussex Academic Press, 2007), p. 58; Tudor Parfitt, *The Road to Redemption: The Jews of Yemen, 1900–1950* (Leiden: EJ Brill, 1996), pp. 188–90; Norman Stillman, *The Jews of Arab Lands in Modern Times* (Philadelphia: Jewish Publication Society, 2003), p. 147.
118. Gilbert, *In Ishmael's House*, p. 193.
119. Baghdad (Wandsworth) to the Secretary of State, 22 April 1948, USNA, 867N.01/4–2448.
120. Gilbert, *In Ishmael's House*, pp. 218–33, 221–3.
121. Secretary of State (Marshall) to USUN, New York, 14 August 1948, USNA, 501.BB Palestine/8-348 CS/A.
122. Shlomo Hillel, *Operation Babylon: Jewish Clandestine Activity in the Middle East 1946–51* (London: Collins, 1988), p. 226.
123. Central Bureau of Statistics, *Statistical Abstract of Israel 2012*, No. 63, Table 4.4: Immigrants, by Period of Immigration, Country of Birth and Last Country of Residence.
124. Elizabeth Monroe, *Philby of Arabia* (London: Pitman Publishing, 1973), p. 223.
125. *Palestine Post*, 14 December 1944; Dalton, *The Fateful Years*, pp. 425–7.
126. Dalton, *The Fateful Years*, pp. 426–7.
127. *The Pittsburgh Press*, 19 November 1945; Ya'akov Meron, 'The Expulsion of Jews from the Arab Countries: The Palestinians Attitude towards it and Their Claims', Malka Hillel Schulewitz, *The Forgotten Millions: The Modern Jewish Exodus from Arab Lands* (London: Continuum, 2000), p.113; Rafael Medoff, *Zionism and the Arabs: An American Jewish Dilemma, 1898–1948* (Westport, CT: Praeger, 1997), pp. 139–61.
128. See Peter Grose, *Israel in the Mind of America* (New York: Alfred a Knopf, 1983); Zaha B. Bustami, *American Foreign Policy and Question of Palestine 1856–1939* (Washington, DC: Georgetown University Press, 1989); Leo V. Kanawada, Jr, *Franklin D. Roosevelt's Diplomacy and American Catholics, Italians, and Jews* (Ann Arbor: University of Michigan Press, 1982).
129. British Middle East Office in Cairo to Foreign Office, 3 August 1948, NA, FO 371/68578 E10456.
130. Ibid.
131. Bagdad (Mack) to Foreign Office, 20 January 1949, NA, FO 371/75336 E1008/G; FO Memorandum (Mack), 19 January 1949, NA, FO 371/75330 E1111.
132. Bagdad (Mack) to Foreign Office, 20 January 1949, NA, FO 371/75336 E1011/G.

133. Yehouda Shenhav, *The Arab Jews: A Postcolonial Reading of Nationalism, Religion, and Ethnicity* (Stanford: Stanford University Press, 2006), p.117.
134. Damascus (Keeley) to Secretary of State, 22 February 1949, USNA, 501.BB Palestine/2-2149.
135. Department of State, Washington, to Certain American Diplomatic and Consular Offices, 7 February 1949, USNA, 867N.48/2-749.
136. Ibid.
137. Egypt (Patterson) to the Secretary of State, 26 February 1949, USNA, 867N.48/2-2649.
138. Bagdad (Mack) to Foreign Office, 13 May 1949, NA, FO 371/75426 E6065.
139. Bagdad (Mack) to Foreign Office, 27 July 1949, NA, FO 371/75334 E9186.
140. Shenhav, *The Arab Jews*, p. 118.
141. Foreign Office to The Chancery, British Embassy, Bagdad, 5 September 1949, NA, FO 371/75152 E9114.
142. Foreign Office to The Chancery, British Embassy, Bagdad, 5 September 1949, NA, FO 371/75152 E9114.
143. British Middle East Office (Cairo) to Middle East Secretariat, Foreign Office, 22 September 1949, NA, FO 371/75152 E11795.
144. Ibid.
145. Ibid.
146. Ibid.
147. Chancery, British Embassy (Bagdad) to Middle East Secretariat, Foreign Office, 29 September 1949, NA, FO 371/75152 E12290.
148. Tel Aviv (Helm) to Middle East Secretariat, Foreign Office, 14 October 1949, NA, FO 371/75152 E12791.
149. FO Minute (Sheringham), 11 November 1949, NA, FO 371/75152 E12791 E13370.
150. Beirut (Houstoun-Boswell) to Foreign Office, 17 October 1949, NA, FO 371/75444 E12637; Nuri Pasha then went on to describe his plan to exchange the Jewish inhabitants of Iraq for Palestinians, but admitted its difficulties; of the 180,000 Jews, two thirds were in Baghdad and the other cities. Many were wealthy and he doubted their wish to go to Palestine even if they were to take their wealth with them and be compensated for loss of real estate. Also see *Palestine Post*, 16 October 1949.
151. Baghdad (Dorsze) to Secretary of State, 19 October 1949, USNA, 501.BB Palestine/10-1549; Tel Aviv (Shiloah) to Washington (Elath), 19 October 1949, *DFPI*, Vol. 4, p. 561.
152. Baghdad (Dorsze) to Secretary of State, 20 October 1949, USNA, 501.BB Palestine/10-2149.
153. Baghdad (Dorsze) to Secretary of State, 21 October 1949, USNA, 501.BB Palestine/10-2149.
154. Chancery, Bagdad to Middle East Secretariat, Foreign Office, 28 October 1949, NA, FO 371/75446 E13568; Bagdad (Mack) to Foreign Office, 21 October 1949, NA, FO 371/75445 E13152.
155. New York (Eban) to Tel Aviv (Sharett), 18 October 1949, *DFPI*, Vol. 4, pp. 555–6.
156. *Palestine Post*, 19 October 1949.
157. Ibid., 9 November 1949.
158. Tel Aviv (Eytan) to Lausanne, 13 September 1949, ISA, LS/118/18.
159. Tel Aviv (Eytan) to Laussane, 13 September 1949, ISA, LS117/20.

160. Baghdad (Dorsze) to Secretary of State, 26 October 1949, USNA, 501.BB Palestine/10-2649.
161. Baghdad (Dorsze) to Secretary of State, 20 October 1949, USNA, 501.BB Palestine/10-2049.
162. Memorandum of Conversation: Jews in Iraq; Proposed Syrian–Iraqi Union; Jerusalem; and Israeli Attack in the Gaza Area, 18 October 1949, USNA, 867N.48/10-1849.
163. Shenhav, *The Arab Jews*, p. 120.
164. Ibid., p. 121.
165. Ibid., pp. 121-2.
166. Fischbach, *Jewish Property Claims*, pp. 57-8; for further explanations see, Itamar Levin, *Locked Doors: The Seizure of Jewish Property in Arab Countries* (Westport: Praeger, 2001), pp. 27-9.
167. Peretz, *Israel and the Palestine Arabs*, p. 76.
168. Memorandum by the Acting Secretary of State to the Executive Secretary of the National Security Council (Lay), 13 September 1950, *FRUS*, 1950, Vol. V, pp. 564-5. p. 1005.
169. Pelcovits, *The Long Armistice*, p. 34.

7 The Birth of UNRWA: The Institutionalization of Failed Diplomacy

1. United Nations General Assembly Resolution 302 (IV). Assistance to Palestinian Refugees, 8 December 1949, A/RES/302 (IV).
2. Ibid.
3. Ibid.
4. UNCCP: ESM Interim Report, 16 November 1949, A/AC.25.6.
5. Ibid.
6. United Nations Assistance to Palestinian Refugees: Interim Report of the Director of the United Nations Relief and Works Agency for Palestinian Refugees in the Near East, General Assembly Official Records: Fifth Session Supplements No. 19, 6 October 1950, A/1451/Rev.1 (hereafter, UNRWA Interim Report, 6 October 1950).
7. Ibid.
8. United Nations Assistance to Palestinian Refugees: Report of the Director of the United Nations Relief and Works Agency for Palestinian Refugees in the Near East, General Assembly Official Records: Sixth Session Supplements No. 16, 28 September 1951, A/1905 (hereafter UNRWA Report, 28 September 1951).
9. UNRWA Interim Report, 6 October 1950, A/1451/Rev.1.
10. Foreign Office to Cairo, 10 November 1949, NA, FO 371/75446 E13588; Beirut (Houstoun-Boswell) to Foreign Office, 12 November 1949, NA, FO 371/75446 E13700.
11. Beirut (Houstoun-Boswell) to Foreign Office, 24 October 1949, NA, FO 371/75445 E12871.
12. See for example, NEA (McGhee) and UNA (Sandifer) to Rusk, 26 September 1949, USNA, 501.BB Palestine/9-2649; Beirut (Pinkerton) to Secretary of State, 18 October 1949, USNA, 501.BB Palestine (E)/10-1849; Beirut

(Pinkerton) to Secretary of State, 25 October 1949, USNA, 501.BB Palestine (E)/10-2549; Department of State (McGhee) to American Legation, Beirut (Clapp), 21 October 1949, USNA, 501.BB Palestine (E)/10-3149; Pinkerton (Beirut) to Department of State, 1 November 1949, USNA, 501.BB Palestine (E)/10-2949.

13. Department of State (McGhee) to American Legation, Beirut (Clapp), 21 October 1949, USNA, 501.BB Palestine (E)/10-3149.

14. Ibid.

15. Foreign Office to Beirut, 3 November 1948, NA, FO 371/75444 E12861.

16. UNCCP: ESM Final Report, 29 December 1949; UNCCP: ESM Interim Report, 16 November 1949, A/AC.25.6.

17. United Nations General Assembly Resolution 302 (IV). Assistance to Palestinian Refugees, 8 December 1949, A/RES/302 (IV).

18. UNCCP: ESM Interim Report, 16 November 1949, A/AC.25.6.

19. UNRWA Interim Report, 6 October 1950, A/1451/Rev.1.

20. Ibid.

21. FO Minute (Evans), 23 December 1949; John Troutbeck, British Middle East Office (Cairo) to Michael Wright, Foreign Office, 20 December 1949, NA, FO 371/82242 EE 1825/2.

22. State Department (Gardiner) to American Embassy, London (Palmer), 21 March 1950, USNA, 357.AC/3-1450 CS/H.

23. British Middle East Office, Cairo (Troutbeck) to Foreign Office (Evans), 26 January 1950, NA, FO 371/82243 EE1825/24.

24. New York (Cadogan) to Foreign Office, 18 January 1950, NA, FO 371/82242 EE1825/5.

25. *Daily Telegraph*, 1 November 1950.

26. FO Minute (Evans), 23 January 1950, NA, FO 371/82242 EE1825/12.

27. Ibid.

28. FO Minute (Evans): Arab Refugees: Advisory Commission of the United Nations' Relief and Works Agency, 10 February 1950, NA, FO 371/82243 EE1825/34.

29. Secretary of State (Acheson) to AmLegation (Damascus), 12 January 1950, USNA, 357.AC/1-1250.

30. NEA, McGhee to Under Secretary of State (Webb), 16 January 1950, USNA, 357.AC/1-1650.

31. Ibid.

32. UKDel, New York (Shone) to Foreign Office, 7 March 1950, NA, FO 371/82244 EE1824/62; Draft: Advisory Committee of the United Nations Relief and Works Agency for Palestine Refugees in the Near East: Note of an Informal Discussion held on Monday Afternoon, 6 March 1950, NA, FO 371/82244 EE1824/62.

33. United Kingdom Delegation to the United Nations, New York to Foreign Office (Evans), 10 March 1950, NA, FO 371/82244 EE1824/62.

34. Foreign Office (Staines) to J.L. Rampton, 3 February 1950, NA, FO 371/82242 EE1825/28.

35. Foreign Office (Evans) to British Embassy, Washington (Greenhill), 18 January 1950, NA, FO 371/82242 EE1825/7.

36. FO Minute (Evans): Relief and Relief Works Agency, 19 December 1949, NA, FO 371/82242 EE1825/22.

37. British Middle East Office, Cairo (Troutbeck) to Foreign Office (Evans), 26 January 1950, NA, FO 371/82242 EE1825/24.
38. Ibid.
39. FO Minute: Palestinian Refugees, Undated, NA, FO 371/82242 EE1825/29.
40. Washington (Franks) to Foreign Office, 19 January 1950, NA, FO 371/82242 EE1825/8.
41. Secretary of State (Acheson) to USUN, New York, 1 February 1950, USNA, 357.AC/1-3150 CS/H.
42. UKdel New York (Cadogan) to Foreign Office, 21 February 1950, NA, FO 371/82242 EE1825/43.
43. Foreign Office to New York, 24 February 1950, NA, FO 371/82242 EE1825/43.
44. New York (Shone) to Foreign Office, 3 March 1950, NA, FO 371/82244 EE1825/58.
45. UNRWA Report, 28 September 1951, A/1905.
46. Ibid.
47. Ibid.
48. Beirut (Pinkerton) to Secretary of State, 10 June 1950, USNA, 320.2-AA/6-1050.
49. UNRWA Interim Report, 6 October 1950, A/1451/Rev.1.
50. The Secretary of State to the Embassy in the France, Washington, 10 January 1950, *FRUS*, 1950, Vol. V, p. 679.
51. The Secretary of State to the Embassy in the United Kingdom, Washington, 5 January 1950, *FRUS*, 1950, Vol. V, pp. 669–70.
52. Sir Oliver Franks (Washington) to Foreign Office, 4 January 1950, NA, FO 371/82236 EE1822/1.
53. FO Minute (Evans) 6 January 1950, NA, FO 371/82236 EE1822/1.
54. American Embassy, London (Palmer) to Department of State (McGhee), 26 January 1950, USNA, 357.AC/1-2650.
55. Ibid.
56. Ibid.; Department of State (McGhee) to American Embassy, London (Palmer), 13 February 1950, USNA, 357.AC/1-2650 CS/C.
57. Minister of State to Sir Stafford Cripps, Treasury, 12 January 1950, NA, FO 371/82236 EE1822/4.
58. Sir Stafford Cripps, Treasury, to Mr McNeil, 19 January 1950, NA, FO 371/82236 EE1822/5.
59. FO Minute (Wright) 23 January 1950, NA, FO 371/82236 EE1822/5.
60. American Embassy, London (Palmer) to Department of State (McGhee), 23 February 1950, USNA, 357.AC/2-2350.
61. Department of State to American Embassy, London (Palmer), 23 February 1950, USNA, 357.AC/2-2750.
62. Editorial Note, *FRUS*, Vol. V, 1950, pp. 860–1.
63. Secretary of State (Acheson) to American Embassy, Paris, 10 January 1950, USNA, 357.AC/1-1050 CS/H; Secretary of State (Acheson) to American Embassy, London, 12 January 1950, USNA, 357.AC/1-1250 CS/H.
64. Secretary of State (Acheson) to American Embassy, Paris, 31 May 1950, USNA, 320.2 AA/5-2550 CS/H.
65. Paris (Bruce) to Secretary of State, 7 June 1950, USNA, 320.2 AA/6-750.

66. Beirut (Pinkerton) to Secretary of State, 27 July 1950, USNA, 320.2-AA/7-2750 HH.
67. FO Minute (Evans): United Nations Relief and Works Agency for Palestine Refugees in the Middle East, 19 April 1950, NA, FO 371/82237 EE1822/30.
68. The Assistant Secretary of State for Near Eastern, South Asian and African Affairs (McGhee) to Dr. Francis Wilcox, Chief of Staff of the Senate Committee on Foreign Affairs, Washington, 26 July 1950, *FRUS*, 1950, Vol. V, pp. 958–9.
69. The Assistant Secretary of State for Near Eastern, South Asian and African Affairs (McGhee) to Dr. Francis Wilcox, Chief of Staff of the Senate Committee on Foreign Affairs, Washington, 26 July 1950, *FRUS*, 1950, Vol. V, pp. 958–60.
70. Washington to Foreign Office, 18 March 1950, NA, FO 371/82244 EE1824/67.
71. UNRWA Interim Report, 6 October 1950, A/1451/Rev.1.
72. The Acting Secretary of State to Ambassador John B. Blandford, at Beirut, Washington, 21 September 1950, *FRUS*, 1950, Vol. V, p. 1018.
73. UNRWA Interim Report, 6 October 1950, A/1451/Rev.1.
74. Ibid.
75. UNRWA Report, 28 September 1951, A/1905.
76. Beirut (Pinkerton) to Secretary of State, 8 July 1950, USNA, 320.2AA/7-850; Beirut (Knight) to Foreign Office (Evans), 18 July 1950, NA, FO 371/82247 EE1825/158.
77. Beirut, UNRWA (Knight) to Foreign Office (Evans), 25 July 1950, NA, FO 371/82248 EE1825/163.
78. Memorandum for Advisory Commission re Problems Met by the Administrative Staff of the Agency and Action Taken to Meet the Situation, Sgd Howard Kennedy, 7 August 1950, NA, FO 371/82248 EE1825/170.
79. Memorandum of Conversation, by Stewart W. Rockwell of the Office of African and Near East Affairs, Washington, 19 April 1950, *FRUS*, 1950, Vol. V, pp. 864–5.
80. Memorandum for Advisory Commission re Problems Met by the Administrative Staff of the Agency and Action Taken to Meet the Situation, Sgd Howard Kennedy, 7 August 1950, NA, FO 371/82248 EE1825/170; Beirut (Pinkerton) to Department of State, 21 June 1950, USNA, 320.2-AA/6-2150 HH.
81. Ibid.; UNCCP: Summary Record of the One Hundred and Seventy-First Meeting, Jerusalem, 7 August 1950, A/AC.25/SR.171.
82. UNRWA, Beirut (Evans) to Foreign Office, 14 November 1950, NA, FO 371/82251 EE1825/261.
83. Memorandum for Advisory Commission re Problems Met by the Administrative Staff of the Agency and Action Taken to Meet the Situation, Sgd Howard Kennedy, 7 August 1950, NA, FO 371/82248 EE1825/170.
84. UNRWA, Beirut (Knight) to Foreign Office, 15 August 1950, NA, FO 371/82248 EE1825/172.
85. The Ambassador in Egypt (Caffery) to Ambassador John B. Blandford, at Beirut, 30 August 1950, *FRUS*, 1950, Vol. V, p. 986; H.F. Knight to Foreign Office (Evans), 21 September 1950, NA, FO 371/82248 EE1825/176.

86. UNRWA Interim Report, 6 October 1950, A/1451/Rev.1.
87. The Ambassador in Egypt (Caffery) to Ambassador John B. Blandford, at Beirut, 30 August 1950, *FRUS*, 1950, Vol. V, p. 986; H.F. Knight to Foreign Office (Evans), 21 September 1950, NA, FO 371/82248 EE1825/176.
88. British Legation, Beirut (Knight) to Foreign Office, 9 May 1950, NA, FO 371/82245 EE1825/105; British Legation, Beirut (Knight) to Foreign Office, 16 May 1950, NA, FO 371/82246 EE1825/115; Beirut to Department of State, 16 May 1950, USNA, 320.2-AA/5-1650 HH; Beirut to Department of State, 24 May 1950, USNA, 320.2-AA/5-2450 HH.
89. UNRWAPR, Beirut (Knight) to Foreign Office, 6 June 1950, NA, FO 371/82246 EE1825/128.
90. Jidda (Childs) to Department of State, 24 May 1950, USNA, 320.2-AA/5-2450 GC.
91. Jidda (Childs) to Department of State, 6 June 1950, USNA, 320.2-AA/6-250 HH.
92. Beirut (Pinkerton) to Department of State, 13 June 1950, USNA, 320.AA/6-1350 HH.
93. Damascus (Harrison) to Secretary of State, 28 July 1950, USNA, 320.AA/7-2850 HH.
94. Beirut to Department of State, 16 May 1950, USNA, 320.2-AA/5-1650.
95. FO Minute (Brief for Sir H. Knight): United Nations Relief and Works Agency for Palestine Refugees in the Middle East, 14 November 1950, NA, FO 371/82245 EE1825/88.
96. Ibid.
97. Secretary of State (Acheson) to American Legation (Beirut), 3 August 1950, USNA, 320.2-AA/7-2850 CS/H.
98. Ibid.
99. ANE (Berry) to NEA (McGhee), Washington, 17 May 1950, USNA, 320.2 AA/5-1750.
100. George C. McGhee, Assistant Secretary, to Dr Francis Wilcox, Chief of Staff, Committee on Foreign Relations, United States Senate, 26 July 1950, USNA, 320.2-AA/7-2650 CS/H.
101. Washington (Greenhill) to Foreign Office (Evans), 23 August 1950, NA, FO 371/82248 EE1825/178.
102. FO Minute (Evans): United Nations Relief and Works Agency for Palestine Refugees: Report to the General Assembly, 2 September 1950, NA, FO 371/82248 EE1825/183.
103. Ibid.
104. Ibid.
105. United State Representative to the Palestine Conciliation Commission (Palmer) to the Secretary of State, 17 August 1950, *FRUS*, 1950, Vol. V, pp. 873–4.
106. Washington (Greenwell) to Foreign Office (Waterlow), 4 September 1950, NA, FO 371/82248 EE1825/184.
107. Foreign Office (Evans) to Washington (Greenhill), 11 September 1950, NA, FO 371/82248 EE1825/184.
108. Washington (Burrows) to Foreign Office (Furlonge), 15 September 1950, NA, FO 371/82249 EE1825/195.

109. Washington (Greenhill) to Foreign Office, 19 April 1951, NA, FO 371/91401 EE1821/62.
110. Amman (Walker) to Foreign Office, 17 May 1951, NA, FO 371/91402 EE1821/77.
111. UNWRA, Beirut (Knight) to Foreign Office (Evans), 31 May 1951, NA, FO 371/91402 EE1821/84.
112. Foreign Office to Washington, 3 October 1950, NA, FO 371/82249 EE1825/206.
113. Ibid.
114. Memorandum of Conversation by the Acting Secretary of State to the Executive Secretary of the National Security Council (Lay), Washington, 13 September 1950, *FRUS*, 1950, Vol. V, p. 1004.
115. Memorandum by the Secretary of State to the President, Washington, 1 November 1950, *FRUS*, 1950, Vol. V, pp. 1039–40.
116. Ibid.
117. UNE (Tomlinson) to UNP (Ludlow), 22 September 1950, 357.USNA, AC/92250 CS/Y.
118. FO Minute (Evans) United Nations Relief and Works Agency for Palestine Refugees: Report, 30 September 1950, NA, FO 371/82249 EE1825/209.
119. The United States Representative at the United Nations (Austin) to the Secretary of State, 2 November 1950, *FRUS*, 1950, Vol. V, pp. 1041–2.
120. The United States Representative at the United Nations (Austin) to the Secretary of State, 3 November 1950, *FRUS*, 1950, Vol. V, pp. 1042–3.
121. Memorandum by the Secretary of State to the President, Washington, 24 November 1950, *FRUS*, 1950, Vol. V, pp. 1061–2.
122. Memorandum by the President to the Secretary of State, Washington, 6 December 1950, *FRUS*, 1950, Vol. V, p. 1071.
123. Memorandum by the President to the Secretary of State, Washington, 20 December 1950, *FRUS*, 1950, Vol. V, p. 1077.
124. United Nations General Assembly 393 (V). Assistance to Palestine refugees, 2 December 1950, A/RES/393 (V).
125. UNRWA Report, 28 September 1951, A/1905.
126. Ibid.
127. British Middle East Office, Cairo (Rapp) to Eastern Department, Foreign Office, 1 February 1951, NA, 371/91399 EE1821/17.
128. H.F. Knight: Discussion with Samir Pasha, Prime Minister of Jordan, 23 May 1951, NA, FO 371/91402 EE1821/80.
129. H.F. Knight, 'Finances: Immediate Problem', 3 February 1951, NA, FO 371/91404 EE1822/8.
130. FO Minute (Evans), 15 January 1951, NA, FO 371/91407 EE1824/1.
131. *New York Times*, 6 March 1951.
132. Harry S. Truman to Kenneth McKeller, 27 July 1951, NA, FO 371/91408 EE1824/41.
133. Treasury (Williams) to Foreign Office (Evans), 2 April 1951, NA, FO 371/91407 EE1824/20.
134. Memorandum by the Deputy Assistant Secretary of State for Near Eastern, South Asian and African Affairs (Berry) to the Secretary of State, 15 March 1951, *FRUS*, 1951, Vol. V, pp. 594–6.

135. Memorandum of Informal United States–United Kingdom Discussions, in Connection with the Visit to London of the Honourable George C. McGhee, 2–3 April 1951, 2 April 1951, *FRUS*, 1951, Vol. V, pp. 612–4.
136. Ibid.
137. Jedda (Trott) to Foreign Office, 21 January 1951, NA, FO 371/91399 EE 1821/13.
138. Amman (Kirkbridge) to Foreign Office, 18 January 1951, NA, FO 371/91399 EE1821/16.
139. FO Minute (Evans), 1 March 1951, NA, FO 371/91400 EE1821/35.
140. British Middle East Office, Cairo (Rapp) to Foreign Office, 13 February 1951, NA, FO 371/91400 EE1821/24.
141. UNRWA, Beirut (Knight) to Foreign Office (Evans), 5 March 1951, NA, FO 371/91401 EE1821/45.
142. The Lebanese Foreign Office to the United Nations Relief and Works Agency for Palestine Refugees, Beirut, 16 April 1951, *FRUS*, 1951, Vol. V, pp. 639–41.
143. Beirut (Bruins) to Department of State, 26 April 1951, USNA, 320.2 AA/4-2651.
144. UNRWA Interim Report, 6 October 1950, A/1451/Rev.1.
145. Beirut (Bruins) to Department of State, 31 August 1951, USNA, 320.2 AA/8-3151.
146. Beirut (Bruins) to Department of State, 7 September 1951, USNA, 320.2 AA/9-751.
147. The Minister in Lebanon (Minor) to the Department of State, 24 October 1951, *FRUS*, 1951, Vol. V, pp. 919–20.
148. The Minister in Lebanon (Minor) to the Department of State, 29 October 1951, *FRUS*, 1951, Vol. V, p. 922.
149. United Nations Conciliation Commission for Palestine: Ninth Progress Report for the period 24 January to 10 March 1951, 22 March 1951, A/1793; for much of the first quarter of 1951, while awaiting the Refugee Office's commencement, the PCC resumed contacts with the sides, receiving views about the General Assembly resolution and words of readiness to cooperate. The PCC also resumed work on blocked accounts.
150. Forsythe, *United Nations Peacemaking*, pp. 84–5.
151. The Secretary of State to the Legation in Lebanon, 23 January 1951, *FRUS*, 1951, Vol. V, pp. 562–3.

Conclusion

1. Progress Report of the United Nations Mediator on Palestine, 16 September 1948, A/648.
2. United Nations General Assembly, 194 (III). Palestine: Progress Report of the United Nations Mediator, 11 December 1948, A/RES/194 (III).
3. Caplan, *Futile Diplomacy, Vol. 3*, pp. 272–4.

Bibliography

Archives

National Archives (NA), Kew, United Kingdom
CAB 128
CAB 129
CAB 134
CAB 195
CO 537
DEFE 5/6
DEFE 6/1
DEFE 6/4
FO 371
FO 816
WO 261
WO 275

The National Archives at College Park (USNA), Maryland, United States
357.AC/1–2850
501.BB Palestine
867N.01
867N.48

Harry S. Truman Library and Museum (TPLA), Independence, Missouri
Clifford Papers
Conway Files, Truman Papers
Elsey Papers
Jacobson Papers
President's Secretary's File, Truman Papers

Israel State Archives, Jerusalem, Israel
Foreign Ministry Papers

Published Documents

Foreign Relations of the United States, 1945, *The Near East, South Asia, and Africa (in Two Parts)*, Vol. VIII (US Government Printing Office, 1948)
——, 1946, *The Near East, South Asia, and Africa (in Two Parts)*, Vol. VII (US Government Printing Office, 1948)

——, 1947, *The Near East, South Asia, and Africa (in Two Parts)*, Vol. V (US Government Printing Office, 1948)

——, 1948, *The Near East, South Asia, and Africa (in Two Parts)*, Vol. V, Part 2 (US Government Printing Office, 1948)

——, 1949, *The Near East, South Asia, and Africa*, Vol. VI (US Government Printing Office, 1949)

——, 1950, *The Near East, South Asia, and Africa*, Vol. V (US Government Printing Office, 1950)

——, 1951, *The Near East and Africa*, Vol. V (US Government Printing Office, 1951)

Yehoshua Freundlich (ed), *Documents on the Foreign Policy of Israel*, Vol. 1, 14 May–30 September 1948 (Jerusalem: Israel State Archives, 1982)

——, *Documents on the Foreign Policy of Israel*, Vol. 2, October 1948–April 1949 (Jerusalem: Israel State Archives, 1984)

——, *Documents on the Foreign Policy of Israel*, Vol. 4, May–December 1949 (Jerusalem: Israel State Archives, 1986)

——, *Documents on the Foreign Policy of Israel*, Vol. 5, 1950 (Jerusalem: Israel State Archives, 1988)

——, *Documents on the Foreign Policy of Israel*, Vol. 6, 1951 (Jerusalem: Israel State Archives, 1991)

Hansard, HC Deb, 25 February 1947, Vol. 433 (cc1901–2007)

Meron Medzini (ed), *Israel's Foreign Relations: Selected Documents, 1947–1974*, Vol. 1 (Jerusalem: Ministry of Foreign Affairs, 1976)

——, *Israel's Foreign Relations: Selected Documents, 1947–1974*, Vol. 2 (Jerusalem: Ministry of Foreign Affairs, 1976)

Statistical Abstract of Israel 2012, *Central Bureau of Statistics*, Jerusalem, 2012, No. 63

United Nations, *Official Records of the General Assembly* (New York: United Nations, 1948–1967)

United Nations Documents

Official Reports

Progress Report of the United Nations Mediator on Palestine Submitted to the Secretary-General for Transmission to the Members of the United Nations, General Assembly Official Records: Third Session Supplement No. 11, 16 September 1948, A/648

Progress Report of the United Nations Acting Mediator on Palestine Submitted to the Secretary-General for Transmission to the Members of the United Nations, Supplement No. 11A, General Assembly Official Records: Third Session, 18 October 1948, A/689, A/689/Corr.1 and A/689/Add.1.

United Nations Assistance to Palestinian Refugees: Interim Report of the Director of the United Nations Relief and Works Agency for Palestinian Refugees in the Near East, General Assembly Official Records: Fifth Session Supplements No. 19, 6 October 1950, A/1451/Rev.1

——, Report of the Director of the United Nations Relief and Works Agency for Palestinian Refugees in the Near East, General Assembly Official Records: Sixth Session Supplements No. 16, 28 September 1951, A/1905

United Nations Conciliation Commission for Palestine: First Progress Report, 15 March 1949, A/819

——, Second Progress Report, 19 April 1949, A/838

——, Third Progress Report, 21 June 1949, A/927

——, Fourth Progress Report For the period 9 June to 15 September 1949 inclusive, 22 September 1949 A/992

——, Fifth Progress Report For the period 16 September to 9 December 1949 inclusive, 14 December 1949 A/1252

——, First Interim Report of the United Nations Economic Survey Mission for the Middle East, 16 November 1949, A/AC.25.6

——, Final Report of the United Nations Economic Survey Mission for the Middle East, 28 December 1949, A/AC.25.6

——, Sixth Progress Report For the period 9 December 1949 to 8 May 1950 inclusive, 29 May 1950, A/1255

——, Seventh Progress Report For the period 8 May to 12 July 1950 inclusive, 17 July 1950, A/1288

——, General Progress Report and Supplementary Report For the period 11 December 1949 to 23 October 1950 inclusive (Eighth Progress Report), 23 October 1950, A/1367/Rev.1

——, Ninth Progress Report For the period 24 January to 10 March 1951, 22 March 1951, A/1793

——, Tenth Progress Report Covering the period from 23 January to 19 November 1951, 20 November 1951 A/1985.

United Nations Special Committee on Palestine: Report to the General Assembly, Vol. 1, New York, 4 September 1947, A/364

Other UN Sources

Palestine Conciliation Commission minutes, summary records of meetings, letters, memos, notes and working papers, available from the United Nations Information System on the Question of Palestine (UNISPAL).

News sources

bbc.co.uk
The Daily Express
The Daily Mail
The Daily Telegraph
The Jerusalem Post
The Jewish Chronicle (The JC)
The Manchester Guardian
The New York Times
The Observer
The Palestine Post
The Pittsburgh Press

The Times (London)
USA Today

Online Documents and Resources

Al-Jazeera Transparency Unit: The Palestine Papers:
www.ajtransparency.com
Avalon Project: Documents in Law, History and Diplomacy:
http://avalon.law.yale.edu
United Nations Documents:
http://www.un.org/en/documents/index.shtml
United Nations Information System on the Question of Palestine (UNISPAL):
http://unispal.un.org/unispal.nsf/udc.htm
Virtual Jewish Library:
http://www.jewishvirtuallibrary.org

Memoirs

Dean Acheson, *Present at Creation: My Years in the State Department* (London: Hamish Hamilton, 1969)

Madeleine Albright, *Madame Secretary* (New York: Hyperion, 2003)

Pablo de Azcarate, *Mission in Palestine, 1948–1952* (Washington, DC: The Middle East Institute, 1966)

David Ben Gurion, *My Talks with Arab Leaders* (New York: The Third Press, 1973)

Bill Clinton *My Life: The Presidential Years* (New York: Doubleday, 2004)

Richard Crossman, *Palestine Mission: A Personal Account* (London: Hamish Hamilton, 1947)

——, *A Nation Reborn: The Israel of Weizmann, Bevin and Ben-Gurion* (London: Hamish Hamilton, 1960)

Bartley C. Crum, *Behind the Silken Curtain: A Personal Account of Anglo-American Diplomacy in Palestine and the Middle East* (New York: Simon & Schuster, 1947)

Hugh Dalton, *The Fateful Years: Memoirs, 1931–1945* (London: Frederick Muller, 1957)

Walter Eytan, *The First Ten Years: A Diplomatic History of Israel* (London: Weidenfeld and Nicolson, 1958)

John Bagot Glubb, *A Soldier with the Arabs* (London: Hodder and Stoughton, 1957)

George Kennan, *Memoirs, 1925–1950* (New York: Pantheon Books, 1967)

Alec Kirkbride, *From the Wings: Amman Memoirs, 1947–1951* (London: Frank Cass, 1976)

Harold Macmillan, *Tides of Fortune, 1945–1955* (London: Macmillan, 1969)

James G. McDonald, *My Mission in Israel, 1948–1951* (London: Victor Gollancz Ltd, 1951)

George McGhee, *Envoy to the Middle World: Adventures in Diplomacy* (New York: Harper & Row, 1984)

Gideon Rafael, *Destination Peace: Three Decades of Israeli Foreign Policy* (London: Weidenfeld and Nicholson, 1981)

Dennis Ross, *The Missing Peace: The Inside Story of the Fight for Middle East Peace* (New York: Farrar, Straus and Giroux, 2005)
Dean Rusk, *As I Saw It* (New York: W.W. Norton, 1990)
Yitzhak Shamir, *Summing Up: An Autobiography* (London: Weidenfeld and Nicolson, 1994)
Harry S. Truman, *Memoirs, Vol. 2: Years of Trial and Hope* (New York: Doubleday, 1956)

Books and Articles

'An Exclusive Interview with Clark Clifford', *American Heritage*, Vol. 28, No. 3, April 1977
Mahmoud Abbas, 'Reports of the Camp David Summit, 9 September 2000', *Journal of Palestine Studies*, Vol. XXX, No. 2 (Winter, 2001), pp. 168–170
Musa Alami, 'The Lesson of Palestine', *The Middle East Journal*, Vol. 4, No. 4 (October 1949), pp. 373–405
Stephen E. Ambrose and Douglas G. Brinkley, *Rise to Globalism: American Foreign Policy Since 1938* (New York: Penguin, 1997)
Avi Beker, *The United Nations and Israel: From Recognition to Reprehension* (Lexington: Lexington Books, 1988)
——, *UNRWA, Terror and the Refugee Conundrum: Perpetuating the Misery* (Jerusalem: Institute of the World Jewish Congress, 2003)
Eliahu Ben-Horion, 'The Soviet Wooing of Palestine', *Harper's Magazine*, vol. 188, (April 1944)
Earl Berger, *The Covenant and the Sword: Arab–Israeli Relations, 1948–56* (London: Routledge & Kegan Paul, 1965)
Nicholas Bethell, *The Palestine Triangle: The Struggle between the British, the Jews and the Arabs, 1935–48* (London: Futura, 1980)
Alexander Blight, 'Israel and the Refugee Problem: From Exodus to Resettlement, 1948–1952', *Middle Eastern Studies*, Vol. 34, No. 1 (1998), pp. 123–147
John Bowyer Bell, *Terror out of Zion: Irgun Zvai Leumi, LEHI, and the Palestine Underground, 1929–1949* (New York: St. Martin's Press, 1977)
Peter G. Boyle, 'The British Foreign Office and American Foreign Policy, 1947–48', *Journal of American Studies*, Vol. 16, No. 3 (December 1982), pp. 373–389
Ahron Bregman, *Elusive Peace: How the Holy Land Defeated America* (New York: Penguin, 2005)
Edward Henry Buehrig, *The UN and the Palestinian Refugees: A Study in Nonterritorial Administration* (Bloomington: Indiana University Press, 1971)
Alan Bullock, *Ernest Bevin: Foreign Secretary, 1945–1951* (London: Heineman, 1983)
Zaha B. Bustami, *American Foreign Policy and Question of Palestine 1856–1939* (Washington, DC: Georgetown University Press, 1989)
Joel Cang, *The Silent Millions: A History of Jews in the Soviet Union* (London: Rapp & Whiting, 1969)
Neil Caplan, *The Lausanne Conference, 1949: A Case Study in Middle East Peacemaking* (Tel Aviv University: The Moshe Dayan Center for Middle Eastern and African Studies, 1993)

——, *Futile Diplomacy Volume Three: The United Nations, the Great Powers, and the Middle East Peacemaking 1948–1954* (London: Frank Cass, 1997)

Youssef Chaitani, *Dissension among Allies: Ernest Bevin's Palestine Policy between Whitehall and the White House, 1945–1947* (London: Saqi, 2002)

Erskine Childers, 'The Other Exodus', *The Spectator* (12 May 1961), pp. 8–11

Thurston Clark, *By Blood and Fire: The Attack on the King David Hotel* (London: Hutchinson, 1981)

Aharon Cohen, *Israel and the Arab World* (London: W.H. Allen, 1970)

Hayyim Cohen, *The Jews of the Middle East, 1860–1972* (New York: Wiley and Kerter, 1973)

Michael J. Cohen, 'The Genesis of the Anglo-American Committee on Palestine, November 1945: A Case Study in the Assertion of American Hegemony', *The Historical Journal*, Vol. 22, No. 1 (March 1979), pp. 185–207

——, *Palestine and the Great Powers, 1945–1948* (Princeton: Princeton University Press, 1982)

——, 'Truman and Palestine, 1945–1948: Revisionism, Politics and Diplomacy', *Modern Judaism*, Vol. 2, No. 1 (February 1982), pp. 1–22

——, *Palestine to Israel: From Mandate to Independence* (London: Frank Cass, 1988)

——, *Truman and Israel* (Berkeley: University of California Press, 1990)

——, *Fighting World War Three from the Middle East: Allied Contingency Plans, 1945–54* (London: Frank Cass, 1997)

Michael J. Cohen and Martin Kolinsky (eds), *Demise of the British Empire in the Middle East* (London: Frank Cass, 1998)

Miles Copeland, *The Game of Nations: The Amorality of Power Politics* (Birkenhead: Wilmer Brothers, 1969)

Campbell Craig and Fredrik Logevall, *America's Cold War: The Politics of Insecurity* (Cambridge: Harvard University Press, 2009)

Richard Crockatt, *The Fifty Years War: The United States and the Soviet Union in World Politics, 1941–1991* (London: Routledge, 1995)

Richard Crossman, *A Nation Reborn: The Israel of Weizmann, Bevin and Ben-Gurion* (London: Hamish Hamilton, 1960)

David R. Devereux, *The Formulation of British Defence Policy towards the Middle East, 1948–56* (London: Macmillan, 1990)

Leonard Dinnerstein, 'America, Britain, and Palestine: The Anglo-American Committee of Inquiry and the Displaced Persons, 1945–46', *Diplomatic History*, Vol. 4, No. 3 (July 1980), pp. 283–302

Michael Dumper, *The Future for Palestinian Refugees: Toward Equity and Peace* (Boulder: Lynne Rienner, 2007)

Martin Ebon, 'Communist Tactics in Palestine', *The Middle East Journal*, Vol. 2, No. 3 (July 1948), pp. 255–269

Zvi Elpeleg, *The Grand Mufti: Haj Amin al-Hussaini, Founder of the Palestinian National Movement* (London: Frank Cass, 1993)

Bruce J. Evensen, 'Truman, Palestine and the Cold War', *Middle Eastern Studies*, Vol. 28, No. 1 (January 1992), pp. 120–156

——, *Truman, Palestine and the Press: Shaping Conventional Wisdom at the Beginning of the Cold War* (New York: Greenwood Press, 1992)

Michael R. Fischbach, *Records of Dispossession: Palestinian Refugees and the Arab–Israel Conflict* (New York: Columbia University Press, 2003)

——, *Jewish Property Claims against Arab Countries* (New York: Columbia University Press, 2008)

David P. Forsythe, *United Nations Peacemaking: The Conciliation Commission for Palestine* (Baltimore: Johns Hopkins University Press, 1972)

Robert Frazier, 'Did Britain Start the Cold War? Bevin and the Truman Doctrine', *The Historical Journal*, Vol. 27, No. 3 (1984), pp. 715–727

Robert Frazier, *Anglo-American Relations with Greece: The Coming of the Cold War* (Baskingstoke: Macmillan, 1991)

Rony E. Gabbay, *A Political Study of the Arab–Jewish Conflict* (Geneva: Libraire E. Droz, 1959)

Zvi Ganin, *Truman, American Jewry, and Israel, 1945–1948* (New York: Holmes & Meier, 1979)

Moshe Gat, *The Jewish Exodus from Iraq, 1948–1951* (London: Frank Cass, 1997)

Mordechai Gazit, 'Ben-Gurion's 1949 Proposal to Incorporate the Gaza Strip with Israel', *Studies in Zionism*, Vol. 8, No. 2 (Autumn, 1987), pp. 223–243

——, 'The Israel–Jordan Peace Negotiations (1949–51): King Abdullah's Lonely Efforts', *Journal of Contemporary History*, Vol. 23, No. 3 (July, 1988), pp. 409–424

Yoav Gelber, *Palestine, 1948: War, Escape and the Emergence of the Palestine Refugee Problem* (Brighton: Sussex Academic Press, 2001)

Klaus Gensicke, *The Mufti of Jerusalem and the Nazis: The Berlin Years* (London: Vallentine Mitchell, 2011)

Martin Gilbert, *In Ishmael's House: A History of Jews in Muslim Lands* (New Haven: Yale University Press, 2010)

Peter Grose, *Israel in the Mind of America* (New York: Alfred A. Knopf, 1983)

Simon Haddad, *The Palestinian Impasse in Lebanon: The Politics of Refugee Integration* (Brighton: Sussex Academic Press, 2003)

Peter L. Hahn, *The United States, Great Britain, and Egypt, 1945–1956: Strategy and Diplomacy in the Early Cold War* (Chapel Hill: University of North Carolina Press, 1991)

——, *Caught in the Middle East: U.S. Policy toward the Arab–Israeli Conflict, 1945–1961* (Chapel Hill: University of North Carolina Press, 2004)

Miriam Joyce Haron, *Anglo-American Relations and the Question of Palestine, 1945–47* (New York: Fordham University, 1979)

——, *Palestine and the Anglo-American Connection, 1945–1950* (New York: Peter Lang, 1986)

Earl G. Harrison, *The Plight of the Displaced Jews in Europe: A Report to President Truman* (New York: Reprinted by United Jewish Appeal for Refugees, 1945)

Ben Hecht, *A Flag Is Born* (American League for a Free Palestine, 1946)

Joseph Heller, *The Stern Gang: Ideology, Politics, and Terror, 1940–1949* (London: Frank Cass, 1994)

Shlomo Hillel, *Operation Babylon: Jewish Clandestine Activity in the Middle East 1946–51* (London: Collins, 1988)

David Hirst, *The Gun and the Olive Branch* (London: Faber and Faber, 2003)

Dennis C. Howley, *The United Nations and the Palestinians* (Hicksville: Exposition Press, 1975)

Michael E Jansen, *The United States and the Palestinian People* (Beirut: Institute For Palestine Studies, 1970)

Martin Jones, *Failure in Palestine: British and the United States Policy after the Second World War* (London: Mansell, 1986)

Leo V. Kanawada, Jr, *Franklin D. Roosevelt's Diplomacy and American Catholics, Italians, and Jews* (Ann Arbor: University of Michigan Press, 1982)

Deborah Kaplan, *The Arab Refugees: An Abnormal Problem* (Jerusalem: Rubin Mass, 1959)

Robert D. Kaplan, *The Arabists: The Romance of an American Elite* (New York: The Free Press, 1993)

Candice Karp, *Missed Opportunities: US Diplomatic Failures and the Arab–Israeli Conflict 1947–1967* (Claremont: Regina Books, 2005)

Efraim Karsh, 'Rewriting Israel's History', *Middle East Quarterly*, Vol. 3, No. 2 (June 1996), pp. 19–29

——, 'Falsifying the Record: Benny Morris, David Ben-Gurion, and the "transfer" idea', *Israel Affairs*, Vol. 4, No. 2 (Winter, 1997), pp. 47–71

——, *Fabricating Israeli History: The 'New Historians'* (London: Frank Cass, 2000)

——, '1948, Israel and the Palestinians: Annotated Text', *Commentary*, May 2008, http://www.commentarymagazine.com/viewarticle.cfm/1948--israel--and-the-palestinians--annotated-text-11373?search=1 (Last visited 31 October 2008)

——, *Palestine Betrayed* (New Haven: Yale University Press, 2010)

Shmuel Katz, *Days of Fire* (London: W.H. Allen, 1968)

I.L. Kenen, *Israel's Defense Line: Her Friends and Foes in Washington* (Buffalo: Prometheus Books, 1981)

John Kent, *British Imperial Strategy and the Origins of the Cold War, 1944–49* (Leicester: Leicester University Press, 1993)

Malcolm Kerr, *The Elusive Peace in the Middle East* (Albany: State University of New York Press, 1975)

Issa Khalaf, *Politics in Palestine* (Albany: State University of New York Press, 1991)

Walid Khalidi, *From Haven to Conquest: Zionism and the Palestinian Problem until 1948* (Beirut: Institute for Palestine Studies, 1987)

——, *All That Remains: The Palestinian Villages Occupied and Depopulated by Israel in 1948* (Beirut: Institute for Palestine Studies, 1992)

——, 'Why Did the Palestinians Leave Revisited', *Journal of Palestine Studies*, Vol. XXXIV, No. 2 (Winter, 2005), pp. 42–54

Fred J. Khouri, *The Arab–Israeli Dilemma* (Syracuse: Syracuse University Press, 1969)

Jon and David Kimche, *Both Sides of the Hill* (London: Secker & Warburg, 1960)

Baruch Kimmerling and Joel Migdal, *Palestinians: Making of a People* (New York: The Free Press, 1993)

Lionel Kochan (ed), *The Jews in Soviet Russia since 1917* (London: Oxford University Press, 1970)

Arthur Koestler, *Promise and Fulfilment: Palestine 1917–1949* (London: Macmillan, 1949)

Arnold Kramer, 'Soviet Motives in the Partition of Palestine, 1947–48', *Journal of Palestine Studies*, Vol. 2, No. 2 (Winter, 1972), pp. 102–119

Bruce Robellet Kuniholm, *The Origins of the Cold War in the Near East* (Princeton: Princeton University Press, 1980)

Dan Kurzman, *Genesis 1948: The First Arab–Israeli War* (New York: Signet, 1972)

Walter Lafeber, *America, Russia and the Cold War* (New York: John Wiley and Sons, 1967)

Ruth Lapidoth, 'Israel and the Palestinians: Some Legal Issues', *The Jerusalem Institute of Israel Studies, The JUS Studies Series*, No. 94 (2003)

Walter Laqueur and Barry Rubin (eds), *The Arab–Israeli Reader: A Documentary History of the Middle East Conflict* (New York: Penguin, 1995)

Walter Laqueur, *The History of Zionism* (New York: Tauris Parke, 2003)

Itamar Levin, *Locked Doors: The Seizure of Jewish Property in Arab Countries* (Westport: Praeger, 2001)

Wm Roger Louis, *The British Empire in the Middle East* (Oxford: Clarendon, 1984)

Wm Roger Louis and Robert W. Stookey, *The End of the Palestine Mandate* (London: I.B. Tauris, 1986)

Bruce Maddy-Weitzmann, *The Crystallization of the Arab State System* (Syracuse: Syracuse University Press, 1993)

Bruce Maddy-Weitzman and Shimon Shamir (eds), *The Camp David Summit: What Went Wrong?* (Brighton: Sussex Academic Press, 2005)

Robert Malley and Hussein Agha, 'Camp David: The Tragedy of Errors', *New York Review of Books*, Vol. 48, No. 13 (9 August 2001)

——, 'Camp David and After: An Exchange', *New York Review of Books*, Vol. 49, No. 11 (13 June 2002)

Nur Masalha, 'A Critique of Benny Morris', *Journal of Palestine Studies*, Vol. 21, No. 1 (Autumn, 1991), pp. 90–97

——, *Expulsion of the Palestinians: The Concept of 'Transfer' in Zionist Political Thought, 1882–1948* (Washington, DC: Institute for Palestine Studies, 1992)

Philip Mattar, *The Mufti of Jerusalem: Al-Hajj Amin al-Husayni and the Palestinian National Movement* (New York: Columbia University Press, 1988)

Daniel McGowan and Marc Ellis (eds), *Remembering Deir Yassin: The Future of Israel and Palestine* (New York: Interlink Publishing Group, 1998)

Rafael Medoff, *Zionism and the Arabs: An American Jewish Dilemma*, 1898–1948 (Westport, CT: Praeger, 1997)

Paul C. Merkley, *The Politics of Christian Zionism 1891–1949* (London: Frank Cass, 1998)

Aaron David Miller, *Much Too Promised Land: America's Elusive Search for Arab–Israeli Peace* (Random House, 2005)

Uri Milstein, *History of the War of Independence: Out of Crisis Came Decision*. Vol. 4 (New York: University Press of America, 1996)

Elizabeth Monroe, *Philby of Arabia* (London: Pitman Publishing, 1973)

——, *Britain's Moment in the Middle East* (London: Chatto & Windus, 1981)

Benny Morris, *The Birth of the Palestinian Refugee Problem* (Cambridge: Cambridge University Press, 1987)

——, *Righteous Victims: A History of the Zionist–Arab Conflict, 1881–2001* (New York: Vintage Books, 2001)

——, 'Camp David and After: An Exchange 1. An Interview with Ehud Barak', *New York Review of Books*, Vol. 49, No. 11, 13 June 2002

——, *The Birth of the Palestinian Refugee Problem Revisited* (Cambridge: Cambridge University Press, 2004)

——, 'Politics by Other Means', *The New Republic*, 22 March 2004

——, 'The Historiography of Deir Yassin,' *Journal of Israeli History*, Vol. 24, No. 1 (2005), pp. 79–107

Amikam Nachmani, *Great Power Discord in Palestine: The Anglo-American Committee of Inquiry into the Problem of European Jewry and Palestine, 194–546* (London: Frank Cass, 1987)

Nafez Nazzal, *The Palestinian Exodus from Galilee 1948* (Beirut: The Institute for Palestine Studies, 1978)

Donald Neff, 'U.S. Policy and the Palestinian Refugees', *Journal of Palestine Studies,* Vol. 18, No. 1 (Autumn, 1988), pp. 96–111

——, *Fallen Pillars: U.S. Policy towards Palestine and Israel Since 1945* (Washington, DC: Institute For Palestine Studies, 2002)

Joseph Nevo, *King Abdallah and Palestine: A Territorial Ambition* (Oxford: Macmillan, 1996)

Arnold A. Offner, *Another Such Victory: President Truman and the Cold War, 1945–1953* (Stanford: Stanford University Press, 2002)

Michael B. Oren, *Power, Faith, and Fantasy: America in the Middle East, 1776 to the Present* (New York: W.W. Norton & Company, 2007)

Ritchie Ovendale, *Britain, the United States, and the End of the Palestine Mandate, 1942–1948* (London: Royal Historical Society, 1989)

——, *Britain, the United States, and the Transfer of Power in the Middle East, 1945–1962* (London: Leicester University Press, 1996)

Ilan Pappé, *Britain and the Arab–Israeli Conflict, 1948–51* (London: MacMillan, 1988)

——, *The Making of the Arab–Israeli Conflict, 1947–51* (London: I.B. Tauris, 1994)

——, *The Ethnic Cleansing of Palestine* (London: Oneworld Publications, 2007)

Tudor Parfitt, *The Road to Redemption: The Jews of Yemen, 1900–1950* (Leiden: E.J. Brill, 1996)

Herbert Parzen, 'The Arab Refugees – Their Origins and Projection into a Problem (1948–1952)', *Jewish Social Studies,* Vol. 31, No. 4 (October 1969), pp. 292–323

Moshe Pearlman, *Mufti of Jerusalem: The Story of Haj Amin el Husseini* (London: Victor Gollancz, 1947)

Nathan A. Pelcovits, *The Long Armistice: UN Peacekeeping and the Arab–Israeli Conflict, 1948–1960* (Boulder: Westview Press, 1993)

Monty Noam Penkower, *Decision on Palestine Deferred: America, Britain and Wartime Diplomacy, 1939–1945* (London: Frank Cass, 2002)

Don Peretz, *Israel and the Palestine Arabs* (Washington, DC: The Middle East Institute, 1959)

Shlomo Perla, 'Israel and the Palestine Conciliation Commission', *Middle Eastern Studies,* Vol. 26, No. 1 (1990), pp. 113–118

Walter Pinner, *How Many Arab Refugees? A Critical Study of UNRWA's Statistics and Reports* (London: Macgibbon & Kee, 1959)

Avi Plascov, *The Palestinian Refugees in Jordan, 1948–1957* (London: Frank Cass, 1981)

William R. Polk, David M. Stamler and Edmund Asfour, *Backdrop to Tragedy: The Struggle for Palestine* (Boston: Beacon Press, 1957)

Ronald E. Powaski, *The Cold War: The United States and the Soviet Union, 1917–1991* (Oxford: Oxford University Press, 1997)

Jeremy Pressman, 'Visions in Collision – What Happened at Camp David and Taba', *International Security,* Vol. 28, No. 2 (Fall, 2003), pp. 5–43

Itamar Rabinovich, *The Road Not Taken: Early Arab–Israeli Negotiations* (Oxford: Oxford University Press, 1991)

——, *Waging Peace: Israel and the Arabs, 1948–2003* (Princeton: Princeton University Press, 2004)

Allis Radosh and Ronald Radosh, *A Safe Haven: Harry S. Truman and the Founding of Israel* (New York: Harper, 2009)

Kermit Roosevelt, 'The Partition of Palestine: A Lesson in Pressure Politics', *Middle East Journal*, Vol. 2, No. 1 (1948), pp. 116

Norman Rose, *'A Senseless, Squalid War': Voices from Palestine, 1945–1948* (London: The Bodley Head, 2009)

Maurice Roumani, *The Jews of Libya: Coexistence, Persecution and Rehabilitation* (Brighton: Sussex Academic Press, 2007)

Joshua Rubenstein and Vladimir P. Naumov (eds), *Stalin's Secret Pogrom: The Postwar Inquisition of the Jewish Anti-Fascist Committee* (New Haven: Yale University Press, 2005)

Barry Rubin, *The Great Powers in the Middle East 1941–1947: The Road to the Cold War* (London: Frank Cass, 1980)

——, *The Arab States and the Palestine Conflict* (Syracuse: Syracuse University Press, 1981)

Howard M. Sachar, *Europe Leaves the Middle East, 1936–1954* (New York: Alfred A. Knopf, 1972)

Nadav Safran, *From War to War: The Arab–Israeli Confrontation, 1948–1967* (New York: Pegasus, 1969)

Joseph B. Schechtman, *The Arab Refugee Problem* (New York: Philosophical Library, 1952)

——, The *Mufti and the Fuehrer: The Rise and Fall of Haj Amin El-Husseini* (New York: T. Yoseloff, 1965)

Benjamin Schiff, *Refugees unto the Third Generation: UN Aid to Palestinians* (Syracuse: Syracuse University Press, 1995)

Malka Hillel Schulewitz, *The Forgotten Millions: The Modern Jewish Exodus from Arab Lands* (London: Continuum, 2000)

Patrick Seale, *The Struggle for Syria: A Study of Post War Arab Politics, 1948–58* (New Haven: Yale University Press, 1987)

Shimon Shamir and Bruce Maddy-Weitzman (eds), *The Camp David Summit – What Went Wrong? Americans, Israelis, and Palestinians Analyze the Failure of the Boldest Attempt Ever to Resolve the Palestinian Israeli Conflict* (Brighton: Sussex Academic Press, 2005)

Anita Shapira, *Land and Power: The Zionist Resort to Force, 1881–1948* (New York: Oxford University Press, 1992)

Gabriel Sheffer, *Moshe Sharrett: Biography of a Political Moderate* (Oxford: Clarendon Press, 1996)

Gilead Sher, *The Israeli – Palestinian Peace Negotiations, 1999–2001* (London: Routledge, 2006)

Colin Shindler, *Israel and the European Left: Between Solidarity and Delegitimization* (New York: Continuum, 2012)

——, 'Can Israel Really Call Itself a 'Jewish State'? *The JC*, (11 October 2012)

Avi Shlaim, 'Husni Za'im and the Plan to Resettle Palestinian Refugees in Syria', *Journal of Palestine Studies*, Vol. 15, No. 4 (Summer, 1986)

——, *Collusion across the Jordan: King Abdullah, the Zionist Movement, and the Partition of Palestine* (Oxford: Clarendon Press, 1988)

——, 'The Debate About 1948', *International Journal of Middle East Studies*, Vol. 27, No. 3 (1995), pp. 287–304

——, *The Iron Wall: Israel and the Arab World* (London: Penguin, 2001)

John Snetsinger, *Truman, the Jewish Vote, and the Creation of Israel* (Stanford: Hoover Institution Press, 1974)

Steven L. Spiegel, *The Other Arab–Israeli Conflict: Making America's Middle East Policy, from Truman to Reagan* (Chicago: University of Chicago Press, 1985)

Cary David Stanger, 'A Haunting Legacy: The Assassination of Count Bernadotte', *Middle East Journal*, Vol. 42, No. 2 (Spring 1988), pp. 260–272

Norman Stillman, *The Jews of Arab Lands in Modern Times* (Philadelphia: Jewish Publication Society, 2003)

Shabtai Teveth, 'The Evolution of "Transfer"', in *Zionist Thinking*, Vol. 107. Moshe Dayan Center for Middle Eastern and African Studies, Shiloah Institute, Tel Aviv University, 1989

——, 'Charging Israel with Original Sin', *Commentary*, Vol. 88, No. 3 (September 1989)

——, 'The Palestine Arab Refugee Problem and Its Origins: Review Article', *Middle Eastern Studies*, Vol. 26, No. 2 (April 1990), pp. 214–249

S.G. Thicknesse, *Arab Refugees: A Survey of Resettlement Possibilities* (London: Royal Institute of International Affairs, 1949)

Saadia Touval, *The Peace Brokers: Mediators in the Arab–Israeli Conflict, 1948–1979* (Princeton: Princeton University Press, 1982)

Jocob Tovy, *Israel and the Palestinian Refugee Issue: The Formation of a Policy, 1948–1956* (London: Routledge, 2014)

Milton Viorst, *UNRWA and Peace in the Middle East* (Washington, DC: Middle East Institute, 1984)

Evan M. Wilson, 'The Palestine Papers, 1943–1947', *Journal of Palestine Studies*, Vol. 2, No. 4 (Summer, 1973), pp. 33–54

——, *Decision on Palestine: How the U.S. Came to Recognize Israel* (Stanford: Stanford University Press, 1979)

'X' (George F. Kennan), 'The Sources of Soviet Conduct', *Foreign Affairs*, Vol. 24, No. 4 (July 1947), pp. 852–868

Daniel Yergin, *Shattered Peace: The Origins of the Cold War and the National Security State* (Boston: Houghton Mifflin Company, 1977)

Saul Zadka, *Blood in Zion: How the Jewish Guerrillas Drove the British out of Palestine* (London: Brassey, 1995)

Index

Israel-Jordan, 65, 71, 140, 141–2,
143–4, 148–53, 165
PCC and, 16, 65, 143–5, 146–7,
150–1, 155–6, 158, 164–5
US and British preference for
multilateral PCC, 15–16, 17,
141, 142, 143, 147, 148, 152,
153, 154, 164, 165
US attitudes towards, 16, 140, 141,
142–3, 144–8, 149, 151, 152,
153, 155, 164, 190
Zaim's overtures to Israel, 140, 141,
145–8, 165, 190
Blandford, John, 123, 124, 134, 170,
172, 174, 180, 183
Boisanger, Claude de, 68, 73, 89, 95,
99, 117–18, 119–20
Britain
Arab hostility over refugee crisis, 42,
44, 61
archival sources, 7–8, 9, 64
attitudes towards Zionism, 8
British Middle East Office, 48
Chiefs of Staff (COS), 20, 21, 23
compensation issue and, 16, 116,
124, 127–8, 129–30, 139
Economic Survey Mission (ESM)
and, 15, 90–1, 101, 103, 105,
106–8, 109, 111, 112
errors over refugee issue, 4, 14, 15,
16, 41, 61, 91, 113, 118, 121,
186–7, 188
Exodus affair, 29–30
fear of Soviet influence in Middle
East, 21–2, 31, 32
foreign policy debate (1946), 20–1
Israel's Gaza Strip proposals, 87–8,
91–2, 94–5
Jewish immigration to Palestine
and, 14, 28–30, 44, 45–6
Lausanne Conference and, 90
military presence in Palestine, 11,
14, 21–2, 186
need for goodwill from Arab States,
14, 19, 22, 29, 31, 33–4, 38, 40,
44, 186
need for US support post-war, 21,
26, 29, 38–9
Paris Conference and, 135

PCC advisory role of, 64, 65,
66–8, 187
PCC's continuance and, 117, 118,
127, 139
population exchange concept and,
159–60, 161–3
post-war economic problems, 21,
23, 29
referral of Palestine question to UN
(1947), 18, 21, 30
repatriation issue and, 61, 78,
79, 106
resettlement issue and, 50–1, 61,
76–80, 90–1, 102, 104, 106, 108
Resolution 194 and, 14–15,
58–61, 62
Suez and, 20, 21, 22
sympathy for Arab position, 33
treaty obligations with Egypt and
Jordan, 22, 24, 33, 135, 154
UNSCOP and, 30–1, 32, 34
winter conditions (1946-47), 18, 23
see also Anglo-American relations
British Mandate, 4, 9–10, 21, 22, 23–4,
31, 34
Bunche, Ralph, 49, 54, 63, 82, 117,
118, 146
Burma, 22
Burns, General James H., 172
Burrows, Bernard, 73, 78, 142–3
Byrnes, James, 22

Cadogan, Sir Alexander, 33, 34,
45, 46
Camp David talks (2000), 2
Canada, 171–2, 180, 182
Caplan, Neil, 64, 78, 86, 143, 187
Central Intelligence Agency (CIA), 104
Childers, Erskine, 6, 8
China, 66, 102, 127
Chirine, Ismail, 143, 154, 157, 183
Churchill, Winston, 28, 152
Cilento, Sir Raphael, 48, 50, 54
Clapp, Gordon, 101, 107, 109, 110,
111, 170, 171
Clayton, Gilbert, 48
Clifford, Clark, 25, 37
Clinton, Bill, 2
Cohen, Aharon, 6

Printed and bound by CPI Group (UK) Ltd, Croydon, CR0 4YY